A History of
Curiosity

Studies in Anthropology and History

Studies in Anthropology and History is a series that will develop new theoretical perspectives, and combine comparative and ethnographic studies with historical research.

Edited by Nicholas Thomas, The Australian National University, Canberra.

VOLUME 1 Structure and Process in a Melanesian Society: Ponam's progress in the Twentieth Century
ACHSAH H. CARRIER AND JAMES G. CARRIER

VOLUME 2 Androgynous Objects: String bags and gender in Central New Guinea
MAUREEN ANNE MACKENZIE

VOLUME 3 Time and the Work of Anthropology: Critical essays 1971–1991
JOHANNES FABIAN

VOLUME 4 Colonial Space: Spatiality in the discourse of German South West Africa 1884–1915
JOHN NOYES

VOLUME 5 Catastrophe and Creation: The transformation of an African culture
KAJSA EKHOLM FRIEDMAN

VOLUME 6 Before Social Anthropology: Essays on the history of British Anthropology
JAMES URRY

VOLUME 7 The *Ghotul* in Muria Society
SIMERAN MAN SINGH GELL

VOLUME 8 Global Culture, Island Identity: Continuity and change in the Afro-Caribbean community of Nevis
KAREN FOG OLWIG

VOLUME 9 The Return of the Ainu: Cultural mobilization and the practice of ethnicity in Japan
KATARINA V. SJÖBERG

VOLUME 10 Tradition and Christianity: The colonial transformation of a Solomon Islands society
BEN BURT

VOLUME 11 Recovering the Orient: Artists, scholars, appropriations
ANDREW GERSTLE AND ANTHONY MILNER

VOLUME 12 Women of the Place: *Kastom*, colonialism and gender in Vanuatu
MARGARET JOLLY

VOLUME 13 A History of Curiosity: The Theory of Travel 1550–1800
JUSTIN STAGL

OTHER VOLUMES IN PREPARATION

VOLUME 14 Exploring Confrontation Sri Lanka: Politics, culture and history
MICHAEL ROBERTS

VOLUME 15 Consumption and Identity
JONATHAN FRIEDMAN

VOLUME 16 Resplendant Sites, Discordant Voices: Sri Lanka and international tourism
MALCOLM CRICK

VOLUME 17 The Rationality of Rural Life
JEFF PRATT

This book is part of a series. The publisher will accept continuation orders which may be cancelled at any time and which provide for automatic billing and shipping of each title in the series upon publication. Please write for details.

Justin Stagl

A History of
Curiosity

The Theory of Travel 1550–1800

Routledge
Taylor & Francis Group

LONDON AND NEW YORK

First Published 1995
By Routledge

Reprinted 2004
By Routledge
2 Park Square, Milton Park, Abingdon, Oxon, OX14 4RN

Transferred to Digital Printing 2006

Routledge is an imprint of the Taylor & Francis Group

BRITISH LIBRARY CATALOGUING IN PUBLICATION DATA

Stagl, Justin
  History of Curiosity: Theory of Travel,
  1550–1800. – (Studies in Anthropology &
  History, ISSN 1055–2464; Vol.13)
  I. Title   II. Series
  910.9

  ISBN 3-7186-5342-7 (hardcover)
  ISBN 3-7186-5621-3 (softcover)
  ISSN 1055-2464

DESIGNED BY   **Maureen Anne MacKenzie**
                Em Squared, Main Street, Michelago, NSW 2620, Australia

FRONT COVER   **Frontispiece of *Der reisende Deutsche*, s.l. 1745. By courtesy of
                the Herzog August Bibliothek, Wolfenbüttel.**

Publisher's Note
The publisher has gone to great lengths to ensure the quality of
this reprint but points out that some imperfections in
the original may be apparent

Printed and bound by CPI Antony Rowe, Eastbourne

Contents

List of Illustrations		vii
Acknowledgements		viii
Introduction		1
ONE	**The Methodizing of Travel in the Sixteenth Century: A Tale of Three Cities**	47
	From Pilgrimage to Educational Journey	47
	Travel Reports	49
	Programmes for the Improvement of Travel	51
	The First Methodologists of Travel	57
	A Tale of Three Cities: Venice, Basel, Paris	65
	The Art of Travel	70
	Further Developments	81
	Postscriptum: On the Practical Utilization of the Ars Apodemica	90
TWO	**Rerum Memoria: Early Modern Enquiries and Documentation Centres**	95
	Preliminary Remark	95
	Travel, Correspondence, Documentation and the "Res Publica Literaria"	97
	The Handling of Empirical Knowledge	100
	The Documentation of Knowledge	110
	The Acquisition and Processing of New Empirical Knowledge	121
THREE	**Imagines Mundi: Allegories of the Continents in the Baroque and the Enlightenment**	155
	Imagines Mundi	155
	An *Imago Mundi* of the Baroque	157
	An *Imago Mundi* of the Enlightenment	163
	Conclusion	166
FOUR	**The Man Who Called Himself George Psalmanazar or: The Problems of the Authenticity of Ethnographic Description**	171
	A Description of Formosa	171
	From the Confessions of an Imposter	178
	An Analysis of "The Description of Formosa"	188
	The Problem of the Authenticity of Ethnographic Description	198

FIVE   **Josephinism and Social Research: The "Patriotic**
            Traveller" of Count Leopold Berchtold   209
            Patriotism, Pietism, Philanthropism, Josephinism   209
            A Josephinist Philanthropist   215
            A Series of Questions for a Patriotic Traveller   221
            A Point of No Return   227

SIX   **August Ludwig Schlözer and the Study of**
            Mankind According to Peoples   233
            On the Early History of "Ethnography", "Ethnology"
                and Related Disciplinal Names   233
            The University of Göttingen   242
            Universal History   249
            The Concept of "People"   254
            The General History of the North   259
            A Discussion of Schlözer's New Terms   262
            Conclusion   267

SEVEN   **From the Private to the Sponsored Traveller:**
            Volney's Reform of Travel Instruction and the
            French Revolution   269
            The Making of a Traveller   269
            Travel and the Questionnaire During the Revolution   273
            From the Art of Travel to Ethnographic Methodology   277
            Travel and the Questionnaire During the Directory   281
            Travel and the Questionnaire During the Consulate and
                Empire   286
            Postscript: Notes and Queries, or Travel and the
                Questionnaire in 19th and 20th Century
                Ethnographic Research   293

            References   297

            Index   331

List of Illustrations

FIGURE 1.   Theodor Zwinger   59

2.   A synopsis of things to be observed during travel   61

3.   Hugo Blotius   63

4.   Petrus Ramus   67

5.   Gulielmus Gratarolus   74

6.   The Grand Tour as part of the educational system of the Baroque   83

7.   Théophraste Renaudot   135

8.   Frontispiece of: Welt-Beschauung   158

9.   Frontispiece of: Der reisende Deutsche   162

10.   ''Formosan'' sedan chair carried by elephants   172

11.   The ''Formosan'' alphabet   174

12.   Mr George Psalmanazar   177

13.   Samples of the ''Formosan'' language   182

14.   ''Formosan'' national costumes   191

15.   ''Formosan'' altar   192

16.   ''Formosan'' diety   194

17.   The geographical position of ''Formosa'' in relation to China and Japan   201

18.   Leopold Berchold   214

19.   The new castle of Buchlau in Moravia   219

20.   August Ludwig Schlözer   245

21.   Le Comte de Volney   271

Acknowledgements

In the academic year 1987/88 I was awarded an "Academy Grant" by the Volkswagen Foundation. This praiseworthy institution paid a substitute to take over my functions at the overcrowded and understaffed University of Bonn, so that I could quietly work on some book. During this period and afterwards Herr Günter Dege of the Volkswagen Foundation gave me his appreciative and unbureaucratic support. Dr. Stefan Hradil, now professor at the University of Mainz, took excellent care of my duties.

My thanks to the *Ecole des Hautes Etudes en Sciences Sociales*, and here especially Dr. Britta Rupp-Eisenreich, who received me from October to December 1987 in Paris; Mme Auffray of the *Institut Francophone de Paris* who arranged for me to live in the beautiful Hôtel Châlons-Luxembourg; Professor Ernest Gellner who first invited me to Cambridge and established contacts with Clare Hall; the President and the Fellows of Clare Hall, Cambridge, who made me a Visiting Fellow from January to August 1988 and elected me a Life Member afterwards; and to Dr. Russell Kirk and his wife Annette Kirk who from September to October of that year took me into their pleasant and scholarly home Piety Hill, Mecosta, Michigan.

Dr. Christopher Pinney of Clare Hall, presently at the London School of Oriental and African Studies, persuaded me to integrate my studies on the art of travel, the history of the survey and the theory of early statistics into one book and to write this book in English. Yet writing in English proved more difficult than I had anticipated, especially after my return to Germany. A residency at the Bellagio Study and Conference Center, Lake Como, Italy, from October to November 1989, for which I am still grateful to the Rockefeller Foundation, permitted a new start. In 1991, I took my present position at the University of Salzburg, which again interrupted my work. Yet now it is finally completed and I am able to reward the patience of my many supporters, among which I also have to thank my family for tolerating my prolonged absences from home. Elizabeth Mortimer, B.Sc., Professor Jane Sayers and Martin Weichbold, M.A. have taken care of my manuscript in the final state, eliminating the last traces of "Austrian English" and standardizing my notes.

The Introduction together with Chapters One and Two give a more or less systematic outline of the problems of pre-modern social research; the remaining chapters deal with particular cases.

Justin Stagl   Salzburg, April 1994

On the Archaeology of Social Research

"The use of the questionnaire has a long past which still waits for its recorder."

(Paul Lazarsfeld)

THE SCOPE OF THIS BOOK

This book discusses the early history of social research. Under that notion I understand the investigation of the "second reality" created by man through social interaction, symbolic communication and the use of tools. This man–made reality is based on the "first reality" of nature; socio–cultural phenomena need the corporal substrata of natural phenomena for their subsistence. Research into social relations, political institutions and cultural peculiarities is thus derived from and proceeds via the exploration of natural phenomena. Because of its indirect and abstract character, social research is commonly thought to have appeared rather late in human history. The present book supports the contrary opinion. I will argue that *some forms* of social research are present in *all* epochs and *all* societies, that social research is therefore coeval with mankind.

I am, however, more concerned with the forms ("methods", "techniques") of such research than with its results. The history of these forms is very little known. This book claims no other merit than that of a first mapping of an unknown land. Historians of empirical social research, such as an Hans Zeisel,[1] Heinz Maus,[2] Anthony Oberschall[3] or Wolfgang Bonß[4] consider it to be characteristic of bourgeois, industrial society. Though they do not claim that its methods were actually *invented* in the late 18th century, they tend to be rather unspecific

---

[1] Zeisel: 1960.

[2] Maus: 1973.

[3] Oberschall: 1972.

[4] Bonß: 1982.

about their origins. Only Paul Lazarsfeld felt that there was something wrong, with this common view.[5]

The present book intends to shed somewhat more light on the *early modern* period, the period preceding the appearance of bourgeois, industrial society. Between ca. 1550 and 1800, social research (I also include under this term political and cultural research) became more systematic than it had ever been before, and its field of application was extended throughout the world. This prepared the emergence of the new socio–cultural sciences (ethnology, folklore, sociology, political science) in about the year 1800. Though treating social research as a requirement of all human societies, this book focuses thus in a Weberian manner on its rationalization in the West and its subsequent globalization. The rest of this Introduction deals, however, with its development *before* the early modern period.

CURIOSITY AND SOCIAL RESEARCH

Having but rudimentary instincts and no specific environment, man depends for his survival on his ability to adapt to new situations. He has to be "world–open".[6] *Curiosity* is a feature of this world–openness. It can be defined as the urge to explore unknown situations.[7] Curiosity and the exploratory activity are so intimately linked that they are considered almost identical.[8] Both appear already in higher animals, such as in mammals or birds. Yet they are nowhere so marked as in man.

Ethologists and psychologists seem to agree that curiosity is (1) a directed activity involving locomotion and the senses; has (2) something to do with new or unknown situations; is (3) "superfluous" activity having no immediate utilitarian goal; is (4) closely connected with play; and leads (5) to indirect, long–range advantages in the form of learning.[9]

An individual with an inquiring mind approaches the objects of its curiosity, explores them through observation, inspection or manipulation, and then relinquishes them, only to return and to repeat this sequence of activities. By thus examining these objects again and again from various angles, he not only comes to know them as identifiable objects in a given situation, but also to connect them with his own experienced world, to transform them into something familiar. After

---

[5] Lazarsfeld: 1961. The quotation above is *op. cit.*, 333.

[6] Gehlen: 1986a, 251ff.

[7] This defination relies on that of Eibl–Eibesfeldt: *"aktiv neue Situationen aufsuchen und erkunden"* (1967, 283).

[8] Wohlwill: 1987.

[9] Berlyne: 1960; cf. also Görlitz–Wohlwill: 1987, 8f, 180f.

this has been achieved, interest subsides. Irenäus Eibl–Eibesfeldt aptly calls this "a dialogue with the environment".[10]

There seem to be "push" and "pull" factors for the exploratory activity. Daniel E. Berlyne regards it as the outlet for a tension occasioned by the appearance of something threatening in the environment, or by boredom;[11] Eibl–Eibesfeldt (following Lorenz and Gehlen) stresses the "superfluous" character of that activity, its exceeding the "normal" functioning of the oganism.[12] In the "curiosity animals" (Konrad Lorenz)[13] this inner urge comes to the fore in the shape of playing and learning as soon as the more utilitarian urges of want and fear are appeased.

Man differs from other "curiosity animals" by his possession of language. This greatly enlarges the field of his curiosity. Berlyne distinguishes accordingly between "perceptive curiosity", the direct sensory motor exploration of objects and situations, and "epistemological curiosity", their indirect exploration via the asking of questions and directed thinking.[14] First signs of "epistemological curiosity" can also be observed in animals, yet it needs the intervention of language to become fully developed. Gehlen thus correctly stresses, as opposed to Lorenz, the higher nature of *research* as an exclusively human activity compared with the exploratory activities of the "curiosity animals":

"The higher intellectual propensity of true research consists in the investigation of certain objective facts according to their proper law, in order to connect them with other facts in a meaningful way."[15]

THREE BASIC RESEARCH METHODS

There seem to be three basic research methods, to which all others can be ultimately reduced. These are (1) *direct exploration* by *means of observation, inspection and manipulation*; (2) *indirect exploration* by *interviewing* others who have done this; and (3) *indirect exploration* via *significant phenomena* (i.e. phenomena refering to other phenomena outside the reach of the explorer, who are collected and manipulated by him to help him to reconstitute the inaccessible phenomena in his mind). The first method derives from perceptive, the second and third from epistemological curiosity.

Every human society has its own system of research techniques, by means of which it investigates its natural and social environment and its own body.

---

[10] Eibl–Eibesfeldt: 1967, 285.

[11] Berlyne: 1960.

[12] Gehlen: 1986a, 57ff, 356ff; Eibl–Eibesfeldt: 1967, 20ff, 282ff.

[13] *Neugiertiere* (Lorenz: 1943 quoted after Gehlen: 1986a, 30f).

[14] Berlyne: 1960; cf. also Moch: 1987.

[15] Gehlen: 1986a, 31.

It is a *system*; the separate techniques being interdependent. This system depends on the structure and cultural tradition of the respective society, a circumstance neglected in Gehlen's definition. All research is undertaken by specific people belonging to definite groups. They undertake it not solely to explore interesting phenomena, but also to connect them with their "experienced world".[16] As hermeneutic theory shows, all research proceeds from certain assumptions ("pre–judgments"), which the researcher shares with the cultural tradition of his society and which he merely *tests* in his research with regard to empirical reality.[17] This is one instance of the well–known "hermeneutic circle".[18]

Research into natural phenomena, being outside the scope of this book, will not be further discussed. For research into socio–cultural phenomena, the three basic methods have taken on a special characteristic about which a few words seem necessary:

(a) direct exploration in the socio–cultural sciences involves a change of place ("locomotion", as mentioned above). This is called *travel* when it leads out of the experienced world of the researcher. Travel can be subdivided into three phases: leaving ones experienced world, entering other spheres where unfamiliar experiences are undergone, and returning to one's normal world. As a method of socio–cultural research, travel comprises the observation of ways of life different of one's own, communication with their representatives, their mental reconstitution as self–contained units, their embodiement in memory, and their depiction to the members of one's own experienced world. Ethnographic fieldwork and sociological participant observation are but modifications of travel so defined.

While entering into other ways of life, the traveller cannot escape remaining a representative of his own: he carries its prejudgments everywhere with him. If these are wholly insufficient to cope with the unfamiliar experience, the traveller will not be able to conceptualize it properly, as is proved by such members of primitive societies which were brought to cities of the West.[19] Travelling has to be learnt, by individuals a well as by societies. A society which cannot evaluate the reports of its travellers will not be able to acquire reliable knowledge about its neighbours, even if its travellers were able to achieve this personally. In any case, however, a returned traveller will become an expert on the societies he has visited. His reports must nevertheless

---

[16] With this expression I render Edmund Husserl's concept of *Lebenswelt*. Cf. also Duerr: 1981.

[17] Gadamer: 1988.

[18] Cf. Conolly–Keutner:1988.

[19] Cf. e.g. Szalay: 1972. The "noble savage", who understands *all* about Western society and *therefore* despises it is a literary fiction. Cf. also ch. four.

be compatible with the pre–judgments of his fellow citizens in order to be understood and accepted by them.

(b) There are two main categories of person which can be interviewed in the social sciences: *experts*, i.e. those who exclusively know some part of socio–cultural reality (everybody is at least an expert on himself), and *representatives* of the various groups making up this reality (either as their leaders and delegates or as their typical members). Interviewing is a method of research, since it proceeds more purposefully than everyday questioning and answering, from which it is however derived. The interviewees are selected and questions are formulated and posed in such a way that the answers can be systematically compared. Not the separate answers, but their entirety is thus the true object of research. The interview takes place, as it were, over the heads of the interviewees. By comparing their answers new knowledge is won.

There are two main forms of methodical questioning. Either several people are asked the same question, respectively series of questions, in which case it is called a *survey*, or several questions are posed after a certain schedule to the same person, in which case it is called an *interrogation*. The latter is frequently used in a juridical or medical contention order to find out circumstances which the interviewee is unable to formulate or does not want to diclose. It is less important to the socio–cultural sciences than the survey and will here not be discussed in detail. Between the survey and travel there are many points of contact. Travel is a kind of survey, since the traveller, lacking the self–evidence of his own way of life, has to question many people — and he himself is frequently questioned by his hosts, who thereby attempt to incorporate him in their own system of knowledge. Travellers can, however, normally not carry out systematic surveys abroad; their hosts can hardly be expected to collaborate with this procedure. In order to comply with a systematic survey, the interviewees must share the interviewer's cultural orientation and feel a certain social solidarity with him. Such surveys are thus normally held only within given communities. They serve their self–exploration, whereas travel serves their exploration of "otherness". If travel can thus be seen as a special kind of survey, the survey can also be seen as a special form of travelling — as locomotion within the experienced world of one's own group. For in order to communicate with the interviewees, the interviewer must visit them or be visited by them. Travel and the survey are thus both mixtures — albeit in different proportions — of perceptive and epistemological curiosity.

(c) Culture has been described by Ernst Cassirer as a "symbolic system": "Human culture derives its specific character and its intellectual and moral values, not from the material of which it consists, but from its form, its architectural structure. And this form may be expressed in any sense material".[20] All cultural phenomena are thus significant, they refer to each other.

These references can, however, only be correctly understood by somebody who has some conception of their entirety, which he connects with his "experienced world" (*Lebenswelt*).[21] Since this is a social world, a world shared with others, culture is inextricably intertwined with society.[22] The architectural structure of culture presents itself as the structure of the mediums of communication within groups of insiders, i.e. language and related symbol systems such as art or ritual. Experiences which have been assigned a definite place in this structure can be called *knowledge*.

If *all* cultural phenomena refer to each other, there are *some* among them for which refering to something else is their main purpose or at least one of their principal purposes. These I call *significant phenomena*. They may be material objects (pieces of evidence, relics, souvenirs, monuments, symbols, graphs, pictures), standardized sequences of actions (techniques, manners, rituals) or recurring forms of speech (names, idioms, formulas, sayings, myths). All these phenomena are less valued for the utilitarian functions they may fulfill than for the "something else" to which they refer. They are in this respect comparable to tools. And they are structured, or at least structurable. This is why they can be used to *document the structure of culture and society*.

A special class of significant objects are the so–called *aides–mémoire*, small, durable and homogeneous[23] objects as for example sticks, stones or knots which are commemoratively associated with certain things or events in the experienced world. *Aides–mémoire* refer thus less to the architectural structure of culture and society than to the material of which they consist, i.e. to empirical reality. The above–mentioned tool–like, structurable character of significant objects is especially marked in them. Being objects which are common and easy to obtain, they may be submitted to operations like addition, subtraction, arrangement in series etc. and stored for unlimited time. *Aides–mémoire* seem to occur in some form or other in almost all human societies. Even if their significative capacity remains restricted

---

[20] Cassirer: 1972, 24, 36

[21] See note 16

[22] I have discussed this more explicitly in Stagl: 1993a.

[23] They have thus a "chartal" (Max Weber) form — like money to which they resemble in many respects (Weber: 1978, 79).

to circles of insiders, they are the true precursors of writing (a form of documentation which can be correctly interpreted also by outsiders).[24] *Aides–mémoire* are the suitable medium for the *documentation of singular things and events* in poorly differentiated societies.

Via the collection, manipulation and arrangement of significant phenomena items of knowledge — knowledge of socio–cultural structure as well as of singular things and events — are related to each other; the mind thus clarifies itself, puts its stock of extant knowledge in order and instructs the senses for purposive further research. This is why I call this a method of research. This research method is especially applicable to socio–cultural phenomena, for these are by their very essence only indirectly accessible. Historical events, cultural traits or social relationships are thus preferably explored via significant phenomena refering to them. This is the research method farthest removed from immediate experience, the method containing the greatest share of epistemological curiosity. Its relative importance has increased during the course of human history. Nevertheless it was already there from the beginning.

On closer examination it appears to be intimately linked with travel and the survey, which can both also be interpreted as the collection and arrangement of significant phenomena. The traveller collects impressions, the surveyer information. Both moreover also manipulate significant objects: travellers bring commercial goods or non–utilitarian souvenirs with them, which by their change of context significantly refer to the sphere of "otherness" from which they have been removed, and surveyers tend to document the collected information by means of *aides–mémoire*.

SOCIAL RESEARCH AND SOCIAL IDENTITY

In order to react adequately to their internal and external problems, human societies need some empirical knowledge of their own body and of their social and natural environment. This knowledge must be public, if united actions are to be taken in response to it.[25] Nevertheless human societies can only deal with a limited amount of empirical knowledge. It is essentially contingent and unpredictable. Even if necessary for survival in a changing environment, it jeopardizes social identity.

---

[24] Newell: 1980; cf. also Goody: 1977; De Francis: 1989.

[25] Gehlen: 1986a, 38ff; cf. also Stagl: 1986b.

This is a basic dilemma. All societies need a "world–view", a conception of the order of the world and their own place in it.[26] At least in its outlines all members of society must be aware of this world–view, and take it for granted, otherwise they would not be prepared to co–ordinate their actions or accept sacrifices for the sake of their community. In order to ensure this the common world–view is sacralized, anchored in the structure of society and in the basic personality of its members, and thus resists falsification.[27] Yet empirical knowledge must allow falsification.

This *antagonism between world–view and empirical knowledge* is especially flagrant in primitive, undifferentiated societies. In these societies everybody is exposed to it. Modern, well–differentiated societies can assimilate disproportionately more empirical knowledge, since they can let this knowledge be handled by specialized institutions, such as bureaucracies or research institutes.

Poorly differentiated (i.e. archaic and primitive) societies have three basic mechanisms for coping with this basic antgonism. These mechanisms are: (a) *the circulation of knowledge between center and periphery*, (b) *the hierarchical structure of memory*, and (c) *the alternation of "opening" and "closing" phases in the system of knowledge*. Together these mechanisms assure that poorly differentiated societies adapt to changing reality (and thus also pursue social research) without endangering their basic identity:

(a) The *center* of socio–cultural unit is made up by those members who either *represent* it as leaders of its constituent groups or as recognized *experts*, such as shamans, priests or scribes. Being socially more conspicuous and better organized than the rest (the *peripheral* members) they form the permanent core of the unit; their fields of vision and action are more extended in space and time than those of the peripheral members. Though these latter too may represent their groups as delegates or typical members and may possess some expert knowledge too, their knowledge of the common cultural tradition tends to be more episodic, less systematic than that of the central members, and they tend to leave its integration into the common world–view to them.

Nevertheless, by communicating on the precondition of the same world–view, both categories contribute to the common system of knowledge. The central members contribute the basic rules and schemata to this communication, the peripheral ones the empirical data.[28] These data may sometimes specify or modify the commonly held pre–judgments, i.e. the basic rules and

---

[26] Müller: 1987; Stagl: 1993a.

[27] This is the cardinal point of Durkheim's sociology of religion, cf. Durkheim: 1964, 206ff. See also Lévi–Strauss: 1958, 303–351; Luhmann: 1971, 113–136; Mol: 1976; Bühl:1986.

[28] Cf. Pitirim Sorokin's considerations about cultural "patterns" and "congeries" in Sorokin: 1957; cf. also Bühl: 1984, 62ff.

schemata of the common system of knowledge. The ongoing circulation of knowledge between both categories thus allows the unit to regenerate its system of knowledge and to adapt it to a changing world. If this circulation would cease, its *identity-establishing knowledge* would become over–rigid and its *empirical knowledge* atomized. In both cases its survival would be endangered.

(b) Knowledge is deposited in *memory*, "the process by which man not only repeats his past experience but also reconstructs this experience".[29] Three forms of memory can be distinguished which form a series of ascending inclusivity: personal, communicative and cultural memory.[30] The first warrants the identity of the individual, the second that of interacting social groups, and the third of the socio–cultural unit itself.

All knowledge must originally be integrated into some personal memory. From there it may enter into communicative and ultimately be incorporated into cultural memory. On all three levels knowledge is thus filtered; incompatible items are sorted out. On the personal level unusable knowledge is banished to the unconscious, whence it can be resuscitated in case of need. On the group level it is excluded from public communication, yet lingers on at least for one more generation in the form of personal knowledge.[31] On the societal level it may remain available for many more generations as the particular knowledge of certain subgroups, such as resident aliens ("strangers" in Simmel's sense), shamans or members of ecstatic cults.[32] In the course of this ascent through successive filters it is abstracted, generalized, streamlined and fitted into the architectural structure of culture. On all three levels, the personal as well as the group and the societal level, official knowledge is thus surrounded by a limbo of unofficial knowledge which cushions it against changing empirical reality.

(c) This system has, moreover, alternating phases of "opening" and "closing" towards empirical reality.[33] Phases of opening accompany situations of crisis. A crisis can be defined as an intensification of the internal/external problems of a social unit drastic enough to jeopardize the customary ways of living

---

[29] Cassirer: 1972, 52.

[30] Assmann: 1988; cf. also Halbwachs: 1950 and Goody–Watt: 1968.

[31] Bühl: 1984, 95ff; cf. also Fürstenberg: 1989 and Stehr: 1992.

[32] See note 62 and 63.

[33] I adopt this dichotomy from Max Weber, who speaks of the alternation between "open" and "closed" states in social relationships (Weber: 1978, 43ff). Weber here means opening and closing against new members, but this can easily be applied to new knowledge. A similar dichotomy is used by Bergson: 1932 and Popper: 1950. Ultimately this dichotomy goes back to St. Augustine; *De civitate dei* 11–14.

and thinking of its members. In such situations the circulation of knowledge described above no longer suffices. The central members, who are
responsible for overcoming the crisis, cannot merely passively wait for the
episodic inflow of relevant empirical knowledge; they must actively explore
the changed conditions. They must thereby admit large quantities of contingent, unpredictable knowledge into the common intellectual household and
eventually even change its basic rules and schemata. Such phases of opening
occur for example in connection with natural or economic catastrophes,[34]
political upheavals or war. Yet the central members attempt to master the
crisis precisely to preserve the identity of the group. If the group succeeds
in reasserting itself, its identity–establishing knowledge, even if somewhat
changed, reasserts itself too; the system of knowledge closes against empirical
reality and the routine circulation of knowledge sets in again.[35]

Thanks to these mutually complementing mechanisms empirical knowledge is always available or at least accessible to poorly differentiated societies,
even if it is not always systematically used. In most occasions such knowledge
remains restricted to certain members or subgroups of society and is only asked
for when a need for it is felt. This *social isolation of empirical knowledge* is
the functional equivalent in these societies for the above–mentioned specialized
institutions handling empirical knowledge in more differentiated societies. It is
also the reason why social research, though coeval with mankind, has made so
little progress in human cultural history up to the early modern period in the
West.

In the following paragraphs I will sketch the peripeties of social research
in relation to the major stages of socio–cultural differentiation, from archaic
(including primitive) societies to the early civilizations, exemplified by the Ancient
Near East, and to the Israelitic, Greek, Roman and medieval roots of early modern
Western culture.

SOCIAL RESEARCH IN POORLY
DIFFERENTIATED SOCIETIES

Little is known about social research before the onset of writing. Yet this
does not prove that no such research existed. Something about it can be inferred
from early written sources and from ethnographic reports.

Primitive societies have a knowledge of their natural and socio–cultural
environment which is both rich and sophisticated, and the same must have
been true for archaic societies. After giving a few pertinent examples, Claude

---

[34] Cf. Clausen: 1994, 13ff.

[35] Müller: 1987, 142ff; cf. also Mühlmann: 1964, 121–133 and Topitsch: 1972, 13ff.

Lévi–Strauss sums up: "This drive for objective knowledge is one of the most neglected aspects of the thought of those which we call 'primitives' ".[36] Without this knowledge our own ethnographic reports could never have been written. Most of the empirical content of these reports has been supplied by "native informants" and has merely been sytematized by the ethnographer.[37] A few more words have to be said on each of the three basic research methods in poorly differentiated societies:

TRAVEL

The Eskimos made journeys with sledges and boats which sometimes took a year or even two. They thereby acquired a detailed knowledge not only of their environment but also of far away regions, a knowledge which was later used by Western explorers. These travels Marcel Mauss compared with "immense feelers" put out by the social organism.[38]

No primitive society is immobile and self–sufficient.[39] Not only nomads, like the Eskimos, but also sedentary group travel. Every society is surrounded by what Friedrich Ratzel called its "spiritual space", the space known to it from reports of travellers.[40] Among these travellers are fugitives and exiles, captives, hostages, women who marry foreigners, children who live for some time in foreign groups in order to learn the language, itinerant merchants and craftsmen, messengers, envoys and spies.

Curiosity can only be a secondary motive for such travellers, since in poorly differentiated societies, where everybody has to earn his own livelihood, travel cannot be legitimized as a goal in itself. Yet at least spies and the abovementioned children, who are exchanged by families belonging to different language groups in order to become interpreters,[41] travel with an express commission for exploration.

By overstepping the horizon of the other members of their group, travellers acquire knowledge inaccessible to these. Travellers moreover learn to know

---

[36] Lévi–Strauss: 1973, 13.

[37] Anthropologists have been rather slow to recognize this debt, cf. however Casagrande: 1960; Redfield: 1968; Fahim: 1982; Stocking: 1983; Clifford–Marcus: 1986. This observation has been anticipated by Goethe: *Wären jedoch Einheimische nicht selbst Freunde ihrer Gegend, nicht selbst bemüht, entweder eines Vorteils oder der Wissenschaft willen, das, was in ihrem Revier merkwürdig ist, zusammenzustellen, so müßte der Reisende sich lang vergebens quälen" (Italienische Reise*, Catania 4. May 1787).

[38] Mauss: 1978, vol. I, 237.

[39] Mühlmann: 1956.

[40] Ratzel: 1897, 263ff.

[41] For New Guinea cf. Behrmann: 1924, 63; le Roux: 1948–50, vol. I, 333. This institution, which seems to occur world–wide, belongs into the context of "fosterage"; cf. Steinmetz: 1928, vol. I, 1–113; Bühler: 1964; Kerlouegan: 1968–71.

their own capacities and limits: during their travels they also explore themselves. Real or imaginary travelling is therefore frequently connected with extraordinary states of consciousness, for example initiation, the quest for visions, ecstasy, shamanism and pilgrimages.[42] A homecomer from a real or imaginary journey is expected to have changed. Like a visitor from abroad he thus becomes a menace to the identity of his group.[43]

If poorly differentiated societies cannot do without knowledge and goods from abroad, they at least regulate their influx as far as possible. This is normally done by means of *rites de passage*, rituals effecting the transition from one social state to the other. These rituals which in some form or other occur in every society, are divided by Arnold van Gennep into three major steps: casting off the old state, staying in a state of limbo where the normal rules of socio–cultural life are suspended, and assuming the new state. Transitions in space (crossing boundaries) are effected by rituals similar to transitions in time (in the annual cycle or in the life cycle). These rituals thus structure space and time, making them equally permeable for change. Thus they combine the unalterable with the contingent.[44]

Visitors from abroad like homecomers are not immediately allowed full contact with the group members. Together with their goods and their knowledge they are detained in a state of social quarantine before the group is prepared to "naturalize" them.[45] Such a quarantine is for example established by the customs of hospitality. In many archaic and primitive societies the guest is so to say monopolized by his host. He must submit to a formal interrogation[46] or is put to the test in some other way.[47] Travellers coming from beyond the group's horizon are thus "explored" by their host group and only admitted — together with their goods and knowledge on that group's terms.

Thus poorly differentiated societies reduce their public knowledge of other ways of life to its essential minimum. Tales told by travellers are distrusted in all societies. Experts on foreign groups are suspect as to the loyalty towards their own. Guests who stay on ("Strangers" in Georg Simmel's sense) are kept in a marginal social position similar to that of border dwellers or group members of mixed origin.[48] Their expert knowledge is thereby both isolated and drawn upon.

---

[42] Cf. Eliade: 1957.

[43] Cf. Schütz: 1972, vol. II, 70–83.

[44] van Gennep: 1960. Cf. also Turner: 1969.

[45] I have expounded this concept of "naturalization" in Stagl: 1981b.

[46] As in *Odyssey* I 169ff, III 69ff and IX 252ff.

[47] Hellmuth: 1984, 82ff: Pitt-Rivers: 1977, 94ff

[48] Simmel: 1958, 509–512. The literature triggered by this seminal essay is meanwhile immeasurable.

SURVEYS

In his *Theaitetos*, Plato mentions an Athenian custom which was apparently self–evident and well established in his time and may serve as an example for archaic surveys: when a child was born, it was carried by the midwife around the circle of bystanders (obviously women of experience) who had to inspect the newborn and then to give their opinion whether it should be nurtured or exposed.[49]

This kind of survey corresponds with the primitive state of socio–political organization with poorly developed bureaucracies and markets. Under these conditions combined actions have to be organized "liturgically", i.e. through the allocation of "burdens which are associated with privileges" (Max Weber).[50]

Such a burden–cum–privilege was the participation in a survey. Jost Trier has disussed ancient Indo–European surveys under the heading of *Reihendienste* (services by taking turns, such as keeping guard, rendering soccage or filling rotating offices).[51] The *Reihendienst* is the basic mechanism for the collection and utilization of goods, services and information not only in archaic but also in contemporary primitive societies.[52] Taking part in a survey is a privilege, since only people who belong to the community and are important in it as experts or representatives are questioned; by giving their answers they contribute to a decision which is binding to the other members. Yet it is also a burden, since no "mere opinion" is required: the participants must be prepared to act according to their answers — and to suffer for them.[53]

The phenomenology of the archaic and primitive survey may be presented according to the following fourteen points:

(a) These surveys are carried out when the life of a community is disturbed by war, illness, crime, witchcraft, civil strife or other catastrophes. Such crises arouse anxiety which leads to ritualization.[54] This yields the social energy necessary for the organization of the *Reihendienst*. Surveys thus take place in a ritualized atmosphere, which moreover, contributes to the standardization of the questioning and answering.

(b) The questioning is done orally; the participants have thus to be assembled in one place. Hence surveys imply locomotion. Considering the arduous

---

[49] 160e–161a.

[50] Weber: 1978, 197.

[51] Trier: 1957; Trier: 1964.

[52] Cf. Leach: 1954; Mair: 1962; Fried: 1967; Abel: 1973; Stagl: 1988.

[53] *"Ein großer Reiz des Studiums primitiver Kulturen liegt darin, ihre plastische Kraft und innere Wahrheit zu erkennen, der Reiz ist ein moralischer. Nichts lag ihnen ferner, als handlungslose Gesinnung durch oratorischen Aufwand glaubhaft zu machen"* (Gehlen: 1986b, 26).

[54] Cf. Eibl–Eibesfeldt: 1967, 262ff; Gehlen: 1986b, 145ff.

conditions for communication and transport, normally only a sample of the total membership is questioned.

(c) In most cases only one question is posed (the main exception is the census which will be discussed below). It is a question of vital importance to the community and presents conflicting courses of action, on which a decision must be taken (for example: Is a newborn fit to become a member of the community or not? In the Athenian case, however, the situation had presumably become so standardized that the question was not posed orally, but deictically, the child being just shown to the interviewees).

(d) The question is posed to the assembled interviewees by an interviewer who is authorized on the part of the community either by virtue of his office (such as the midwife in Athens) or by a special commission. The interviewer thus represents the community itself.

(e) In posing the question successively to the assembled, the interviewer makes a round or circuit of them. (If all the interviewees cannot be summoned to one place, the question may be carried to them by messengers, who likewise represent the community). This explains why I consider the survey to be a special form of travel.

(f) The interviewees are selected from the total membership of the commu- nity either as representatives of its (familial, local, religious or military) constituent groups, as for example the participants in a war council, or as experts possessing some special knowledge relevant to the situation, as for example the experienced women in the Athenian case. In both capacities they represent in their entirety the community itself.

(g) Whereas experts supply objective data as parameters for the impending decision, representatives convey insights into subjective states (their own and those of their followers) and thereby elucidate the morale of the community's constituent groups, whose knowledge is important for the implementation of that decision.

(h) Objective data and subjective states are seen as interrelated, for knowledge is not yet separated from its bearers.[55] As highly dramatic procedures, surveys in poorly differentiated societies hardly leave space for impartial discussion and exlude intellectual curiosity as a primary motive.

(i) The interviewees have to give their answers publicly. These can thus be controlled and in case of need corrected by the bystanders. The answers hence exert a certain influence on each other, by means of which a common

---

[55] This explains seemingly irrational behaviour like the punishing of the bringers of bad news or the seeking of scapegoats; cf. Clausen: 1994, 37ff.

opinion is built up in the course of the survey. This unification of opinion prepares the impending decision.

(j) Opinion–making is affected by the order of precedence in the questioning. The more important interviewees give their answers first, which therefore carry more weight, yet also the greater risk of being dissident. Lesser participants, being questioned later, can imperceptibly hide behind the emerging common opinion.

(k) By giving their answers, interviewees commit themselves — together with their followers — to one of the possible courses of action defined in the question. They moreover assume responsibility for its implementation. If their opinion turns out to be a dissident one, they may be made to pay for it.

(l) There is thus a latent resistance against answering, which manifests itself in not telling everything one could, in hiding one's "true" opinion or in dodging the survey altogether. This resistance may be overcome by rational insight into the danger of the situation, by hallowed custom (an infortituous connection is often made between surveys and *rites de passage*, as also in the Athenian case), and ultimately by political coercion.

(m) The information collected in archaic and primitive surveys must be stored in the memories of the participants — a further incentive to hold surveys publicly. Yet the amount and the standardized character of the information eventually leads to the use of technical aids (*aides–mémoire*). Even if knowledge is not yet separated from its bearers, this is a first step in that direction.

(n) By means of such surveys poorly differentiated societies concentrate their extant empirical knowledge, which is normally broadly scattered over their members. Yet they achieve this only at certain points and temporarily in order to master emergencies. After the decision has been reached, only that evidence is permitted to remain public knowledge which supports the "right" course of action; conflicting evidence is quietly forgotten or even consciously suppressed by intimidation, ridicule or physical violence.[56] Hence this occasional concentration of knowledge does not lead to its ongoing accumulation.

MANIPULATION OF THE SIGNIFICANT PHENOMENA

As has been shown,[57] significant phenomena are closely interwoven with the architectural structure of culture. The third basic research method is thus

---

[56] Cf. the war council in *Iliad* II 73–399.

[57] See § *Three Basic Research Methods*, (d): Indirect exploration via significant phenomena.

more difficult to set off against the general socio–cultural background than the first and the second. This requires some interpretation. Nevertheless I hope to do this convincingly by interpreting two types of primitive rituals: (a) *community rituals* and (b) *rituals of "otherness"*.

(a) Among the many functions rituals have is the visualization of socio–cultural relationships. In this respect the performance of rituals can be seen as a self–exploration of the organizing group, whose results are presented by significant actions instead of significant words or objects, that is, deictically. Community rituals are rituals wherein a whole community takes part as organizers, contributors, performers and spectators. Among these are the "corroborees" of the Australian Aborigines, the pig slaughter feasts in New Guinea, circumcision rituals in Central Africa and comparable cults of primitive societies in many other parts of the world. They involve the contribution of personal goods and services to a common funds and their subsequent public display and consumption in connection with religious ceremonies, dances, parades and other "shows". Their main goal is the re–structuring of the community by the collective performance of its rites of passage (initiations, marriages, burials, in addition the settling of lawsuits and the conclusion of political alliances). Besides their goods and services the participants also contribute information, for by performing this ritual the community demonstrates its morale, producing power, size, political unity and military strength to its own members and to interested guests from abroad.[58] Quoting Niklas Luhmann one can call this a "self–thematization of the social system".[59]

Organized as *Reihendienste*, community rituals are obviously related to surveys. By demonstrating the structure and strength of the organizing community at periodical intervals, such as the harvest seasons or the climaxes in the reproductory cycles of the herds and of the community itself (initiation and marriage ceremonies!), they *invite comparison* between the achievements of various subgroups and individuals within the community, between its past and present state, and between itself and other groups. They thus permit an empirically substantiated assessment of the relevant social forces.[60] They can be seen from this angle as a further development of the survey in the direction of the *systematic documentation* of the total community. The masses of empirical information necessary for the organization of such rituals

---

[58] A good description and analysis from the Highlands of New Guinea is given in Rappaport: 1968. Cf. also Durkheim: 1964, 371ff; Turner: 1969; Mol: 1976; Tambiah: 1984.

[59] Luhmann: 1975. Cf. also Hahn–Kapp: 1987.

[60] I have expounded my thesis of the origin of the census from the community rituals in Stagl: 1992. Cf. also Stagl: 1974a, 272ff.

(their "logistic") are frequently mastered with the help of *aide–mémoire*.[61] As will be shown below, community rituals are the archetype of the *census*.

(b) There are other rituals less central to the self–image of primitive societies which apply the manipulation of significant phenomena to the exploration of cultural "otherness". Among the Songhai on the northern bend of the Niger emerged about 1920 an ecstatic cult called *hauka* which represented the French and the British as well as the Muslim by means of symbolic objects (sculptures, flags, whistles etc.) and symbolic actions (imitating and parodying these powerful "others" by means of characteristic disguise and behaviour and breaking their characteristic taboos).[62] The Cuna of Panama, whose official mythology contains no conception of the white man, reconstitute him nevertheless as a dreaded, demonic being in shamanic rituals for the treatment of mental illness.[63]

THE ANCIENT NEAR EAST

Large–scale polities and written records appeared in Egypt and Mesopotamia in the late fourth millennium B.C. and gradually spread to the intermediate and adjacent regions, eventually to form an area of more or less common culture called the Ancient Near East. The end of this culture is conventionally seen as the point where all the major Ancient Near Eastern polities were incorporated either in the Persian (late 6th century B.C.) or in the Macedonian universal monarchy (late 4th century B.C.). I discuss the Ancient Near East here as a transitional form between archaic, poorly differentiated societies and classical antiquity, and at the same time as a model for other "early civilizations" such as the Indian, Chinese, Andean and Mexican.

These civilizations brought distinctive advance in social, political and cultural differentiations over the archaic societies:

"consider ..... a fairly stable, but complex, large and well–stratified ..... society. At its base, there is a large number of rural, servile, inward–turned food–producing communities, tied to the land, and obliged to surrender their surplus produce. Above them, a self–insulating ruling elite of warriors/administrators controls the means of coercion and the channels of communication, and is legally entitled to act as a cohesive body (a right denied to the peasant category). This enables it to maintain

---

[61] Cf. for New Guinea Strathern: 1979, 116, 120; Wassmann: 1982, 65f.

[62] Kramer: 1987, 153ff, Kramer points out that in many primitive societies this "interpretation of the other through mimesis" is much more "realistic" than the rituals and works of art which represent the self–image of the society and thus are more stylized and abstract (*op. cit.*, 242ff, cf. also Lips: 1937). This corresponds to my own distinction between "empirical" and "identity–establishing" knowledge.

[63] Severi: 1993, 7ff.

its domination. Alongside it, there is a parallel religious hierarchy, comprising both monastic communities and individual officiating priests, who provide ritual services to other segments of the population. In between the rural communities on the one hand and the military–clerical elite, there is a layer of craftsmen and traders, some settled in small pockets in the countryside, or living as perpetual migrants, and others living in more concentrated urban agglomerations."

(Ernest Gellner)[64]

This political, religious and economic centralization created an immense social distance between rulers and ruled. The subject communities retained something of their original independence only thanks to the still archaic conditions of transport and communication. Nevertheless they had to surrender their surplus produce in goods and manpower to the rulers. These used it partly for their own purposes and redistributed the other part among the ruled according to necessity. The advantage of rational, large–scale, long–range planning over the contingencies of situation–related measures contributed greatly to the stability of the system.[65]

The habit of planning furthered two important developments: a new technology of documentation, *writing*, and the emergence of *bureaucracies*. This intermediate class somehow bridged the abyss between rulers and ruled, chanelling the flow of goods, services and information from the bottom to the top of the political pyramid and back again.[66]

Writing apparently originated as an advancement of traditional *aides–mémoire* among merchants and was subsequently taken over by governments.[67] (New features frequently appear at the periphery of society and only after having been put to the test are they adopted at the centre.)[68] Unlike *aides–mémoire*, writing can be read (i.e. univocally interpreted) by outsiders. It thus breaks the spell of the immediate, places things and events far away in time, space and consequence within intellectual reach, and constitutes an artificial memory. By

---

[64] Gellner: 1987, 13. It has to be said that Gellner paints here an "ideal type" of the "traditional society" general enough to be applicable also to other epochs and parts of the world.

[65] Cf. Wittfogel: 1962; Polanyi–Arensberg–Pearson: 1962; Fried: 1968; Service: 1977; Claesen–Skalnik: 1978; Haas: 1982; Saggs: 1989; Eisenstadt: 1993; Ferguson–Mansbach: 1994, ch. III and IV.

[66] The literature on orality and literacy is meanwhile immeasurable; cf. note 57. For the literature on early bureaucracies cf. note 65.

[67] Schmandt–Basserat: 1978. For the history of writing see moreover Diringer: 1962; Gelb: 1963; De Francis: 1989.

[68] See the *Social Research and Social Identity* above.

handling it, the new class of bureaucrats, called "scribe", created the prerequisites for the functioning of the large–scale polities.[69]

Originally writing was mainly used for the keeping of lists.[70] Lists replace the spontaneity of perception by *method* and chart the mental field. Since they require completion they encourage inquisitiveness. The habit of keeping lists was soon extended from present (inventories) to past (registers) and even future phenomena (prescriptions). It led thus to an increased awareness of temporal–spatial continuity and reinforced the tendency of social planning. The conception of national territories emerged[71] and eventually the idea of the *cosmos* as a homogeneous field of experience subject everywhere to the same laws — which implied the idea of an *impersonal science*.[72] This science has been aptly described by Wolfram von Soden as "list science" (*Listenwissenschaft*).[73] Though triggered by tasks of commerce and administration, it achieved its most spectacular triumph in the registration and evaluation of natural phenomena (Babylonian astronomy!) — which, however, had also significance for social life. List science was also applied with some success in the socio–cultural sciences. Babylonians, Egyptians and Phoenicians reduced the report of their traveller to a systematic geography–ethnography.[74]

Writing and lists also moulded empirical social research. Governments undertook written surveys within the bureaucracy, where the center of power (the court of the monarch) posed the questions and the administrators at the local level answered them. Some lists of human beings, goods and services are so detailed and standardized[75] that they only can be interpreted as answers to equally standardized lists of questions, or *questionnaires*.[76] These were no doubt also sent to other places so that the answers given independently could be compared.

Besides such surveys within the ruling group there were also stocktakings of the whole population. Given the illiteracy of the masses and the still archaic

---

[69] See note 65. There is, however, the aberrant case of ancient Peru, a bureaucratic empire whose administration solely relied on *aides–mémoire* (the famous *quipus*; cf. Gelb: 1963, 57f; Morris: 1976). This case shows that bureaucratization preceded writing.

[70] Cf. Goody: 1977, 74ff; Ong: 1982, 99ff.

[71] "Contrary to the impression that "territoriality" is an invention of the modern state, ancient (Near Eastern, J.S.) rulers were keenly aware of the territorial limits of their political jurisdiction." (Ferguson–Mansbach: 1992, ch. three, 21).

[72] Kranz: 1955; Goody: 1977, 148ff; cf. also *op. cit.*, 53ff. Cf. also ch. three.

[73] Soden: 1965, 66ff.

[74] Müller: 1972–80 vol. I, 74ff.

[75] See note 70.

[76] A series of questions is called a "questionnaire" when it is administered in written form; when it is administered orally, so that direct interaction between interviewer and interviewee takes place, it is called an "interview schedule". Yet in any case they must not merely be questions; there must be a research design behind them (Manheim: 1977, 210f).

conditions of communication and transport they had to be conducted orally, utilizing the old *Reihendienst* pattern. The Ancient Near Eastern censuses, which seem never to have been comprehensively studied,[77] superimposed thus on the archaic community rituals the new model of the bureaucratized written survey. For it must be presumed that the same series of questions which had been written down in advance were posed (where necessary in translated form) simultaneously to all local communities within the national territory and that the answers were written down in order to be compared and totaled up at the centre.[78]

In bureaucratized censuses the socio–cultural distance between researchers and objects of research is so great that both categories no longer share the same experienced world. The former thus no longer implicitly understand the latter. They also can no longer count on their voluntary cooperation, but have to enforce their compliance. They take away something of the latter's insider *knowledge* and convert it into impersonal *information* which from now on can be handled by outsiders.

This also implies a shift of emphasis from *quality* to *quantity*: more questions are posed by more interviewers to more interviewees, and proportionately more information is gathered. Yet it is information of indifferent quality. For it is by no means the same if a self–determinating community puts one question of vital importance to its central members or if a series of questions is forced by remote rulers on a "servile, inward–turned" population. In this latter case the always latent resistance against answering questions[79] becomes virulent. Being explored entails being exploited. The ruled withhold thus as much information as they can from their rulers, knowing quite well that surrendering it means that they soon also will have to surrender their goods and services too. In the Old Testament censuses are said to entail the wrath of the Lord in the shape of plagues.[80] Such beliefs can be interpreted as a reaction of formerly independent communities, who feel their tribal gods offended by the arrogation of their census–rituals by a remote government.

Written surveys among the bureaucracy too brought far from satisfactory results. Peripheral administrators show little interest in undermining their own position by making their activity too transparent to the center of power.[81]

Bureaucratic collection of information had thus to be standardized at the lowest common denominator. Since large distances in space and time intervened between its collection and its use, the information currently available

---

[77] Jan Assmann, personal information. For short summing–ups cf. John: 1884, 17ff; Wittfogel: 1962, 80ff; Gladden: 1972, vol. I, 18ff.

[78] For examples cf. the *Israel*.

[79] See *Early Social Research, Surveys*, point (1).

[80] See the *Israel*.

[81] Eisenstadt: 1993, 157ff.

was necessarily of different provenance, age and reliability. It would thus have been self–defeating to aim at a too high degree of exactness in its collection. The information at the disposal of the rulers represented the actual state of the polity merely by what is now called the fiction of an "ethnographic present".

Governments were well aware of this state of affairs. To counteract it they created travelling officials called the "eyes" or "ears" of the monarch. Being thus parts of the body of the monarch, these officials represented him wherever they went, carrying as it were a state of emergency with them. Their commission overrode those of the local administrators, they verified information submitted by these and heard complaints by the local population, spied on both categories alike, investigated critical situations and redressed abuses. The "eyes" and "ears" of the monarch complemented thus the broad, quantifying, routine research of the bureaucratic machinery by selective, yet intensive and qualitative research.[82]

This semi–secret service was closely allied to the diplomatic service which emerged as a regular feature of international politics in the second millennium B.C. Diplomats were a category of travelling officials representing the monarch abroad. In order to be able to report on foreign polities, they explored them by their own travels and the interviewing of other travellers; after their return home they frequently functioned as expert advisers to the monarch. The explorative journey abroad was thus bureaucratized in a similar way as the circuit within the national territory.[83]

Through all this extensive data collecting, a systematic socio–politico–economic science became at least a remote possibility in the Ancient Near East. Thus, acccording to Sir Leonard Woolley, Egyptian bureaucrats arrived at an abstract concept of "labour" which served them as a common denominator for various goods and services:

> "All taxes were paid in kind and stored in the royal magazines; it is illuminating to find that all the goods thus brought in, grain, cattle, wine, linen, are invoiced indiscriminately as "labour"; in other words, they are put on precisely the same basis as the *corvée* whereby Pharaoh's serfs, the people of Egypt, were called up to build a pyramid or to clean out a canal."[84]

Yet this involvement with bureaucratic practice both hindered and furthered the rise of a social science. The bureaucracies were prevented from reducing the vast amounts of diverse information they handled to a body of verifiable and teachable doctrine by (a) the *topical* nature and (b) the *secrecy* of that information:

---

[82] Dwornik: 1974, 6f, 15, 23f; Eisenstadt: 1993, 144ff.

[83] Oates: 1986, 70ff; Saggs: 1989, ch. 9; Ferguson–Mansbach: 1994, ch. 3.

[84] Woolley: 1963, 624; cf. also Goody: 1977, 88.

(a) Permanent documentation of information in writing poses the question of sorting out unneeded items. Yet under the fiction of the "ethnographic present" it is not so easy to decide whether a piece of information is already obsolete or not. Thus after being no longer regularly used, files and even entire archives were often allowed to quietly rot away (luckily for the archaeologists). Sometimes, however, they were purposely destroyed.

Even if practically used, the results of bureaucratic research were thus not *accumulated*; they were collected, used, and eliminated in ever repeated cycles. Empirical social knowledge was a useful if not a highly esteemed kind of knowledge — which is precisely why it was permitted to be handled by the intermediate class of the scribes. What reason was there to preserve it forever? This topicality of empirical knowledge was very well compatible with a high regard for changelessness. Ancient Near Eastern polities were usually "divine kingships"; the government was supported by the "parallel religious hierarchy" which extolled the political order as an emanation of the unchanging order of the cosmos.[85] At the same time they were rational administrations adapting to change. The combination of these two features caused the essential immobility of Ancient Near Eastern polities as well as their attempts to "rewrite history".[86]

(b) The rulers had to keep their stock of information secret in order to guard the parameters of their decisions against outsiders (*arcana imperii*). This was originally not so difficult to achieve: the *literati* were only a tiny fraction of the population and guarded the secrets of their art jealously.[87] The government had virtually a monopoly of demand for writing skills and could thus easily control the *literati*.[88] It was more difficult to keep the *arcana imperii* from disloyal fractions within the ruling elite — a difficulty never really overcome. In order to forestall palace revolutions, high treason or rebellions, the available stock of empirical social knowledge was split up in so far as it was feasible among mutually isolated departments. The coordination of this scattered information was left to the leaders at the very top of the political pyramid. Yet up to about 1000 BC Ancient Near Eastern monarchs and aristocrats were usually illiterate.[89]

---

[85] Frankfort: 1978; cf. also Engnell: 1967 and Saggs:1989.

[86] This is a central thesis of Wittfogel's study of "oriental despotism (Wittfogel: 1962). It is the work of a disillusioned former communist written with the hindsight of modern totalitarian systems, which show indeed the same tendencies of immobilism and "rewriting history". On the latter see also Kees: 1952 and Assmann: 1983.

[87] Goody–Watt: 1968.

[88] Religion and commerce being also virtually branches of government, cf. Polanyi–Arensberg– Pearson: 1962; Saggs: 1989, 130ff; Ferguson– Mansbach: 1994, ch.4.

[89] Goody–Watt: 1968.

To the *arcana imperii* corresponded the *arcana populi* which have already been discussed. In an inverted way the belief in divine punishment of censuses can be said to correspond to the ideology of "divine kinship".

On a closer consideration of these two requirements one realizes that the Ancient Near East (as well as other comparable civilizations) is not so different from poorly differentiated societies with respect to its techniques of social research as it first appears. As archaic "experts" remain subordinated to "representatives", so in the early civilizations the bureaucracies — despite their important functions — remain subordinated to aristocratic rulers who make do with an implicit, orally transmitted political wisdom close to the empirical world, just like archaic chieftains.[90] This imbalance made the political systems of the early civilizations vulnerable. It forced them to arrogate as many powers as feasible to the very top of the pyramid, to guard the *arcana imperii* ferociously, and even to spy upon themselves. One gets the impression that empirical social knowledge, though indispensable, was considered as extremely dangerous by these governments — about as necessary and dangerous as atomic energy is to us.

If nevertheless there was *some* progress of the social sciences in the Ancient Near East, it can be attributed to a slow and gradual mutual opening of its socio–cultural communities, thanks to which the entire region eventually became one interacting system (an *oikouméne*, as the Greeks later called it.)[91] As amazing concurrences between Egypt, Mesopotamia and other regions show, travelling and the diffusion of cultural traits had already taken place before 3000 and occurred increasingly afterwards. It was furthered by mounting international competition: between 3500 and 500, when they all became engulfed by the Persian Empire, the Ancient Near Eastern polities grew in size and complexity but diminished in numbers: from tribal and city states to kingdoms and empires.[92] In order to survive as independent units, the competing polities had to keep pace with their neighbours; thus technological and organizational innovations spread over the whole region. Among the latter were standing armies, the above–mentioned institutions of diplomats and "eyes and ears of the monarch", and a

---

[90] The Great King Xerxes, possibly the most powerful monarch in all the history of the Ancient Near East conducted at least his war council wholly like an archaic survey. According to Herodotus, Xerxes summoned preceding the battle of Salamis all naval commanders and vassal princes to his camp, where he seated them according to their rank. "When they had sat down in order one after another, Xerxes sent (the commander–in–chief, J.S.) and put each to the test by questioning if the Persian ships should offer battle. (The commander–in–chief) went about questioning them, from the Sidonian (The King of Sidon in Phoenicia, J.S.) onwards....." (VIII 67–68). On the norms and mores of Ancient Near Eastern government cf. Ferguson–Mansbach: 1994, ch. 4.

[91] Cf. Tenbruck: 1968, 331ff; Tenbruck: 1989.

[92] Cf. Ferguson–Mansbach: 1994, ch. 4.

centralization of the bureaucratic machinery culminating in the office of "grand vizier", a second, more secular power center after the divine monarch.[93]

All this eventually led to the appearance of common cultural identity and common behavioural standards in the Ancient Near East. Travelling became more common, and many rulers "naturalized" foreigners who had proved their special worth as soldiers, craftsmen, commercial agents, administrators or advisers.[94] Empires are by their very nature multi–national, and, as is known from the Old Testament, whole peoples were either invited to settle or forcibly re–settled by them.[95] International relations and the conquest of formerly independent polities by kingdoms and empires created a need for intersocietal and inter-cultural mediation. "Translating" socio–cultural features into corresponding ones of other groups led to the search for their largest common denominator, to a comparing and abstracting attitude.[96] If the need to remain in control over the increasingly rationalized bureaucratic machine had forced monarchs, hierocrats and aristocrats to become literate and thus had upgraded literacy socially, members of the elites of subordinated polities, being relieved of govern-mental functions, were now free to turn into "intellectuals" mediating between socio–cultural groups and contributing to a common literary education.

There were also attempts to bridge the abyss between ruling and ruled groups. Faced with expansive neigbhours and the always latent possibility of revolts, the rulers had to open up to the people to a certain extent in order to mobilize popular support. They had somehow to acquaint them with their plans and listen to their complaints. The Babylonian King was the "ultimate rectifier of wrongs", to whom private citizens could appeal directly.[97] The Egyptian literary masterpiece *The complaint of the peasant* describes a similar appeal to Pharaoh, which shows a residual trust in the integrity of at least the higher echelons of the ruling elite.[98]

This mutual opening of hitherto closed communities and social groups spread the idea of the universalization of knowledge. Closed communities have a *magical* attitude: the world appears in principle to be already known to them.[99] Only an *oikouméne*, a polycentric system of communities with perme-able boundaries who nevertheless retain their basic self–assertion, allows for the *scientific* attitude, which assumes an unknown, yet knowable world. It was

---

[93] *Op. cit.*; cf. also Gladden: 1972 and Eisenstadt: 1993, ch. 10.

[94] Ferguson-Mansbach: 1984, ch. 4.

[95] Ibidem.

[96] Already Durkheim has shown that the (intellectualist) idea of an international or intertribal religion follows from regular communication between different communities (Durkheim: 1964, 295ff). See also the writings of Friedrich Tenbruck indicated in note 91.

[97] Tadmor: 1986, 216.

[98] Cf. Herrmann: 1957, 79ff.

[99] Goody: 1977, ch. 8; Bühl: 1984, ch. 4 and 5; Müller: 1987, part II.

the self–organization of the Ancient Near East as an *oikouméne* which gave this attitude its chance to become a primary motive,[100] and eventually led to further progress in the methodology of the social sciences.

ISRAEL

The fourth book of Moses, called Numbers, though in this form considered unhistorical by modern Old Testament scholarship, nevertheless provides an insight into the techniques and mentality of social research towards the end of the second millennium.[101] By being incorporated, into the Bible, it moreover became known to the whole Christian world and influenced social research in the West.

As the story goes (4 Mos. 1–4), the people of Israel were gathered in the desert of Sinai to be counted, reviewed and assesed. This was carried out by a commission of twelve respected men, one for each of the twelve tribes, under the direction of Moses and his brother Aaron. All males above the age of twenty and fit for military service were registered according to their tribe, lineage and family. Their total number is given as 603,550. Subsequently those males were counted that did not serve, yet were politically important: the Levites (22,000), the first–born boys in every family (22,273) and the persons suitable for priestly service (8,580). A poll tax had to be paid for everyone registered and further tributes were levied. This census inaugurated sweeping military, fiscal, political and religious reforms, which were interpreted as a purification of the community. It met with strong opposition from the people who were punished by the Lord with fire, plague and leprosy (cf. also 4 Mos. 11,33 and 2 Mos. 30,12).

After having carried out this census, Moses organized the reconnoitring of the land Canaan. Again a commission of twelve men was appointed, one for each tribe. This commission had a research mandate in the form of a list of questions (no doubt the census had likewise been carried out with the help of such a list, an "interview schedule" to be precise). The instruction for the reconnoitring of Canaan reads as follows:

"Get you up this way southward, and go up into the mountain: And see the land, what it is: and the people that dwelleth therein, whether they be strong or weak, few or many; And what the land is they dwell in, whether it be good or bad; and what cities they be that they dwell in, whether in tents or in strong holds; And what the land is, whether it be fat or lean, whether there be wood therein or not."

In addition this explorative expedition was requested to bring back significant objects, that is to say samples of the "fruit of the land" (4 Mos. 13,17–20).

---

[100] See the preceding note and Nestle: 1940; Popper: 1950; Jaspers: 1957, part I; Altheim: 1960, 17ff; Topitsch: 1972, 124ff; Müller: 1972–80, vol. I, 29ff; Eisenstadt: 1986.

[101] Rad: 1957, vol. I, 279ff, 288ff.

After having safely returned, the twelve commissioners reported to a public meeting presided over by Moses and Aaron. Ten among them warned against attempting a conquest since they considered the Canaanites to be too strong. Two advised venturing it. These two narrowly escaped being stoned by the crowd who were afraid of this campaign. In the end, however, the minority opinion, supported by Moses and Aaron, prevailed. Yet the people of Israel were punished by the Lord for their lack of conquering spirit. They suffered a crushing defeat. Appropriately, the ten cautious commissioners then perished in a plague. The two fearless ones, however, survived the forty years of wandering in the desert following thereon, eventually to lead a second, more successful invasion into Canaan (4 Mos. 13–44).[102]

Among the other examples of social research in the Old Testament, the census of David still deserves mention. After David had usurped the kingship of Israel (about 1000), he instructed his commander–in–chief Joab as follows: "Go, number Israel from Beersheba even to Dan; and bring the number of them to me, that I may know it" (1 Chron. 21,2). Joab and his sub–commanders were installed as a travelling commission making a circuit of the country. They were to register all males belonging to the people of Israel who were over twenty and fit for military service (the subjugated Canaanites were thus not registered). This took the commission almost ten months. It met with sullen resistence. David's census was not successful. The people looked upon it as sinful. Prophets arose to preach against it. Joab executed his orders without enthusiasm. Eventually a plague broke out. It was immediately called a judgment of the Lord on king and people. The census had to be abandoned (2 Sam. 24; 1 Chron. 21 and 27, 23–24).[103]

In Moses' time, Israel was a tribal confederation marginal to the centres of civilization of the Ancient Near East. Accordingly the census as described in 4 Mos. 1–4 shows many archaic features. All full members of the community were questioned (i.e. the adult men, who apparently represented their womenfolk, children and slaves). They were assembled in one place. The interviewing was organized as *Reihendienst*. The census took place publicly. The interviewers formed a commission which represented all constituent tribes plus the central government. By answering their questions, the interviewees committed themselves, together with their dependents, to the future policy of their leaders. At the same time the census was a community ritual. In it the community displayed its social structure, economic capacity and military strength to its own members. Lepers and other unclean persons were banished and the community members

---

[102] Rad: 1957, vol. I, 295ff.

[103] There seems to be more historical substance in the report on David's census than on Moses' census; cf. Carlson: 1964; Beek: 1973, 53ff.

had to confess their sins (4 Mos. 5). Several other decrees by Moses in the name of the Lord followed.

It frequently happened that the influx of new social forces intensifies for the moment the existing institutions and extends them to the very limits of their capacity, before they give way to new, more fitting institutions.[104] This must have happened here with the archaic community ritual under the influence of writing and bureaucratization. List–keeping is expressly mentioned in the Book of Numbers.[105] The commission headed by Moses and Aaron kept registers for the whole community, which is inconceivable without the aid of a clerical staff. These bureaucratic features, which were obviously adopted from Egypt, were grafted on the archaic pattern of the community ritual.

The procedure of the reconnoitring of Canaan was very similar to that of the census. It, too, was organized as a *Reihendienst*. There was a commission of twelve scouts, one for each tribe of the Israelitic confederacy. They had got a research mandate in the form of a questionnaire, orally no doubt, but significant for the mentality of bureaucratized social research. By means of it, the twelve representatives of Israel were to make themselves experts on the land of Canaan. Their mission thus transferred the principle of systematic self–exploration of the community of Israel to foreign people: what had been social research turned into ethnography.

The questioning of the returned scouts by Moses and Aaron before a public meeting was also very similar to an archaic survey. This was patently a situation of crisis and tension. The leaders aimed at an invasion, the people dreaded it — the samples of the "fruit of the land" were intended by the leaders to whet the appetite of the rank and file. In this situation the twelve commissioners could not report impartially: as representatives of their own tribes they had to make political decisions. The theocratic government felt strong enough to disregard the popular discontent voiced by ten (83%) among them. By the defeat of Israel their "wrong" opinion turned out to have been the "right" one. Yet the government persevered. The cautious scouts perished together with their evidence. The two fearless ones (representing 17% of the popular opinion) survived. Their evidence was kept alive too by the government's propaganda for a second invasion. By leading it, they successfully completed their *Reihendienst*.

Like the social research undertaken by Moses and Aaron three centuries ago, David's census was part of a programme of sweeping political and religious reorganization. David's rule was new and unlawful, and he attempted to stabilize it by moulding the tribal confederation into a centralized monarchy according to the Egyptian–Mesopotamian pattern.[106] His census was a provincial version of

---

[104] Stagl: 1971,40. Walter J. Ong applied a similar consideration to the transition from orality to literacy (Ong: 1982,9, 108ff).

[105] 4 Mos. 1,18 and 11,26.

their practices. Since he was concerned with a partly nomadic, partly sedentary population he could no longer assemble it in one place; he had to explore it by means of a commission making the circuit of the country. For this he relied on the main instrument of his power, the army (interviewing was no longer a *Reihendienst* but an assignment by the very center of power). There was thus a hitherto unaccustomed measure of constraint in this census.

We are not told how the census actually took place, yet we must assume that the commission of officers ordered the local headmen to convoke their retainers in one place and then attempted to proceed in a similar fashion to that of Moses.[107] The census was thus subdivided into successive oral surveys whose results were correlated by the commission (apparently helped by a clerical staff). This was thus ethnographic and statistical exploration of the ruled by the rulers rather than self–exploration of interacting local communities. The immense social distance implied in this procedure provoked the resistance of the people, which eventually proved successful.

Unlike the Book of Numbers, our sources on David take the side of the people against the government. Yet David's programme of reorganization was not dissimilar from that of Moses. Like Moses he even turned the force of popular resistance into an impetus for his policy of centralization: as Moses had done with his poll tax,[108] David justified his new temple in Jerusalem, which was to supersede all local sanctuaries and for which the people had moreover to pay, as an atonement of *all* Israel to the Lord for the sin of this census[109]

HELLAS

Like Israel and neighbouring Phoenicia, Hellas was situated on the periphery of the Ancient Near Eastern world; unlike them, the many small Hellenic polities had never been subject to a bureaucratized divine kingship. They were thus able to adopt many achievements of these superior civilizations without the corresponding institutions. Writing, list–keeping and bureaucratic administration were made known to the Hellenes by the preceding Minoan (c. 2000–1600) and Mycenaean (c. 1600–1200) civilizations.[110] Their skills in navigation, seafaring and commerce were improved by their rivalry with the Phoenicians, who transmitted to them at the beginning of the first millennium, also their great invention, alphabetical writing.[111] The Hellenes improved it by introducing signs

---

[106] See note 103.

[107] It could well have been that the Biblical report of Moses' census was coloured by memories of this census of David.

[108] 2 Mos. 30, 12–16.

[109] 2 Sam. 24, 10–25.

[110] Andrewes: 1967; Chadwick: 1976; Deger–Jalkotzy: 1978; Finley: 1981; Murray: 1993.

for the vowels. This first fully phonetic writing left no room any longer for the interpretative wisdom of insiders. Greek society was thus the first society which can rightly be called literate.[112]

The many small polities — tribal and city states — which emerged after the "dark age" following the downfall of the Mycenaean civilization joined the flexibility of archaic communities with the intellectual refinement of a great civilization. Filtering through Phoenicia and Asia Minor, the scientific attitude took roots among the Greeks, who due to their greater freedom from the 6th century onwards began to surpass their masters.[113] The Greek polities were too small and too numerous to be able to control the minds of their citizens.[114] There was no clergy and no bureaucracy to monopolize intellectual freedom. Seafarers and merchants, the Greeks were a mobile people. Political upheavals in the many city states produced a never–ending stream of expatriates, who, as educated members of the ruling elite, were temporarily relieved from their functions. There were thus everywhere foreigners present with a large horizon, able to compare and to abstract. All this created an intellectual milieu where curiosity could become a primary motive:

> "All men by nature desire to know. An indication of this is the delight we take in our senses; for even apart from their usefulness they are loved for themselves...... (They make us know and bring) to light many differences between things."

These sentences from the introduction to Aristotle's *Metaphysics* (980a) would have been inconceivable in the Ancient Near East. They aptly characterize the mentality of the educated during the heyday of Hellenic culture.

The well–attested exploratory voyages of the Phoenicians had little advanced geographic–ethnographic science, since they mostly were kept secret for reasons of commercial rivalry.[115] Trade secrets have the same effect as *arcana imperii*. Yet for the Greeks travel became for the first time in history an instrument of pure objective research. The *Odyssey* (8th century) praises its hero, the archetypal Greek intellectual, for his having "seen many cities of man and studied their customs" (I 3). Ulysses still had utiliarian reasons to travel, but from the 6th century we hear of travels undertaken for intellectual curiosity. Herodotus makes King Croesus say to Solon (c. 550):

---

[111] Barnett: 1958.

[112] Goody–Watt: 1968.

[113] Kranz: 1955; Kranz: 1971, 22ff. (The question of Ancient Near Eastern influence on Greek thought was a main issue in the late 19th century, which had certain ideological overtones. Today it has become so well attested that it is no longer deniable. Yet the Greeks developed something peculiar to themselves from these Oriental stimuli. This can also be said of their scientific research.)

[114] In the Hellenic world from Asia Minor to Italy some fifteen hundred city polities are said to have co–existed (Starr: 1986, 46 quoted after Ferguson–Mansbach: 1994, ch. 5).

[115] Müller: 1972–80, vol. I, 29ff.

"Our Athenian guest, we have heard much of you, by reason of your wisdom and your wanderings, how that you have travelled far to seek knowledge and to see the world." (I 30).

Herodotus himself (5th century) did the same. Like Solon he had left his native city (Halicarnassus in Asia Minor) for political reasons and then travelled for many years, apparently on his own means, in Egypt, Mesopotamia, Syria, Asia Minor, around the Black Sea and in southern Italy. He did this obviously to collect the material for his *History* by studying the scenes and interrogating witnesses of the Greco–Persian war. This pattern of travelling for the preparation of a great historical–geographical–ethnographical work remained alive for the next thousand years and even beyond. It was followed for example by Thucydides, Polybius, Poseidonius, Strabo, Arrian, Pausanias, and later also the Romans, the Byzantines and the Arabs.[116]

I can mention here only those aspects of the Greek scientific attitude which had a marked influence on social research in the West. The most important of these seem to have been: (1) *rhetoric*, (2) *dialectic* and (3) *empiricism versus science*:

RHETORIC

When the Greeks turned literate, they also studied the old oral techniques of handling knowledge.[117] From the 5th century the art of speaking in public was reduced to a body of formal doctrine, *rhetoric*.[118]

Rhetoric dealt with "words and things",[119] with the manner and the matter of speech. Of the matter there existed a maximalist and a minimalist construction: rhetoric could claim all knowledge as its province, or focus on knowledge relevant for ethical and political decisions.[120] Accordingly it had two major fields of application: education and politico–legal action in assemblies, courts and council meetings. Rhetoric was thus outstandingly important in the small Hellenic polities with their large percentage of educated citizens and broad political participation.[121] As an educationalist discipline it was concerned with the encyclopaedic[122] digestion of knowledge of all sorts, as a politico–legal

---

[116] Cf. Fritz: 1971; Müller: 1972–80, vol I; Strasburger: 1977; Hartog: 1980; Nippel: 1990, 11–29.

[117] An instance of the tendency of new social forces initially to extend the old institutional patterns, cf. note 104.

[118] Cf. Norden: 1958; Perelmann and Olbrechts–Tyteca: 1971; Mooney: 1985; Lausberg: 1990.

[119] *"Omnia autem oratio constat aut ex iis quae significantur aut ex iis quae significant, id est rebus et verbis"* Quintilian 3,5,1; cf. also Cicero, *de oratore* III 19.

[120] Lausberg: 1990, §§ 47–52 (48ff).

[121] Cf. Ferguson–Mansbach: 1994, ch. 6.

[122] *Enkýklios paideia* (Quintilian 1,10,1) means the integration of all the "liberal arts" (*téchnai enkýklioi = artes liberales*) into a program of education apt for all free citizens who take re-

discipline it handled socio–cultural knowledge and guided the corresponding research. After the loss of Hellenic freedom at the end of the 4th century rhetoric in this second sense declined; yet as an educationalist discipline it remained fundamental for the Greeks, the Romans and the Christian Middle Ages up to the time of the Humanists.[123]

Rhetorical theory structured speech according to points of controversy (*problémata = quaestiones*). It advised the orator to collect the evidence for his various points by searching his memory, interviewing experts, or looking into the facts personally, and then to classify this evidence. It moreover told him to relate each class of evidence to a separate part of his memory and place it there. Memory was thus conceived spatially, for example as a building,[124] which could be subdivided into separate "places" (*tópoi = loci*). Orators were free to employ their own system of "places", yet for influencing public opinion it was considered expedient to appeal to "common places" (*koinói tópoi = loci communes*). These were "intellectual themes" or "headings" to which the orator and his audience were alike accustomed, allowing the former to arrange his speech in a way acceptable to the latter. After having thus digested the matter of his speech, the orator could easily "find" the arguments relevant to any point of controversy, a process called *heúresis = inventio*.[125]

Structuring speech thus also meant structuring the mind. Whoever was trained in this way was more thorough in his utterances, be these oral or written. This initial cross–fertilization of oral tradition and literacy contributed to the height of Greek civilization in the 5th and 4th centuries.[126]

Rhetoric as a method of social research provided instructions for the acquisition, documentation and presentation of empirical socio–political knowledge. Thus Xenophon (c. 430 — after 355) advised the would–be orator to acquaint himself with the matter of his maiden speech, for example some recent discontent with the police or a decline in the production of the public silver mines, by interviewing experts or by personal investigation on the spot. Over and above that, the young man had to get to know his own city state if he wanted to be part of the circle of citizens "who understand what they are saying and doing". The knowledge of one's own polity Xenophon organizes under the following; five *tópoi*: (1) public revenue and expenditure, (2) the means of power of the

---

sponsibly part in public affairs, *"wobei das Wort enkýklios 'im Kreise der freien Bürger als Reihendienst herumgehend, also keine Spezialausbildung erfordernd (von Ämtern); gewöhnlich, alltäglich' auf den allgemein–verbindlich–elementaren (nicht spezialisiert–beruflichen) Charakter dieser artes hinweist"* Lausberg: 1990, 33f. The passage put by Lausberg in quotation marks refers to Trier: 1957 (cf. note 42). See also Koller: 1955.

[123] Curtius: 1973, ch. 4.

[124] Lausberg: 1990, § 1087 (526).

[125] See the pertinent keywords in Lausberg: 1990. For "common places" as "headings" cf. Ong: 1982, 110f; Ong: 1971, 147ff; for "intellectual themes" cf. Curtius: 1973, 79.

[126] Goody: 1987.

city and its neighbours, (3) the strength of the respective armies and navies, (4) local food production and imports, and (5) further needs of the city and means for their fulfilment.[127]

A similar system of *tópoi* is supplied in Aristotle's *Rhetoric*: (1) ways and means, (2) war and peace, (3) national defence, (4) imports and exports, and (5) legislation. All five points are further subdivided, and empirical information, including exact numbers, are called for wherever possible. As in Xenophon's system, *tópos* (5) is a residual category, for under "legislation" Aristotle also includes the socio–cultural conditions under which the laws have to be applied, i.e. the general living condition of the polity. He goes on to state that this schema can only be correctly applied in the comparative perspective, either diachronically (the present state of the city is compared with past ones) or synchronically (the city under discussion is compared with other cities): "From this we can see that books of travel are useful aids to legislation, since from these we may learn the laws and customs of different races."[128]

If social research thus profited from free political discussion among the Greeks both in substance and in method, it still suffered from the other great impediment to which it was subjected in the ancient civilizations: the requirement of topicality still remained effective. The need for empirical social knowledge to be topical was even greater in Hellas because of the many small polities with frequently changing constitutions; the viewpoints of relevance changed thus much faster.

Knowledge organized by rhetoric had serious limitations. Bound to practical issues and in most cases not written down it could hardly be accumulated. The securing, arrangement and presentation of such knowledge remained a personal, situation–related achievement. Thus it soon came to be regarded as superficial by more scientific minds. One of these, Aristotle himself, even though he was the author of the most celebrated rhetorical handbooks of the Greeks, remarks in the passage just quoted that he would have preferred to deal with the "usual subjects of public business" not, as tradition would have it, in the context of rhetoric; by right this important province of knowledge should belong to "a more instructive art."[129]

---

[127] *Mem. Socr.* III 6. This little dialogue is paralleled by another addressed to an elderly man with the required capacities who does not speak in public. Incidentally, both adressees are close kinsmen of Plato (one was the brother, the other the uncle). Their interlocutor is Socrates, who appears here as a champion of rhetoric (cf. Xen. *mem. Socr.* III 7).

[128] 1359a–1360b.

[129] 1359b

DIALECTIC

Such an art actually existed. Like rhetoric, dialectic codified something of the oral culture of small polities. Canvassing was probably as important there as public oratory. Being addressed to the few instead of the many, the "art of conversation" had always been elitist.

The key figure in the transformation of dialectic from a technique of political dispute into one of philosophical investigation, which eventually led to a socio–political science, was Socrates (c. 470–399). He had been the teacher of Aristotle's teacher Plato. Socrates and his circle turned dialectic into an art of the common search of truth.

Instead of one orator playing on the emotions of a crowd, dialectic presupposed a restrained circle of equals or near equals taking turns in structured conversation. Instead of histrionic talent it required cogent reasoning. Socratic dialectic led to the splitting up of speeches into dialogues, where different standpoints were apportioned to different interlocutors.[130]

Socrates dominated this circle by his personal force and intellectual ascendancy. His technique of conversation consisted in guiding the process of reasoning of his interlocutors by his questions link by link until they arrived at the right answer "themselves". He compared this to the art of his mother, who had been a midwife.[131] Like the newborn child carried around by the midwife in the circle of bystanders, any assertion maintained by an interlocutor was examined by Socrates with the help of other participants in order to ascertain whether it be true or not.[132]

This questioning technique implied that the true answers were in a certain sense already "known" to the interlocutors. It could thus not be applied to the exploration of the external world (Socrates accordingly professed to show no interest in the *kósmos*). He used it instead for human self–exploration. Socrates himself was exclusively interested in ethical questions. Yet as the great sociologist Vilfredo Pareto has pointed out, his dialectic method showed the potential for a social science. Socrates' interlocutors, though often historical persons, are in fact typical cases, being either spokesmen for given philosophical tenets or representatives of certain human categories or of man in general.[133] Had it been otherwise, he would not have been a philosopher, but a therapist or a social researcher. The main difference between Socrates' questioning technique and an opinion poll was that the former strove to rule out false answers and to establish

---

[130] Socrates himself ascribes the invention of this method to Zeno, pupil of Parmenides. Yet he used it paradigmatically for later generations; cf. Zeller: 1883, §§ 28, 30–34 (91f, 99ff); Robinson: 1953; Kranz: 1971, 84ff; Windelband: 1980, §§ 8, 1; 11, 2.

[131] *Theaitetos* 150b–151d, 161a–b; *Phaidon* 73a; *Gorgias* 487d–e.

[132] *Theaitetos; loc. cit.*

[133] Pareto: 1935, vol. I, § 612 (368f); cf. also Perelman Olbrechts–Tyteca: 1971, 36f.

the true one instead, whereas the latter ascertains which opinions are majoritary and which minoritary. The last appeal instance for Socrates is reason (*lógos*), for the opinion researcher it is society.

Socrates addressed himself over the heads of his individual interlocutors to a "universal audience".[134] He put thus the exploration of man on the same footing as the exploration of the *kósmos*, by his predecessors the "natural philosophers" of the 6th and 5th centuries.[135] These philosophers had been pan–Hellenic intellectuals which did not identify with particular polities. Socrates, though taking part dutifully in the public affairs of his own city, was like them primarily concerned with the *lógos* valid for all men alike. His circle consisted of foreigners as well as Athenians, and was looked upon by patriotic Athenians with suspicion. Infortuitously, the concept "cosmopolitan" (*kosmopolites* = citizen of the *kósmos*) stems from Socrates' circle.[136]

The social foundation of Socratic dialectic were private gatherings of the "select few".[137] Yet however productive intellectually, this was too flimsy a basis to permit a continuous progress of knowledge. In order to bring non–perishable fruits to the "universal audience", the common pursuit of truth in elitist circles had to be *institutionalized*.

The first step in that direction was the publication of Socrates' dialogues by his pupils, the most important of whom was Platon (428–348).[138] Though still a product of oral culture, Socratic dialogues had apparently been jotted down at once by pupils. *Theaitetos* shows us one of them completing his notes by repeatedly interrogating the master himself. The reconstruction of Socrates' dialogues after his death could thus rely on an infrastructure of systematic questioning and record–keeping. Written versions of Socratic dialogues circulated in the milieu of philosophers probably even before the master's death, extending thus his Athenian circle into the "universal audience".[139] One can regard this as a precursor of the early modern "republic of letters".[140]

---

[134] Perelman Olbrechts–Tyteca: 1971, 31ff, 37.

[135] Kranz: 1971, 26ff.

[136] According to Diogenes Laërtius, this word was first used by Diogenes (412? — 323), the founder of Cynicism (Diog. Laërt. VI 63). Gehlen: 1986c, 15 ascribes its coinage to Antisthenes (441? — c.365), who had been Diogenes' teacher and Socrates' pupil, and like the cynics advocated the retreat of the philosophers from public affairs. Gehlen does, however, not tell us on what authority. In any case, cosmopolitanism became a fashion in 4th century philosophy, corresponding to the decline of the Hellenic *pólis* (*op. cit.*, 13ff).

[137] Cf. *Symposion*.

[138] Cf. notes 131 and 137; two of Xenophon's Socratic dialogues are mentioned in note 127.

[139] Cf. the classical study of Gigon: 1947.

[140] The Humanist *res publica literaria* looked back to Socrates and Platon as their founding fathers, cf. ch. II, § *Travel, Correspondence, Documentation and the 'Res Publica Literaria'* of the present book.

The second and decisive step was the establishment of philosophical schools. These provided the emerging international network of intellectuals with permanent institutions of its own. Plato's "Academy" (c. 387) and Aristotle's "Lyceum" (c. 335) formalized the master–pupil–relationship as hierarchic structures. Both were organized as colleges where the masters lived together with their pupils. The masters were thus relieved from the struggle for existence and could pursue their search for truth professionally. The pupils tended to be no longer fellow intellectuals, but young men from good families finishing their education. This brought about a decline of Socratic dialogue. In the Academy *problémata* were posed to the students in the form of questions which had to be solved by common discussion, and thus still by a kind of *Reihendienst*.[141] (Their solution was, however, already known to the masters.) In the Lyceum the dialogue dried up into catechisms for the students.[142] The Lyceum was moreover also a research institute, and in so far similar to a modern university.[143]

The cosmopolitan milieu of philosophers had thus created proper institutions for the free pursuit of intellectual curiosity, institutions which attempted to keep aloof from topical interest and considerations of political expediency (even if they were financed and protected by well–wishers concerned with practical politics). These institutions formed a private area where a social–cultural–political science not committed to any existing polity could originate.

EMPIRICISM VERSUS SCIENCE

In 6th century Hellas scholars called *logográphoi*, "writers of stories", began to record the mythologies, genealogies, memorable events, customs and sights of their cities. Though oriented towards concrete communities, the *logográphoi* stimulated detached, objective research, for their writings became known abroad and were compared with each other. This research into local traditions Herodotus called *historía*, a term which originally meant the interrogation of witnesses in law courts:

> "What Herodotus the Halicarnassian has learnt by inquiry (historía, J.S.) is here set forth: in order that so the memory of the past may not be blotted out from among men by time, and that great and marvellous deeds done by Greeks and foreigners and especially the reason why they warred against each other may not lack renown" (I 1).

---

[141] Jaeger: 1948, 13ff.

[142] Hirzel: 1895, vol. I, 307ff; vol. II, 346.

[143] Jaeger: 1948, 312ff, 337ff.

It was the example of Herodotus' *History* which made this the general term for antiquarian–historical–ethnographical research and by extension for empirical research in general.[144]

The Greeks contrasted *historía*, as the knowledge of changeable phenomena, with *epistème*, the knowledge of the unchanging order of the *kósmos*. In this distinction the time–hallowed opposition between empirical and identity–establishing knowledge[145] became even more virulent than it had been in archaic societies and the early civilizations, since knowledge of both kinds was now fixed in writing and detached from concrete communities. By the activity of the *logográphoi*, much of what had been *epistème* for their fellow citizens, was degraded to *historía*.

Herodotus' great "historical" synthesis had nevertheless had a universal significance: he wanted to celebrate the decisive achievements of the Greeks against the Persian world power as a success due to Greek political freedom. The philosophers, however, did not believe in concrete communities, not even in that of all Hellenes; they believed in the universal *lógos*. They accordingly denigrated *historía*. Platon taught that sense experiences are not truly real, since they are always changing, and that they thus can merely be objects of opinion, but not of true knowledge (*epistème*). He was not interested in *men*, like Herodotus, but in *man*. Plato's socio–political science was therefore not empiricist. It consisted in the construction of an ideal polity by means of a dialectical inquiry into the idea of justice.[146] Its significance was not a pan–Hellenic, it was a worldwide and timeless one.

It was left to Aristotle (384–322) to achieve a synthesis between Herodotus and Plato, *historía* and *epistème*. Aristotle taught that ideas ("forms") cannot exist independently of matter, yet matter can only in so far be experienced by the senses as it is "formed", i.e. moulded by ideas. In this way empirical reality becomes accessible to scientific method, and inversely science can be based on empirical research. Aristotle's method essentially consisted in "applying the principle of form to the details of reality" (Werner Jaeger).[147] Having started as a pupil of Plato, he developed into an empirical scientist, whose universal curiosity even surpassed that of Herodotus.

Aristotle's great chance came when he was appointed as tutor to the young Alexander of Macedonia (356–323). He was now in a position of authority which he could use in the interest of research. He also succeeded in imbuing his royal pupil with the spirit of systematic curiosity. When Persian ambassadors paid a

---

[144] Strasburger: 1966, 47ff; Müller: 1972–80, vol. I, 111ff; Meier: 1975; Seifert: 1976, 12ff; Nippel: 1990, 12ff.

[145] See above, § *Social Research and Social Identity*.

[146] Kranz: 1971, 140ff; cf. also Menzel: 1936.

[147] Jaeger: 1948, 328; cf. also *op. cit.*, 68ff, 376ff and Bien: 1980.

courtesy visit to the young prince, the latter "instead of posing them childish or trifling questions inquired after the mileage of the roads and the manner of travel in the interior of Asia, then after the king himself, how he behaved toward his enemies, and how great the power of the Persians was. About that the Persians marvelled....".[148] It is thus not surprising that Alexander set out for his Persian expedition "surrounded by historians and scholars",[149] who sent much information on the conquered countries back home.[150] One of the scholars entrusted with the digestion of this information was Aristotle.

Yet he was not content merely to work on the material his former pupil had sent him. I have mentioned that his Lyceum was organized as a research institute. It was from there that Aristotle undertook, among other kinds of research, empirical research by means of written surveys. In this way he collected bodies of evidence (*historia*) on various aspects of empirical reality, which formed the basis of his treatises on nature, the arts, science and government. Aristotle's questions — or questionnaires — have not survived, yet some of his data have.

Aristotelian social research consisted in collecting evidence on as many Hellenic polities as possible. He thus organized a written survey covering the whole Hellenic world from Asia Minor to Southern France. The returns were integrated in the so-called *Constitutions*, a body of monographs on 158 polities.[151] All monographs were drawn up according to the same schema. The first one, the *Constitution of Athens*, had apparently been written by Aristotle himself as a model for the rest. His descriptive schema is divided into two major parts: (1) an outline of the constitutional history of the polity and (2) the description of its actual constitution. The basic units of the description, the pegs on which so to say each *Constitution* is hung, are the public offices. By explaining how they came into being, by enumerating them and depicting their competences and the procedures related to them, Aristotle portrays the dynamics of a Greek polity's constitution. Interwoven with it he also portrays its way of life, its individual character. Most of these offices still had very short terms, and were filled by means of *Reihendienst* among the local ruling stratum; describing them meant thus also describing the activities of those citizens who mattered. Moreover offices outlasted the life-spans of their incumbents and altogether formed a reasonable system. Focusing on them enabled Aristotle to steer a middling course between ephemeral and enduring knowledge, *historia* and *epistème*.

---

[148] Plutarch, *Alexander* 5. Of course this has been written with the hindsight of Alexander's conquest of the Persian Empire.

[149] Jaeger: 1948, 122.

[150] Droysen: s.a., 90, 290, 476, 482ff; Pfister: 1961; Müller: 1972–80, vol. I, 232ff.

[151] Cf. Aristotle: 1961 (Introduction by H. Rackham).

A survey of that scope could only have been carried out by a scholar of pan–Hellenic reputation. Moreover Aristotle had clerical staff and sufficient means at his disposal and correspondents in all parts of the Hellenic world. The *Constitutions* belong to Aristotle's last years; they were probably still unfinished at his death.[152] No doubt this survey also profited from his well–known relationship to the new ruler of the world. Some contemporaries, not believing in condition–free social research, regarded the Lyceum as "a Macedonian secret service bureau".[153] Even if Aristotle himself was solely motivated by intellectual curiosity (he fed the evidence of the *Constitutions* in his theoretical exposition of his socio–political science, the *Politics*, especially in books IV–VI dealing with constitutional developments), the compliance of others to answer his questions could have been motivated by subservience to the new world power.

Alongside the *Constitutions* Aristotle carried out yet another gigantic survey. It covered the non–Hellenic part of the *oikouméne* and was called *Barbarian Customs* (*nómima barbariká*). Obviously Aristotle regarded the customs of non–Greek peoples as fulfilling the same function as the offices in Greek polities — in full agreement with Herodotus' opposition between Oriental servility and Greek freedom.[154] Being under despotic rule, and thus not under state of law, the "Barbarians" could not be described in terms of constitutions, but only in an antiquarian–ethnographic way (in which the *logográphoi* had described Greek cities a few generations earlier). Yet Aristotle considered barbarian peoples as *functioning wholes* just like Greek cities, the reference system for the description being in both cases "the way of life (the *bíos*) of an organized community".[155]

For the non–Greek peoples, where he hardly could have corresponded with like–minded scholars, Aristotle relied on the information sent to him by Alexander's staff and no doubt on an evaluation of the "books of travel" he had mentioned in his *Rhetoric* as "useful aids to legislation".[156] The latter must have been excerpted systematically, remaining gaps being filled in by questioning people who had travelled in the respective countries or correspondents in Alexander's army.[157]

With these two surveys, which covered the whole *oikouméne*, Aristotle marks the zenith of Hellenic social research. Yet the zenith is, alas, a temporary position. Aristotelian social research was not developed further by his successors. His loving description and conscious analysis of scores of small city states still breathes a republican spirit, whereas the opportunity to explore them all, and

---

[152] Jaeger: 1948, 265f, 285f, 327ff; Müller: 1972–80, vol. I, 198ff.

[153] Jaeger: 1948, 314.

[154] Cf. Herodotus VII 101–104; cf. also Aristotle, *Politics* I.

[155] Müller: 1972–80, vol. I, 199.

[156] See note 129.

[157] Müller: 1972–80, vol. I, 198ff; Strasburger: 1977, 40f; Nippel: 1990, 25f.

to carry out a research design covering the whole *oikouméne*, presupposes a monarchical world power. Aristotelian social research thus exactly fits into the transitional period when Greek political freedom whithered to be superseded by the Hellenistic monarchies,[158] events already casting their shadows before them in the 4th century. Sharing in the prestige of the new universal monarch, Aristotle could collect like stamps constitutions which were about to lose their importance. And he could likewise collect the customs of foreign peoples recently subjugated. It is said, moreover, that Aristotle was at the point of falling out with Alexander on account of his republicanism, but then both men died within a short time of each other.

Alexander's empire and the subsequent Hellenistic monarchies were syntheses between Hellas and the Ancient Near East. They were thus unfavourably disposed towards free social research. The small polities that were tolerated to function under their overlordship were no longer rewarding objects of study for a general socio–political science. These polities continued, however, to be described in an antiquarian fashion, as in Pausanias.[159] The envisaged liberation of the cosmopolitan elite of philosophers–scientists from all political commitments had turned out to be an illusion.[160]

The Aristotelian spirit of systematic inquiry survived much longer in philosophy and the natural sciences than in the — politically more dangerous — social sciences. Yet interest in Aristotle's writings declined. The *Constitutions* and the *Barbarian Customs* were lost except for a few mentions in later writers.[161] "On the Hellenistic age this giant mass of knowledge had an amazingly insignificant influence".[162]

ROME

Rome's position to the Hellenic *oikouméne* was as marginal as that of Israel towards the Ancient Near Eastern *oikouméne*. Roman social research thus preserved similar archaic features, which were nevertheless intensified by the contact with a literate society.

---

[158] Cf. Ferguson–Mansbach: 1994, ch. 6.

[159] Cf. Müller: 1972–80, vol. I, 176ff.

[160] The Academy continued nevertheless as a centre of philosophical research and teaching even under the Romans, until it was closed in A.D. 529 by the emperor Justinian in order to please Christian public opinion.

[161] Though some authors, Cicero among them, referred to the *Constitutions*, they "were not preserved through the Middle Ages in the Aristotelian Corpus". Only in 1880–90 was most of the *Constitution of Athens* recovered (Rackham: 1961, 2f).

[162] Jaeger: 1948, 317.

The *census* of republican Rome resembled still a community ritual: every fifth year all citizens liable for military service were arrayed on an open space outside the city, the *Campus Martius*, in order to be reviewed, judged for their past conduct and assessed. Fitness, conduct and property determined their ranks in military as well as in civil life, and these ranks were either confirmed or changed at the *census*. It was thus a matter of supreme importance to the polity. The *census* was carried out until 443 B.C. by the highest Roman magistrates, the consuls, and after that date by the censors, whose office became the most prestigious one in Rome. A clerical staff was available to them. It grew in size over the years proportionally with the extension of the Roman polity.

The questioning followed as with court procedure, the interviewees being put under oath and the bystanders serving as witnesses. It was guided by an interview schedule, a list of standardized questions (*formula census*). The answers were written down. These bureaucratic features were superimposed on the archaic community ritual. For the *census* was also a periodic purification of the Roman people wherein the magistrates were assisted by priests. The Roman state was thus symbolically refounded every fifth year.[163]

In the Roman senate, too, oral surveys were carried out. These surveys showed archaic features, which were, however, highly formalized. When questioned in the prescribed form (*rogare, interrogare*) by an authorized person, the senators were obliged to give their official opinion (*sententia*). These were obviously questions of vital importance to the state. The questioning followed an order of rank, the more important senators being questioned first. Another form of social research for senators, which too was organized as *Reihendienst*, was the appointment as travelling commissioners. These commissioners were empowered to inquire into some local problem or charged to sound out the intentions of foreign potentates.[164]

Despite its foreign conquests, which eventually turned it into an empire, Rome remained constitutionally a city state until the end of the republic. Rhetoric, which had suffered from the decline of the city state in Hellas, had thus a second heyday in republican Rome. Through its influence on the formation and the political practice of the Roman elite, rhetoric later became the basic all–round educational discipline for the West.[165]

The greatest of the Roman orators, Marcus Tullius Cicero (106–43), was a cultural mediator between Hellas and Rome. He was also a champion of the republican constitution. Since Rome had by his time actually become an empire, Cicero's political wisdom, however brilliantly expounded, was already old–fashioned. He favoured a personalized and situation–related knowledge of

---

[163] Mommsen: 1871–88, vol. II, 333ff.

[164] Mommsen: 1871–88, vol. III, 965, 977, 988; cf. also Moore: 1935.

[165] Curtius: 1973, 70ff.

political affairs instead of an impersonal, universally applicable political doctrine. Two of Cicero's dicta became well known afterwards by frequent repetition: *"Est senatori necessarium, nosse rempublicam"* ("The senator must know the state")[166] and *"Ad consilium de republica dandam, caput esse, nosse rempublicam"* ("In giving counsel on state affairs, the main thing is to know the state").[167] Cicero thereby meant that the elite had to know their polity at least in the outline — the specialized knowledge of bureaucrats could not be expected of gentlemen.[168] As latter comparable utterances by Plutarch[169] and Tacitus[170] show, this republican–aristocratic ideal died hard in the ruling stratum. Yet under the principate it eventually faded into a nostalgic reminiscence.

Under the founder of the principate, Gaius Iulius Caesar (100–44), a new attitude towards social research appeared, which recalls the transition from city state to a universal monarchy under Alexander: a combination of bureaucracy and propaganda. As new régimes generally do, that of Caesar invested much energy into social planning, which presupposed systematic social research and documentation. Thus Caesar collected books for state library and worked on the codification of "the best and most necessary" in Roman law.[171] In order to mobilize broader popular support, the new régime also opened itself up to the people. Thus Caesar ordered the protocols of the senate meetings to be published — an anti–oligarchic measure, which exposed the traditional political wisdom of the senators to rational criticism.[172] Caesar was, moreover, his own chief propagandist. He published reports of his campaigns. The ethnographic descriptions in these writings, which were based on systematic reconnoitring organized by Caesar, became models for later Roman and Renaissance ethnography.[173]

This characteristic combination of bureaucratic research and opening up to the public was upheld by the principate as long as it had to struggle with the remnants of the republican spirit.

Augustus (63 B.C. — A.D. 14), though keeping up the appearances of the republican constitution, actually governed a universal monarchy which also included the former Hellenistic states. Like Alexander before him, he had recourse to techniques of Ancient Near Eastern government. His survey of the Roman empire in A.D. 6–7, the *"descriptio universus orbis"* of the Gospel,

---

166 *De legib.* III 8.

167 *De orat.* II 337.

168 Meier: 1986, 76ff.

169 *An seni r. p. g. s. c.* 11, 12.

170 *Dial. de oratorib.* 28–32.

171 Meier: 1986, 551f; cf. also Syme: s.a., 405ff.

172 Meier: 1986, 258f.

173 Müller: 1972–80. vol. II, 67ff.

followed the pattern exemplified by David's census rather than the *census* of republican Rome.[174] Its results were treated as *arcana imperii*. Augustus condensed them into a booklet (*breviarium*) reserved for his personal use. Thus he was able to integrate the specialized knowledge of all his subordinates like an Ancient Near Eastern monarch.[175]

This *breviarium* was destined to play an important role in the on–going struggle between the republican and the imperial spirit in Rome. After Augustus' death his successor Tiberius had it brought and read to the senate:

> "It was a description of the instruments of power of the empire, and indicated the number of the troops consisting of Roman citizens or confederates and of the navy, the number of kingdoms and provinces (under Roman rule, J.S.), the excises and taxes, moreover the neccesary expenses and donations. All this information Augustus had written down in his own hand..... „[176]

According to Tacitus' report, Tiberius (reigned 14–37) gained his end by thus opening up to the senate. He succeeded to demonstrate to it that such large and complex instruments of power could only be directed by one single will — that of the *princeps*.[177]

The first *principes* still used the senate as an audience for making things public among the traditional Roman elite.[178] Yet public discussion of information relevant to their decisions ceased in the measure in which they felt secure in their possession of the instruments of power. The last time the senate was used for that purpose by a princeps was under Caligula (reigned 37–41).[179] Knowledge of the Roman empire and the surrounding "barbarians" was still discussed in circles close to the government. It was used by the great political, geographical and ethnographical writers of the second century, such as Tacitus, Plinius, Strabo or Pausanias, who supplemented it according to the age–old pattern by their own private travels and surveys. After their period, this tradition of privately undertaken social research stagnated. With the last vestiges of the republican spirit, rhetorical culture lost its research aspect and turned into a mere educational technique.[180] The development of social research in Rome thus took a course similar to Hellas.

---

[174] The census taken at the time of the birth of Jesus Christ must have been a test–run to this greater one. The story told in Luke 2, 1–7 gives a glimpse of the inconveniences for the people concerned. The discontent which was aroused stimulated the political terrorism of the Zealots: cf. Meyer: s.a., vol. II, 51; Beek: 1973, 158ff; Syme: s.a., 368, 378, 403f.

[175] Suetonius, *Augustus* 101.

[176] Tacitus, *Ann.* I 11.

[177] *Ibidem.*

[178] Mommsen: 1871–88, vol. III, 1265; cf. also Syme: s.a. 425ff.

[179] Mommsen: 1871–88, vol. III, 1025.

[180] Marrou: 1957; Lausberg: 1990, §§ 12–15 (33ff).

There was an aftermath to that story which had repercussions on Western social science: towards the end of the fourth century the imperial chancellery (*schola notariorum*) collected information relevant to the administration of the whole empire. This collection had something to do with Stilicho's reforms, which centralized the military administration. Yet contrary to bureaucratic usage, this collection of information was neither destroyed nor allowed to decay after it had lost its topicality. One generation later, about 425, a description of the empire was compiled on this basis, which came to be called *Notitia omnium dignitatum tam civilium quam militarium*. It could not have served as a "manual" of the Roman Empire, as Humanist scholars assumed, for the material it contained was certainly outdated. So why was it compiled at all? There is only one answer imaginable: pure intellectual curiosity.[181]

Being educated men, the imperial *notarii* described the empire as a structure of offices together with their fields of competence. The pattern they followed was not the cold political anatomy of Augustus, but the loving description of political forms whose archetype were Aristotle's *Constitutions*. The *Notitia dignitatum* is thus the last document of the inquisitive spirit of classical social science. It was preserved through the Middle Ages in one codex in the cathedral library of Speyer, one of the capitals of the Holy Roman Empire. This codex is now lost. Yet in the 15th century, when interest in classical social science revived in the West, it was transcribed and eventually printed in 1552.[182] It was immediately considered as exemplary. Early modern descriptions of polities, called *Notitiae rerum publicarum*, refered with this very designation to Cicero's *"nosse rempublicam"* as well as to the *"Notitia dignitatum"*.[183]

THE MIDDLE AGES

The downfall of the Roman empire meant decentralization, and the return to more primitive political forms. Popular literacy almost disappeared in the West, and with it secular bureaucracies. Only the church preserved something of the universal spirit of the empire, together with the Latin language and culture. Yet the clergy guarded the traditional cultural techniques of writing and administration almost like an Ancient Near Eastern guild of scribes. In connection with this, it tended to denigrate free intellectual curiosity as sinful.[184] Up to the 12th century, higher intellectual activities were thus almost exclusively confined within the premises of the Christian world–view.[185]

---

[181] Böcking: 1834; Polaschek: 1936.

[182] Polaschek: 1936, *col.* 1114.

[183] Seifert: 1980, 219f, 236.

[184] Zacher: 1976, ch. 2. Cf. also notes 2 and 9 to ch one.

[185] Curtius: 1973, 37ff; Haskins: 1979, ch. 1.

This led again to a strict separation between theoretical and empirical knowledge. The knowledge of social, political and cultural facts was handled mostly orally and topically: if such facts were written down at all it was in the style of *Listenwissenschaft* (for example the *urbarii*). Such registers were normally kept in only one copy, which was used by authorized persons, yet not publicly discussed.

Bureaucratic rationality was not completely lost, however; it revived wherever favourable conditions arose. This was the case under Charlemagne, when also the idea of the Roman empire was revived in the West. From that time on the secular power rivalled the church in its pretension to universality.[186] Charlemagne (Emperor 800–814) did his utmost to subject his vast dominions to rational, standardized administrative control. He also revived the ancient office of the "eyes and ears of the monarch" by appointing travelling commissioners (*missi dominici*).[187] Yet in the subsequent centuries bureaucratic rationality declined together with the Carolingian empire. It was revived to some extent by the emerging national monarchies, such as those of France or England.

The best known medieval survey due to this bureaucratic rationality was the *Domesday Book* of 1086. It was organized by William the Conqueror as a stocktaking of his newly won English territory, primarily for tax purposes. The king appointed panels of travelling commissioners (*legati*) who made circuits through separate parts of the country. In one location after the other they commanded the attendance of the local officials, clergy and landowners. These had to serve as experts on local tenure and tenants. They were put under oath as jurors and interrogated with the help of a list of precisely formulated questions. The whole procedure was that of sworn inquest. The standardization of the questions made the answers from all parts of the country comparable. The interrogation itself was oral and public; the local experts thus answered under each other's control. Their answers were returned to the royal treasury at Winchester. From these returns a concise summary was made which was kept at Winchester and later called *Domesday Book* — a name which still testifies to the popular restistance against this form of social research. From the planning to the compilation of the results this survey took little more than one year.[188]

Comparable surveys were carried out in southern Italy by the Norman–Sicilian bureaucracy under the Hohenstaufen and Anjou rulers. To what extent these were connected with the Anglo–Norman survey of the *Domesday Book* seems still to be an open matter.[189]

---

[186] Halphen: 1947.

[187] The "missatic system" (Weber: 1978, vol. II, 1042), which was also used by William the Conqueror; see the following note.

[188] Galbraith: 1961; Finn: 1963.

[189] Personal communication by Heinz Thomas. Cf. Haskins: 1911 and Wittfogel: 1962, 274ff.

When emperor Charles IV. took stock of his newly acquired territory, the margraviate of Brandenburg, he followed a similar pattern of research. The results were compiled in the *Landbuch* of 1375. Charles' questionnaires, "if it were put in modern form, would not differ in anything from the question cards used presently (1905, J.S) for statistical surveys in Prussia" (Otto Behre).[190] There were still other surveys of this kind in the Middle Ages. Yet their results were not publicly discussed and therefore not accumulated.

Besides these there existed also non–utilitarian surveys which obviously carried on the Aristotelian tradition of research by questioning experts. The *Solutiones* of Priscianus Lydus (6th century), a main source for natural philosophy in the West, were composed in form of answers to *problémata* posed by the Persian Great King Chosroes (reigned 531–579).[191] Similar lists of *quaestiones* worth discussion or investigation continued to circulate among physicians and scientists of the Christian as well as the Muslim *oikouméne*.[192] Frederick II of Hohenstaufen (Emperor 1220–1250) used to pose *quaestiones* orally to scholars at his court, a court which also had aspects of a research institute,[193] or to send his questions in written form to scholars all over the civilized world, thus for example the *Sicilian questions* on philosophy, posed in 1240 in identical form to seven Christian and Muslim philosophers.[194]

Yet even this intellectual Emperor separated the utilitarian surveys of his bureaucracy strictly from his own non–utilitarian surveys dedicated to the collection of scientific and philosophical knowledge. As usual in the Middle Ages, the "raw materials" of actual facts and events[195] was left to practical men, yet left outside the realm of true knowledge. This was especially the case with empirical social, political and cultural knowledge, as state of affairs which prevented an independent social science in the Middle Ages. Systematic discussion was restricted to philosophy and the natural sciences. This was not in Aristotle's spirit but it was certainly in the spirit of Hellenistic Aristotelianism which avoided a too close involvement with politics.

The first attempts at a systematic collection and free discussion of such knowledge date from the high Middle Ages. From the 13th and 14th centuries, the interest of the intellectuals in heavenly things began to subside, whereas their concern with earthly things increased. Delight in the senses and in the free play

---

[190] Behre: 1905, 28.

[191] Lawn: 1963, 1f.

[192] *Op. cit.*

[193] In his work on falconry the Emperor says; "Not without great expense did we call to ourselves from afar those who were expert in this art, extracting from them whatever they knew best and committing to memory their sayings and practices" (quoted in Haskins: 1979, 333). Cf. also Kantorowicz: 1927, 323ff.

[194] Haskins: 1927, 265.

[195] Auerbach: 1988, 77.

of the mind began to lose its sinful connotation.[196] At the same time the secular power began to get the upper hand over the church. The rise of lay literacy brought about more mutual opening of various social groups and a more easy flow of information between them.

This led to an intellectual constellation somewhat similar to that in Hellas at the time of Aristotle or to that in Rome at the time of Cicero, and eventually to the pan–European movement of Humanism (14–16th centuries). The gap between scientific method and empirical knowledge began thus to be bridged even in the social, political and cultural sciences. Some implications of this rehabilitation of intellectual curiosity will be explored in the following chapters.

---

[196] Zacher: 1976, 37ff.

CHAPTER ONE

The Methodising of Travel
in the 16th Century

"Segnius irritant animos dimissa per aurem quam quae sunt oculis subiectae
fidelibus et quae ipse sibi tradit spectator".

Q. Horatius Flaccus, Epist. II 3, 180–182

FROM PILGRIMAGE TO EDUCATIONAL JOURNEY

In the Christian Middle Ages the main model for non-utilitarian travel had been the *pilgrimage*. It had been a multifarious activity where curiosity, boredom, enthusiasm for travel and other less innocent secular motives intermingled with the religious purpose.[1] Towards the end of the Middle Ages the secular components were clearly on the advance against the religious one. Pilgrimages tended to degenerate into a mere pretext for other things. A comparison of late medieval pilgrim reports shows that less and less attention was paid to religious actions and sentiments, whereas the distance covered became increasingly more important. This tallies with contemporary complaints that *pietas* meant less to many pilgrims than *curiositas*.[2] Pilgrimage was losing its legitimacy. The humanists treated it with irony, the reformators openly attacked it, and the counter-reformators defended it but half-heartedly.[3] About the year 1550 pilgrimage had ceased to be a plausible justification for travel. A new legitimation was needed.

It was found in *education*. In his *Colloquia familiaria*, Erasmus of Rotterdam (c. 1466–1536) extolled the pious work of self-improvement against the useless, expensive and morally corruptive pilgrimage.[4] His pupil Joachim Fortius

---

[1] Turner and Turner: 1978

[2] Sommerfeld: 1924; Zacher: 1976, 3ff; Huschenbett: 1985, 29ff; Wolf: 1989, 90ff.

[3] Turner and Turner: 1978; Rothkrug: 1980.

[4] Desiderius Erasmus Roterodamus *Familiarum Colloquiorum Opus, Basel (1542). De utilitate colloquiorum, ad lectorem*.

Ringelbergius (Sterck van Ringelbergh, 1499 – c.1536) praised the wandering life in a tone of religious enthusiasm: only by constantly changing one's abode one could avoid being taken in by everyday life and becoming a commonplace person; only thus one could educate oneself.[5] Such were the arguments by which the humanists redefined pilgrimage as a journey of education.

In the Middle Ages too education had presupposed mobility. The page training for knighthood, the apprentice entering the service of some master, the student going to an educational institution - they all had to change their abode and be frequently on the road. The *peregrinatio academia* was especially identified with a pilgrimage. From such socially recognized models the humanists could proceed. Yet they no longer privileged the university towns: the whole earth was for them a place where something could be learnt and where one could improve oneself. Even the old Christian concept of the *peregrinatio vitae* could be used for this re-evaluation of travel: if life itself was a pilgrimage, why should one go to one special place? And why perform external actions without internal benefit? And why accumulate meaningless indulgences instead of meaningful knowledge and useful accomplishments? Thus the *peregrinatio animi causa* came to be regarded as a crucial means of education.[6] A popular humanist *tópos* was the astonishing diversity of localities and human beings with the concomitant unequal distribution of useful goods and knowledge over the surface of the earth. If this was so, they had to be related to each other and thus to be made even more useful by means of travel.[7]

The only remaining privileged places for the humanists were those where the ancients had dwelt, where taste could be schooled on the remains of classical antiquity, and where the memory of a higher form of civilization still lingered on. These were more important than the places of pilgrimage. The aura of papal Rome was giving way to the aura of classical Rome.[8] Even a semi-barbarian from the North of Europe could educate himself by entering this classical sphere. This was more useful than so many pilgrimages.

This new emphasis on spatial mobility was linked with a reassessment of intellectual curiosity. Mobility and curiosity had always been seen together. For medieval moralists *curiositas* was "a wandering, unstable state of mind", which was "exemplified in metaphors of motion and in the act of travel". *Curiositas* was thus opposed to *stabilitas*. It was seen as a vice leading man away from God, 'a fastidious, excessive, morally diverting interest in things and people".[9]

---

[5] Joachim Fortius Ringelbergius *De Ratione Studii Liber*, ed. Thomas Erpenius, Leiden, (1622) 146–160.

[6] Bates: 1911

[7] Lohmeier: 1979.

[8] Howard: 1914;3ff; cf also Schudt: 1959 and Jedin: 1951.

[9] Zacher: 1976,21,20; cf also Newhauser: 1982 and Peters: 1983, 1994.

Yet from the 14th century, *curiositas* slowly gained more positive significance. The interest of the humanists in the external world as well as their enthusiasm for travel were epiphenomena of this change of mentality which prepared for the "age of discoveries". The total sum of human knowledge came to be seen as something expandable and improvable.[10] Summing up this development till the end of the 15th century Margaret Aston states: "Much travel will no more make a philosopher than much reading. But the exploration of places, like the exploration of books, can act as a powerful stimulus to the philosophically inclined, and in the fifteenth century increased travel and increased reading were both leading to new questioning. 'The further you go, the more you shall see and know', as a travel treatise of the period put it. Curiosity breeds criticism and, then as now, travel could help to promote empirical inquiry .... To travel well is to question well and, as both the writing and reading of books (travel books and others) shows, the fifteenth century became increasingly appreciative of the virtues of the good traveller. More people were undertaking more travel of various sorts, and their explorations, intellectual and geographical, made an important contribution to the outlook of the age".[11]

This change in the intellectual climate prompted the humanists to value mobility over stability and to redefine pilgrimage as an educational journey.[12] For many humanists, such as Erasmus and Fortius Ringelbergius, their wandering life was a conscious programme. This programme began to be defined about 1550, especially by North European humanists, such as the Englishmen Andrew Boorde (c. 1490–1559) and Thomas Wilson (1525–1581)[13]. In the following period too the *methodizing of travel* was mainly advanced by scholars from the "semi-barbarian" countries of the North.

TRAVEL REPORTS

The upgrading of mobility led to a new concept of the travel report. Medieval travel reports had organized their material according to the criteria of special genres. Thus secular travels had been dealt with by the genre *navigatio*, which also comprised geography and trade, whereas religious travels were described in pilgrims' reports, a branch of theological literature which attempted to authenticate the history of salvation through the experiences of present-day pilgrims. A third genre was formed by fabulous travel reports which were mainly

---

[10] See also the *Documentation of Knowledge*, in ch. two.

[11] Aston: 1968, 85.

[12] Howard: 1914; 1ff. Loebenstein: 1966, 80.

[13] Andrew Boorde *The fyrst boke of the Introduction of knowledge*, London; (1542) Thomas Wilson *The Arte of Rhetorique, for the use of all such as are studious of eloquence....*, London. (1553)

intended to entertain. There had been little effort to integrate all this into a coherent body of knowledge.

This changed with the advent of the humanist doctrine that the whole earth was a place where something was to be learnt. Now a new genre emerged: the multipurpose travel report. It became a receptacle for empirical information of various sorts.[14] Early modern travel reports were classified with the genre *historia*, which included, in addition to historiography proper, the description of empirical facts of various kinds. As loosely connected knowledge, *historia* was opposed to *scientia*, systematically deduced knowledge, which was considered as more reliable. *Historia* was dealt with by rhetoric, *scientia* by philosophy.[15]

The typical manner of presenting "historical" knowledge was to string single pieces of information together. This was often called the *ordo naturalis*.[16] In the case of travel reports, a series of observations and remarks was arranged chronologically, each of them in addition provided with the name of the place to which it pertained. The singular facts were thus localized in a temporal-spatial system of coordinates. The chronological order derived in many cases from that of a *diary*. Travel diaries had already been known in the late Middle Ages. They originated from the chronologically arranged catalogues of expenses which were kept by some pilgrims. This habit of bookkeeping in connection with travel was transferred to the psychological sphere by humanists like Fortius Ringelbergius. He advised the traveller to observe himself daily and to register his mental states in a diary, where also his observations of the external world should also find their place.[17]

There was little or no methodological reflection on the selection of the facts which were to be observed and reported. This was left to the judgement of the traveller. He was supposed to turn his attention to all those facts which were extraordinary, which on the strength of their peculiarity stood out in the field of common experience. Special rhetoric attention was given to such facts and events, which were called *memorabilia, insignia, curiosa, visu ac scitu digna* (things memorable, striking, curious, worth seeing and knowing).[18]

By ascribing these qualities to the things *themselves* — and not to the system of references of the observer — and by leaving the selection of the things to be reported completely to the judgement of the traveller, the rhetorical theory of knowledge gave to the latter an almost sovereign disposal over his data. At home he could recount what he thought fit. But none the less those left at

---

[14] Neuber: 1989; Neuber: 1991; Ertzdorff and Neukirch: 1992.

[15] Seifert: 1976; Seifert: 1980. See also the *"Empiricism versus Science"* in the Introduction.

[16] Neuber: 1989,55.

[17] Sommerfeld: 1924, 830f; Huschenbett: 1985, 39ff; Fortius Ringelbergius: 1622 (as in note 5), *loc. cit.*

[18] I have elaborated this in Stagl: 1980a, 143f. cf. Seifert: 1976 and Stewart: 1978.

home had one means of checking: they could refuse to believe the traveller. Travel reports had always laboured under a reduced trustworthiness, yet in early modern times, when the interest in the external world became rampant, their *authentication* became a basic problem.[19] There were various strategies of authentication. The traveller could attempt to impress his public through the weight of his own personality, that of his patron or of the recipient of his dedication. He could quote authorities, especially classical ones. Yet the principal strategy consisted in adopting a deliberately plain, dry and realistic style. This was looked upon as especially trustworthy.[20] Thus Montaigne in his essay *Des Cannibales* authenticated the informant who had furnished his ethnographic information by telling the reader that this man was "simple and coarse" and thus incapable of inventing lies.[21]

In spite of their self-chosen plainness travel reports became increasingly popular during the 16th century. There was a tremendous interest for everything concerned with travel. The humanists edited the ancient geographers, ethnographers and travel writers in order to offer them as models to their contemporaries.[22] Antique travel poetry was revived in the *Hodoeporica* of Conrad Celtis (1502), a work which found many imitations, and whose polished Latin shed some splendour on the *genus humile* of the travel reports.[23] In addition, the writings of the humanists contain many reflections on travel in the form of letters, orations, aphorisms, maxims, proverbs and emblems, which as yet have not been studied systematically.[24]

PROGRAMMES FOR THE IMPROVEMENT OF TRAVEL

Such reflections had a *programmatic* intent. They purported to give the travellers self-confidence *vis-à-vis* the unknown, to divert their attention from trivial things to those worth seeing and knowing, and to tell them what to do with their newly acquired knowledge. They can thus be seen as attempts to *codify the cultural patterns of travelling* of that period. Not everything which they contained was new. Their main innovative features were their *systematic character* and their *publication*.

---

[19] See ch. four.

[20] Cf. Neuber: 1989, 57ff.

[21] *"Cet homme que j'avais, était homme simple et grossier, qui est une condition propre à rendre véritable témoignage; car les fines gens remarquent bien plus curieusement et plus des choses, mais ils glosent (...). Ou il faut un homme très fidèle, ou si simple qu'il n'ait pas de quoi bâtir et donner de la vraisemblance à des inventions fausses, et qui n'ait rien épousé. Le mien était tel (...)."* (Michel de Montaigne: *Essais* I, Ch. XXXI, *Des Cannibales*, 1580. Ed. Pierre Michel, Paris 1965, 261f.

[22] Cf. Dainville: 1940, Momigliano: 1966, 127–142; Oestreich: 1976.

[23] Wiegand: 1984; Wiegand: 1989.

[24] Cf Stagl: 1980a, 140, with further literature.

People have probably never travelled completely unadvised. Travelling in the Middle Ages was risky, trying and expensive, and thus connected with anxiety.[25] Good advice could minimize these negative factors and assuage concern. Yet advice to travellers in the Middle Ages must in most cases have been given *privately* and *orally*. It was thus not apt for cumulation. Nevertheless, written instructions for travellers existed, and some of them have survived in manuscript form. A methodically minded man such as Conrad von Grünemberg (1486) could work out his journey to the Holy Land beforehand, utilizing oral advice as well as written pilgrim's guides (see below).[26] High nobles could commission an experienced cleric to do this work for them. Thus in 1333 the Bishop of Limoges, of the house of Talleyrand, employed Wilhelm von Boldensele, a runaway Dominican from Minden, for that purpose, and in 1484 Count Ludwig von Hanau-Lichtenberg did the same with Bernhard von Breidenbach.[27] The best known and most important travelling instructions were, however, those worked out for ambassadors. Chanceries influenced by the new spirit of humanism, such as those of the Papal court and of the republic of Venice, worked out regularized and detailed instructions for their ambassadors. These were moreover trained in observing and reporting. The reports of the Venetian ambassadors are among the best examples of late medieval and early modern descriptive literature.[28] They were albeit to a certain extent standardized, and built upon each other, the knowledge contained in them, however, was not for general use and thus could hardly be accumulated. After they had ceased to be topical they were allowed to moulder in the archives.

The humanists attempted instead to *generalize* and *systematize* such advice in order to increase the intellectual profit of contemporary enthusiasm for travel. This was in keeping with their striving for educational reform and with Renaissance empirism.[29] A more regularized manner of travelling could avail the *res publica literaria*.[30] in two ways: it would help the travellers to become more accomplished, versatile personalities, and it would further human knowledge through better travel reports written by such men. If in the Middle Ages advice to travellers had been given *privately* and *orally*, the humanists addressed them *publicly* and in *writing*. Thereby they somehow abstracted from the individual traveller and his personal needs. Instead, they aimed at the standardization of the practice of travelling and the possible accumulation of its results. These attempts to regularize travelling confirmed with a tendency to subject as many aspects of

---

[25] See among others Wolf: 1989; Althoff: 1992; Moraw: 1992.

[26] Goldfriedrich and Fränzel, s.a.; Wolf: 1989,87f.

[27] Sommerfeld: 1924, 829; Huschenbett: 1985, 29ff.

[28] Andreas: 1943; Venturi: 1976; Toscani: 1980; Jensen:1988.

[29] Cf Stagl: 1980a, 135ff.

[30] See ch. two.

life as possible to planned control, a tendency which had always been present in humanism but which came especially to the fore in the 16th century:[31] "Since the first half of the 16th century the initial universalism of Renaissance humanism began to break down, to be replaced by institutions with strict regulations that aimed at researching precisely within the framework of a normally closely circumscribed program" (R. and M. Wittkower).[32] The regularization of travel was part of a contemporary penchant for *rational planning*. This had led to the emergence of *method* as the central problem of philosophy and educational reform. In the second half of the 16th and in the early 17th centuries an incredible numbers of tracts appeared that "methodized" different activities and areas of life — down to the correct way of dying.[33] Why should travel be an exception to this? The rational planning of travel manifested itself at first in two literary genres: *advisory writings* and *compendia* of empirical knowledge on the external world.

The advisory writings continued traditions which already existed in the Middle Ages. Thus *technical advice for seafaring* (included in the genre *navigatio*)[34] were expanded and systematized in the spirit of Renaissance empirism, e.g. by Lilius Gregorius Giraldus (*De re nautica*, Basel 1533) or by William Bourne (*A booke called the Treasure for Traveilers*, London 1578).[35] The medieval *pilgrim's guides*,[36] which had instructed pilgrims what to do at the sacred places and how to get there, were developed into two forms: (1) tracts for the justification of pilgrimages and their spiritual use by Catholic humanists (e.g. E. Maignan, *Petit Discours de l'Utilité des voyages ou Pelerinages*, Paris 1578[37] or Johannes Pitsius, *De peregrinatione*, Düsseldorf 1602,[38] and (2) "road-books", functional literature written by men engaged in the postal service and carrying trade, such as Jörg Gail's *Ein neuwes nützliches Raiß Büchlin der fürnesmesten Land vnnd Stett*, Augsburg 1563. (Such works were compilations of *"itineraries"*,

---

[31] Neal:1960; Risse:1963. The wider socio-cultural connotations of this tendency for regulation have been explored by Norbert Elias in his famous theory of the process of civilization, cf Elias: 1962.

[32] Wittkower: s.a., 273.

[33] Neal: 1960,69ff.

[34] Eis: 1962,22ff; Neuber: 1989, 56.

[35] Lilius Gregorius Giraldus (also Gyraldus, 1479–1552): *De re nautica libellus, admiranda quadam et recondita eruditione refertus, nunc primum natus et aeditus* Basel 1540. William Bourne: *A booke called the Treasure for Traveilers, devided into five Bookes or partes, contaynyng very necessary matters, for all sortes of Traveilers, eyther by Sea or by Lande.* London 1578. This practically minded little book was still in circulation in 1641 under the title *A Mate for Mariners*.

[36] Cf Howard: 1914,4ff; Sommerfeld: 1924, 831ff; Wolf: 1989,87f; Bremer: 1992,329ff.

[37] E. Maignan: *Petit Discours de l'Utilité des voyages ou Pelerinages, tiré de plusieurs passages de la Saincte Escriture, & autres Autheurs. Mis en lumiere du Commandement de la Royne de France, par E. Maignan, Chanoine de Reims.* Paris 1578. The true author of this rare work is "frère Claude Vicar, Cordelier".

[38] Johannes Pitsius: *De peregrinatione libri septem.* Düsseldorf 1602.

descriptions of ways and their stations, such as had been used in the Middle Ages by pilgrims, merchants, seamen or ambassadors).[39] A further medieval genre to be perfected in the 16th century were the *"travel regimina"*, collections of hygienic and dietary advice for the preservation of health during travels by land and sea.[40] Humanist doctors such as Georg Pictorius of Villingen (*Raiß Büchlin*, Strasbourg and Mühlhausen 1557)[41] or Guilhelmus Gratarolus (*De regimine iter agentium*, Basel 1561)[42] codified this advice and supplemented it with moral and practical instruction for travellers.

Whereas such treatises could build upon written predecessors, the above-mentioned humanist reflections on travel attempted to standardize a hitherto mainly oral tradition. Letters on travel method such as that of Hubert Languet to Sir Philip Sidney from 18. December 1573[43] or that of Justus Lipsius to Philippe de Lannoy from 3. April 1578,[44] albeit addressed to individual persons, were actually intended to be published by being shown around and eventually they were printed. Both give well-considered advice to politically interested travellers in a terse form. Comparable were academic orations in praise of travel. In 1566 Laurentius Gryllus published a eulogy of the educational journey for physicians,[45] Nathan Chytraeus in 1575 another one for the travels of humanist-antiquarians.[46] Georg Fabricus (1516–1571) and Johannes Caselius gave special

---

[39] Jörg Gail: *Ein neuwes nützliches Raiß Büchlin der fürnemesten Land vnnd Stett. Durch mich Jörg Gail, Bürger zu Augsburg in truck verfertiget*. Augsburg 1563. On the "road Books" see Bates: 1911,15ff; Fordham: 1912; Fordham: 1926; Denecke: 1992.

[40] Cf Sudhoff; 1911; Vermeer: 1972.

[41] Georg Pictorius (=Jörg Maler): *Raiss Büchlin. Ordnung wie sich zu halten/ so einaer raisen will in weite und onerfarne Land/ unnd wie man allen zufällen/ so dem raisenden zustehn mögen/ mit guten mitteln der artzney begegnen soll*. Strasbourg-Mühlhausen 1557 (further editions Mühlhausen 1558, Frankfurt am Main 1566). On Pictorius see Kurz: 1895.

[42] Guilhelmus Gratarolus (=Guilelmo Grataroli): *De Regimine iter agentium, vel equitum, vel peditum, vel navi, vel curru seu rheda, & c. viatoribus & peregrinatoribus quibusque utilissimi libri duo, nunc primum editi*. Basel 1561 (further editions Cologne 1561, Strasbourg 1563, Cologne 1571, Nürnberg 1591). On Grataroli see Bietenholz: 1959,131ff.

[43] First published in Hubert Languet: *Epistolae Politicae et Historicae, Scripta quondam Ad Illustrem, & Generosum Dominum Philippum Sydnaeum*. Frankfurt 1633.

[44] Justus Lipsius: *De Ratione cum fructu peregrinandi, & praesertim in Italia Epistola ad Ph. Lanoyum*, in *Justi Lipsii epistolarum selectarum chilias centuria prima*. Antwerp 1586, No XXII. This little treatise in the form of an elegant letter was very influential, often republished (cf. Stagl: 1983,66f) and also translated into English (with commentaries) by Sir John Stradling *A Direction for Traueilers. Taken out of Justus Lipsius, and enlarged for the behoofe of the right honorable Lord, the young Earl of Bedford, being now ready to travell*. London 1592.

[45] Laurentius Gryllus: *Oratio de peregrinatione studii medicinalis ergo suscepta, deque summa vtilitate eius Medicinae partis, quae medicamentorum simplicium facultates explicat*. s.l. 1566.

[46] Nathan Chytraeus: *Hodoeporica, sive Itineraria, a diversis clariss. Doctissimisq; viris, tum veteribus, tum recentioribus... carmine conscripta. Item: Epigrammata de praeclaris urbibus, studio Nathanis Chytraei poetae laureati, & professoris in Academia Rostochiensi, publici, in gratiam doctae iuventutis et peregrinationum avidae, collecta*. Frankfurt 1575. Chytraeus (Nathan Kochhafe, 1543–1598) was highly regarded in his time as a Latin poet. The *Hodoeporica*, an anthology of classical and modern travel literature, including his own

instructions for the journey to Italy (printed in 1575 and c. 1578 respectively).[47]
The last four authors were German, and indeed this genre was preferred by
humanists from north of the Alps, the principal country to be toured in such
a methodical way being Italy.

Besides such advice for specialized travels other more general recommendations were published. From the second half of the 16th century writings
on worldly wisdom (*prudentia civilis*) contained special chapters on travel,
such as the *Proxeneta* of Hieronymus Cardanus (1501–1576).[48] Writers on
education also discussed travel, e.g. Michel de Montaigne in various places of
his *Essais* (1680).[49] The publication of ancient travel writers by humanists was
also expected to have a beneficial influence on contemporary travelling practice.
Finally Theodor Zwinger in his *Theatrum vitae humanae* (Basel 1565), the most
important humanist encyclopedia, provided classical examples for the use and
abuse of travel.[50]

This leads to the other example of the tendency to regularize travel:
compendia of empirical knowledge collected by travellers. There were three main
types of such compendia:

(a) *Collections of Travel Reports*: The first such collection seems to have been
that published by the German printer Valentin Fernandez in Lisbon in 1502.
Yet their great vogue came only in the second half of the 16th century. By that
time the great voyages of discovery had subsided and scholars set to work on
the empirical knowledge produced through them.[51] This desk-work actually
completed the "age of discoveries". For " 'to discover' means more than to
see for the first time; it also means the joining together of new knowledge
with the old in the evaluation of what has been seen" (F.C. Lane).[52] Thus
in these collections old and new travel reports, mainly of extra-European
countries, were edited and arranged beside one another. They were large-
scale publishing enterprises, requiring the collaboration of scholars, nautical

---

ὑπομνήματα ὁδοιποϱικά was intended to give models of observation and description to contemporary travellers. With the same intent he published his own Italian travel
1565–1567, cf Chytraeus: 1568; Chytraeus: 1594. On Chytraeus cf. Pettke:1994.

[47] Georg Fabricius: *Hypomnemata hodoeporika ad Christophorum Leuschnerum in Italiam
euntem*; in Chytraeus: 1575 (see note 46); Johannes Caselius: Διάσϰεψις *Qui doctrinae
virtutisque gratia peregrinari animum inducunt, quas gentes potissimum adeant eo nomine
Italiam autem minime omnium praetereundam, quidque ex ea talis hospes emolumenti
capiat*, in: *Collectio Caselianorum*, ed. Joh. Chr. Kieswetter. Rudelstadt s.a.

[48] Hieronymus Cardanus: *Proxeneta, seu De Prudentia Civilis Liber; Recens in Lucem protractus
vel e tenebris erutus*. Leiden 1627.

[49] Michel de Montaigne: *Del'Institution des Enfants, à Madame Diane de Foix, Comtesse de
Gurson*, in: Michel de Montaigne: *Essais ... livre premier et second*. Bordeaux 1580. Cf. also
note 21.

[50] On Zwinger see below. On the *Theatrum Vitae Humanae* see ch. two.

[51] Broc: 1980, 37ff.

[52] Lane: 1981,275

experts and printers. Continuing the medieval "*navigationes*", they were aptly enough published especially in leading seaports, such as Lisbon, Venice, or London. The most influential of these collections were *Delle Navigationi et viaggi* (Venice 1550, 1556, 1559) compiled by Giovanni Battista Ramusio, a high functionary of the Venetian Republic. It dealt with the earth as with "one single world consisting of homogeneous regions" (Marica Milanesi).[53] The best known English work of that kind are the "Navigations" (London 1589) of Richard Hakluyt.[54]

(b) *Cosmographies*: In these works geographical/ethnographical knowledge was somewhat more systematically arranged. It was taken from its original context and reorganized in the form of descriptions of continents, countries and cities, which altogether covered the whole earth (thence "cosmographies"), but actually centred on its best known part, i.e. on Europe, and within it on Germany. These works were something like a German speciality, being closely connected with commercial towns such as Basel or Strasbourg. The best known work of that kind is the *Cosmographia* (Basel 1544) of the theologian and orientalist Sebastian Münster.[55] Besides perusing the ancient and modern geographical and travel literature, Münster also travelled himself and collected additional information by systematically questioning his correspondents.[56]

(c) *"Statistical" works*: In 1561 Francesco Sansovino (1521–1583), a miscellaneous writer and publisher in Venice, brought out his *Del Governo de i regni et delle republiche cosi antiche come moderne*. Purporting to continue Aristotle's "Polities" and drawing on written sources as well as on the Venetian trade in news, this work consists of descriptions of 18 ancient, modern and even future political systems (it even contains an abridgement of Thomas Morus' *Utopia*).[57] It is thus a description of the world according to *polities* ("kingdoms and republics"). *Del Governo* inaugurated a stream of works called "*notitiae rerum publicarum*" in the 17th and "statistics" in the 18th century (the latter concept derives from *statista*, statesman, and originally designated the knowledge necessary for such a person). These works con-

---

[53] Milanesi: 1982, 35. Cf also Milanesi: 1976 and Donattini: 1980.

[54] On the collections of travel reports see Böhme: 1904; Penrose: 1975, ch. 17; Broc: 1980, 37ff; Neuber: 1991,183ff.

[55] On Münster's *Cosmographia* see ch. two. § *Compendia*.

[56] Ibidem

[57] Francesco Sansovino: *Del Governo de i regni et delle republiche cosi antiche come moderne Libri XVIII ne quali se contengono i Magistrati, gli Offizi, & gli ordini proprii che s'osservano ne predetti Principati. Dove si ha cognitione di molte historie particolari, utili & necessarie al viver civile*. Venice 1561. 2nd ed.: *Del Governo e amministrazione di diversi regni e republiche cosi antiche come moderne Libris XXII*. Venice 1562. On Sansovino see Grendler: 1969.

tained comprehensive descriptions of countries and peoples organized by their constitution and hierarchy of offices. They were the main receptacles for political, social and cultural information during the early modern period.[58]

With these programmes for a more efficient organization of travelling and these new literary forms for the presentation of its results, the time had come when something qualitatively new could arise. This happened about 1570. In the last third of the 16th century a formal methodology of travel called *ars apodemica* appeared. It was expounded from that time on till the end of the 18th century in many treatises in Latin and in the vernaculars.[59]

THE FIRST METHODOLOGISTS OF TRAVEL

In the academic year 1568/69 two aspiring scholars and a celebrated philosopher met in the university town of Basel. The *ars apodemica* goes back to discussions between these three men.

Their common problem was the growing mass of empirical knowledge. It was a typical problem of the age of discoveries and of printing, which had already alarmed Juan Luis Vives (1492–1540), the Spaniard who went to the Netherlands and became a figurehead of northern, practically oriented humanism. Our three men were followers of Vives, and like him concerned with education and the organization of knowledge. The rapid growth in the 16th century of empirical knowledge, which was obviously practically useful, but could no longer be mastered intellectually, endangered traditional patterns of thought. Vives' solution had been the setting up of collections of notes classified according to specialized subjects.[60] Yet this method could avail the individual scholar, but certainly not the *res publica literaria*, the scholarly community. Thirty years after Vives' death it seemed clearly insufficient. It was felt that there must be some way to separate the chaff from the wheat by common effort, to order the really useful knowledge, and to teach scholars how to handle it.

In the said academic year 1568/69 Theodor Zwinger from Basel and the Dutchman Hugo Blotius commenced their humanist friendship. Zwinger (1533–1588) was undoubtedly the more important of the two men. A scion of a family of printers and scholars, he had left school as a boy and led the life of a vagrant student. For some time he was a printer's apprentice in Lyons. Then he went to Paris where he became a student of Petrus Ramus, whose attempted reform of Aristotelian logic was having an enormous impact at that time. Besides, Zwinger became well versed in theology, oriental languages and even the Cabbala. He then read medicine in Padua. In 1568 he was at the beginning of a splendid

---

[58] Rassem/Stagl: 1980; Rassem/Stagl 1994. Cf also Introduction § Rome.

[59] Bibliography in Stagl: 1983.

[60] Cf Buck: 1991,11ff.

career in the university of his native town. He had recently reaped literary laurels by finishing and editing the *Theatrum vitae humanae*, which his stepfather Conrad Lycosthenes had left unfinished after his death. We have already met this work, and still more on it will be said in the next chapter. An encyclopedic collection of excerpts from classical and modern literature, which were intended as examples to shed light on every possible problem of human life, it became one of the great literary successes of the time.[61] Zwinger was remarkable for his systematizing mind and his capacity for hard work. He was to become both as a physician and as a humanist, one of the luminaries of the University of Basel.[62]

In 1577 Zwinger's *Methodus apodemica in eorum gratiam qui cum fructu in quocunque tandem vitae genere peregrinari cupiunt* was published in Basel. This work, a bulky quarto volume, whose second edition appeared in Strasbourg in 1594, remained an accepted authority on the theory of travel until late into the 17th century, although it was always more praised than read. In the preface Zwinger tells the story of his misguided youth and his overhasty acquisition of heterogeneous knowledge. He wants to save coming generations of scholars from this fate by instructing them to gain and to digest their knowledge in a more orderly manner. His argument proceeds in accordance with Aristotelian logic. In Book I Zwinger gives an overview of the different kinds and forms of travel by means of definitions together with examples from literature which are arranged in tabular form. Book II supplied moral and practical advice for travellers intending to improve themselves; it is arranged in the same manner. Book III, which is the most voluminous, contains four descriptions of cities, namely, of Basel, Paris, Padua and classical Athens. They are intended as models for the descriptions of cities by future travellers. Starting with the discussion of the ancient and new names of the city, they deal successively with its territory, history, constitution, principal sights and the occupations of the inhabitants. Zwinger acknowledges the uneven coverage of his descriptions; he is often reduced by lack of material to catalogue-like enumeration. Book IV contains plans for the description of tangible life abroad according to the three categories, *locus, locatum,* and *actio.* They are not fully worked out, only given as exemplary sketches. As patterns for "*locatum*" and "*actio*" Zwinger gives tabular descriptions of the equestrian statue of Colleoni in Venice and of the art of printing. It was clear to Zwinger that his programme was over-ambitious and that his examples were defective. But he addressed, as it were, the ideal traveller, the community of scholarly travellers, and encouraged these, each according to his special preferences, to develop his basic suggestions.

---

[61] See also note 50.

[62] No biography of Zwinger has been written yet. Cf however Vetter 1952, Gilly 1977, 1979, Stagl 1980a and ch. two § *Treasure Houses for Knowledge.*

THEODORVS ZVINGERVS
BASIL. MEDICVS.

Quæ mihi Zuingeri mentem, qua pectoris artes
Pinget, & ò terras pinget & astra manus.

V. T. L.

TRINV.

FIGURE 1: THEODOR ZWINGER. From: Nicolaus Reusner: Icones aliquot virorum clarorum. Basel 1589. By courtesy of the Herzog August Bibliothek, Wolfenbüttel.

As a thorough worker and occupied with many other tasks, Zwinger had taken eight years to draw up his arguments. But he mentions in his preface that they had been conceived in 1568/69 in his discussions with Blotius. In the meantime two other books containing general directions had appeared. As I have shown in the preceding paragraph and as is frequently borne out by intellectual history,[63] the time was ripe for something qualitatively new to appear in the field of knowledge, which was thus "discovered" simultaneously by several men working independently of each other.

In 1574 the Saxonian jurist Hieronymus Turler (c.1520 – c.1602) had published a travel method in Strasbourg, called *De peregrinatione et agro Neapolitano* (reprinted in *De arte peregrinandi*, Nüremberg, 1591; English translation: *The Traveiler*, London 1575).[64] Like Zwinger, Turler starts with a definition and subdivision of the concept of travel and proceeds to give moral and practical advice as well as classical examples. As the title shows, he adds a model description to his advice, for which he chooses the Kingdom of Naples, a territorial state, being himself not the burgher of a city state, but the subject of a prince. Turler had studied at several universities – Leipzig, Louvain and Padua (where he had met Zwinger)[65] - and travelled in Italy, France and England. Then he became professor of law at the newly founded University of Marburg. Like Zwinger, Turler was aware that he broke new ground with his method for travel.[66]

In 1577, but still before Zwinger's book, where it is already mentioned, yet another method of travel appeared. This was the *Commentariolus de arte apodemica seu vera peregrinandi ratione* (Ingolstadt 1577) bei Hilarius Pyrckmair (also reprinted in *De arte pereginandi*, Nüremberg 1591).[67] Pyrckmair, whose dates are unknown, was a doctor and a humanist. Born in Landshut in Bavaria, he had visited the University of Freiburg and had travelled to Prague, Rome, Venice and Padua, partly in the service of the house of Fugger. The *Commentariolus* he wrote, as he informs us, for the preparation of a second tour

---

[63] Merton: 1985, 258ff.

[64] Hieronymus Turler *De peregrinatione et agro Neapolitano Libri II. Scripti ab Hieronymo Turlero. Omnibus peregrinantibus utiles ac necessarii; ac in eorum gratiam nunc primum editi.* Strasbourg: 1574. English: *The Traveiler, devided into two Bookes. The first conteyning a notable discourse of the maner, and order of travelling oversea, or into straynge and forein Countreys the second comprehending an excelent description of the most delicious realme of Naples in Italy. A Woorke very pleasaunt for all persons to reade; and right profitable and necessarie unto all such as are minded to Traveyll.* London 1575. Reprint Gainesville, Florida 1951. There is as yet no study of this author, who has also translated Machiavelli and Castiglione into German and dealt with the philosophy of history. Cf. Stagl: 1980a, 131f, 146, and ch. two.

[65] Zwinger mentions that he had met Turler about twenty years before (i.e. 1557–58) in Padua (Zwinger: 1577, *Praefatio*).

[66] Turler's letter from Weissenfels in 1572 to Gregor Bersmann, printed in *Nova Literaria Germaniae Anni* 1703.

[67] Hilarius Pyrckmair: *Commentariolus de Arte Apodemica, seu Vera Peregrinandi Ratione. Auctore H.P. Landeshutano.* Ingolstadt 1577.

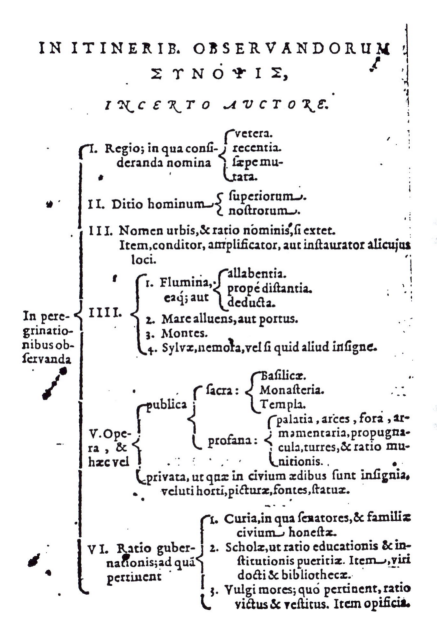

IN ITINERIB. OBSERVANDORUM
ΣΥΝΌΨΙΣ,

INCERTO AUCTORE.

In pere-
grinatio-
nibus ob-
servanda

I. Regio; in qua confi-
deranda nomina
- vetera.
- recentia.
- fæpe mu-
  tata.

II. Ditio hominum
- superiorum.
- nostrorum.

III. Nomen urbis, & ratio nominis, fi extet.
Item, conditor, amplificator, aut instaurator alicujus loci.

IIII.
1. Flumina,
eaq; aut
- allabentia.
- propé distantia.
- deducta.
2. Mare alluens, aut portus.
3. Montes.
4. Sylvæ, nemora, vel si quid aliud insigne.

V. Ope-
ra, &
hæc vel
publica
- sacra:
  - Basilicæ.
  - Monasteria.
  - Templa.
- profana:
  - palatia, arces, fora, ar-
    mamentaria, propugna-
    cula, turres, & ratio mu-
    nitionis.
privata, ut quæ in civium ædibus sunt insignia,
veluti horti, picturæ, fontes, statuæ.

VI. Ratio guber-
nationis; ad quã
pertinent
1. Curia, in qua senatores, & familiæ
civium honestæ.
2. Scholæ, ut ratio educationis & in-
stitutionis pueritiæ. Item, viri
docti & bibliothecæ.
3. Vulgi mores; quo pertinent, ratio
victus & vestitus. Item opificia.

FIGURE 2: Anonymous author: A synopsis of things to be observed during travel. From: Nathan Chytraeus: Variorum in Europa Itinerum Deliciae....., Herborn 1594. By courtesy of the Herzog August Bibliothek, Wolfenbüttel.

to Italy, which he was to undertake as a private tutor to three young counts of Sulz, who had been with him at the University of Freiburg.[68] Since he published nothing afterwards, Pyrckmair probably died during this journey. The *Commentariolus* is an elegant little volume in duodecimo, which in contrast to Zwinger's quarto volume could easily be taken with one whilst travelling. Its contents are similar to those of Zwinger's and Turler's work, but rather more "chatty". Pyrckmair also gives a schema for the description of countries, cities and peoples, which probably had more impact than the model descriptions of the other two authors. Condensed by some unknown author into an easily manageable synopsis, this schema was printed in the *Variorum in Europae itinerum Deliciae* (Herborn 1594) of Nathan Chytraeus, whom we have already met.[69]

In this anonymized and simplified form, Pyrckmair's descriptive schema appears in the preface of many travel books, whose arrangement it obviously influenced, until late into the 17th century.[70]

And Zwinger's friend Blotius? If he ever wrote his own travel method it remained unpublished. Hugo Blotius (de Bloote, 1534–1608) was no doubt less of a scholar than Zwinger, but he too was to have a successful career. Born in Delft, he had read law in Louvain, Toledo, Paris and Orleans, where he had taken his doctorate. He had combined this *peregrinatio academica* with private tutorships in influential families. His habits were rather those of a bibliophile than those of an investigator. In Basel he moved mainly in the circles of humanists and printers. The connections he established there proved extremely helpful to his career. They led him first to a chair of ethics in Strasbourg, then to a tour of Italy and finally smoothed the way for him in Vienna, where he acquired an influential position despite his lack of published work and his Calvinism: Court Librarian to the Emperor Maximilian II in 1575, Professor of Rhetoric at the university in 1576, Imperial Historiographer in 1578.[71]

During his whole career Blotius carried on an extended scholarly correspondence with many partners in different countries. His relationship with Zwinger remained close. From Strasbourg and from Italy he sent him models and materials for the description of cities. Zwinger used them in his *Methodus*, as he did with many suggestions from Turler and Pyrckmair. (Contrary to the custom of the time, Zwinger was generous enough to mention all three names.) As Court Librarian, Blotius continued to collect information and to organize projects, which will be dealt with more extensively in the next chapter.[72] He was apparently

---

[68] For Pyrckmair's biography see Stagl: 1980a, 132f, 147.

[69] See note 46.

[70] Schudt: 1959, 139.

[71] Cf Brummel: 1972.

[72] See ch. two. § *Treasure houses for knowledge.*

FIGURE 3: Hugo Blotius. A medal in possession of the Münzkabinett, Kunsthistorisches Museum, Vienna

the type of organizer of scholarship who shuns publication and prefers to work behind the scenes. He had moreover to watch his steps after the death of the crypto-protestant Emperor Maximilian II in 1576, for the Counter-Reformation was now in ascendance at the imperial court. Blotius died as an embittered and ineffective man.

There is, however, a small text on the method of travel by Blotius, that has survived and had a certain impact. In the supplement to the third edition of Paul Hentzner's *Itinerarium Germaniae, Galliae, Angliae, Italiae* (Nürnberg 1629) is to be found a *Tabula Peregrinationis continens capita Politica* by "Hugo Plotius" otherwise unknown.[73] It is a list of 117 questions with the help of which a city could be described. The questions do not follow any obvious order. They refer to various aspects: constitution and administration, churches and schools, food and dress, criminals, the poor, lepers, the disposal of refuse.... The internal evidence of the *Tabula Peregrinationis* leaves no doubt that its author was in fact Hugo Blotius and that it was written during his time in Strasbourg, i.e. immediately after his meeting with Zwinger.[74] Ernest S. Bates, who was the first to draw attention to it, envisages its author as a superannuated,

---

[73] Hugo Plotius (*recte* Blotius): *Tabula Peregrinationis continens capita Politica*, in: Paul Hentzner: *Itinerarium Germaniae, Galliae, Angliae, Italiae*. 3rd ed. Nuremberg 1629.

[74] Stagl: 1979, 614. The change from "Blotius" to "Plotius" may have been brought about by the Austrian tendency not to differentiate between b and p. Instead of "hot cross bun" an Austrian would say "hot cross pun".

pedantic old private tutor.[75] This is not completely wrong, as we have seen, but Blotius was more than that and his *Tabula Peregrinationis* was more than a mere exercise in pedantry. It was conceived as an auxiliary for gathering empirical knowledge during travel. It was directed at travellers in general, through whose collaboration Blotius apparently hoped to establish an institution for the permanent documentation of such knowledge. A similar institution was propounded in Zwinger's *Methodus Apodemica*.[76] The story of such institutions, which I call "documentation centres" and which led to the establishment of permanent statistical offices at the end of the early modern period, will be told in the next chapter.[77] Related to the idea of such a centre, and to the idea of a science dealing with the problems of human life, the *Tabula Peregrinationis* was actually the first *sociological questionnaire*.[78]

These four founders of the methodology of travel had many things in common. It is obvious why many "discoveries" in intellectual history are made simultaneously and independently by several men. When a certain height is reached on a mountain tour, the horizon suddenly changes and reveals new sights. When a party of mountaineers reaches this height, they see these new sights at the same time. Concerning travel, such a "rise" had been reached about 1570, as has been shown in the preceding paragraph, and the first methodologists of travel formed such a "party".

They were humanists from Germany and the Low Countries, and were thus especially dependent on the educational journey to Italy. They were moreover personally fond of travel, having extended the customary *peregrinatio academica* to a great number of universities and in addition had been to many other places in Europe, as vagrant scholar, private tutor, employee of a merchant firm or on their own means. Coming from the educated fraction of the burgher class, they had special connections with university towns along the Rhine valley from Basel to Louvain, a region rising in economic importance and soon to rival Italy in cultural splendour, a region moreover on the margins of different national cultures. Born around 1530, they had been formed by a later strand of humanism, the humanism of Vives, whose mainstay was not so much Italy, but the Low Countries and Germany, and whose social centres were not so much princely courts, but universities, publishing firms and commercial towns. They supported the Reformation or at least sympathized with it. Yet their religious attitude was – like

---

75 Bates: 1911,35ff.

76 Stagl: 1979, 615. More on the *Tabula Peregrinationis* will also be said in ch. two § *Treasure houses for knowledge*.

77 See ch. two § *Treasure houses for knowledge*.

78 Stagl: 1979, 615.

that of many humanists - not clear-cut. They were open to heterodox currents of thought, like Neoplatonism and the Cabbala.[79]

First and foremost, the founders of travel methodology were Renaissance empirists. They strove for the extension, purification and digestion of empirical knowledge, not for its own sake, but to improve mankind in wisdom, virtue and happiness according to the humanist ideal of *studia humanitatis*.[80] This is why they became interested in travel. Travel gave to the members of the *res publica literaria* the opportunity to cultivate themselves as well as to acquire true knowledge - knowledge gained through observation rather than through mere transmission of belief or hearsay. Though being useful to its owner, such knowledge was not to remain restricted to him, but to be disseminated over the *res publica literaria* by means of travel reports, letters, and collections of material objects made during the journey.[81] Thus it could be best utilized for the advancement of its original owner, his city or country, and mankind in general. This rootedness of the *ars apodemica* in Renaissance empirism explains why, till the end of the early modern period, it never clearly made a distinction between travel as a means for the formation of the individual personality and as a means for the gathering of useful knowledge (between "*virtus*" and "*doctrina*").[82]

A TALE OF THREE CITIES: VENICE, BASEL, PARIS

The methodizing of travel occurred in countries marginal to the original area of humanism. Humanists from these countries emulated the models coming from the area of origin, and therefore developed a specially sharpened consciousness for these models. Three cities in this marginal area became most important for the methodizing of travel: Venice (with Padua), Basel and Paris.

Zwinger, Turler, Pyrckmair and Blotius had all travelled in Italy, yet had shown conspicuously less interest in its classical remains, art treasures and splendid courts than in the merchant republic of *Venice* and its "Quartier Latin", the University of *Padua*. This had no doubt to do with their northern and burgher origins and with their religious attitude (Pyrckmair was the only Catholic among them and apparently a rather doubtful one). The republic of Venice was tolerant

---

[79] For the religious attitudes of Zwinger, Turler, Pyrckmair and Blotius see Stagl: 1980a, 139; for that of the humanists in general see Heer: 1959.

[80] Cf Buck: 1975a; Buck: 1986.

[81] Hodgen: 1964, 114ff.

[82] These concepts appear juxtaposed in the title of Johannes Caselius's Διάσκεψις cf note 47.

in religious matters and Padua was therefore the favourite Italian university for German and other North European students.[83]

Venice had not been among the original centres of Italian humanism. It had for a long time clung to its medieval tradition. The University of Padua, conspicuous in the rediscovery of Aristotle for the West, continued as a centre of Aristotelianism till the 16th century. Yet it also became a centre for medical and scientific studies, and its Aristotelianism soon turned anti-scholastic, promoting not so much abstract discussions as questions concerning the foundations and practical use of empirical knowledge. It had a leading position in the methodological discussion of the 16th century.[84] By that time Venice had opened up to humanism, but rather to its later, empirically and didactically oriented form.[85] This opening up was connected with its flourishing printing and publishing trade (for which the religious tolerance of the republic proved very advantageous). In these fields it was the leading Italian city, in the second half of the 16th century turning out three and a half times as many books as Milan, Florence and Rome combined.[86] Moreover, the aristocratic merchant republic with its traditional links to the Orient and to Germany, its diplomats trained in the observation of foreign countries and its efficient secret service had also become an emporium for the trade in information, the "metropolis of the news", as described by German student in 1567 in Padua.[87]

A comparable centre north of the Alps was *Basel*. A merchant town at the edge of different countries and cultures, it belonged to the Swiss confederation and was governed by a burgher oligarchy. In 1529 it had accepted the Reformation. It had a famous university, had since the days of Erasmus been the mainstay of extra-Italian humanism, and was also a centre of the printing and publishing trade. In the words of Friedrich Heer, it was in the 16th century the "capital of educated Europe".[88] Its links with Venice were especially close. Many Basileans finished their education in Padua, and through the connectioh with Venetian firms and the good offices of Italian emigrants, many Italian authors were published in Basel.[89]

The third important city for the methodizing of travel was *Paris*. Formerly the European centre of scholasticism, in the 16th century it had become with Padua the centre of methodological discussion. In 1543 Petrus Ramus had published there his enormously influential *Dialecticae Institutiones*. Ramus claimed

---

[83] Brugi: 1905.

[84] Randall: 1940; Neal: 1960,69ff; Giard: 1983, 1984, 1985.

[85] Branca: 1963.

[86] Febvre and Martin: 1958, quoted after Lane: 1973, 311.

[87] Brugi: 1905,27.

[88] Heer: 1959,238.

[89] Vetter: 1952; Bietenholz: 1959.

PIERRE RAMUS
Mathematicien né a Cuth en
Vermandois en 1515. et Assassiné a Paris
le jour de S.t Barthelemi en 1572.

Rame tuis Gallis es, quod latio fuit olim.
Romani princeps Tullius eloquij.

à Paris chés Daumont rue S.t Martin

FIGURE 4:   Petrus Ramus. From the portrait collection of the Herzog August Bibliothek, Wolfenbüttel.

to have "improved" Aristotelian logic and to have forged it into a practically oriented universal method for all arts and sciences - an aggressively advocated claim, that had brought him both deadly enmity and world-wide fame.

The celebrated philosopher living in Basel in 1568–69 was none other than Petrus Ramus (Pierre de la Ramée, 1515–1572). To escape the civil war in France and the no less dangerous hostility of his scholastic opponents at the University of Paris, Ramus had begun a circular tour of German universities, starting with Strasbourg, also a minor centre of methodological discussion.[90] This tour, intended to propagate his doctrine in Germany, had developed into a veritable "triumphal procession"[91] and along the way Ramus had openly professed the Reformed confession. He was thus very well received in Basel, where he spent the winter 1568–69 and for which he acquired a special liking. He publicly eulogized the city in his *Basilea*,[92] where among other things he praised the *Theatrum vitae humanae* of his former pupil Theodor Zwinger, with whom his renewed acquaintance had grown so intimate that he was asked to be godfather for Zwinger's son.[93]

There was no such close personal connection between Ramus and the other three methodologists of travel, yet the influence of the Ramist method was certainly felt. Turler and Blotius had been to Paris, and, given the special direction of their interests and the celebrity of the philosopher, it is unlikely that they did not hear him. Blotius, moreover through his friendship with Zwinger, had ample opportunity to meet him in Basel. The ambitious Dutchman was quick to ingratiate himself with important people, and one can surmise that his call to Strasbourg shortly afterwards would not have come about without a recommendation from Ramus.[94] If Turler met Ramus personally I cannot say. In any case he became an early convert to his method when he was Professor of Roman Law at Marburg (1560–1564), he taught it in a Ramist fashion.[95] Pyrckmair's relationship to Ramus was indirect yet strong. At Freiburg he had been a student of Johann Thomas Freige (1543–1583). Freige visited Ramus at Basel in the *annus mirabilis* 1568–69, becoming afterwards a downright fanatical

---

[90] Schindling: 1977, 162.

[91] Desmaze: 1864, 89.

[92] Petrus Ramus: *Basilea ad Senatum Populumque Basiliensem* (1569), ed. Hans Fleig, Basel 1944. On Zwinger *op. cit.*, 18.

[93] Bietenholz: 1971,153ff.

[94] Besides Zwinger, Ramus and Blotius had at least another common friend and patron in Basel, the Jewish merchant Marco Perez, who had converted to Calvinism and who continued to correspond with Blotius on geographical issues. Cf Ramus: 1944,32 and Brummel: 1972,22.26f.

[95] Cf Turler: 1569 (This work is an educational aid for his students in Marburg in the shape of a folder with a synoptic table that gives a disposition of the contents of the Institutions).

Ramist, who adapted the subject matter of all the moral sciences in the Ramist fashion and posed as "Ramus's heir" in Germany.[96]

After this momentous tour of Germany, Ramus returned to Paris, where he was killed in the massacres following St. Bartholemew's night in 1572; possibly at the instigation of his enemies from the university. This martyr's death sealed the success of Ramism, which now spread with the suddenness of an explosion over the Reformed and, to a lesser extent also, over the Protestant areas of Europe (and America). It exerted a deep influence on higher education in these areas, that lasted at least until 1630, and was centred in Germany.[97] The greatest number of tracts on the method of travel appeared in this period and in this area, and they are obviously influenced by Ramism.[98]

Ramism was a *universal method*, purporting to be able to deal with empirical and non-empirical knowledge alike. As a self-confessed follower of Vives,[99] Ramus attempted to transform Aristotelian logic from an instrument of debate into one for the acquisition and suitable arrangement of *useful* knowledge. More on this method will be said in the next chapter. Here suffice it to say that it required every topic under consideration to be investigated by means of ten standard questions, called "*loci*" ("places"), in order to derive propositions from it which could be tested through experience. The sum of the thus gained propositions on some topic, called the "discourse", was then to be ordered appropriately according to the "natural method". It consisted of a classification of all assertions forming the discourse which descended from the more general to the more particular. First one had to give a definition of what was evident. The conception gained in this was then to be divided into sub-classifications. These were again to be defined, and so on, down the hierarchy of assertions, until nothing more remained to be defined and divided: at this point, Ramus pretended, one left the sphere of conception and arrived at the essential nature of the things themselves.[100]

This arrangement of discourses was often represented in "synoptic tables", where homogeneous concepts were linked by brackets, such as in the "synopsis" reproduced above. Ramus did not invent these tables – they were already common in the medical school of Padua – but they became so popular in Ramist writings, that they almost function as a "leading fossil" of Ramism.[101] They are also prominent in Zwinger's *Methodus*. This work consists essentially in a

---

[96] Cf the article on Freige in *Allgemeine Deutsche Biographie* and Ong: 1958,298ff; Bietenholz: 1971,156.

[97] The standard work on Ramus and Ramism is Ong: 1958. Older, uncritical representations are Waddington: 1855 and Desmaze: 1864. See also Graves: 1912 and Hooykaas: 1958.

[98] Stagl: 1980a, 131ff; Stagl: 1983.

[99] Hooykaas: 1958, 28.

[100] Ramée: 1555,119ff.

[101] Höltgen: 1964; Yates: 1966,185ff.

framework of genealogical trees of conceptions, which sprout from each other, to form one single immense "*arbor scientiae*", in whose branches definitions and appropriate examples from the literature are arranged. The other early travel methods also show the influence of Ramism, even if they are not so conspicuous.

In this way, any subject matter could be "methodized" with comparative ease. This is what Ramists did in the following decennia. The success of this method was based on its universal applicability. In view of the immense expansion of the cultural horizon in the 16th century, Ramism gave its adherents gratifying security. All knowledge, even future knowledge, could be organized according to the same "natural method" (a principle of success, by the way, that Ramism shares with similar later movements, such as dialectical materialism or systems theory). In practice, however, it soon became evident that the method of Ramus never led to the real thing. It always remained in the conceptual sphere in which areas of knowledge were merely regrouped. Ramism had its greatest impact not on the acquisition of new and useful knowledge, as Ramus had hoped, but on the organization and unification of available knowledge, as in higher education and in the writing of encyclopedic compendia.[102]

THE ART OF TRAVEL

Zwinger, Turler, Pyrckmair and Blotius brought together various literary traditions and tendencies of their times and integrated them into a formal doctrine of travel. For this achievement Ramist methodology furnished, as it were, the "primer detonation". Following their attempts to methodize travel a stream of books and booklets aimed at the travelling public continued till the end of the early modern period. A preliminary study has revealed about 300 of these texts from the late 16th to the late 18th century.[103] The names which the founders gave to this doctrine, "*ars apodemica*" or "*prudentia peregrinandi*", have stuck and were used till the end of that period (English "art of travel", French "*art de voyager*", German "*Reisekunst*" or "*Reiseklugheit*"). Founded by Germans who had seen Venice and had become Ramists in Paris or Basel, the *ars apodemica* combined German didacticism, Italian realism and French methodology. It was thus a true all-European phenomenon, though its main field continued to be Northern and Western Europe, and especially Germany. Proceeding from the late medieval and Renaissance travelling practice, it attempted to codify and to improve it. Its influence is attested by the demand for these texts on the book market. It extended from the observational schemas which travellers brought with them to the actual realisation of the journey and the subsequent composition

---

[102] Ong: 1961; Risse: 1963; Henningsen: 1966; Joachimsen: 1970; Stark: 1972,332ff; Jardine: 1974,29ff.

[103] Stagl: 1983.

of travel reports or arrangement of collections. Even if not all travellers allowed themselves to be guided by the *ars apodemica*, the more scholarly minded among them certainly did. It is thus a cultural-historical phenomenon of the first order, which has hitherto been unduly neglected.[104]

What is the content of these texts? I will restrict myself to a list of the topics that recur frequently, especially in the early treatises. This list enumerates the contents of an ideal travel method. As will be noticed, one could easily write a paper on any one of these points:

(a) A *definition* of travel. (I have already pointed out that Ramism was addicted to definitions.) In these definitions the utility of travel for education and research is stressed. This is done by means of a characteristic distinction: *true* travel ("*peregrinari*") is contrasted with aimless and useless rambling ("*vagari*").[105] The best short definition is probably that given by S. Zwicker (*Breviarium apodemicum methodice concinnatum*, Danzig 1638): "*Est igitur Peregrinatio profectio quaedam cupiditate et desiderio extera loca perlustrandi, invisendi et cognoscendi ab idoneo homine suscepta, ad bonum aliquod inde aquirendam, quod vel Patriae et amicis, vel nobis ipsis prodesse posset*" ("Travel is thus a certain journey, undertaken by a suitable man out of the desire and wish to wander through, inspect and get to know external places, in order to acquire from there some good or other, which could be useful either to the fatherland and the friends or to ourselves").[106]

(b) A *subdivision* of the conception thus gained. (Ramus's "natural method" consisted after all in the definition and subdivision of concepts. It was retained in the "apodemic" treatises till well into the 17th century.) Zwinger is especially systematic here. His classification of ways of travel may thus serve as an example. Zwinger divides the conception of travel according to the four Aristotelian "causes",[107] viz. (I) the object (travels of scholars, merchants, artists, craftsmen); (II) the means (spiritual means, such as power

---

[104] Cf Stagl: 1979, 1980a, 1980b, 1981a, 1989a, 1990, 1992; Kutter: 1980; Witthöft: 1980.

[105] Turler writes: "*Perigrinatio nihil aliud sit quam labor ivisendi et perlustrandi alienas terras, non a quibusvis, nec temere, sed ab idoneis suscipendus, ut vel artem, quam addiscere vel exercere cupiunt, probe tandem calleant, vel ea, quorum usus aliquis in communi vita est apud exteros videant, discant, et diligenter observant, iisque sibi suis, et patriae, si opus sit, prodesse possint*" (1574,3). Zwinger's definition is very similar (1577, Praefatio). Pyrckmair defines the traveller as "*aliarum terrarum idoneum perlustratorem & diligentem harum rerum observatorem, quae scitu sunt & neccessariae & utiles, quique suam peregrinationem non temeritate quadam, sed utilitate publica, honestate & gloria motus prudenter instituat, neque levi caussa se a proposito suo distrahi aut impediri patiatur, sed iis rebus, quarum gratia peregrinatur, subinde sedulo invigilet*" (1577, *fol.* 6f).

[106] S. Zwicker: *Brevarium apodemicum methodice concinnatum*. Danzig 1638.

[107] When Zwinger conceived his *Methodus*, he was no longer a strict adherent of Ramus, but had returned to a more sober Aristotelianism through the influence of his studies in Padua, cf. Bietenholz: 1971,153ff. He thus arranged his subject matter in an orthodox Aristotelian fashion.

of observation, corporal means, such as health, and material means, such as money, maps, and compasses); (III) the form (travels by land, which can again be subdivided into travels on foot, on horseback or with a coach, travels by water and even travels by air, for which Zwinger refers to the examples of Daedalus and of the Angels); and (IV) the matter of travel (destination, routes, and different species of travellers. These latter are hierarchically subdivided into saints and their relics, men of different estates from high to low, animals, and finally things, such as merchandise). In Aristotelian logic the "accidences" and the "species" follow the "causes". As accidences of travel Zwinger discusses time, place, state of health, the conjunction of the stars and the fellowship of travel, as species of travel sacral and profane, public and private, old and new ones. All these points are elucidated by means of examples and further subdivided if necessary.[108] Other authors are less systematic, but they all take the educational journey as the basic idea of travel, against which all other forms are measured.

(c) A *consideration of the arguments* for and against travel. This continued the dispute on the use and abuse of pilgrimages.[109] The humanists had always defended travelling for the sake of the mind (*animi causa*) against the Stoic and medieval disparagement of mobility and the *vitium curiositatis*, which had been taken up by the Reformers as well as by the rising absolutist state, who aimed at restricting the freedom of movement of its subjects.[110] Zwinger had handily combined the pros and cons in his *Theatrum vitae humanae*,[111] Stephanus Vinandus Pighius (1520–1604) had opposed them in dialogue form[112] and Melchior Junius (1545–1604) at Strasbourg had set his students the task of presenting them in academic orations.[113] The counter-arguments were weighty indeed: according to them, travelling turned the mind away from God towards irrelevant things; it loosened social and political ties and thus endangered the morals, manners and health of the traveller; it encouraged the spread of new ideas menacing the stability of government;

---

[108] Zwinger: 1577,149ff.

[109] Cf. the paragraph *From Pilgrimage to Educational Journey* above

[110] Conrads: 1982.

[111] Theodor Zwinger: *Theatrum vitae humanae*.... Basel 1565, I,13f; I,1.

[112] Stephanus Vinandus Pighius: *Hercules Prodicius, Seu Principis Iuventutis Vita Et Pergrinatio ... Historia Principis adolescentis institutrix: & antiquitatum, rerumque scitu dignarum varietate non minus utilis quam iucunda*.... Antwerp 1587, 131ff.

[113] Melchior Junius: *Utrum peregrinationes sind bene constitua in Repub. permittendae? Orationes aliquot, exercitationis causa, ab Eloquentiae scriptae studiosis*.... In: Junius: 1595, 35–86.

and last but not least it was expensive.[114] The travel methodologists could no longer celebrate mobility with the naive frankness of a Fortius Ringelbergius. They had to take the counter arguments seriously. From merely opposing the pros and cons they thus proceeded to strike the balance. Only after having weighed them against each other, the arguments for travel are given the preference. The travel methodologists achieve this by making use of the abovementioned distinction between *"peregrinari"* and *"vagari"*. They thus justify travel mainly by its educational value. This justification can be seen as a means of self-defence of the humanist *res publica literaria* against the pretension to exclusiveness of church and state in the age of confessionalism and absolutism. The *ars apodemica* neutralized the arguments against travel by assimilating them in the shape of the methodical self-control of the traveller. This justification of travel occurs especially in the earlier treatises; in the later ones it is taken for granted. In the 17th century, moreover, the self-control of the mature travelling humanist was increasingly replaced by the external control of a youthful, immature traveller on his "grand tour" by a private tutor who acted on the instructions of the traveller's family.[115]

(d) *Medical advice.* This part of the *ars apodemica* was derived from the old "travel regimina".[116] Many of the counsels for preserving the traveller's health are directly taken over from them. From here and from other medical writings, the travel methodologists also took over the doctrine of the "climates" which will be discussed below. As will be remembered, physicians were conspicuous among the founders of the *ars apodemica*. A more than passing mention is deserved here by Guilhelmo Grataroli (1516–1568), a physician from Padua, who had fled for religious reasons to Germany, where he taught at Marburg as Turler's colleague and as Zwinger's in Basel. Grataroli's *De Regimine iter agentium* (Basel 1561) is the most

---

[114] These counter-arguments are especially forcefully presented in Joseph Hall: *Quo vadis? A Iust Censure of Travell as it is commonly undertaken by the Gentlemen of our Nation.* London 1617. Hall (1574–1656), Bishop of Exeter and Norwich, called the "English Seneca", was a highly regarded preacher and theological writer. By using arguments from the Stoics and fathers of the church, he condemns the educational journey of the English upper classes as "private and publike meschiefe". England being an "abridgement of (God's) whole Earth and possessing the best constitution and the best universities in Europe, there is actually no need for English gentlemen to travel. These became standard arguments of the English critics of the "grand tour". They were elaborated by the philosopher John Locke (*Some thoughts concerning education*, London 1693, 189–201) and by Richard Hurd (1720–1808), Bishop of Worcester (*Dialogues on the Uses of Foreign Travel; considered as part of an English gentlemen's education: between Lord Shaftesbury and Mr. Locke. London 1764*).

[115] The transition between *ars apodemica* and the special literature for private tutors offers Petrus Mieszkowski: *Institutio peregrinationum peregrinantibus peropportuna.* Louvain 1625. Cf also Schwart: 1693. On the "grand tour" much has been written. Cf Bates: 1911; Mead: 1914 (reprint 1972); Michéa: 1945; Loebenstein: 1966; Hibbert: 1969; Shackleton: 1971.

[116] Cf note 40.

FIGURE 5: Gulielmus Gratarolus. From: The portrait collection of the Herzog August Bibliothek, Wolfenbüttel.

systematic travel regimen and the link between that genre and the nascent *ars apodemica*.[117] It was excerpted by many later travel methodologies such as Zwicker's *Breviarium*.[118] The section on medicine did not, however, develop significantly in the later treatises. The same advice was repeated all over again. This is not astonishing, since much of this advice was sound and had a timeless value. Such advice can still be found in the introductory chapter of modern tourist guides.

(e) *Religious advice*, derived from the old pilgrims directories.[119] The *ars apodemica* is surprisingly detailed on religious issues. From the pilgrims directories it takes over many pietistic practices and a tripartition of the journey in preparation, execution and evaluation.[120] Its founders even wanted to retain for travellers *"animi causa"* the privileges pilgrims and clerics had enjoyed in the Middle Ages.[121]

The main problem the travel writers had to cope with in this respect was the religious diversity of late 16th and 17th century Europe. Roughly speaking the countries from which most travellers and travel writers came (Germany, the Low Countries, England, Scandinavia) were Protestant, and the countries to which they went were Catholic (Italy, later also France). This raised a matter of conscience: to what extent should a traveller conform to foreign usages or even conceal his confession without betraying it? Sometimes it was labelled the *problema machiavellisticum*.[122] It was predominantly discussed - with a fine sense for nuances – by theologically trained travel writers. Most of them chose to quote St. Ambrose: If you are in Rome do as the Romans do.[123] Theologian travel writers were especially numerous in the 17th century, when the humanist educational journey was superseded by the "grand tour". The theory of travel then became a typical theme for theologians at German universities preparing for a career as private

---

[117] Cf note 42. On Grataroli cf Gallizioli: 1788; Bietenholz: 1959,131ff.

[118] Cf note 106.

[119] Cf note 36.

[120] Pitsius: 1602 calls the three phases *"praeparatio"*, *"opus ipse"* and *"operis terminis"* (lib. V, cap. III, cf note 36); Zwicker: 1638,6 calls them *"Itio"*, *"Commoratio"*, *"Reditio"*. A leading modern author on scientific travel speaks of the *"Dreiklang von Vorbereitung, Ausführung und Auswertung"* (Beck: 1959,228).

[121] Turler: 1474, *cap.* VI; Pyrckmair: 1577, *fol.* 11; Salomon Neugebauer: *Tractatus de peregrinatione. Methodo naturali constriptus, ac Historicis, Ethicis, Politicisque exemplis illustratus...* Basel: 1605?, 130ff; David Frölich: *Bibliotheca sive Cynosura Peregrinantium, hoc est, Viatorium...* Ulm 1643–44, vol.I, 99f.

[122] Daniel Gruber: *Discursus Historico-Politicus de Peregrinatione Studiosorum...* Strasbourg: 1619,24; Johann Paul Felwinger: *De Peregrinatione*, in Felwinger 1666, 665.

[123] For many variants of that proverb see Benham (s.a.), col. 917b

tutor.[124] It was no easy thing for theologians to come to terms with travelling "*anima causa*". It proceeded from considerations of innerworldly utility and acknowledged the intrinsic value of every country travelled through and therefore led to *relativism*.[125] If we ask why Protestant travel writers showed themselves to be so tolerant and why so many pious Protestants continued to endanger their spiritual welfare by travelling to Italy, we must take into account the continuing intellectual force of humanism. Certainly by the end of the 16th century the inhabitants of northern countries no longer considered themselves as "barbarians". However, immersion in the sphere of classical Rome and the education of taste by the standards of classical antiquity involved bridging an abyss that the Reformation had opened up between Rome and northern and western Europe.[126]

It is noticeable that the religious advice of the "apodemic" writers is in most cases formulated in a confessionally neutral way. The Catholics are treated with respect and the difference between Lutherans and Calvinists is played down. Only the Anglicans stick to the point of religious diversity, since every journey to the continent forced them to travel in confessionally different areas. They were especially concerned with the proselytism of the Jesuits.[127] The neutralism of most travel methods had certainly to do with marketing considerations - books on travel must be read everywhere -, but also with the surviving irenic attitude of humanism. This attitude came again to the fore in the 18th century, when confessionalism declined. Then the religious part of the travel directions also declined in importance.

(f) *Practical advice* for travellers, often divided according to three stages; i. preparation of the journey, ii. its completion and iii. behaviour after the return. This tripartition was taken over from the pilgrims guides.[128] I also follow it here:

i. The apodemic treatises were written with the intent of preparing the traveller for his journey. They had thus to be studied beforehand. In addition, some knowledge of the countries travelled through and their languages was to be acquired. It was important to take sufficient money, preferably in the form of bills of exchange. Another important asset were letters of introduction to important men abroad (*viri illustres*). Only a journey thoroughly prepared in that way could bear the expected fruits.

---

[124] Cf Stagl: 1980a, 159, note 107. See also note 115 of the present chapter.

[125] Cf. Atkinson: 1924.

[126] Jedin: 1951,45. See also Michéa: 1945 and Schudt: 1959.

[127] Hall: 1617 is especially eloquent about this. See note 110.

[128] Cf. note 120.

ii. Some of the advice on behaviour during the journey is timeless: the traveller had to beware of excesses of every kind, to refrain from open comparisons between the country visited and the native country, to adapt himself to the local customs, not to be over-confident, and certainly not to enter into discussion of religion or politics. Other counsels are period-bound. From what is told on the post and conveyance, on behaviour in inns, on payment systems and so on, one could easily write a cultural history of travel in early modern times. Finally there are place-bound counsels on how to tour particular countries and cities and what to observe in them. Generally speaking, such advice was derived from long practice and certainly handed down from one generation of travellers to the next before it became codified in the *ars apodemica*. The main characteristic of that genre is its *openness to reality*. The travellers are repeatedly admonished to suspend their judgments, to be open to everything strange and new, to observe and listen rather than to talk, or, as one author sums it up, to be *"emax"* rather than *"vendax"*.[129] This attitude sometimes borders on Machiavellian amoralism. Being reticent without seeming so, drawing people out and exploring places without arising suspicion - in other words, spying - is taught in some 17th century treatises as a merely technical problem, or even as a fine art.[130]

iii. After returning the traveller is advised to resume his native dress and customs, not to show off with foreign expressions or make himself ridiculous by telling incredible stories[131] and not to despise his old friends at home. He nevertheless should cultivate his newly acquired friendships abroad by writing letters. This point is especially stressed. The exchange of letters somehow continued the journey with different means. It entitled the returned traveller to ask for new information and write letters of introduction for other travellers; it also obliged them to receive foreigners recommended by his correspondents. Thus the network of the *res publica literaria* continued to be woven.[132]

(g) Short *descriptions* of the principal nations of Europe, their countries, ways of life and political systems. Sometimes these sketches also include a rudimentary psychology of people based on the theory of the "climates" which

---

[129] Julius Bellus: *Hermes Politicus Sive De Peregrinatoria Prudentia libri tres.* Frankfurt 1608,97.

[130] e.g. Bellus: 1608 (see the preceding note); Hermann Conring: *De civili Prudentia liber unus.* Helmstedt 1662, cap. XIII and the anonymous treatise *L'art de voyager utilement.* Amsterdam 1698.

[131] On the topos of the untrustworthiness of the traveller cf. ch. tour.

[132] See ch. two § *Travel, correspondence, documentation and the "res publica literaria".*

in the 16th century had been renewed by Jean Bodin.[133] This survey of the national dissimilarity of Europe was intended to prepare the traveller what to expect abroad; it worked, however, against the openness required of the traveller by supplying him with stereotypes and strengthening his prejudices. Finally, the sketches of the various nations indicate the close link between the *ars apodemica* and the above-mentioned "statistical" compendia.

(h) Hints for the use of *travel contrivances* such as maps, compasses, nautical instruments, itineraries and travel guides. Such technical hints connect the *ars apodemica* with the medieval and Renaissance genre of *navigatio*.[134] Among the travel contrivances discussed were some which would be called "magical" today, such as astrological, physiognomic and magical diagrams, whose practical use for the traveller was taken for granted by most authors. This was in the spirit of the period, but it has also to be remembered that many early writers of the *ars apodemica* adhered to the cabbalistic-neo-Platonic doctrine of the harmony between macrocosmos and microcosmos favourable to the occult sciences.[135] In order to avoid confusion a few words have to be said on travel guides. They were a separate genre different from travel methods, even if there was some overlap. They had no moral or intellectual goal, but only a practical one which was efficient travel. Travel guides are a much older genre than travel methods, going back to pilgrims' guides, itineraries and "road books" (see above) and they survived the travel methods, being still in use today.[136]

(i) Instructions for the *direction of the attention* of the traveller. Travel methods contain instructions on what to observe, how to make observations and how to record and evaluate the information gained. These are of special interest to the historian of the social sciences. The traveller is urged to ascertain interesting facts from everywhere and everybody; not only from statesmen, scholars and artists, but also from craftsmen, sailors, merchants, peasants and "wise women".[137] Thus the entire spectrum of mankind becomes the unit of observation. The traveller is expected to communicate with people of all estates and trades, attend council meetings and court sessions, visit churches, schools, workshops and hospitals, and be as perspicacious and persistent as possible in his observations without becoming irksome or suspicious.

---

[133] Cf Jean Bodin: *Methodus ad facilem historiarum cognitionem.* Paris 1566, cap. V.

[134] See above; see also Penrose: 1975,329ff.

[135] Especially prolific in this respect is the most comprehensive - and bulky - apodemic treatise, David Frölich: *Bibliotheca, seu Cynosur Peregrinantium....* 2 vols., Ulm 1643–44. On the whole matter see Shumaker: 1972. See also ch. two, § Ars memoratira.

[136] Cf Schudt: 1959,18ff.

[137] This had already been required by Vives and Ramus. Cf Hooykaas: 1958,28.

In this way, a wealth of information is reaped during a journey. In order not to be forgotten it was to be fixed in *writing*. The *ars apodemica* was a major aspect of the early modern culture of literacy. Its authors turned against the totalizing mode of perception characteristic of oral culture, intending to break it down into specific, verifiable items. I have mentioned that the story-telling of returned travellers was disparaged. Instead these were urged to fix their experiences in their diary, where they could be checked. Generally speaking, the 16th century distrusted memory. What was told and had to be believed on the strength of the narrator's personality was no longer considered as trustworthy, but only what was experienced and presented methodically. Method began to replace memory.[138] The early authors of the *ars apodemica* polemize at some length against hearsay and instead extol autopsy, quoting to a man Horace's *Ars poetica* 180–182.[139] This emphasis on autopsy explains why travelling was deemed so important in the early modern curriculum and why it had to be methodized.

Besides the notes in their diaries, the travellers were also advised to collect excerpts from rare works, copies of inscriptions, drawings in their sketch-book and, according to their means, coins, medals, works of art, specimens of natural history, ethnographica and other "curiosities".[140]

These written and tangible yields of a journey were to be classified according to "*loci communes*". These were conventional heads or rubrics under which one could classify anything heard, seen, read, experienced or thought about, in order to have it ready for later use. They were developed by humanism for the written registration of all loosely connected ("historical") knowledge (as has been mentioned in connection with Vives and Ramus). *Loci communes* were thus especially important for the traveller exposed to a wealth of new and heterogeneous knowledge. They enabled him not to be completely overwhelmed by it, but to give it a preliminary order. Scrupulous authors like Thomas Erpenius (1584–1624) or Johann Heinrich Boecler (1611–1672) even recommended the traveller to keep two notebooks. In the first he had to note down everything memorable that he came across or that occurred to him, promptly but discretely, while his memory was still fresh. In the evening, or whenever else he had leisure, he was to transcribe the most important notes into the second book which was to be subdivided into *loci communes*.[141] This procedure closely resembled

---

[138] Yates: 1966,185ff. Cf also ch. two, § Ars memoratira.

[139] See the motto of this chapter.

[140] Chytraeus: 1594 and Erpenius: 1631 are especially detailed in that respect. For the sketch-book cf. James Howell: *Instructions for Forreine Travell*. London 1642,32. Among the founders of the *ars apodemica* Turler is most interested in collecting.

[141] Erpenius: 1631,20; Boecler: 1701,21.

"double bookkeeping" which had recently been perfected in Venice[142] The two principal forms of the travel report, narration and description, obviously go back to the chronological order of the diary and to the synchronistic order of the traveller's notes according to the *loci communes*.[143]

It is also obvious that *loci communes* concentrated the attention of the traveller. By showing him where to register his experiences they also showed him where to make new ones. For *loci* could be formulated not only as *rubrics*, but also as *questions*, under which the answers obtained could be classified. An example for a system of *loci* formulated as a questionnaire is the *Tabula Peregrinationis continens capita Politica* by Hugo Blotius. This will be more fully discussed in the next chapter.

(j) *Descriptive schemata*: The *loci* furnished to the travellers by the *ars apodemica* were not isolated. Together they formed schemata which codified the patterns of observation and description. One of these has been reproduced above (p.61). A first impression on reading the early treatises is that every author proposes his own schema. Yet this is misleading. They all are variations of a few traditional patterns of description. The most important of these was the rhetorical technique of *praise*. Since late antiquity there had been standard formulas for the praise of places.[144] They formed the starting point for the humanist "praise of cities" and "praise of countries", a popular genre especially cultivated in the above-mentioned "travel poetry" (e.g. the famous praise of Nuremberg by Conrad Celtis). Cities or countries could be praised on the strength of their natural beauty and produce, the magnificence of their fortifications and buildings, the number, excellence and special way of life of the population, their history, noble families and *viri illustres*, the virtue of their ruler or rulers and their means of power, the piety of their worship and the excellence of their constitution.[145] From this encomiastic literature developed the more soberly descriptive one, viz. the "cosmographic" and "statistical" works. A second model for description was contained in ancient medical and scientific literature, where the connections between places, their climate and the human type inhabiting them was explored.[146] It was especially taken up by physicians like Zwinger and

---

[142] Cf Luca Pacioli: *Summa de Arithmetica, Geometria, Proportioni e Proportionalità*. Venice 1492.

[143] Cf also ch. four, § *False ethnography. For the "loci communes" cf. Introduction § Rhetoric, and ch. two. § Ars memoratira.*

[144] Reproduced in Halm: 1863, 556ff, 569, 587, also Lausberg 1990, § 247.

[145] Buck: 1975b; Schmidt: 1978.

[146] This goes back to the pseudo-Hippocratic text *De aere, aquis et locis*. The *Corpus Hippocraticum* had been edited by Zwinger. This text was the point of departure of the "doctrine of the climates". Cf note 133.

Pyrckmair. Still further models were provided by antique ethnographers like Herodotus, travel writers like Pausanias, geographers like Strabo and the "Polities" of Aristotle, which were, as has been shown, much imitated during the Renaissance. The most important impulse for the integration of these traditions and examples into a coherent scheme for the exploration and description of foreign countries or cites came, however, from Arab geography. It had been transmitted to the *ars apodemica* via Ramusio. In the preface to the second volume of his *Navigationi* the Venetian recommended this scheme as "*ordine veramente belissimo*". It contained (1) the names (ancient and modern), (2) the history according to the authoritative writers, and (3) the situation of the place, its climate, and a short description of the most important local phenomena.[147] This was the pattern for Zwinger's exemplary descriptions of cities as well as for the *Synopsis* reproduced above.

FURTHER DEVELOPMENTS

The *ars apodemica* imposed an encyclopedic programme on travellers. How could a single person manage all this? In order to keep their programme manageable, the authors told the travellers to restrict their attention to the really important matters. This tallied with the outlook of early modern empiricism, which had adopted from rhetoric the focusing on *memorabilia, insignia, curiosa, visu ac scitu digna*.[148]

The world, as it was explored by the early modern traveller, did not have the homogeneousity of our present scientific worldview. It was conceived as qualitatively heterogeneous. Every thing or event occurring in it was something special in itself. Such phenomena could not easily be classified according to cause and effect, yet they could be subsumed under heading or rubrics. If - in the ideal case - all noteworthy things and events were subsumed under their headings, completeness would be achieved. This world allowed thus for intellectual progress. But it was difficult to analyze and almost impossible to quantify.

The autonomy of the singular phenomena led to a surprising objectivity in the observer. The personality of the reporter is hardly evident. The stock of information which the travellers brought back from their journeys already pre-structured by the *loci* or their notebooks was typically processed into travel reports and compendia. These literary genres have already been discussed. They had a dry, matter-of-fact style and an enumerative character. If this enumeration

---

[147] Ramusio: 1556, Prefatione. For the Arab schema in general see Miquel: 1967, vol. I, 281. Such conventional schemas continue in geographical (and ethnographical) descriptions, cf Hettner: 1932, Spethmann: 1932.

[148] Cf note 18.

followed the chronology of a travel diary, it took the shape of a travel report (*rela-tio, historia*), if it followed the schema of a notebook, it resulted in a synchronistic description (*descriptio, status, notitia*). There were several transitional stages and mixed forms between those extremes. The information contained in such works was not the exclusive intellectual property of the author. Sometimes the person who wrote or edited a travel report included at the appropriate places all kinds of interesting and noteworthy things from other books. This person was very often not identical with the traveller. The printed report or description became rather far removed from the original experience of the traveller. Faced with this free-floating and unverifiable information, it was easy to invent travels which had never taken place, to foist incorrect facts on true travel reports, or to take this genre with its conventions as a starting point for free flights of imagination ("imaginary travels"). This possibility of easy distortion impaired also the credibility of true and sober reports and descriptions. Nevertheless these genres remained extremely popular during the whole early modern period.[149] And despite their shortcomings, they brought about progress in knowledge of each other and of the rest of the world by the European nations. The same *loci communes* were ready for everybody to subsume his experiences into. Thus the thousands of works of these genres can almost be considered as so many attempts by the "ideal traveller" to describe the world.

This mode of experiencing and describing the world reached its limits when all "noteworthy" things were more or less known. For the main European nations this happened in the late 17th century. By then, descriptions of the relevant countries, regions and cities which were complete according to the standards of the *ars apodemica* were accessible to the public in printed, their major "sights", in engraved form. The *ars apodemica* had achieved its goal. Its descriptive schemata could of course be further refined and the descriptions could be brought up to date more rapidly - but this was already routine. The excitement of European self-discovery had evaporated.

This development had important social consequences. The *ars apodemica* survived, yet its market changed. I have mentioned that its founders had written for mature men in search of self-improvement and useful knowledge. From the mid 17th century on, the writers aimed at young men who for the finishing of their education wanted to gain some experience of the world, represent the splendour of their family and establish useful connections abroad. Such young men were supervised by private tutors functioning, as it were, as a portable *ars apodemica*. The family sometimes employed this tutor also for the editing of the travel report - the traveller himself being by his social rank above an author's ambition. Thus humanist travel "*animi causa*" became superseded by the "grand tour". However great the latter's educational and social value - its yield

---

[149] Cf note 115, cf also Wuthenow: 1980; Brenner 1989; Griep: 1991; and ch. four.

FIGURE 6: The Grand Tour as part of the educational system of the Baroque. Frontispiece of Anton Wilhelm Schwart:Der Adeliche Hofmeister, Frankfurt 1693. By courtesy of the Herzog August Bibliothek, Wolfenbüttel.

in information was almost negligible. Explorative journeys in the more civilized and better known parts of Europe began to stagnate. If the *ars apodemica* survived this change, it lost its significance - qualitatively and quantitatively.[150]

The first creative period subsided after about 1630. The genre then became a recognised part of educational literature, a playground for professional polygraphs (among whom one pillaged the other), and a standard topic for dissertations at German protestant universities (who followed the same course). It kept its Ramist stance up to the late 17th century. At that time, the absolutist state succeeded in making the "grand tour's" educational aspiration more or less superfluous by the establishment of local universities. The "grand tour" degenerated into a mere scoring of "sights" and became as ritualised as the late medieval pilgrimage had been. "With the year 1740 the epoch of the 'grand tours' can be considered to have reached its end"[151] – at least for continental Europe; the English, prompted by their insular situation, continued their tours till the wars of the French Revolution. But this decline of the "grand tour" is not yet the end of the story.

Even if the recipes of the *ars apodemica* had become stale, travelling and collecting continued to be the main means of gaining empirical knowledge. Educational travel - guided by methodical treatises - was preserved in certain professions, especially in medicine.[152] Indeed travels for vocational training by non-gentlemanly and even non-academic classes were now also methodized. The *Hand- und Reisebuch für alle in die Fremde ziehende junge Personen* ("Manual and travel-book for all young persons going abroad"), which Ernst Friedrich Zobel published in Altdorf in 1734, and had at least six editions till 1795 – the second edition being printed in 10,000 copies - addressed explicitly "shop assistants, artisans, craftsmen".[153] Even women were not forgotten: Mademoiselle Sidonia Hedwig Zäunemannin's *Curieuser und immer währender Astronomisch-Meteorologisch-Oeconomischer Frauenzimmer-Reise-und-Hand-Kalender* ("Curious and everlasting astronomic-meteorologic-economic travel-and hand-almanac for women") appeared in Erfurt in 1737.[154]

---

[150] Cf. Loebenstein: 1980; de Ridder-Symoens: 1989 and note 115.

[151] Conrads: 1982,47.

[152] Medicine had been an itinerant profession in the Middle Ages and the early modern period. The *"peregrinatio medica"*, the journey of young physicians in order to complete their education, was thus a well-established custom. The Danish anatomist Thomas Bartholinus (1616–1680) had written the best-known instruction for the *peregrinatio medica* (Bartholinus: 1674). The celebrated Johann Peter Frank (1745–1821), one of the pioneers of modern medicine, had still defended it in an academic oration (Frank: 1792).

[153] Zobel: 1734, Preface. Zobel (1687–1756) was first bookbinder, then schoolmaster and finally Imperial notary in Altdorf, owner of a publishing firm and Pietist church politician.

[154] Mlle Zäunemannin was not the editor of this work, but only wrote the introduction to its sixth edition (Erfurt 1737), the one I have consulted. Sidonia Hedwig Zäunemannin (1714–1740) was crowned as "Imperial Poetess" by the University of Göttingen in 1738. She was fond of travelling disguised as a man, and thus met her accidental death (Pelz: 1991).

Just as the *ars apodemica* itself and its audience became more peripheral so also the travellers who wanted to experience and learn something new shifted their attention from the centres to the periphery of civilization. Besides Italy and France, the less well known European countries, such as Spain, Sweden or Russia, were explored; more frequent and regular travels overseas were attempted; and one's own country became more pertinent. In all these three cases, the aim of travel shifted from the improvement of the traveller's personality to the gathering of knowledge. The balance, which the *ars apodemica* had tried to maintain between these two goals was upset. The travel methods which reacted to this new trend form a transition to the methodology of expeditions.

I sketch here only four major elements of this transition:

(i) At the end of the 17th century, the instructions for copying inscriptions, using libraries and collections etc. grew into special methods guiding "literary travels" and "antiquarian" research. From this type of research the auxiliary disciplines of history developed in the 18th century.[155]

(ii) The same happened in natural history for the collection and conservation of minerals, fossils, plants, and animals.[156] Here there were close connections with the instructions for the *peregrinatio medica*, travel for the vocational training of physicians.[157] The transition between these technical instructions for collecting and the methodology of exploratory expeditions is exemplified by the two influential texts by Carl von Linné (1707–1778). The *Oratio, qua peregrinationum intra patriam asseritur necessitas* (Upsala 1741) was an exhortation, accompanied by methodological hints, to explore the native country (which Linné himself had done with his voyage to Lapland in 1732); the *Instructio Peregrinatoris* (actually a dissertation by Erik Nordblad supervised by Linné) gave a comprehensive programme for the gathering of medical and scientific information.[158]

(iii) In the 17th century questionnaires were systematically employed by the scientific academies for the collection, comparison and verification of information on native or foreign countries supplied by travellers and correspondents. This will be more fully discussed in the next chapter.[159]

---

[155] The best known treatise was Baudelot de Dairval (1686). On "literary travels" see Heer: 1938. Johann David Köhler (1684–1755), Professor of History in Göttingen, wrote a guide for the proper use of libraries and collections, which was published in 1762 by his son and successor Tobias (1720–1768) and became a standard work (Köhler: 1762). On the origins of the auxiliary sciences of history in Göttingen see ch. six.

[156] E.g. Duhamel de Monceau: 1752; Turgot: 1758; Forster: 1771; see also ch. seven.

[157] Cf note 152.

[158] Linnaeus: 1741 (frequently re-edited); Nordblad: 1759 (frequently re-edited under Linnaeus' name).

[159] See ch. two.

(iv) From the early 18th century onwards, these academies sent out scientific travellers with specialized instructions. As has been mentioned above, individual travel instructions had preceded the more general precepts of the *ars apodemica*, and continued to exist alongside it, going into the particulars of specially planned voyages.[160] After the decline of the *ars apodemica* they gained new significance.[161] The travellers of the 18th century were almost overwhelmed with questions especially posed for them by various academies and learned societies. These public instructions were sometimes supplemented by secret ones from the government which financed their journey. These are less concerned with the progress of knowledge than with commercial, political and colonial aims. Many of these secret instructions are certainly lost, and many remain unpublished.[162] Those for the voyage of Bougainville survive and show that the traveller himself had had a hand in the formulation of his instructions – which apparently were the result of discussions between nautical experts, scientists and government officials.[163] The public and secret instructions for overseas voyages would merit a special monograph. They were often methodologically innovative due to their proximity to current problems. Thus the unpublished questions on anthropology and ethnography which the *Société Royale de Médicine* drew up in 1785 for the expedition of Lapérouse[164] were an important early contribution to the methodology of ethnographic fieldwork, to be further developed by the well-known *Considérations sur les diverses méthodes à suivre dans l'observation des peuples sauvages* (1800) de Joseph-Marie de Gérando.[165]

These four developments had the same effect: the hitherto holistic encyclopedic mode of travelling was split up and specialized, and the self-improvement of the traveller receded into the background as against the acquisition of new knowledge. This took place in connection with a conflict of two world-views. Early modern empiricism had been based on the idea of a *discontinuous* world full of phenomena which were *in themselves* important and existed in their own right independently of an observer. Yet the modern scientific outlook, on which

---

160 For example, the great Colbert wrote a special instruction for the travel of his son, the Marquis de Seignelay, in Italy. Its demands on the young man, whose observance was supervised by his tutor, were atrocious (Clément: 1867,95–103). Seignelay later became Minister of Naval Affairs, in which position he, like his father, conducted many statistical inquiries (Rothkrug: 1965,215).

161 The Silesian mathematician and scientist Ehrenfried Walther v. Tschirnhaus auf Kißlingswaldau (1651–1708) remarks about 1700 that individual instructions for young travellers had recently come into fashion (cf Tschirnhaus auf Hackenau: 1727).

162 Cf Faivre 1967, Moravia 1967, Broc 1984, 287ff.

163 Martin-Allanic 1964, I, 475f.

164 Bibliothéque Mazarine, Paris, Ms 1546. For the inquests of the *Société Royale de Médicine* cf Bourget 1976 and Moravia 1982, 109ff.

165 See ch. seven.

the exact sciences are based, is founded on the idea of *continuity*, as Husserl among others has shown.[166] The triumph of this new world-view was inevitable, as it was the only way in which the immense mass of knowledge gathered by early modern empiricism could be dealt with. This meant a scientific revolution no less important than that between the late Middle Ages and the Renaissance. What happened about 1800 has been called the "temporalization of taxonomy".[167] The *form* of knowledge became more important than the *substance* of it; method eclipsed material; empirical knowledge ceased to be arranged synchronistically, but was arranged in succession, in temporal series. This scientific revolution signified also the *terminus ad quem* for the art of travel.

There were, however, rearguard actions. Modern scientific travellers faced objections that they would no longer focus on what was "considerable", but instead overwhelmed and confused the reading public with "inconsiderable" details.[168] A chasm had opened between the new type of travel and the public. Details hitherto judged "inconsiderable" included the individual personality of the traveller and his exact movements in space and time. Both now became important, since the precise description of the observer's situation was now felt to be relevant.

Thus the advancement of the scientific world-view also called for the evaluation of subjectivity. One could even say that the inexplicable, which was excluded from the world of objects, found a new refuge in the mind of the observing subject. Thus, whilst travelling developed from an "art" to a "science", Laurence Sterne's *A Sentimental Journey through France and Italy* made its appearance (London 1768), which triggered the vogue of "sentimental journeys". These threw the objectivism of the *ars apodemica* (of which Sterne made fun) overboard, restricting themselves solely to "objects of feeling".[169] The "sentimental" traveller was not a teller of fairy tales. He was as truthful as the scientific traveller, yet not to the outer world but to his inner experiences.[170]

It is not by chance that these examples of scientific travel and the "sentimental" reaction to it came from western Europe rather than Germany. Germany had lost its leadership in this field and had become a backwater. Considering again the axis Venice-Basel-Paris, which had been central to the methodizing of travel in the late 16th century, one might say that the innovative centre shifted after the 16th century to the west, to Paris and further on to London. Yet Germany, or to be precise, those Protestant parts that had been touched by

---

[166] Husserl: 1954, Part 2.

[167] Lepenies: 1976,101. Cf also chs. three and seven.

[168] Stewart: 1978, ch. 2.

[169] Sauder: 1983,305.

[170] See also ch. four.

Ramism, remained its true home from the beginning of the *ars apodemica* until its demise about 1800.

How can this German backwardness be explained? No doubt the Thirty Years War and the ensuing politico-religious fragmentation had something to do with it. Without a proper capital, the German upper class had to travel in order to avoid provincialism. Thus an interest in travel for education and its methodology was preserved there until the middle of the 18th century. After then, the rising class of the bourgeoisie brought a new impetus into the established pattern of travelling. Having developed into an all-German group interconnected by commercial, intellectual and matrimonial exchanges that suffered under the particularism of the German Empire, it contended with the nobility for the privilege of making educational journeys. It firmly believed in the enlightening value of travel. Thus the fashion of travelling and travel books, which in western Europe had already begun to subside about 1750, came to the fore in landlocked, colony-less Germany precisely at that time.[171]

This granted an unexpected "Indian Summer" to the moribund *ars apodemica*. It especially flourished at the new universities founded by enlightened governments for the education of statesmen, civil servants and the liberal professions. The most famous of these universities was Göttingen, established in 1734 by the elector of Hanover.[172] Here the stagnant discipline of *notitia rerum publicarum* was revived about 1750. The leading figures of this revival were Gottfried Achenwall (1719–1772) and August Ludwig Schlözer (1735–1809). They modernized it into an empirical description of the demographic, economic, political, military, social and cultural forces of all known political states, which they called "*Statistics*", a term which gained European currency about 1800 thanks to the close connections between Göttingen and England.[173] In the context of "statistics" also the *ars apodemica* became a university subject. From 1777 to 1795, Schlözer taught every alternating term a course on the method of travel and another one on the evaluation of journals - the two main sources of information for "statistic" description.[174] The success of the new universities like Göttingen gave a new self-confidence to the collecting and registering type of empirism which was essentially pre-modern. This explains why the main opposition to the modern scientific way of travel came from Göttingen, Halle

---

[171] Moravia: 1967,943ff. See also ch. three.

[172] On the intellectual climate and influence of Göttingen see ch. six. § The University of Göttingen.

[173] See note 58.

[174] August Ludwig Schlözer, *Entwurf zu einem Reises-Collegio .. nebst einer Anzeige seines Zeitungs-Collegii*. Göttingen 1777. Cf also August Ludwig Schlözer, *Theorie der Statistik. Nebst Ideen über das Studium der Politik überhaupt...* Göttingen 1804, 97–109. On Schlözer see ch. six.

and other similar places.[175] These were the same places where after 1770 the new discipline of "ethnography" originated.

The very last and at the same time most comprehensive treatises on travel method were both connected with Göttingen. They were written by Austrian partisans of enlightened absolutism who had both been there, a nobleman and a middle-class university man. Count Leopold Berchtold (1759–1809), a Moravian landowner who travelled for seventeen years in Europe and the Near East, published *An Essay to direct and extend the Inquiries of patriotic travellers* in English (2 vols, London 1789, German ed. Braunscweig 1791, French ed. Paris 1797).[176] This manual contains (1) general reflections on travel method, (2) an immense questionnaire intended to guide the inquiries of the traveller into every conceivable aspect of the nation he wanted to describe, and (3) catalogues of methodological treatises and travel books "from the earliest times, down to September 8th 1787".[177] Berchtold, who was also an orientalist, had especially close connections with Carsten Niebuhr, who had taken part in the Arabian expedition organized at Göttingen and who had a hand in the German edition of the *Patriotic Traveller*. The other work in question is called *Apodemik oder die Kunst zu reisen. Ein systematischer Versuch zum Gebrauch junger Reisenden aus den gebildeten Ständen überhaupt und angehender Gelehrten und Künstler insbesondere* ("Apodemics, or The Art of Travel, A systematic essay for the use of young travellers of the educated classes in general, and would-be scholars and artists in particular"), 2 vols, Leipzig 1795. Its author, Franz Posselt, whose dates I have not been able to find out, was a librarian from Bohemia who had spent one year at Göttingen, also attending Schlözer's courses for travellers and users of journals. In his well-considered and thorough book Posselt aspires to give, and indeed achieves, a comprehensive theory of travel as a means for the education of heart, taste and reason.

These two works consciously sum up the more than two-hundred-year old tradition of the *ars apodemica*. But they are swansongs. Immediately after their publication educational travel stopped in Europe because of the French Revolution. It was not resumed after the return of peace. The old encyclopedic style of travelling was superseded by scientific expeditions on the one hand and "tourism" on the other. Thus the *ars apodemica* became obsolete. The explorer contented himself with the methodology of his subject, and the tourist with his travel guide. If the *ars apodemica* survived in a changed shape, it was in the most archaic scientific method in existence, *ethnographic fieldwork*, which has preserved the encyclopedic outlook of Renaissance empirism and is at the same

---

[175] Stewart: 1978, ch. 2.

[176] On Berchtold see ch. five.

[177] The full title of Berchtold's *Patriotic Traveller* is specified in note 38 to ch. five.

time a basic personal experience, a travel *animi causa*.[178] More will be said on the hidden connection between ethnographic method and the *ars apodemica* in the last three chapters of this book.

POSTSCRIPTUM: ON THE PRACTICAL UTILIZATION OF THE ARS APODEMICA:

I have sometimes been asked whether the *ars apodemica* had any effect on actual travelling in its epoch. This question is easier posed than answered and is slightly absurd. Would hundreds of travel methods have been published between 1570 and 1800, some of them by authors of the first rank,[179] if travellers had been completely uninterested in them and unprepared to follow their advice? This thought is indeed so unrealistic that the burden of proof should be reversed and the sceptics made to state their reason for assuming the ineffectualness of the *ars apodemica*. Is it not much more sensible to assume that these treatises were bought by the contemporaries as guidelines for their travels? I do not pretend that they were followed in every respect. They asked too much from the average traveller for that. I rather think that they shared the fate of other works of instruction, e.g. cookbooks or books on etiquette, which are usually consulted in special cases rather than followed throughout. Yet after they had once codified the contemporary patterns of travelling, the educational journey and the observation and description of countries and peoples, they came to form the *last stage of appeal*[180] for correct travelling - at least for the educated classes. Yet via the imitation of one's betters they most probably even influenced such travellers who had never read any of them.

Nevertheless I do not want to answer this sceptical objection merely with general considerations. There are after all concrete examples. I mention three of these, all from the formative period around 1600. They are chance findings I met with during my research on the *ars apodemica*. No doubt many others could be quoted. It would be highly desirable, though unfeasible in the present context, to make a more systematic study of the utilization of the *ars apodemica* by various categories of travellers. These three cases are merely "*exempla*" in the humanist sense, characteristic instances carrying the force of arguments:

(a) *Ludwig Iselin*: A bundle of notes has survived in the university library of Basel which Ludwig Iselin (1559–1612) had brought back from his Italian journey. Iselin, a lawyer, belonged to a prominent Basilean family. He was closely

---

[178] Much has been written on this double aspect of fieldwork in the last years; cf Kohl: 1987; Stagl: 1993a.

[179] See Stagl: 1983.

[180] On high culture as the last stage of appeal for popular culture I have said more in Stagl: 1989b, 49ff and Stagl: 1993b

related to and influenced by Theodor Zwinger. As his notes prove, during his journey (1586–1589) he followed the latter's *Methodus Apodemica* as closely as possible. He even attempted to improve it. Thus he extended Zwinger's schema for the description of cities as follows: (1) ancient and modern place names and names of *viri illustres*, (2) the origins, the founder and the patrons of the city, (3) its site, (4) its remarkable buildings and other sights, (5) its public life, (6) the manners and customs of the people. Following this schema, Iselin had explored and described various Italian cities, hoping that other travellers would follow his lead (*Brevis..... designatio eorum, quae aliqout Italiae urbes atque loca peregrinantibus investiganda sunt*). This had remained a fragment. Possibly after his return Iselin had been prevented by his various official duties (he became Professor of Roman Law at the university and legal advisor to the city of Basel) from completing it. Yet possibly there was also another, deeper reason: Iselin had followed Zwinger's advice too literally. Iselin was an epigone, the son, great-grandson and nephew of important men, whose tradition of Basel humanism he continued without condensing it in works of his own. Thus he probably lacked the force to digest the wealth of his Italian notes in a "Zwingerian" travel report.[181]

(b) *Mihály Forgách*: Justus Lipsius' instructions for the voyage to Italy made a great impression on the contemporaries.[182] After having published it in 1586, Lipsius was addressed by several humanists planning their Italian voyage for additional advice and letters of introduction. Among these was a young Hungarian, Mihály Forgách, baron of Ghymes. Forgách had spent one year in Strasbourg and was now, in 1587, pursuing his studies in Wittenberg. It is understandable that a Hungarian, whom his *peregrinatio academica* had led to Germany, should prove himself responsive for reflections on travel. After having read Lipsius' letter he employed all the rhetorical technique he had acquired under Junius[183] in Strasbourg to write a eulogy on travel containing the usual *tópoi*. He recited it to the society of his compatriots in Wittenberg and had it published there under the title *Oratio de peregrinatione et eius laudibus* in 1588.[184]

---

[181] On Iselin see Vetter: 1952,122ff. (Ms C VI 40, University Library of Basel, fol. 73–79t, 166–179t, 182,186–198t, 202).

[182] It was re-edited up until 1721. Bibliography in Stagl: 1983,66f.

[183] The academic orations for and against travel delivered under Junius' direction had only been held in 1593 and published in 1595 (cf note 123). Yet there was already a tradition of rhetorical exercises on this theme in Strasbourg, as Forgách's *Oratio* proves, which is very similar to Junius' *Orationes*. Cf the following note.

[184] Michael Forgacz, *Oratio de peregrinatione et eius laudibus: cum ex insigni Argentoratensi quo ante missus fuerat in celeberrimam Witebergensem Academiam venisset: in inclyto nationis Ungaricae Coetu Witebergae scripta et habita a Michaele Forgacz, Libero Barone in Gymes.* Wittenberg 1588.

In this booklet Forgách especially stressed Lipsius' advice to profit from the association of *viri illustres*. He also followed it. Shortly before setting out for Italy, on November 14, 1588, he wrote a letter to Lipsius, wherein he elegantly paraphrased this advice and applied it to the master himself, asking to be admitted at least to the privilege of his correspondence. Lipsius seems to have been flattered. He included his very friendly response, which must have reached Forgách already in Italy, in his printed correspondence. In it he mainly expatiates on the education of young noblemen for the service of the state. It is not known whether Forgách had actually followed Lipsius' advice on his Italian journey, for he left no travel report. Yet it is highly probable, since Forgách continued to pride himself on his correspondence with the master in Leiden. After his return, in 1592 he became co-founder of a society of noble humanists which called itself, taking up a formulation from Lipsius' letter to Forgách, "*proles Hungaricae Palladis*". From this circle emerged some eminent Hungarian statesmen and historians.[185]

(c) *Márton Szepsi Csombor*: If Iselin and Forgách left no travel reports, Márton Szepsi Csombor (1595–1622) did. As a schoolmaster and son of a family of craftsmen, "Martin the student" belonged to a more modest social sphere than the other two. Born in the Upper Hungarian mining district (present-day Slovakia) he acquired a good education, learnt German and made a first journey to Transylvania. In 1616 he went to pursue his studies at the "Athenäum" in Danzig, a Calvinist institution of higher learning. He studied there under the philosopher and geographer Bartholomäus Keckermann, one of the pioneers of the "statistical" genre.[186] After having taken his degree, Szepsi Csombor embarked on his journey. Proceeding by ship from Danzig, he skirted Denmark, Holland and England and finally landed at Dieppe. He passed through France, mostly on foot, via Rouen, Paris and Nancy to Strasbourg, which was still German and a centre of humanist studies at that time. He spent one month at Strasbourg and then returned via Germany, Bohemia and Poland to Hungary. True to the precepts of the *ars apodemica* he had filled his diary with notes which he had systematically ordered afterwards. Appointed as schoolmaster in Kaschau (Košice) after his return, he created from these notes a description of his journey and the countries he had travelled through. He did this with such intensity and rapidity (he did the printing himself) that he neglected the duties of his office and had to be dismissed in 1620. In that year also his book *Europica Varietas* appeared.[187] Written in Hungarian, it has the subtitle " A short description of

---

[185] On Forgách cf. Klaniczay: 1988.

[186] On Keckermann see ch. two, § *Dialectic*.

[187] Márton Szepsi Csombor, *Europica Varietas*. Kaschau 1620.

the countries: Poland, Mazovia, Prussia, Denmark, Frisia, Holland, Zeeland, England, France, Germany and Bohemia; Things seen and described by Márton Szepsi Csombor, not only for the pleasure of all readers, but also for their greatest profit".[188] Shortly afterwards, the author obtained the position of private tutor to a family of Hungarian magnates. He wrote a second book on the education of young noblemen, yet died of the plague in 1622.[189]

In the introduction to *Europica Varietas*, Szepsi Csombor develops a programme for description which heavily draws on the *ars apodemica*. His main authorities are Turler and Pyrckmair; he does not seem to know Zwinger. His principles of description are taken from the rules laid down for "*descriptio singularis*" by his master Keckermann.[190] In the main part of his book he gives the realization of this programme for the countries he had visited. Although he had, with the exception of Poland and France, but spent little time there, he nevertheless had the legitimation of autopsy; the lacunae in his notes he supplemented with excerpts from books and information from experts he had questioned either orally or per letter. As announced in the subtitle, Szepsi Csombor's descriptions are terse as well as systematic; occasionally he even cites numerical data. As counterpoise to these dry and matter-of-fact descriptions he quotes anecdotes and personal experiences, as Pyrckmair had also done, and intersperses his prosa with travel poems of considerable literary merit. All this makes the "first work of Hungarian descriptive statistics" also into "one of the most precious Renaissance documents".[191]

(d) *Conclusion:* As Szepsi Csombor's example shows, the programme of the *ars apodemica* could be put into effect by an exceptionally gifted and devoted traveller and thus contribute to the progress of the social sciences. Nevertheless the examples of Iselin and Forgách prove that this programme was too ambitious for most travellers, however enthusiastic they were, at least in so far as the working out of travel reports was concerned. Yet it has to be admitted that Iselin and Forgách had successful public careers after their return, to which the exacting and many-sided style of travelling required by the *ars apodemica* had no doubt prepared them well, whereas Szepsi Csombor, who seems to have had the monomaniac temperament of the true scholar, was so concerned with his book that he proved unable to fulfil his other duties. Thus the essential tension between self-education and

---

[188] Márton Szepsi Csombor, *Complete Works* (in Hungarian). Ed. Sándor I. Kovacs and P. Kulcsár. Budapest 1968.

[189] Horváth: 1985.

[190] Cf Seifert: 1980,218ff.

[191] Horváth: 1985,344,335.

the gathering of new knowledge, which had characterized the *ars apodemica* since its origins, is palpable also in these few examples. However short individual travellers fell behind the requirements of the *ars apodemica*, it remained an ideal standard for early modern travelling which was repeatedly pronounced till the end of that period. As Iselin's and Forgách's example shows, the personal inadequacy of a traveller could be compensated by his turning into a travel methodologist himself (I cannot refrain from observing here that this holds true for many methodological writers even today). And what surpassed the forces of the individual traveller - comprehensive descriptions of cities, countries, polities and peoples based on autopsy - has at last been furnished by the mutually supporting and regulating detailed work of many generations of travellers educated by the *ars apodemica*: first for Italy, then for the civilized parts of Europe and finally for its fringe areas and the other continents.

Rerum Memoria: Early Modern Surveys and Documentation Centres

"For *knowledge* itself is *power*"

(Francis Bacon, Essayes)

PRELIMINARY REMARK

What would an educated European in the Middle Ages have known of foreign countries? Or even his own? Apparently very little. There were no reliable descriptions of countries and cities, and no handbooks describing their various constitutions and ways of life. Pertinent information had been collected, of course, but was stored in chanceries and archives, out of reach of the unauthorized eye. People knew their own spheres of life well enough and some, such as nobles, ecclesiastics, diplomats, missionaries, sailors and merchants, had spheres of life which extended farther. Yet even their knowledge implied practical mastery rather than intellectual penetration. Characteristically, the most reliable geographical descriptions were "itineraries", guides telling travellers how to reach their destination.[1] Yet the descriptions of the destinations themselves were tantalizingly imprecise and poetically embellished, interspersed with monsters and marvels in direct proportion to the remoteness of the place described.[2] They offered entertainment rather than being of practical use.

Until the late Middle Ages an educated European would have had no more reliable information about the rest of the world than an educated Muslim, Hindu, Chinese or Aztec of the same period. In all of those civilizations people travelled, and some knowledge of cities, countries and peoples existed. Yet little need was felt for a systematic collection of precise and trustworthy information on foreign social, cultural and political conditions. Even someone with an empirical mind would have been in no position to distinguish the true from the false in these matters.

---

[1] Schudt: 1959, 18ff; cf also Fordham: 1912, Fordham: 1926; Baudet: 1965 and ch. one. note 1.

[2] Allen: 1976; Harbsmeier: 1982; Huschenbett: 1985.

In the West this situation changed in the subsequent centuries. By the 18th century, comprehensive and reliable descriptions of most European and many non-European places had been formed and moreover were easily available to the public, as were pictorial representations of their principal sights. Collections of natural and cultural objects from these places could be seen and products from many countries were on the market. All this contributed to an enormous mass of empirical information; tangible proof of the diversity of the world and of mankind. The 'true' could now be distinguished from the 'false' and formed into organized provinces of knowledge. All civilizations had hitherto been content to live surrounded by the unknown. For the West at the end of the early modern period, the unknown had been reduced to "white spots" awaiting exploration.[3]

This amazing intellectual progress was one of the preconditions for the expansion of the West into the rest of the world. The knowledge thus accumulated had been collected by means of the three basic techniques of socio-politico-cultural research, namely travel, the survey and systematic documentation.[4] These research techniques were not expanded in the early modern period, but they were *methodized*. Moreover, there were attempts to base a science of human action on the knowledge gained by means of them (e.g. Machiavelli, Bodin, Botero or Hobbes).[5] These attempts to methodically explore, understand and thereby to control human action is one of the characteristics of Western "disenchantment of the world".[6]

Whereas the preceding chapter dealt with travel, the present one focuses on the survey and documentation. While the travel chapter could rely on the writings of the *ars apodemica*, no contemporary body of printed reflexion exists for the other two techniques. Yet contemporary lists of questions — precursors of our present questionnaires — do exist which were used, or were intended to be used, for the collection of social, cultural and political knowledge. Various forms of documentation of such knowledge also exist, and there were attempts to establish institutions to collect and to register the information even more systematically, thereby bringing it continuously up to date. However this whole field is under-researched; there has been no attempt to treat these developments - some of which are well known to historians of the early modern period - from a methodological point of view. Here I can give only a preliminary synthesis of those facts which came to light during my research into the methodology of travel. This chapter is thus hardly more than a series of footnotes to chapter one.

---

[3] Rassem and Stagl: 1980.

[4] See Introduction, § *Three basic research methods*.

[5] Meinecke: 1929; Franklin: 1963, 28ff, 61f, 69ff; Salomon-Delatour: 1965, 143ff, 164ff; Zacharasiewicz: 1977; Crick: 1987.

[6] Weber: 1958, 13ff, 76ff, 182f.

TRAVEL, CORRESPONDENCE, DOCUMENTATION AND
THE *"RES PUBLICA LITERARIA"*

Somebody seeking an education in early modern times was expected to travel, and travelling meant, among other things, visiting important and famous men (*viri illustres*). A wise traveller would continue to profit from their acquaintance by exchanging letters with them after his return home. The *ars apodemica* considered this to be one of the main advantages of travel.[7] Like travel, correspondence meant an extension of the usual sphere of life, permitting the educated a more multifarious experience of the world. Having many partners in correspondence was a cultural as well as a social asset.

Through travel and correspondence, enduring personal relationships were established among the educated across Europe.[8] Informal and polycentric, this network of relationships escaped the control of the established powers of church and state. Moreover it perpetuated itself through the stream of new travellers and new exchanges of letters initiated by them. The educated classes participating in this network made up a self-conscious and interactive group, called by its most famous leader, Erasmus of Rotterdam, the "Republic of Letters" (*res publica literaria*).[9]

Founded in Italy in the 14th and 15th centuries and extending to countries north of the Alps in the 15th and 16th centuries, the "republic of letters" was socially integrated through the common efforts of its members, the "humanists", for secular (in contrast to religious) knowledge and by a system of rewards and punishments based on the management of publicity. By offering their skills in handling knowledge and language to ecclesiastic or secular employers, the humanists were able to establish a coexistence between the *res publica literaria* and church and state, exploiting the latter two institutions for the goals of the former. For example, they published information which had accumulated in ecclesiastic or secular chanceries and archives in order to win literary fame and to augment mankind's store of knowledge. Thus, much official information which would otherwise have perished because of its highly specific nature, survived and began to be related to other such pieces of knowledge. Moreover, officially employed humanists rationalized administration by prompting it to take heed of current social, political and cultural conditions. Thus travel, correspondence and documentation became more closely interwoven than they had ever been before. They began to form an integrated system of empirical research set in motion through the diverging, yet interconnected interests of the *res publica literaria*, church and state.

---

[7] Cf ch. one and Klaniczay: 1988.

[8] Cf ch. one, especially the paragraph *From pilgrimage to educational journey*.

[9] Schalk: 1977; Reinhard: 1984.

The sociologically decisive factor in this system was *private initiative*. Early modern travel in search of education was an essentially private undertaking as was letter writing. Both pastimes brought individualistic rewards, personal friendships and public fame. Thus a new driving force came into play in socio-politico-cultural research: whereas medieval surveys had been carried out by public authorities against the will of the subjects, early modern researchers could rely on their voluntary cooperation as long as their research remained within the sphere of the *res publica literaria*. Friendship, vanity or the chance to spread one's pet ideas prompted many a humanist to show a stranger around or to answer the troublesome questions of a correspondence partner. However, this information system presupposed mutuality and equality and as such could only be maintained by giving the questioned some share in the fame resulting from the enterprise and the discussion of its results.

The urge for publication was thus closely connected with this type of research. Humanist letters were semi-public documents intended for display. The *res publica literaria* was already in existence when printing was invented in the 15th century, and this new technique for duplicating written text merely intensified the developments outlined above. Thus "public opinion" arose as a political force, a force which could not be completely controlled by church or state, and which was upheld by educated, self-reliant individuals.[10] Through the writings of the humanists, more information regarding social, political and cultural conditions was made accessible to private persons than ever before. Public opinion was thereby enabled to judge the actions of church and state.

Pertinent information was collected and discussed in two institutions peculiar to the *res publica literaria*: the academies and the offices of the printer-publishers. Emerging in Italy in the 14th century and modeled after Plato's "Academy", the academies were places where like-minded persons met to discuss topics of common interest. Insisting on mutuality and equality, these academies counterbalanced the hierarchical organizations of church and state. Yet though the academies started as voluntary meetings of private persons, they were also intended to be permanent institutions influencing public opinion with the weight of the combined intellectual power and fame of their members. They were also better able to collect and to handle large bodies of empirical knowledge than isolated scholars.[11]

Like the academies, the offices of the printer-publishers functioned as points of intersection in the network of the "republic of letters". Printing began as a private business, which however soon attracted the humanists. As business enterprises working for the public market, the printer's shops were nevertheless managed by scholar-craftsmen and often employed scholars as correctors and

---

[10] Mandrou: 1973.

[11] Kristeller: 1974-1976, vol. I, 50ff, vol. II, 101ff; Bauer: 1969; Buck: 1981.

advisors. This staff also served as a clearing house for information floating in the network of the "republic of letters". Sometimes these offices were even formally organized as a kind of academy.[12] There was, however, a specific difference between the two kinds of institutions: for the academies mutual self-improvement of their members and guests was the more important goal, but for the printer's shops the production of tangible and marketable results had greater significance. In the printer's shops, all intellectual activities focused on products which were to be alienated from their makers - even if those products were organized bodies of knowledge. If they were less elitist, the printer's shops collected and interconnected the information floating in the "republic of letters" even more effectively than the academies.

The concentration of social, political and cultural information by academies and printer's shops triggered a need to improve the collection of such information. Travel was the basic technique for this and the *ars apodemica* strove to produce better educated travellers and to encourage these to collect and report more varied and more reliable information. It also attempted to improve the quality of foreign correspondence. Generally humanist education reformers set great store on the observation of empirical reality and the careful registration of these observations.

Humanist philosophers contrived new organizational systems for the handling of this information. The self-assurance of the *res publica literaria* found an expression since the 16th century in projects of institutions for the collection, digestion and propagation of all practically useful knowledge. These institutions, which will be called "documentation centres" here, were to provide rational foundations for human thought and action. By their means the "documentation centres" aspired to a quasi-religious and quasi-political role.

There had been a utopian moment in humanism from its beginnings: a tendency to under-estimate the irrational in man and consequently to over-estimate the beneficial aspects of rational planning. This tendency also implied the idea of *progress*. Following the example of the humanists, all men were ultimately destined to become wise and virtuous, fit to be denizens of a terrestrial paradise. This utopian bent was shared by the information system of the *res publica literaria*. Depending on free cooperation within a small elite, it nevertheless presupposed the voluntary and complete collaboration of all the rest. The ensuing contradictions unfolded themselves during the early modern period. This is a principal theme of the present book.

On the supposition that everybody would gladly cooperate in its endeavours, the humanist idea of a documentation centre actually required the inclusion of the whole population, and ultimately the inclusion of all mankind, into the *res publica literaria*. Implicitly or explicitly, the proponents of documentation

---

[12] Eisenstein: 1979.

centres aimed at a kind of "educational dictatorship". The moment of the terrestrial paradise would come when the *res publica literaria*, by its accumulation
of useful knowledge translated into rational and beneficial planning, would have
made church and state superfluous, taking over the guidance of the people from
them. This programme had been spelt out in Plato's *Republic* and *Nomoi*. It was
especially taken up by humanist neo-Platonism.[13]

Though increasingly dependent on literate manpower and in consequence
interspersed with humanist ideas and values in the early modern period, church
and state could never accept this programme without giving themselves up.
Thus tensions developed between them and the *res publica literaria*.[14] The
latter had the one decisive weakness of being restricted to the small coterie
of the educated. By offering its fragile institutions on the one hand protection, financial support, privileges and prestige, and by controlling them on
the other hand through censorship, church and state attempted to keep it
on a tight rein in leading strings. The *res publica literaria* tried to re-assert
itself through its wealth of expert knowledge and its management of public
opinion. The conflict between these three parties did, however, not exclude
cooperation. As we shall see, they moved closer together in situations of
socio-cultural crises, such as the menace to civilization by barbarism (exemplified
by the Turks), deadly inner strife within Christendom (e.g. Reformation and
the ensuing civil wars), and finally encounters with other cultures (such as in
colonizing or missionising). These were the historic moments for the progress of
socio-cultural research.

THE HANDLING OF EMPIRICAL KNOWLEDGE

A distinctive achievement of humanism was the synthesis of intellectual
rigor with practical skills. It was preceded by a gradual shift of emphasis in the late
Middle Ages from reason to the senses. In this period the belief in a meaningful
system of the universe governed by a personal God whose intentions were
known to man began to crumble among the intellectual élite. This decay of the
absolute increased the appreciation of immediate experience and thus stimulated
the exploration of external reality. The empirical and practical orientation of
Humanism was no doubt also connected with the fact that many of the early
humanists were sons of peasants, craftsmen, or merchants, and did not obliterate
these origins by becoming clerics. Yet even if they could no longer believe in
a meaningful system of the universe mediated by the church, the longing for
such a system had been imprinted on them by their Christian education. Thus

---

[13] Cf especially the paragraph *The acquisition of new empirical knowledge: treasure houses of
knowledge* in this chapter.

[14] Heer: 1959.

they transferred their search for meaning into their exploration of external reality. Humanism launched a research programme embracing the whole range of human experience. By attempting to decipher the "book of nature" — this metaphor implied that external reality was at least as expressive of the Creator's intentions as the Bible — humanism hoped eventually to reestablish the lost meaning of the universe. In anticipation of this expected harmony, it held empirical research to be as pleasing to God as it was useful to man.[15] The humanists thus re-evaluated the two disciplines traditionally handling knowledge; rhetoric and dialectic.[16]

RHETORIC

Rhetoric is the theory of organised speech. Moreover it has been the basic educational discipline in the West since classical times. It was also an epistemological discipline which dealt with *accepted* as well as with *new knowledge*.[17] — both being represented in organised speech.

In spite of its permitting the flexible handling of a broad range of knowledge, rhetoric was looked down upon by those who strove for intellectual rigour and who had therefore to master the more demanding art of *dialectic*, the theory of argument according to formal rules of thought. After the revival of classical dialectic in the High Middle Ages, its practitioners, the "scholastics" (schoolmen) formed the leading group of intellectuals in the West. Yet dialectic was rather concerned with the formed than with the substance of knowledge. It was thus badly suited to the exploration of external reality.

The humanists originally had had a humbler position than the scholastics. They were first and foremost teachers and practitioners of rhetoric. Their skills were not so much in demand at the centres of learning, the universities, as in institutions with *practical* aims, such as chanceries and schools, or the faculties of arts at the universities, which prepared the students for the "higher" (and more profitable) faculties of theology, jurisprudence and medicine. In chanceries the humanists dealt with new knowledge, in schools and faculties of arts they mediated the accepted one. Yet both endeavours influenced each other. In the research programme launched by this rising group of intellectuals, accepted knowledge was enriched by new information, and the new information was systematized by the knowledge already accepted.

At the end of the Middle Ages, this interconnection between "old" and "new" knowledge led to a revival of interest in the theory of rhetoric. Dialectic, on the other hand, became discredited by the loss in confidence in a meaningful system of the universe. The highly technical form of logical reasoning employed

---

[15] Heer: 1953, ch. IX-XVII; Koyré: 1957; Debus: 1968; Blumenberg: 1966, esp. part II; Blumenberg: 1975, 247ff, 667ff; Krafft: 1982.

[16] Curtius: 1973, 46ff.

[17] Cf Introduction, § *Rhetoric* and Neuber: 1989.

by the scholastics for the classification of theological and philosophical issues was now denounced by the humanists as having no practical use. The scholastics as a class were degraded by this argument. Instead of the penetrating metaphysicians and great scientists admired in the Middle Ages, humanists hero-worshipped great orators and eclectics like Cicero or Erasmus. They disparaged the intellectual rigour of the scholastics as "pedantism" and extolled against it the "common sense" of the layman.[18]

There was, however, a decisive difference between ancient and humanist rhetoric. Ancient rhetoric was primarily concerned with *oral*, humanist rhetoric with *written* speech. Actually, the theory of written speech had preceded the rise of humanism. In the High Middle Ages, a process of rationalization in commerce, jurisdiction and administration had set in. A wealth of new information concerning the actual state of society had therefore to be considered as a basis for national policy making. As a corollary of this development, the art of writing letters(*ars dictaminis, ars epistolaria*) had evolved from a modest branch of rhetoric into a "super discipline".[19] In that context the medieval schemas for describing cities and countries were expanded, refined and systematized.[20] This proved significant for the development of social research in early modern times. By supplementing the crowded and fickle individual memory with durable signs in ink on vellum which could also be read by other persons, writing enlarged man's ability to represent his word. And unlike oral speech, written speech does not need to hold the attention of its audience all the time. Manuscripts therefore can afford to be more involved and detailed than orations; they are thus more suitable for describing a complex reality.[21]

The appearance of such descriptive schemes in the *ars epistolaria* signified decisive progress in the documentation of social, cultural and political facts. Instead of merely *presenting* them, such schemas *organized* them. They thereby stimulated *additional research* to fill in the gaps. Such schemas could moreover be applied to different clusters of facts, making *comparison* possible. Finally they paved the way for the above mentioned attempts at a science of human action.

Humanists employed in chanceries were especially favourably placed to fill out the gaps in these schemes with information taken from their files.[22] In the 15th century, Leonardo Bruni,[23] Enea Silvio Piccolomini (Pope Pius II),[24] Flavio

---

[18] Kristeller: 1956, 553ff; Blumenberg: 1981, 58ff; Mouchel: 1990, part I.

[19] Curtius: 1973, 85ff, 158ff. Cf also Gerlo: 1971.

[20] See ch. one esp. the paragraph *Programmes for the improvement of travel*.

[21] Ong: 1982, 78ff; Goody: 1990, 152ff; Assmann: 1992.

[22] See note 19.

[23] Leonardo Bruni, *Historia florentini populi*, ed. Emilio Santini, Città di Castello 1927 (Rerum Italicarum Scriptores, n.s. XIX/3); cf *The Humanism of Leonardo Bruni, Selected Texts*. Binghampton 1987.

[24] *Cosmographia* Pii Papae.....Paris 1509.

Biondo[25] or Marcantonio Coccio Sabellico[26] wrote comprehensive descriptions of cities and countries including details of their politico-legal institutions, cultural life, and history. The schemas of the *ars epistolaria* also proved very helpful for the digestion of the inflowing masses of knowledge in the "age of discoveries".[27] These models of description were first perfected in Italy, but since the early 16th century they were also followed by humanists from other nations.[28]

Being experts in the management of public opinion, the humanists knew well that describing a human group as a self-contained unit can strengthen the distinctive consciousness of that group. Description makes the object described available to purposeful action.[29] Besides being pieces of literary creation expressing a pure delight in the manifoldness of God's creation,[30] the above mentioned descriptions of cities and countries had also more practical aims. By strengthening the fellow feeling of its members and enhancing its reputation abroad, the unit described should be defended against some interior or exterior menace. A thorough description could also prepare a political reform or a conquest.[31] This principle, which today would be called the social effect of social research, was especially utilized by trans-Alpine humanists. By applying the Italian models of description to their own country, they wanted to demonstrate that their compatriots were no mere barbarians. Moreover they wanted to stimulate the pride of their compatriots and incite them eventually to surpass the Italians.

This principle was expressed e.g. by Conrad Celtis (1459-1508) in his inaugural lecture at Ingolstadt gymnasium (1492), a rousing piece of rhetoric which has now become famous. Celtis chafed at the cultural backwardness of the Germans, who were still called "barbarians" by the Italian humanists. Assuming the directorship of a German establishment of higher learning, he recommended rhetoric as the foundation of all education, denounced scholasticism as barren and misleading intellectual gymnastics, and instead extolled the experience of the world through the senses. With this programme he called upon the Germans to explore and describe their own country. Celtis did not doubt that by realizing their own forces his compatriots would grow into a self-confident nation and

---

[25] Flavio Biondo, *Italiae Illustratae libri VIII*. Rome 1474.

[26] Marcantonio Coccio Sabellico, *Historiae rerum venetiarum*. Venice 1487; *De venetis magistratibus*. Venice 1488.

[27] Voigt: 1880/1881, vol. I, 158, 204, vol. II, 494, 513ff; Dainville: 1940; Neuber: 1991.

[28] Burckhardt: s.a., ch. 4, *Die Entdeckung der Welt und des Menschen*; Strauss: 1959; Büttner: 1979; Kulcsár: 1988.

[29] Stagl: 1981b.

[30] This has been especially stressed by Burckhardt; see note 28.

[31] Kulcsár: 1988 (with further literature).

qualify themselves for the great role history had in store for them.[32] This lecture inaugurated a programme of geographical, historical and social research which applied Italian descriptive models to Germany and was put into effect over the following century by patriotic humanists.[33]

Yet however successful it proved for the time being, humanist reliance on rhetoric and rejection of the technicalities of pure reasoning also had their price. They implied a certain superficiality. The facts were not thoroughly analyzed and compared and were only marshalled enough to be given a smooth wording — which only too often concealed their heterogeneity or even their lack of truth. The practical orientation of the knowledge handled by rhetoric impeded its general acceptance and thus its accumulation. Humanist descriptions of empirical reality soon reached their limits and began to ring hollow.

Yet there were some critics of this superficiality in the ranks of the humanists themselves who strove for more rigorous thinking and therefore tackled the art of dialectic which had so far been avoided.

DIALECTIC

Not all humanists despised dialectic altogether. Some among them, like Lorenzo Valla or Rudolph Agricola, attempted to appropriate it to the humanist research programme by reforming it. In order to wrench dialectic from the scholastics, early humanists turned from Aristotle, who had systematized dialectic, to Socrates and Plato who had invented it. This led to a repetition of the development of the organization of intellectual pursuits which had taken place in Athens in the 5th and 4th centuries B.C.

Contrary to the universities dominated by scholastics, the "sodalities" and "academies" of the humanists arranged discussions as freely and as flexibly as possible as they were thought to have been in the circles around Socrates and Plato. They could certainly not agree to strictly formalized discussions supervised by professors. Unconstrained gatherings of intellectual equals were the first nuclei of the *res publica literaria*.[34] Yet like in Athens this formative period, however fruitful, was not destined to last. Having their origin in the 14th and their heyday in the 15th century, humanist academies showed signs of ossification by the 16th century. They became specialized and formalized. Aristotelian dialectic came back, though not as a logic of disputation but as one of research.[35] Here lay the roots of early modern social research methodology.

---

[32] Conradus Celtis Protucius, *Oratio in gymnasio in Ingeldstadio publice recitata cum carminibus ad orationem pertinentibus*. Ed. Rupprich, Leipzig 1932. Cf Rassem/Stagl: 1994, 51ff.

[33] Joachimsen, 1910, 21ff, 87, 110ff, 155ff, 167ff, 188ff; Strauss: 1959, 19ff; Seidlmayr: 1965, 183ff.

[34] Cf note 11.

[35] Schüling: 1963.

A common feature of the discussion in universities and academies was that they were being generated by means of lists of problems, sometimes formulated as questions (*quaestiones*). The publication of such discussions in the 15th century in the form of so-called "problem-books"[36] strengthened the impression that there were basically two categories of *quaestiones*: (1) those that could be answered by appeal to reason alone and (2) those that needed to ascertain the facts in question through sensual experience. By the 16th century, emphasis had clearly shifted from category (1) to (2). This development had been accelerated by the religious controversies of the century. Colloquies among intellectuals tended to become envenomed by religion, whereas empirical research — a dialogue, as it were, not between man and man, but between man and nature — promised a less controversial and more rewarding knowledge. Religion thereby became disparaged and science upgraded.[37]

The idea of transforming dialectic from technique of reasoning into a technique of research was thus in the air. This was first attempted by Rudolph Agricola (1443–1485). In his *De inventione dialectica* the Frisian humanist gave a scathing critique of prevailing dialectical method and at the same time a new start.[38] Socrates and Plato had separated dialectic from rhetoric, and they had been kept separate from that time. By a bold stroke, Agricola brought them together again. He emphasized the concept of "places" which was after all a piece of doctrine common to rhetoric and dialectic. In his *Topic* Aristotle defines the "places" as "opinions" which are "reputable" since they are "accepted by everyone or by the majority or by the wise". Everybody who intends to "reason........ about any subject presented" can thus appeal to them.[39] Being the gist of thinking habits that had proved their worth without being strictly deducible from basic principles, they are indispensable for the arrangement of generally accepted knowledge. A preliminary arrangement according to them is even to be preferred to strict reasoning if one deals with new, empirical knowledge having as yet no place in the established system of thought.

This was Agricola's starting point. He elevated the "places" into the key position of his modernized dialectic. Taking up the contemporary shift of emphasis from ratio to the senses, he no longer intended dialectic method for the correct discussion of metaphysical questions, but rather for the efficient handling of large masses of knowledge of all sorts. Whoever wanted to argue convincingly on any subject was advised by Agricola to (1) procure himself a clear conception

---

[36] Lawn: 1963. On *quaestiones* (*problémata*) see the Introduction, § *Rhetoric.*

[37] Krafft: 1982: cf also Yates: 1964, 314f.

[38] Rudolph Agricola, *De inventione dialectica*. Cologne 1528 (orig. 1479). Reprint with introduction by Wilhelm Risse Hildesheim 1976. It is fair to say that Agricola was preceded by Lorenzo Valla (14077–1457), *Dialecticae disputationes contra Aristoteleos*, which was, however, only printed in Venice in 1499.

[39] Aristotle, Topic 100a-b.

of that subject including empirical information, and (2) to explore its scope by means of a list of "places" applicable to all subjects. He arrived at this list by combining basic concepts of Aristotelian logic (categories such as time, place, quality, quantity or relation) with basic concepts from Ciceronian rhetoric (e.g. the name of the topic under discussion, its comparables, its opposites, etc.). By thus exploring the scope of one's mental concept of the subject on which one intended to argue, one became able to "find" pertinent statements (*inventio*, which appears in the title of Agricola's treatise and thereafter gained increased prominence in humanist dialectic). The same "places" also helped in arranging the discourse which was thus generated (an operation called *iudicium*). It is obvious that by this method the content of the discourse outweighed its logical stringency. Proceeding from the implicit assumption of the identity between the order of the discourse and the order of the world, Agricola's logic dealt with words and things, with the intellectual and the sensible world, as with one homogeneous field accessible to the same method. This method aimed at the unification of all knowledge.[40]

Conrad Celtis had been Agricola's pupil, and the programme of education and research in his Ingoldstadt lecture had been inspired by Agricola.[41] But only after *De inventione dialectica* was re-issued at Louvain in 1515 did Agricola's impact become pervasive, especially north of the Alps where humanism had always been more dialectically oriented than in Italy. In the following generation the Dutchman Erasmus, the Spaniard Vives and the Frenchman Budé, the "triumvirs of the republic of letters in the early 16th century"[42] were affected by Agricola's influence: "instead of concepts they called for things".[43] Consequently many popular handbooks of dialectic were published in which the general rules of thought and speech were given less attention and special rules for the teaching and improvement of particular subjects (*artes, prudentiae*) were stressed instead.[44] This empiristic turn of dialectic had important consequences for socio-cultural research. It encouraged the dialogue between intellectuals and men of practical experience. The former were instructed to question the latter in order to incorporate their experiences into the stock of recognized knowledge. This procedure upgraded the "common man"; if laymen were repositories of truth, meaningful research could be done by questioning them.

---

[40] On *inventio* and *iudicium* in rhetorical theory see Lausberg: 1990, ch. two. On humanist dialectic and Agricola's part in it see Joachimsen: 1926; Gilbert: 1960, 119ff; Jardine: 1974, 2ff; Schmidt-Biggemann: 1983, 3ff; Mouchel: 1990, 126ff.

[41] Strauss: 1959, 22, 135.

[42] Thorndike: 1966, 126.

[43] Windelband: 1980, 308.

[44] Jardine: 1974, 5, 25.

Humanist dialectic no longer aimed at making implicit truths explicit. It aimed instead at the collection of empirical truths dispersed among the people. This was for example Martin Luther's procedure in translating the Bible. Not exactly a humanist, yet touched by humanism, Luther turned to socio-linguistic research, looking for the true vernacular equivalent of the sacred original. He would ask "the mother in her home, the children in the streets, the common man at the market........and look him on his mouth".[45] The same striving for empirical truth led Luther to ask craftsmen to explain their tools to him or a butcher to cut up a ram, so that he could get a clearer conception of its entrails.[46] When Juan Luis Vives announced his programme for pedagogical-technological reform (*De disciplinis*, Antwerp 1531), he postulated that in order to learn the true nature of all things, peasants and craftsmen should be questioned rather than dialecticians.[47]

Humanist dialectic or logic (the latter term was increasingly used as the former became disparaged) was moreover conceived as an instrument of practical utility. Petrus Ramus (1515–1572) became the most famous proponent of this doctrine. His *Instituiones Dialecticae*, first published in 1543 and constantly revised and reissued by him until the year of his death, became "the most influential textbook of the 16th century".[48] Its bearing on the *ars apodemica* has already been discussed. Travelling was just one of the many activities reduced to a formal "art" under the influence of Ramus. Avowedly following Agricola and Vives, the French logician even more radically renounced metaphysics and pure reasoning. Instead, he attempted to weld rhetoric and dialectic into a unified instrument of discourse and thought equally suitable for education and research. Following Agricola, Ramus subdivided this instrument into two parts, *inventio* and *iudicium*, standardizing both with the help of "places". Ramus imitated and attempted to surpass Aristotle by "reforming" him. He adopted Aristotle's categories, supplementing them with "places" taken from various authors. Compared with Aristotelianism, Ramism played down the doctrine of inference (syllogistic), stressing instead the doctrine of classificatory description (topic).[49]

Ramist logic presupposed, like that of Agricola, the common identity of the order of the world with that of the mind: "a correct doctrine of discourse

---

[45] Martin Luther, *Sendbrief für Dolmetscher*, quoted after Friedenthal: 1982, 373.

[46] Friedenthal: 1982, 378.

[47] cf. Hooykaas: 1958, 26ff.

[48] Schmidt-Biggemann: 1983, 41. I have used the French edition (Pierre de la Ramée, *Dialectique*. Paris 1555). On the various editions see Ong: 1958b.

[49] The authoritative study on Ramus is Ong: 1958a. see also paragraph *A tale of three cities* in ch. one and note 40.

is a replica and description of nature".[50] It attempted thus to reconstruct reality by structuring discourse. While encouraging empirical research, Ramism actually relied on information already extant, though dispersed, in the shape of the subject-matters of all arts, sciences and poetry, as well as in narrations and descriptions (*historiae*).[51] The Ramists "processed" such information by subjecting it to the logical operations of *inventio* and *iudicium*. In order to standardize *inventio*, Ramus had proposed fourteen "places", his list being simpler, more homogeneous and closer to Aristotle than Agricola's.[52] By applying it in the form of a series of standard questions to any subject matter, everybody was supposed to be able to "find" pertinent propositions which, in their entirety, formed the "discourse" on the said subject-matter. Subjecting all extant and possible knowledge to the same procedure in this way, Ramus implicitly treated it as belonging to one homogeneous field. In this he can be regarded as an early representative of the attempt to create a scientific method applicable both to nature and history, and thus of a socio-cultural science.

The discourse generated by *inventio* was to be structured by *iudicium*. Ramus' theory of *iudicium* was his principal achievement. He divided it into three parts: (1) truth or falsehood of single proposition had to be examined by means of syllogisms; Ramus considered this part rather unimportant, disposing thus of traditional Aristotelian logic. He stressed instead (2) that part of *inventio* that dealt with the interconnection of propositions, and thus by implication also with the structure of reality. He called it "method". It consisted of the exploration of concepts by defining, dividing, subdefining and subdividing them again and again in order to arrive at a hierarchy of concatenated concepts descending from the general to the particular: "Method is the cognition of various axioms which are homogeneous and, because of the clearness of the nature of that cognition, put in front; proceeding from these the concordance of all things is judged and incorporated into memory",[53] (3) The third and last part consisted of the interconnection of all possible discourses ("*coniunctio artium*

---

[50] In the first edition of the *Institutiones Dialecticae*, which appeared under the title *Aristotelis Animadversiones* (1543), Ramus declares: "*Vera ut dixi, legitimaque disserendi doctrina, est imago, et pictura naturae*" (*Dialecticae Institutiones*, reprint Stuttgart-Bad Cannstatt 1964, *fol.* 8). Ramus later renounced this Platonic theory of correspondence, which nevertheless remained implicitly present in his method, cf Schmidt-Biggemann 1983, 44f.

[51] See ch. one, paragraph *Travel reports*, and Seifert: 1976.

[52] Ramus "places" were: *Causae, Effectum, Subjectum, Adjunctum, Dissentanei, Genus, Species, Nomen, Notatio, Conjugatum, Testimonium, Comparatum, Distributio, Definitio.*

[53] "*Methodus est dianoia variorum axiomatum homogeneorum pro naturae suae claritate praepositorum, unde omnium inter se convenientia judicatur memoriaque comprehenditur*". This is the last version of his definition cf. *Dialecticae libri duo*, Paris 1572, p. 87, cf. Schmidt-Biggemann: 1983, 45, 49. (Ramus used *axioma* for any general proposition, not only for the first principles of knowledge, cf Jardine: 1974, 78).

omnium et ad deum relatio".[54]) All actual and potential knowledge was thus destined to ultimately be included into one system, a hierarchy of hierarchies, ascending towards the most general entity, God, and descending towards the most particular, the singular, empirical, things and events.

Method is a democratic concept. Whoever applies it to the same initial situation must arrive at the same result; his personality, his inspiration, do not matter. By its claim to universal validity, Ramus' method implicitly denied privileged sources of knowledge, such as the Bible, classical antiquity, or individual genius, and instead aimed at the accumulation of all knowledge by the exertions of many likeminded researchers working in different fields. Yet his method, impressive as it was, had one flaw. Proceeding from intellectual evidence, and thus deductively, there were problems showing exactly how the singular, empirical, things and events fitted into its general concepts. The Ramists helped this situation by introducing empirical facts in the shape of "examples", which were assumed to be representative of general concepts. This worked well in compendia and encyclopedias, which accordingly became the main field of application of the Ramist method. It did not work in the domain of empirical research. Here the Ramists did not prove in what respect their examples — which they mainly took from books anyway — represented their concepts. These concepts were eventually realized to be congeries of "places" traditionally used in the various disciplines rather than self-evident axioms structuring all knowledge in a natural way. This realisation initiated the decline of Ramism.[55]

Among the foremost critics of these deficiencies of Ramism were two logicians of the next generation, Francis Bacon of Verulam and Bartholomäus Keckermann. Both upheld the Ramist claim to combine all human knowledge into one system, yet they attempted to base this knowledge on genuine experience alone. Bacon will be discussed in greater detail below. Keckermann, who taught at Danzig, published in his short life (1571–1608) a series of compendia covering almost all branches of knowledge, whose titles invariably begin with *Systema*, and which were later aptly collected as *Systema Systematum* (Hanau, 1613).[56] Keckermann's basic problem was to prove that singular things and events could be dealt with scientifically. He solved it by dividing every discipline into two stages, which he called *historia* and *scientia*, the former being a collection of relevant, yet unstructured facts, the latter their subsumption under a structure of general concepts. He tackled the problem of the transition from the first to the second stage in an ingenious way; he condensed the collected

---

[54] Petrus Ramus, *Dialecticae Instituiones* (1543), reprint Stuttgart-Bad Cannstatt 1964, fol. 57; cf. Schmidt-Biggemann: 1983, 41f.

[55] See Ch. one, § *A tale of three cities* and note 40.

[56] On Keckermann cf Seifert: 1976, 89ff; Büttner: 1979, 153-172; Schmidt-Biggemann: 1983, 89ff.

facts into generalizing propositions (*praecepta*), which he then discussed in the light of current scientific opinion. Those *praecepta* that passed this critique were eventually included in his system.

By "inventing" *praecepta* and then "judging" them, Keckermann transformed *historia* into *scientia*. Yet his *praecepta* were neither traditional *quaestiones* nor lists of catch-all "places" like those in Agricola's or Ramus' logic; they were organizing principles specific to each discipline and derived from enquiry. Each discipline thereby got its own topic. Even if Keckermann did not use these specially designed lists of "places" as instruments for empirical research, as Bacon later did, their methods converged in the same direction. Some of Keckermann's "systems", though mere compendia, were seminal for later developments. He was especially interested in geography and politics. His *Systema geographicum* (Hanau, 1611) and *Systema Disciplinae Politicae* (Hanau, 1608) provided theoretical superstructures for the Renaissance collections of empirical descriptions of countries and polities (see below). They thereby inaugurated the empirical science of politics (*notitia rerum publicarum*) flourishing especially at German Protestant universities from the 17th to the late 18th century.[57]

THE DOCUMENTATION OF KNOWLEDGE

ARS MEMORATIVA

All documentation builds upon memory, which it relieves and supports. In classical rhetoric, memory had been conceived as a treasure-house where knowledge is stored in some order. Classical rhetoric also included a technique for tapping this store (mnemonics). "It consisted of memorising a series of places in a building, and attaching to these memorised places, images to remind one of points of speech. The orator when delivering his speech, passed in imagination along the order of memorised places, plucking from them the images which were to remind him of his notions".[58] The "places" were thus originally a mnemonic device. The "images" attached to them, being thoroughly visualized, were internal signs used to document one's knowledge to oneself.[59]

It is very likely that these "images" were mental projections of *aides-mémoire* which have been used since time immemorial for the remembrance of things and events, and are considered to be the antecedents of writing. The forms of documentation created by writing — manuscripts and books, archives and libraries — had to show some structure compatible with memory if they were to fulfil their function to relieve and to support it. Yet since these forms of

---

[57] Seifert: 1980, 218ff.

[58] Yates: 1964, 191.

[59] Yates: 1966, 2ff: Joachimsen: 1926; Ong: 1958a, 75ff, 307ff.

documentation are based on durable material objects, they are even better suited to systematic arrangement and intricate subdivision than the fleeting "images" of memory.[60]

Classical rhetoric had focused on oral speech. The arrangement of "places" and "images" in classical mnemonics had therefore been flexible and modest in scale. Yet in the High Middle Ages when written speech gained in importance, the *ars epistolaria* provided more stable and thorough topical arrangements (see above). It thus became a discipline competing with mnemonics, or *ars memorativa*, as it was now called. Both disciplines dealt with the structure of human knowledge and by implication with the structure of reality, but whereas the *ars epistolaria* proceeded from its multifariousness, the *ars memorativa* stressed its fundamental unity.

Struggling to hold its own in the face of an ever increasing store of written — and later also of printed — knowledge, the *ars memorativa* evolved from a technique of marshalling personal knowledge into one of handling all extant knowledge. Allying itself with the neo-Platonic/cabbalistic current in Renaissance thought, the *ars memorative* proceeded from the assumption of a close correspondence between "microcosm", man, and the "macrocosm", the universe. According to the influential writings of Theophrastus Paracelsus (1493–1541), the universe is mysteriously mirrored in man (the optical metaphor played an important role for this school of thought).[61] The microcosm-macrocosm philosophy established a precarious balance between the waning medieval conception of a meaningful universe and the Renaissance emphasis on the individual. This balance could, however, only be achieved by the outstanding individual, who had attuned himself with the cosmos, and was able to memorize everything at its right "place". The outstanding individual could, moreover, apply this knowledge magically to the external world, since microcosm and macrocosm were believed to interact.[62]

16th century *ars memorativa* (e.g. Giordano Bruno) attempted to imprint the cosmic order itself as a "place" system into the mind; its "images" were conceived as archetypal Platonic ideas and at the same time as something like magical talismans. This should enable the outstanding individual — the magus — to control the increasing mass of heterogeneous knowledge instead of being controlled by it. For that purpose phantastically involved mnemonic systems were constructed by Bruno and others, where "places" and "images" were no longer related to one single building, but to a whole imaginary town. Such ideal towns no longer only symbolized the harmoniously ordered mind and

---

[60] Cf Introduction, § *Three basic research methods, (a): Indirect exploration via significant phenomina* and Ong, 1982, 57ff,139ff.

[61] Kaiser: 1969, 29ff; Schipperges: 1989, 99, 116. Cf also note 161.

[62] Heer: 1953, 15f, 230ff; Yates 1964; Kristeller: 1963; Gilly: 1977–79.

universe, but also the right order of all knowledge and of human life.[63] They were offshoots of Platonic utopism which had been revived in the 16th century by Thomas Morus' *Utopia* (1517).[64] The microcosm-macrocosm philosophy, by stressing the unity and order of all knowledge, the desirability to collect it at one place, and its technical-magical-utopian applicability, became the native soil of the many early modern centres for the collection, preservation and practical application of knowledge, of which some are presented below.

COLLECTIONS: MUSEUMS, ARCHIVES, LIBRARIES, ACADEMIES

All objects associated with certain memories are apt to resuscitate them. Treasures, relics, monuments etc. function thus as *aides-mémoire*. The Renaissance was a period when precious or curious objects of various description were systematically collected. Such collections were the origin of our present-day *museums*. They had a pecuniary value, and also a commemorative one. They were thus not only treasures, but were also considered as representative for some aspect of the order of reality. *Archives* and *libraries* are also collections of precious or curious objects, yet in these objects (manuscripts and books) the commemorative function is not a by-product, but the essential thing. In archives and libraries thus the commemorative value outweighs the pecuniary one. Archives are the memories of institutions and thus there is a tendency to restrict access to them. Libraries are the memories of whole communities (or at least of their educated fraction); they therefore need to be more accessible and less specialised. *Academies* belong to the same context. They too are collections, if not of precious objects or information-bearing signs, yet of subjects pooling their faculties for certain purposes.

These four types of collections (museums, archives, libraries, and academies) can be conceived as externalized super-memories, or centres of documentation. They all experienced an accelerated development in the 15th and 16th centuries, influencing each other, and closely connecting with contemporary efforts to improve the educational and informational value of travel and correspondence.

We can outline the development of collections in general by focusing specifically on collections of precious or curious objects. In 16th century Italy it was no longer fashionable to store away such objects, but rather to display them ostentatiously. The rooms dedicated to that purpose were called *musei*. This was soon imitated north of the Alps (French: *cabinets de curiosités*; German: *Kunst- und Raritätenkammern*; English: "curio galleries"). A group of savants also emerged who were specially interested in them (*curieux*, *virtuosi*). Though often doing valuable work — especially in archaeology and natural history — they were looked down upon by more methodical scholars and held up to ridicule

---

[63] Yates: 1966.

[64] Thomas Morus, *De optimo reip. statu, deque nova insula Utopia*........Basel 1517.

for their aimless and boundless curiosity. The curio galleries were indeed an omnium-gatherum — works of art, relics, antiques, coins and medals, tools and weapons, pre-historic finds, minerals, dried plants, stuffed animals, monstrosities — united by their one common feature of being extraordinary.[65]

Any collection aims at completeness, an aim which can never be reached, especially by an omnium-gatherum. Early modern collecting had thus a utopian, futile aspect, which explains why the *curieux* were so easily held up to ridicule. More sober and methodical minds therefore began specialized collections, e.g. of statues, pictures, manuscripts, archaeological finds, specimina of natural history. Here the aim of completeness could be pursued with more justification in one particular field. This tendency came to the fore in the second third of the 16th century.[66] It led to a bifurcation: the universalistic curio galleries increasingly turned into places for ostentation and amusement; the specialized collections become ever more documentation-, research- and education-oriented.

Collecting was closely linked to travel and correspondence. Famous collections were "sights" which were visited by travellers for the schooling of their taste and for their general education. As has been shown in the preceding chapter, the *ars apodemica* provided a programme of general education and advancement of knowledge whose principal means was autopsy; the travellers therefore were instructed in how to profit from visiting foreign collections and how to lay out their own. In this way travelling and collecting became systematizing activities. Like the mind of the humanist traveller, like the place system in his note book, a collection was intended for structured growth. Early modern collecting replicated the rhetorical arrangement of discourse: by judiciously arranging the collected objects, lacunae between them were revealed, which had to be filled by the collector by means of "inventing" (i.e. tracing out and purchasing) new specimina.

For this the collector had to rely on the agency of knowledgeable travellers and correspondents, any significant collection depending thus on the network of the *res publica literaria*. Famous collections were described in catalogues, which were printed in order to make them better known to the literati abroad. Local literati tended to form learned societies around collections which provided visual aids to their discussions. The boundaries between *musei*, books and academies were thus fluid.

In early modern collections the rhetorical metaphor of the treasure-house was applied literally. The objects classified together were also exhibited together in their "places", e.g. in separate rooms or different cabinets or cupboards, "cunningly designed by skilful artisans, and equipped with small drawers, trays and

---

[65] Bastian: 1881, 125ff; Berliner: 1928; Anderson: 1947; Hodgen: 1964, ch. 4 and 5; Momigliano: 1966; Langmeyer/Peters: 1979; Alpers: 1983, esp. 163f.

[66] Wittkower: s.a. 273.

pigeonholes to make their contents readily accessible".[67] Topically arranged in this way, the exhibits somehow lost their extraordinariness and turned into mere *specimina*; visible examples of their categories. A topically organised collection was no longer a mere treasure only serving ostentation. By representing the universe (or at least in one of its aspects) locally, it had turned into a "mirror" or "theatre of the world",[68] a microcosm suitable for the instruction of mankind.

This spiritualization of the human proclivity to hoard and to show off was especially propagated by Protestant humanists from western and northern Europe influenced by the logical reforms of Agricola and Ramus. In 1565 Samuel Quichelberg, a Fleming in the service of the Duke of Bavaria, postulated that a true museum should represent the universe by means of a systematic classification of all subject matters.[69] The plan of a *museum generis humani* (1575) by his countryman Hugo Blotius will be discussed below. In the 17th century naturalist-antiquarians like the Dane Ole Worm and the Englishmen Elias Ashmole (a founding member of the Royal Society) and Sir Hans Sloane (Ashmole's friend and pupil and president of the Royal Society) built up large, topically arranged *musei* of man-made objects and specimina of natural history, which formed the nuclei of the present-day museums of Copenhagen, Oxford (Ashmolean) and London (British Museum). The idea that a good museum should replicate the macrocosm was renewed on a technically more sophisticated level in the *Museographia* (1727) of the German F.C. Neickel.[70]

Specialized collections, e.g. of plants or animals, tended to be even more research-oriented. Botanical gardens and herbaria had always served medicine, and by extension, natural history. Around 1550 many botanical gardens were founded in Italian university towns. About the same time, the Swiss naturalist, antiquarian and linguist Conrad von Gesner (1516–1565) collected and described biological specimina or pictures of such "sent from every corner of the world". In the next century the English divine, traveller, naturalist and linguist John Ray (1627–1705), "realizing the need for precise and ordered knowledge of the flora of the world, first studied and collated existing literature, then turned to the accumulation of examples of mammals, birds, fishes, cryptogams, and all known plants........Distant friends, 'skilful in Herbary,' were called upon to ransack their neighbourhoods. Many plants and flowers, having once been dried and sewn to large sheets of paper, went into his *Hortus siccus*, a work of twenty volumes. Ray

---

[67] Hodgen: 1964, 121.

[68] The metaphor "theatre of the world" goes back to Plato, *Nomoi* I, 644d-e. That of the "mirror" is classical as well as biblical (Curtius: 1973, 341f; Gabriel: 1967, 17ff; Yates: 1969)

[69] Samuel Quichelberg, *Inscriptiones vel tituli theatri amplissimi*. Munich 1565.

[70] C.F. Neickel, *Museographia Oder Anleitung Zum rechten Begriff und nützlicher Anlegung der Museorum, Oder Raritäten-Kammern... In beliebter Kürtze zusammengetragen und curiösen Gemüthern dargestellt*. Leipzig-Breslau 1727 (the author's name is an anagram for Einckel). Cf. Fechner: 1977.

also pioneered the stocktaking of local forms of speech, "a kind of *herbarium* of dialects".[71] In the 18th century, the classificatory system of Linnaeus (Carl von Linné) became the paradigm for collection and registration.[72]

COMPENDIA

The literary genre of the *compendium* corresponded to this form of collecting empirism. A compendium is a systematically arranged collection of written information. Compendia existed already in Antiquity and the Middle Ages (Strabo, Varro, Plinius, Vincent of Beauvais, Aeneas Sylvius, etc.); yet they became extremely popular with the appearance of humanism and the spread of printing. "Inventing" pertinent information from dispersed manuscripts and inaccessible books and arranging them "judiciously" was, even in the first century or two of printing, a form of empirical research. Thus the desire to represent the world or one of its major aspects between two book covers emerged concurrently with the *musei*. Erasmus' *Adagia* (Paris, 1500) is a case in point. An extremely successful collection of classical proverbs and sayings, and thus a guide through the vicissitudes of life, it appeared in over 150 editions, was translated into many languages, and inspired scores of successors, among them the above-mentioned John Ray, who in 1670 published a "Collection of British Proverbs".[73]

From the collection of proverbs to the collection of folklore is an easy step, facilitated by the claim of rhetoric to deal equally with "words and things".[74] In 1520, the German hebraist Ioannes Boemus published his trailblazing *Omnium Gentium Mores, Leges et Ritus*, the first of a long series of early modern ethnographic compendia.[75] Claiming to represent the whole of a subject by means of some judiciously chosen excerpts, such works were indeed microcosms like the *musei*. Both forms of collection could, moreover, be "translated" into each other. Thus *musei* were turned into books by being described, as has been mentioned, in catalogues, and books into *musei* by becoming lavishly and systematically illustrated, such as in the albums with portraits of illustrious men, views of famous cities, or depictions of national costumes (*Trachtenbücher*) which came into fashion around 1550.[76] (Ray's *Hortus Siccus* too belongs to this genre of

---

[71] Hodgen: 1964, 117ff, quotations 117, 126.

[72] Lepenies: 1976, 55f. Cf also Hagberg: 1946.

[73] Heer: 1962, 7–47, esp. 14f. Cf. also Schoeck: 1990.

[74] Cicero: *De oratore* III, 19. Cf also the Introduction to the present book *Rhetoric* and Mooney: 1985, 24ff.

[75] Ioannes Boemus, *Repertorium librorum trium de omnium gentium ritibus*. Augsburg 1520; here used in the ed. Lyons 1536 (*Omnium Gentium Mores, Leges & Ritus ex multis clarissimis rerum scriptoribus, a Ioanne Boemo Aubano Tuetonico nuper collecti & novissime reogniti. Tribus libris absolutum opus, Aphricam, Asiam & Europam describentibus. Non sine Indice locupletissimo*).

published *musei*.) Such works stimulated research among the author's friends and correspondents, as shown by the examples of Gesner and Ray.

The first scholar to attempt a compendium of the whole world seems to have been the Swiss humanist Christophorus Mylaeus (Millieu), who in 1548 published his *Consilium historiae unversitatis scribendae* in Florence. When travelling in Greece, Mylaeus fell ill and whiled away — or so he tells us — a long and bookless recovery by arranging the contents of his prodigious memory into one topically structured discourse. Thrown back to the sole resources of his mind by being helplessly stranded in barbarian surroundings, he discarded the traditional wisdom of the schools and rebuilt the system of knowledge in a "natural way", i.e. in a way conforming to the "book of nature".[77] This is possibly the first of the modern intellectual "robinsonades", where a mental reconstruction of the world is authenticated by a paradigmatic experience of the author — a strategy later made famous by Descartes and Comte.

Mylaeus's method was not actually as "natural" as he believed it to be. His classification of knowledge into *historia naturalis, h. prudentiae* and *h. sapientiae* goes back to that of Aristotle ("practical", "poetical", and "theoretical knowledge") and to the tripartitions of medieval and early modern encyclopedias based on it.[78] An avowed disciple of Agricola, Mylaeus further subdivided his subject matter according to "places" taken from the various disciplines them-selves. Thus, like his contemporary Ramus, many traditional thinking patterns crept in.[79] Yet Mylaeus was trend-setting in that he focused where ever possible on factual knowledge (*est enim expeditor rerum, quam verborum memoria*) and consequently presented his material in the form of enumerations (*historiae*).[80] His book is the first in a long series of polymath compendia, books wherein the

---

[76] Koch: 1991.

[77] Christophorus Mylaeus, *De scribenda universitatis rerum historia libri quinque.* Basel 1551, Dedication. Cf Schmidt-Biggemann: 1983, 23ff.

[78] Mylaeus, *op. cit.*, p. 124 links his tripartition to the three "higher" faculties of the university (medicine, jurisprudence, theology). For medieval and Renaissance encyclopedias with basic tripartition cf Vincent of Beauvais (cf. note 68), who divides his *Speculum majus* in: Sp *naturale, historale,* and *doctrinale* (1256). Raimundus Lullus (d. 1315), language, grammar, meaning of words; Pierre Bersuire (Berchorius, d. 1362): Bible, things, words; Raphael Maffei (Volterranus), *Commentarii urbani,* 8 eds. 1506–1603: Geography, Anthropology, Philology; Giorgio Valla (d. 1499): mental, bodily and external things; Theodor Zwinger (d. 1588): practice, poiesis, theory; Francis Bacon (d. 1626): history, poetry, knowledge; Jan Amos Komensky (Comenius, d. 1670): Pansophia, Panhistoria, Pandogmatica; Daniel Georg Morhof, *Polyhistor* (1688): *P. literarius, P. philosophicus and P. practicus*; John Locke (d. 1704): things, actions, signs. Cf. art *Encyclopedia in Encyclopedia Britannica,* ed. 1966, vol. 8, 365f; Dangelmayr: 1974; Gilly: 1977–79, part 2, 166ff.

[79] Seifert: 1976, 39; Schmidt-Biggemann: 1983, 26ff.

[80] Mylaeus: 1551, 303f. In this work, Mylaeus gives a commentated bibliography called *historia litteraria,* and described by Schmidt-Biggemann: 1983, 28f as the first true history of science. Mylaeus especially extols here Agricola's *De inventione dialectica.* Morhof (see note 78) traces back the genre of the polymath compendium to Mylaeus (Daniel Georg Morhof, *Polyhistor.* Lübeck [4] 1747, vol I, p. 10).

basic principles and main results of all disciplines are collected, a series which culminated in Daniel Georg Morhof's *Polyhistor* (1688).

Mylaeus did not attempt to document all positive knowledge. Rather than an encyclopedia, his book is an educational programme. He restricts himself to the basic principles of all knowledge which he wishes to transmit to posterity to enable it to "reinvent" civilization in case of its destruction. Like many humanists before and after him, Mylaeus lived in the fear of a new "age of barbarism". After all, he had seen the havoc made of Byzantine civilization by the Turks.[81]

This concentration of the basic principles of a spatially ordered memory in the form of a written compendium Mylaeus calls a *universitas*. His reconstruction of the "book of nature" in printing testifies to a (modern) bent to conceive mental activity as a form of construction. Mylaeus himself speaks of his book as an "edifice" which he entrusts — like a Noah's ark — to Maximilian II and Philip II, the two universal monarchs championing Christendom against the infidel.[82]

A second edition of Mylaeus' book was published in Basel in 1551 (it continued to be published until 1668).[83] Basel, the city most deeply imprinted with the Humanism of Erasmus, also became the publishing centre of a multitude of systematizing compendia. Some personalities should be mentioned in this context who have already appeared in Chapter I.

Simultaneously with Mylaeus, the Basilean humanist Conrad Lycosthenes also attempted to concentrate the gist of all useful knowledge single-handedly into one book. Lycosthenes was, however, more interested in positive knowledge than in basic principles and therefore his compendium was organised according to situations typically occurring in human life. He died prematurely in 1561, apparently from overwork. His stepson Theodor Zwinger took up the torch. Zwinger was the son of a former husband of Lycosthenes' wife, a sister of the scholar-printer Johannes Oporinus (who in his youth had been Paracelsus' amanuensis and was incidentally also Mylaeus' Basilean publisher). Published in 1565 by Oporinus, the *Theatrum vitae humanae* of Lycosthenes-Zwinger

---

[81] Mylaeus: 1551, Dedication. On the humanist fear of a new "age of barbarism" cf Heer: 1953 31f, 41f.

[82] Mylaeus: 1551, Dedication and 5f. Cf his definition of a universitas: "*Sit igitur........Universitas nihil aliud, quam rerum omnium in Naturae varietate, in communis vitae usu ac tractatione, atque in doctrinis, et studiis literarum, singulis, et iis accomodatis partibus, ad debitam integritatem complendam, et ad incolumitatem retinendam, in unum aliquod totum divinitus apte coniunctis, collatis, atque compositis, servatus, et ad suum propositum finem relatus ordo, commoda inter se distinctio, collocatio, mutuus consensus: ac ut quindque aliud alio prius in tanta varietate, quasi discors concordia: ut non potuerit vox alia in omne sermone Latino, his omnibus generatim comprehendendis, plenior inveniri, et accomodatior*" (op. cit., 15).

[83] This is the edition from which I have quoted. The bibliography of this work is as follows: Christophorus Mylaeus, *Consilium historiae universitatis scribendae*. Florence 1548, 1668. *De scribenda universitatis rerum historia libri quinque*. Basel 1551 (the text of both versions is identical; in the Basel edition only the dedication to the two kings is added). Further editions of this version: Basel 1576, 1579, Jena 1624.

was a resounding success[84] and "the first modern encyclopedia with a practical purpose".[85] It kept Zwinger busy for the rest of his life, swelling from a 1426 page folio volume in the first edition of 1565 to four times this size in the third edition of 1596. This enormous mass of knowledge was intended as an empirical foundation for a *historia naturalis humana* and as a guide to right actions. It was arranged in the Ramist fashion, descending from the general to the particular by means of definitions, divisions and "places". In the third edition, this arrangement had become so intricate that it surpassed the capacity of everybody's memory; the book had thus become rather difficult to use. Therefore in a still later edition (Cologne, 1631) the new editor abandoned the systematic superstructure altogether and rearranged the matter alphabetically, converting the *Theatrum* thereby into a mere work of reference.[86] The "places" were after all a mnemotechnic device and retained their limitations, even in printing!

In compendia restricting themselves to more specialized fields of knowledge the topical arrangement proved more serviceable. Sebastian Münster's *Cosmographia* (Basel, 1544), Giovanni Battista Ramusio's *Delle Navigationi et viaggi* (Venice, 1550–1559) and Francesco Sansovino's *Del Governo de i regni et delle republiche cosi antiche come moderne* (Venice, 1561) were, as has been shown[87] organic advancements of the descriptive technique of the *ars epistolaria*. Such works differed significantly from polymath compendia à la Mylaeus and Zwinger. The latter were mainly used in higher education or for the adornment of polished speech and were therefore published in Latin; they contained a basic stock of knowledge which could not be fundamentally changed, but only added to. The former were used by professional men such as officials, merchants, soldiers and sailors and therefore published in the vernacular instead. Most of their material was taken from a quickly changing socio-political-cultural reality; in other words, they dealt with the information which they offered being more like perishable objects than eternal words.

Such compilations had to be brought up to date; otherwise they soon became obsolete. Politico-socio-cultural compendia were thus no self-contained

---

[84] Cf. the preceding chapter. The subtitle of this work is: "*Omnium fere eorum, quae in hominum cadere possunt, Bonorum atque malorum EXEMPLA historica, Ethicae philosophiae preceptis accomodata, et in XIX LIBROS digesta, comprehendens: Ut non immeritò Historiae PROMTUARIUM, Vitaeque humanae SPECULUM nuncupari poßit.*" Cf Ong: 1976, Schmidt-Biggemann: 1983, 59ff. On the metaphors of the theatre and the mirror cf note 68. Lycosthenes had already published a predecessor of his great collection, *Apophthegmatum sive responsorum memorabilium........ex autoribus priscis pariter atque recentioribus collect. Loci communes.* Basel 1555, as well as other books where the subject matter was digested according to loci communes.

[85] Schmidt-Biggemann: 1983, 62.

[86] Theodor Zwinger, *Magnum Theatrum Vitae Humanae........*ed. Laurentius Beyerlinck, 8 vols. in folio, Cologne 1631 (re-edited Venice 1707). Beyerlinck's abandonment of systematic arrangement of the *Theatrum* was still deplored by Leibniz (Schmidt-Biggemann: 1983, 64f, 251; Gilly: 1977–79, part 2, 148ff).

[87] See ch. one, § *Programmes for the improvement of travel.*

achievements, but "works in progress". In order to keep themselves on the book market they had to be updated with new editions. In this they were akin to periodicals, which developed at about the same time from a need to document a changing reality. Actually, the origin of periodicals was closely connected with that of these compendia.[88] Moreover, they were no mere receptacles for empirical data; as the examples of Gesner and Ray have already shown, they could themselves be turned into instruments of empirical inquiry. The information they contained came to a large extent from the reports of travellers and correspondents. Instead of merely passively registering them according to his place system, the author could actively look out for further pertinent information by systematically questioning knowledgeable persons.

Thus Sebastian Münster built up a "system of local surveys",[89] questioning humanists and statesmen all over Europe in order to fill the gaps of his *Cosmographia* in its later editions. His partners were of course glad to answer him in order to get their town or country adequately documented in this standard work.[90] In the same way Münster also collected maps, views of towns, coins, and other objects of documentary value,[91] exemplifying the close connection between collecting material objects and information. After his death, the *Cosmographia* continued to be updated by successive editors (there were 21 editions between 1544 and 1628).

Other compendia obtained comparable positions as "books of authority".[92] Like archives, libraries, and *musei*, such quasi-periodical compendia can be seen as microcosms representing one aspect of the macrocosm by means of characteristic items taken from their original context and rearranged according to a place system.

The social milieu in which these micorcosmoi were assembled gravitated around the universities (especially the Protestant, anti-scholastic ones), the academies and learned societies, and the workshops of the printer-publishers. Systematic collecting of information and objects alike were favoured by a growth of wealth and security and by the establishment of regular postal services from the 16th century. Collecting valuable objects, such as works of art or exotic animals, was of course restricted to the wealthy and powerful, but in order to start a collection of instructive objects, gathering information together or compiling a compendium, one needed only determination, industry and a good standing in

---

[88] Schöne: 1924.

[89] Beck: 1973, 98.

[90] Rassem-Stagl: 1994, 87ff. Cf also Strauss: 1959, 111ff.

[91] Ibidem.

[92] Ob. "books of authority" cf Koschaker: 1947, 99ff.

the *res publica literaria*. The printing press and the spirit of bookkeeping shaped and pervaded this social milieu.[93]

A good example of this milieu is the above-mentioned genealogical, scholarly and commercial connections between Lycosthenes, Oporinus and Zwinger. The network, of which these men formed part, encompassed the Basilean university, the city's economic life and government, and extended to southern Germany, northern Italy and French Switzerland. Sebastian Münster belonged to the same network. Coming from southern Germany like Lycosthenes, he had been a pupil of the latter's uncle, the Hebrew scholar and geographer Conrad Pellicanus. Master and pupil came to Basel, accepted the reformed faith and worked in a printer's office. Münster later married his employer's widow, his stepson thereby becoming his publisher. He rose from being a printer's corrector to an important chair and the rectorate of the university;[94] Theodor Zwinger repeated this career path in the next generation.[95]

In Venice the printer-publishers played a similar role. Sansovino owed his commercial success as an author to the fact the he ran his own publishing firm.[96] Since the Venetian university was in Padua, the printers in Venice itself became more closely connected with academies; the most famous of them, Erasmus' friend Aldus Manutius, even founded his own academy (*Neacademia*, later called *Accademia della Fama*) which met in his house and served as a braintrust to his publishing firm.[97]

Venetian and Basilean publishers closely collaborated, thereby bridging the abyss between the confessions.[98] These few examples may give a glimpse of the network, in which politico-socio-cultural data were collected, condensed, systematized and redistributed, in which the *ars epistolaria* was cultivated and the *ars apodemica* invented.

If printed compendia relieved memory, they nevertheless became part of the rhetorical organization of knowledge whose shortcomings they shared. Their heyday was in the early age of printing, when knowledge hidden away in hardly accessible manuscripts was assembled, multiplied, distributed, and thus democratized. Yet after they had fulfilled this mission, their shortcomings began to appear. By continuing to employ the mnemotechnic model of the spatially organized treasure-house for a continuously and tremendously increasing mass of knowledge, they overtaxed human receptivity. The story of the early modern

---

[93] Gilbert: 1960, 233ff; Ong: 1961.

[94] Burmeister: 1969.

[95] See ch. one, paragraphs *The first methodologists of travel* and *A tale of three cities*.

[96] Rassem-Stagl: 1994, 105ff.

[97] Brown: 1891; Febvre - Martin: 1958.

[98] Bietenholz: 1959.

compendia polymath as well as specialized - mirrors that of the *ars apodemica*.[99] The genre was doomed from the beginning. After its first organization of hitherto scattered knowledge it lost its fascination.   Other ways of dealing with that knowledge had to be found, and they were found in the "scientific revolution" of the 17th century.

THE ACQUISITION AND PROCESSING OF NEW EMPIRICAL KNOWLEDGE

TREASURE HOUSES FOR KNOWLEDGE

Old-established thinking habits are not so easily discarded. Though the shortcomings of the topical model for organizing knowledge became increasingly apparent, it was still destined for an astonishing career, by which it contributed to the "scientific revolution" of the 17th century.

A convenient starting point for this career of the ancient model of the treasure-house was reached in the *annus mirabilis* 1568/69, when Theodor Zwinger discussed the ways of dealing with all knowledge with Ramus and Blotius. It seems that they had become aware of the limitations of the model of the treasure-house, which derived from and ultimately depended on individual memory. Could not a remedy be found in a collective memory maintained and filled up by the collaboration of many scholars? If a permanent, well-protected, well-endowed centre for the collection, inspection, preservation and redistribution of all knowledge could be created, this institution would be the most perfect microcosm, combining the advantages and avoiding the limitations of memory, archive, library, collection, compendium, printer's office and academy. This centre would make the systematic improvement of all crafts, arts and sciences and the rational planning of human life possible. Its only prerequisite was the unreserved collaboration of all the scholars involved – a condition which these members of the *res publica literaria* thought easily achievable.

Zwinger's *Methodus apodemica* was a fruit of these deliberations. An improvement to the current practices of travel and correspondence was necessary for the establishment of such an institution, whose outlines are for the first time sketched in the *Praefatio* to Zwinger's book:

"Like precious goods are transported from the whole world to the most famous emporia and are exported from the same competitively, so treasures of wisdom and virtue of all types, which are diffused over the whole earth, can be brought together into a Republic (such as Plato wanted to be created in his book

---

[99] Henningsen: 1966; Stewart: 1978, ch. two.

of that name) or into an Academy, or even into one church by the zeal of the travellers, and they can be recaptured from there, just as from a Trojan horse, so that by this type of reasoning clearly, travels may be known to have considerable importance for every type of life."[100]

Zwinger introduces his new institution by comparing it with others already known to the reader. The "emporia" alluded to must be Venice and Basel or other city states prominent in the traffic of goods and information. To those existing bodies he links three other more or less utopian, yet prestigious ones: Plato's *Republic*, the model of the Platonizing academy and the super-confessional church which Zwinger, like other humanists (including Emperor Maximilian II), was working towards.[101] The new institution, as yet unnamed, was to collect the dispersed "treasures of wisdom and virtue" and to transform them by means of "reasoning clearly" into precepts for "everyday life". In this it resembles the *Theatrum vitae humanae*. Yet it was not to be the work of one single man and no mere book. It was conceived as a union of intellectuals monopolizing the traffic in knowledge. The "treasures of wisdom and virtue" are not merely to be passively registered by them, they are actively to be inquired into, scientifically processed and redistributed for the instruction of mankind. Actually, Zwinger's documentation-and-research centre is conceived as the centre of a church – state governed by philosopher-rulers rationally planning all aspects of human life. It is the capital of a sovereign "republic of letters".

As Plato had done in his *Republic*.[102] Zwinger assigns the task of collecting the dispersed treasures of knowledge to the travellers, for whose education he has written his *Methodus apodemica*. They — and by implication also the correspondents[103] — fulfil the same function for the "republic of letters" as merchants, diplomats and missionaries do for state and church. The task of processing this knowledge and redistributing the results he apparently assigns to sedentary scholars — Plato's philosopher-kings — who form an academy. He envisages men from all walks of life, and its implication, all mankind as recipients.

While inaugurating great vistas for the future, this seminal passage of the *Methodus apodemica* also expresses a certain uneasiness. In using the metaphor

---

[100] *"Ut ergo è toto terrarum orbe preciosae merces in celeberrima convehuntur emporia, & ex iisdem certatim evehuntur; ita omnigenae sapientiae & virtutis thesauri per totum universum disseminati, vel in unam Remp. (quod Plato in sua fieri volebat), vel in unam Academiam, vel etiam in unam Ecclesiam, peregrinantium studio, convectae, inde rursus tamquam ex equo Troiano peti possunt, ut hac sane ratione peregrinationes ad omne genus vitae non exiguum habere momentum intelligantur."* (Zwinger: 1577, *Praefatio*).

[101] Zwinger organized interconfessional discussions, cf Thommen: 1889, 241ff; Bonjour: 1960 182ff; Gilly: 1977–79, part 2, 209ff.

[102] 950d-952a. On the significance of the *Republic* for the present context cf also Bietenholz: 1959, 115.

[103] The relationship between travel and correspondence is of course dealt with in the *Methodus apodemica*.

of the "Trojan horse", Zwinger involuntarily reveals himself. It is no doubt an apt metaphor for the collection and redistribution of knowledge, but is also a bad omen. In the late 16th century the "spell of Plato"[104] was still unbroken. Social engineering appeared as an unmitigated positive force. The sinister side of institutions converting knowledge into power only became apparent when they ceased to be involved in utopian projects. It was left to the "reign of terror" in revolutionary France to create a *Bureau de renseignements* to keep all citizens under surveillance and control.[105]

Theodor Zwinger merits more attention than he has hereto received by historians of ideas. He has been depicted as a diligent compiler and scholarly editor, a successful teacher and respectable savant, who nevertheless embodies Basel's decline from universal significance to self-centred provincialism.[106] Only now does one begin to see that he was a thinker in his own right and an early herald of scientific empiricism. His bad luck was that his encyclopedia and his editions were so successful that scholars of the next century such as Bacon and Comenius used them without caring to quote them. Zwinger was thus reduced to the rank of an unoriginal, if useful author. Yet in carrying the model of the treasure-house for knowledge to its utmost limits, he has however, at least three universally significant achievements to his credit: the main humanist encyclopedia, the *Methodus apodemica* and the seminal idea of the research-and-documentation centre.

An early proponent of this last idea was Hugo Blotius. After having met Zwinger at Basel in 1568/69, Blotius started one of those pan-European correspondences which were the Renaissance equivalent of modern scientific journals.[107] From Strasbourg and Venice he sent Zwinger drafts of city descriptions which were used by the latter for his own model descriptions in the *Methodus apodemica*.[108] As has been told in ch. I, he also wrote instructions for travellers in the form of a list of 117 numbered questions, which followed the rhetorical schema for the praise of cities, but on a more intricate level. Focusing on government, law and adminstration, Blotius' questionnaire also considers the natural features of the surroundings of the city and their economic use, the fortifications and architectonic landmarks of the city, its past and present state, population, occupations and ways of life, ecclesiastic and scholastic institutions, illustrious men, weights and measures, sanitary conditions, warlike exercises,

---

[104] This formulation refers to Popper: 1950.

[105] See ch. seven.

[106] Cf note 101; Vetter: 1952 73ff; Bietenholz: 1971, 153ff; Seifert: 1976, 79ff; Ong: 1976; Schmidt-Biggemann: 1983, 59ff.

[107] Rühl: 1958; Leitner: 1968. Cf also ch. one: *The first methologists of travel*.

[108] L. Brummel, *Twee Ballingen s'Lands Tijdens Onze Opstand Tegen Spanje. Hugo Blotius (1534–1608) Emanuel van Meteren (1535–1612)*. s'Gravenhage 1972, pp. 26f; Zwinger, *Methodus apodemica*, Descriptions of Basel and Padua.

food, clothing, festivities and other interesting features. A spirit of systematic stock-taking pervades this questionnaire; objective and even quantitative data are called for wherever possible.[109] By answering them a traveller could complete a full description of any city. Yet Blotius' questions had no immediate practical purpose; they were addressed to his humanist peers and were meant as an instrument of research. Yet they were not particularly well designed; the questions are imprecise and sometimes rambling, divided into sub-questions and explained by examples. It is difficult to imagine that a traveller could actually work with them; and I know of no city description drawn up with their help. They were eventually published only sixty years after having been written (*Tabula Peregrinationis continens capita Policica*, 1629).[110]

Even if the practical significance of the *Tabula Peregrinationis* remained insignificant, it is still interesting from a theoretical point of view. In writing detailed instructions for the description of any city, Blotius obviously attempted to standardize politico-socio-cultural research and to make the concomitant descriptions comparable. This in its turn presupposed a documentation centre to which the travellers would submit their descriptions. A centre for the documentation of this kind of empirical data was very much in the air. Only a few years earlier Sansovino had compiled such data in his *Del Governo* (1561) yet Blotius came to Venice in 1570/71 having already written his *Tabula Peregrinationis* and there is no indication that he was influenced by Sansovino's work. As a humanist from western Europe, he was more influenced by the logical reforms of Agricola and Ramus, by Münster's *Cosmographia* and by Zwinger's *Theatrum vitae humanae*. Yet unlike these three figures he did not inquire into everything, instead he focused on political, social and cultural data. He must have been influenced, however, by the most famous antique collection of such data, Aristotle's "Polities" which were also the avowed model of *Del Governo*.[111] The decisive impulse certainly came from discussions with Zwinger, which led to the latter's *Methodus apodemica*. Zwinger's four city descriptions contained in this work are built on a similar place system (...*quid observatum vel observandum sit, locorum Topica, respectu Rerumque pragmatica certaque sane Historica expendamus...*).[112]

Yet Blotius did not merely intend to write a compendium. After having been appointed *praefectus Bibliothecae* to Emperor Maximilian II in 1575, he advanced ambitious plans. Besides starting a portrait collection, a concordance of coins, weights and measures, and a lexicon of Roman proper names,[113]

---

[109] Blotius: 1629; cf Stagl: 1978, 614f.

[110] A German translation of Blotius' questionnaire is given in Stagl: 1978, 631–638; cf also the paragraph *The first methodologists of travel* in ch. one.

[111] See note 57 to ch. one.

[112] Zwinger: 1577, 159.

[113] Menhardt: 1957; Unterkirchner: 1968, 81ff, cf also note 107.

he also developed a plan for two interconnected documentation centres. A *Bibliotheca Generis Humani Europaea* should be established in Speier and a *Musaeum Generis humani Blotianum* in Frankfurt. These were free cities of the Empire which were closely connected with the office of the Emperor and both showed some degree of religious tolerance.[114] Like Mylaeus, Blotius was deeply impressed by the Turkish threat and proposed transfering the Imperial treasures from the specially exposed capital Vienna to safer locations in the interior of Germany.[115] This would also give him the opportunity of rearranging these treasures into topically structured microcosmoi open for further growth. The project of a super-library is rather conventional; that of a super-museum is more interesting. Obviously the city descriptions of the travellers responding to the *Tabula Peregrinationis* were to be kept there. The *Musaeum* should moreover contain a portrait gallery of past, present and future *viri illustres* (including scholars and *homines mechanici*), pictures of the racial appearance and national costumes of all peoples, *specimina* of ancient and modern weights, measures and coins, as well as models made of wood, metal or cardboard of weapons, coaches and wagons, ships, buildings, tools and other useful devices of all nations. On this geographico-historico-ethnographico-technological microcosm Blotius bestowed his own name![116]

Blotius' documentation centres were conceived as fruits of an alliance between the *res publica literaria* and the empire. Both were powers with universal pretensions. Their alliance seemed necessary in view of the weakening of Christendom through its religious self-laceration and the Turkish menace to civilization. The naming of both centres expresses Blotius' faith in the underlying unity and universal validity of Western Christian culture.

Under Maximilian II, these projects were not wholly "phantastic plans", as Blotius' biographer believes them to have been.[117] Allegedly a crypto-Protestant, Maximilian went farthest of all Habsburgs in his efforts to placate the Protestants; he was moreover an energetic, if unlucky, fighter against the Turks. And he courted humanist public opinion. Yet Maximilian died in 1576 and Blotius' plans came to nothing. Never a productive scholar and always depending on the collaboration of others, under the new and more orthodox régime Blotius wisely took a back seat where he stayed for the rest of life.

SOME ATTEMPTS AT PRACTICAL REALIZATION

The alliance between political humanism and a modernizing, centralizing tendency in church and state in the second half of the 16th century led to many

---

[114] Blotius: 1629, questions 4 and 17; Brummel: 1972, 45f, 65f.

[115] Leitner: 1968, 154ff, 216f, 236ff; Brummel: 1972, 45f, 65f.

[116] Leitner: 1968, 37ff.

[117] Brummel: 1972, 45f.

attempts at stock taking social, cultural and political reality. The churches and governments alike strove to become acquainted with the conditions under which they confronted each other and the situation of the peoples for whose allegiance they contended.[118]

The continuous and systematic surveying and documentation of such data was especially attempted by missionary orders such as the Franciscans, Dominicans and Jesuits. Tightly and centrally organized bodies, these orders — like the Holy See itself — had to rely on correspondence and on files for the coordination of their worldwide activities. Since the last third of the 16th century, they conducted large-scale written inquiries among their members all over the world, evaluating the returns at their headquarters in Rome for administrative purposes and publishing some of them for propaganda. This led to a truly scientific spirit: "What the superiors really had to know in order to enlighten their decisions or to direct the activities of the other members was not the abnormal, the exceptional, but on the contrary the average, the common usage, the type".[119] Humanist members of missionary orders achieved splendid works of empirical socio-cultural and political science on this basis. Thus the Franciscan Bernardino de Sahagún (1499–1590) based his comprehensive survey of Aztec language, culture and religion on oral and written interviews following standardized lists of questions (*Historia general de las cosas de Nueva España*, written in 1569–1575).[120] Giovanni Botero (1540–1617), ex-Jesuit, functionary of the Counter Reformation and political theorist, compiled from data collected by the Holy See and the missionary orders descriptions of the political and religious state of all countries and peoples (*Relationi Universali*, 1591–1596).[121] These were, however, incompletely published, whereas Sahagún's work remained unpublished in the archives till 1829.

Colonial administration was similar to missionary work in its dependence on written files. Especially important in this respect was the foremost colonial power of the 16th century, Spain. For historical reasons, Spanish humanism was closely connected with Dutch humanism, and humanists played an important part in colonial administration. All letters to and from the Spanish territories in America had to pass through the supreme administrative authority, the "Council of the Indies". The functionaries in that office not only evaluated this information, but also gathered in new ones by posing questions to their correspondents, (local officials and missionaries). In 1577, King Philip II conducted an immense survey in this manner, which encompassed all his possessions in the New World.

---

[118] Cf Muchembled: 1978, ch. 4; Rassem: 1979; Rothkrug: 1980.

[119] Dainville: 1940, 121ff. Cf also Brou: 1929; Ricard: 1933; Todorov: 1985.

[120] D'Olwer-Cline: 1973.

[121] Part 5 of the *Relationi Universali* was only published in 1895. Cf Fischer: 1952; Firpo: 1971; Rassem-Stagl: 1994, 183ff.

This survey was a result of the king's reform of the Council of the Indies. In 1567, he had appointed the humanist lawyer Juan de Ovando y Godoy as its revisor ("visitor") and Juan López de Velasco as the latter's secretary. These two intellectuals became the figure heads of a reform intending to turn the Council of the Indies into a scientific advisory bureau for long-range administrative action. In 1571 López de Velasco was created Principal Royal Chronicler-Cosmographer with the task of forming a volume of files describing all aspects of the Indies. He immediately started his immensely valuable compilation *Geografía y descripción universal de las Indias*, a stock-taking of the information already extant in the council, which remained, however, buried in the archives till 1894. Yet it fulfilled its main function of directing the collecting of new information. In 1573, Ovando wrote an instruction for colonial administrators to improve and to standardize their reports (*descriptiones y relaciones*). Containing 135 paragraphs on 60 folio pages, this instruction was obviously too cumbersome to be put into practice. Owing to the personal intervention of the king it was cut down to a manageable list of 39 precisely formulated questions. This list — with some additional questions for coastal towns — was distributed among the American officials of the crown. Beyond their practical aim of taking stock of recently acquired possessions they show the humanist delight in socio-cultural variability and a special interest in the living conditions of the native Indians. This scholarly striving for completeness of information links Philip II's questionnaire with literary productions like Blotius' *Tabula Peregrinationis*. This similarity is not fortuitous. Both questionnaires were rooted in the practical humanism of Agricola and Vives. Yet it was precisely this scholarly over-ambition which contributed to the failure of the survey. Only thanks to the immense power and energy of the King did it almost become a success. But the field of investigation was too large, transport and communication were too cumbersome, and intellectual categories were insufficient for the further processing of this mass of data. Most questionnaires eventually returned with some answers but these came too late to be of practical administrative use. These answers, the so-called *relaciones geográficas*, were however preserved for their scholarly value.[122] In the same year, 1577, the King started a similar inquiry with equal success in Spain itself.[123] Philip II was certainly the most important patron of the project of a bureaucratic research centre in the 16th century. If he did not completely succeed in both inquiries, he remained undeterred and continued to employ his humanist advisors. In 1591 he promoted López de Velasco to be Secretary to the King.

In Germany the humanist-bureaucratic research programme was implemented on a smaller scale. In 1587, a certain Albertus Meierus (Albrecht Meier,

---

[122] Konetzke: 1970; Cline: 1972; Rassem-Stagl: 1994, 131ff.

[123] Vinas y Mey: 1951.

1528–1603) published a *Methodus describendi regiones, urbes & arces, & quid singulis locis praecipue in peregrinationibus homines nobiles ac docti animadvertere, observare et annotare debeant*. Written under the direction and at the expense ("..*auspicio atque impensis..*") of Henricus Ranzovius (Heinrich Rantzau, Herr von Bredenberg, 1526–1599), it resembles both Blotius' and Zwinger's descriptive schemas and the cooperation between Juan de Ovando and Philip II. It is well thought out and tightly structured, yet somewhat large for practical use, consisting of 186 "places" frequently formulated as questions, and classified into 12 chapters. Written in unadorned Latin quaintly interspersed with German and Low German expressions, it was reissued in 1588 under the Zwingererian title *Methodus apodemica*, translated in 1589 into English, and continued to be published until 1699.[124] Rantzau was the Danish governor of Schleswig-Holstein (*Produx Cimbricus*) and a scholar, patron and collector with many interests, among these the occult, which he shared with the country parson, mathematician, astrologer and alchemist, Meier. Educated as page to Emperor Charles V in the Netherlands and at the University of Wittenberg, Rantzau entertained a pan-European correspondence with scholars and statesmen which he also exploited as an intelligence service for his king. He had been instrumental in the subjugation of the peasant republic of Dithmarschen and the ensuing reorganization of the two duchies. As an accomplished scholar he had also written a comprehensive study of their geography, history and institutions organized after a place system which reappears in a more elaborate form in the *Methodus*, which he had commissioned Meier to write.[125] Similar lists of "places" for description, often formulated as questions, continued to be published in Germany until the 18th century.[126]

These few examples clearly show how uneasy the alliance between the *res publica literaria* and the church or state was. They drew closer to each other in situations of crisis, such as external menace (the Turkish danger), the encounter with other peoples and cultures (missions) or the forcible reorganization of society (colonies, "internal colonization"). Yet both parties retained their prejudice against the other. The humanists feared the loss of their credibility by becoming too deeply entangled in the politico-ideological aims of their employers; the established powers feared that their means could be diverted to high-sounding and impracticable projects and eventually turned against them. Thus all of the inquiries mentioned above were somehow obstructed and the publication of their results was restricted or prevented; hidden in archives rather than

---

[124] German editions: Helmstedt: 1587, Leipzig: 1588, Rostock: 1591, Strasbourg: 1608, Leiden: 1699; English edition: London: 1589. Cf. Stagl:1983, 71f, 85f; Rassem Stagl: 1994, 157ff.

[125] Henricus Ranzovius, *Cimbricae Chersonesi eiusdemque partium, urbium, insularum, et fluminum.... descripto nova*. First published in E.J. de Westphalen, *Monumenta inedita* I, 1739. On Ranzovius cf also Brandt: 1927 and Fuhrmann: 1959.

[126] See ch. seven.

displayed in libraries, where they could have furnished occasions for public discussions. Yet the more the internal contradictions of a "political humanism" became apparent.[127] the more the idea of a centre for the collection, preservation and processing of all useful knowledge merged with utopian or chiliastic schemes for the total reformation of human society. The heyday of such schemes was the first half of the 17th century.

UTOPIAN RESEARCH AND DOCUMENTATION CENTRES

In 1602, while languishing as an unsuccessful revolutionary in a Neapolitan dungeon, the polymath neo-Platonic philosopher Thomaso Campenella (1568–1639), a Dominican friar, imagined an ideal polity. His *Civitas Solis, Idea Reipublicae Philosphicae* was only published in 1623.[128] The "City of the Sun" is governed by a kind of president-pope called "The Sun" since he sees and knows everything. Under him stands a triumvirate of dignitaries called "Power", "Wisdom" and "Love" and a corporation of priestly intellectuals. They are responsible for a purely rational administration. The stability and prosperity of this polity is founded on continuous, systematic research. It dispatches travellers to explore all nations of the world and investigates its own people by means of spies reporting to an "office of enquiry".[129] Compulsory confession is also used as a means of social research: the confessors reporting regularly, "yet in general, without giving anybody's name", to the governing body.[130] The rulers can thus always take the appropriate measures.

These data are continuously brought up to date. Together with philosophical, scientific and technical knowledge, which is collected in a similar way, they are condensed by the rulers into a book called "The Wisdom". It is apparently the only book extant and there is only one copy of it. This is kept in the temple in the centre of the city. Its contents are, however, visualized for the benefit of the citizens in paintings which are fixed in a topical arrangement on the walls at the periphery of the city. Here among many other images, depictions of all countries of the world can be seen, and "the manners and customs, laws, origins, and means of power of the inhabitants are explained in terse words".[131] The "City of the Sun" is thus a mnemonic town in the sense of the *ars memorativa*. Its rulers are Renaissance magi. Their researchers serve the best interests of their subjects, but they also serve mankind. Adopting sensible laws and useful inventions from every where, the "City of the Sun" will eventually become "the teacher of all".[132]

---

[127] Cf Heer: 1953, ch. 12

[128] Quoted hereafter from the edition of Heinisch: 1960. On Campanella cf Heinisch: 224ff; Schmidt-Biggemann: 1983, 40ff; Blumenberg: 1966, 78ff.

[129] *Op. cit.*, pp. 122, 137, 150, 154.

[130] *Op. cit.*, p. 153.

[131] *Op. cit.*, pp. 120f.

All nations will become convinced that joining this "philosophical republic" is the best solution to their problems.[133]

It is now recognized that the "scientific revolution" of the 17th century was deeply indebted to this neo-Platonic utopism. In the first half of that century several men projected and attempted to realize schemes for encyclopedic research, systematic documentation of all useful knowledge, and a total reform of human society. Among them were the Germans Andreae and Hartlib, the Englishmen Bacon and Petty, the Frenchman Renaudot and the Bohemian Comenius.

Johann Valentin Andreae (1586–1654), a Protestant theologian, had in his youth been deeply impressed by Zwinger's *Theatrum vitae humanae*. Open to many heterodox currents of thought, he had read Campanella's *Civitas Solis* in the manuscript and had a hand in its belated publication in 1623 in Frankfurt. In the years from 1614 to 1620 Andreae pursued three interrelated undertakings: he started rumours of a secret society preparing a general reform of Christendom (the so-called "Rosicrucians"); he attempted to found a *Societas Christiana*; and he wrote the first German utopia, *Rei Christianopolitanae descriptio*.[134]

The basic ideas behind those activities are by now already familiar: the collection of knowledge dispersed over the world; its topical arrangement in a *universi compendium*[135] and its mnemonic-pedagogic representation through pictures and material *specimina*; its utilization for the improvement of arts, crafts, sciences and society in general as well as for the erection of a "new stronghold of truth" after a cultural deluge (*totius rei literariae interitus*).[136]

Andreae hoped that mankind could thus return to its pristine glory before the Fall. It should be guided in this by an order of priestly intellectuals which was obviously modelled upon the Catholic missionary orders (the Rosicrucians were to be the Protestant response to the challenge of the Jesuits).[137] Faced with many dangers because of the politico-religious strife of Christendom, this order should keep its aims and much of its knowledge secret,[138] yet work for the ultimate good of mankind.

The republic of Christianopolis is an anticipation of the terrestrian paradise Andreae hoped to bring about. Its citizens are learned yet pious, knowing

---

[132] *Op. cit.,*p. 142.

[133] *Op. cit.,*p. 146.

[134] (Anon.), *Fama fraternitatis Rosae Crucis*, Kassel 1614; *Confessio oder Bekenntnis der Societät und Bruderschaft Rosenkreuz*, Kassel 1615; *Rei publicae Christianopolitanae descriptio*, Strasbourg 1619 (here used in the edition of W. Biesterfeld, Stuttgart 1975). Cf Yates: 1972; van Dülmen: 1978, 148ff. 163ff; Fischer: 1982; Schmidt-Biggemann: 1983, 214ff; Péter: 1987; Fischer-Strasser: 1992. On the influence of Zwinger and Campanella on Andreae cf. esp. Yates: 1964, 413ff; Gilly: 1977–79, part 2, 192ff; van Dülmen: 1978, 32, 149ff, 166ff.

[135] *Fama fraternitatis* (as in note 134); Andreae also speaks of a *rerum compendium* (*ibid.*)

[136] *Confessio* (as in note 134), Section 4.

[137] Yates: 1972, *passim.*

[138] Yates: 1972, 162ff.

yet innocent. The city is laid out geometrically. In its centre rises a temple which is surrounded by a college with libraries, archives, lecture halls, a printing office, workshops, musea and a botanical garden. All knowledge collected there is topically organized and adapted to pedagogical use. The government of the city has three departments; Theology, Justice, and Learning. It is also much concerned with the temporal welfare and happiness of the citizens; its philanthropic spirit also extends to foreigners, the old, the poor and the sick.[139] Though opposed to and remote from the worldliness of contemporary Christendom, it expects that in the fullness of time all men will follow its example.[140]

Francis Bacon, Lord Verulam (1561–1625) has already been mentioned as a logical reformer and a critic of Ramism. Objecting to Ramism's preoccupation with *iudicium* and its consequent inability to produce new knowledge, Bacon worked for a "universally appropriate model for the procedure of scientific discovery".[141] Bacon had little confidence in the human intellect and thought thus that logic should rather accompany scientific discovery than guide it. He conceived scientific discovery as an ongoing process where method develops *pari passu* with positive knowledge. This process represents the true history of mankind. Though it cannot be anticipated by a universally valid logic, it can yet be controlled and directed by a scientific élite. The fate of mankind had thus to be managed in a responsible way.[142]

The object of all scientific discovery for Bacon was nature, an entity unknown, but most certainly homogeneous.[143] In order to discover new aspects of nature, one has to pose the right questions. For this purpose Bacon used unstructured lists of heterogenous "places"[144] which he called "particular topicks, that is, places or directions of invention and enquiry in every particular knowledge,........ being mixtures of logick with the matter of sciences: for in these it holdeth: 'Ars inveniendi adolescit cum inventis' ".[145] Bacon called catalogues of such "places" formulated as questions *interrogatoria*. Their aim was to make gaps in the extant knowledge obvious and to direct research to fill these gaps. He composed himself *interrogatoria*, e.g. for the winds (important for a seafaring nation!) and for longevity (always a major concern for scientific utopism!).[146]

---

139   Andreae: 1975, 96ff.

140   Andreae: 1975, *finis*. Cf. also Biesterfeld's Postface in Andreae: 1975.

141   Jardine: 1974, 2.

142   Growther: 1960, 28ff.

143   Schmidt-Biggemann: 1983, 215ff, 219ff.

144   *Op. cit.*, 218ff.

145   Bacon: *Of the Proficience and Advancement of Learning, Divine and Humane* (1605), in Bacon: 1740, vol. II, 491f.

146   Bacon: *Topica Particularia, sive Articuli de Ventis*, in Bacon: 1740, vol. II, 25–29; *Topica Particularia: sive Articuli inquisitionis de Vita et Morte, ibidem* 112–113.

It has not been sufficiently stressed that Baconian empiricism consisted not so much of questioning nature herself (by experiment or guided observation) but of questioning human beings about their knowledge of nature.[147] In the spirit of the logical reform of Agricola, the Lord Chancellor propounded the methodical questioning of the common man. Yet unlike the modern sociologist he was more interested in his memory than in his opinions. "The same places, which will help us what to produce of that which we know already, will also help us, if a man of experience were before us, what questions to ask".[148] By methodically tapping the memories of such men, the knowledge dispersed among the people could be collected. Scientific observation and experiments are subsidiary to this basic technique. They have to follow the same topical principle.[149] This *ars inveniendi* is apparently modelled upon the inquiry in the judiciary and the secret service which were Bacon's main occupation during the first half of his life.[150]

After having been collected in this way, empirical knowledge had to be digested into "primary histories" of the particular fields. From these, general propositions had to be derived by applying formal logic to them. Bacon called these propositions, which closely resembled the *praecepta* of his contemporary Keckermann (see above), "aphorisms". He intended them as the seeds of further discoveries.[151] Processing of the collected knowledge was to be the task of the scientific élite.

As a cooperative and responsibly managed task, Baconian science presupposed a permanent institution coordinating its various efforts. It had appeared already in the *Advancement of Learning* (1605) in the rather modest shape of a "kalendar resembling an inventory of the estate of man, containing all the inventions, (being the works or fruits of nature or art) which are now extant, and whereof man is already possessed, out of which does naturally result a note, what things are yet held impossible or not invented".[152] This idea is elaborated in the *Novum organum* (1620) where he propounded the systematic collection of all relevant facts for a "natural and experimental history" and, among other things, a compendium describing all technologies.[153]

---

[147] Experiments were for Bacon not a technique for *inventio*, but for *demonstratio* of discoveries made otherwise (*demonstratio* being the equivalent for the Ramist *iudicium*). Cf. Jardine: 1974, 136f; Schmidt-Biggemann: 1983, 218; Martin: 1988, 154f.

[148] Bacon, *Advancement of Learning* (cf note 145), 491.

[149] Purver: 1967, 43.

[150] Martin: 1988, 105ff.

[151] Bacon, *Advancement of Learning* (cf note 145), 491; cf Jardine: 1974, 174ff; Hattaway: 1978.

[152] Bacon, *Advancement of Learning* (cf note 145), 475f.

[153] Bacon, *Parasceve, or preparative toward a natural and experimental history*, an appendix to the *Novum organum*. Cf Houghton: 1941; Jardine: 1974, 138, 154.

Bacon, who said that "knowledge itself is power",[154] did not share the humanists' naive love of knowledge for its own sake. A "kalendar" or compendium accessible to everybody was not his last word on the issue of documentation. He also imagined a permanent institution supported by and working for the government and therefore necessarily secret for political reasons. This was not outrightly cynical. Like Comte after him, Bacon was concerned with order as well as with progress. He condemned privately undertaken research as something akin to sectarianism.[155]

The formula "an inventory of the estate of man" has a juridical, but also a utopian flavour; Bacon's indebtedness to Renaissance magic and utopianism (e.g. to Campanella and Andreae) can no longer be denied.[156] It is less obvious in his two great works mentioned above, which he had addressed to his master, King James I of England, than in his last work, the unfinished utopia *New Atlantis*, which he wrote after he had been dismissed from his offices in disgrace, and which was published posthumously in 1627. Here he no longer lets one single country profit from "an inventory of the estate of man", but instead mankind itself profits.[157]

Bacon describes in his utopia an ideal Christian community. Yet he shows little interest in the organization of the community itself; his work focuses on an institution for research and documentation called "Salomon's House". It is run by a self-perpetuating "order" of priestly intellectuals, who monopolize scientific knowledge for the benefit of the community. Though called the government's "eye", Salomon's House is actually an independent power, advising the rulers or withholding information from them at will.[158] It also directly influences the people's actions by predicting natural and cosmic events. The power of the "Fellows or Brethren of Salomon's House" is moreover founded on their ability to prolong human life, on their manufacturing medicaments, drugs, and even food, and on their technological wonders which must appear to the common people as magic.[159] They are thus generally revered. In contrast the position of the rulers (king and senate) remains shadowy.

Yet the government greatly benefits from their research: though unknown to all peoples, "New Atlantis" knows them all. Every twelfth year, some brethren of Salomon's House are dispatched to foreign countries, where they live incognito, adapting to local conditions. They are called "merchants of light". Their

---

[154] Published first in Latin (*Nam et ipsa scientia potestas est*) in Bacon, *Meditationes sacrae*, Sect. 11, *De haeresibus* (1597); English: "For *knowledge* itself is *power*" in Essayes, 2nd ed., part II, 1598.

[155] Martin: 1988, 163ff.

[156] Rossi: 1968, 128ff; Yates: 1972, ch. IX.

[157] Yates: 1964, 450; Yates: 1972, ch. IX.

[158] Bacon's *New Atlantis* is quoted here after Heinisch: 1960 (see note 128); here §§ II, 2, IV, 3.

[159] *Loc. cit.*

errand is "to give us knowledge of the affairs and state of those countries to which they are designated, and especially of the sciences, arts, manufacturing, and inventions around the world; and withal to bring us books, instruments, and patterns of every kind".[160] Thus they are late humanist travellers as well as ethnographers and spies. The "light" which by their activities is collected in the "eye" of Salomon's House is useful knowledge,[161] and therefore also power. It is thus only a matter of time[162] that all mankind will be governed by the "Fellows or Brethren" of that order.

"Salomon's House" is a compendium of the world. It is dedicated to the study of the works of God and the extension of human power over nature.[163] Like the "City of the Sun" and "Christianopolis" it also seems to have mnemonic-pedagogic aims, for it visualizes the ongoing process of scientific discovery in a museum of "inventions" and a gallery of statues of famous "inventors".[164]

The staff of this institution constitutes a hierarchy. The "merchants of light" forms the lowest grade; above it are others who also collect facts by excerpting them from books, questioning people, or making experiments. Above these are those who compile such facts in tables or "titles" (most probably "particular topics" or *interrogatoria*, J.S.) and apply this knowledge in new "inventions". The higher grades inquire into the hidden forces of nature by means of solitary thought, discussion, and experiments of a "higher light". The highest of all, called "Interpreters of Nature", reduce all knowledge accumulated by the rest "into greater observations, axioms, and aphorisms".[165]

BUREAUX D'ADRESSE

To a certain extent, the utopia of a universal research-and-documentation centre was actually realized in the *Bureau d'adresse* of Théophraste Renaudot

---

[160] *Op. cit.*, § II, 7. Bacon speaks here of six brethren, in IV, 3, however, of twelve.

[161] On the optical metaphor for knowledge (physical light = mental enlightenment) and on the metaphor of the mirror cf notes 61 and 68. Bacon uses it consistently in *New Atlantis*, cf. Jardine: 1974, 202. This is Frances A Yates' main argument for her thesis that Bacon stood in the Hermetic-Cabbalistic tradition together Campanella and Andreae, cf. Yates: 1972, ch. IX. This can be corroborated by the fact that Andreae too spoke of "merchants of light". In connection with his project *Societas christiana* he wrote (ca 1620): *Wenn es Kaufleuten erlaubt ist, ihre Güter auszutauschen, sollte es uns nicht erlaubt sein, im gleichen Sinne zu verfahren, wo es um Geschäfte und Forschung des christlichen Reiches handelt?* (van Dülmen's translation, cf van Dülmen: 1978, 153).

[162] The only reason why "New Atlantis" has not established regular contacts with the other world is – rather inconvincingly – the backwardness of its navy (§ II, 5). If this technological lag could be overcome, "New Atlantis" would no doubt be superior to all other countries and able to conquer them.

[163] Bacon: *New Atlantis* (cf note 128), § II, 7.

[164] *Op. cit.*, § IV, 2.

[165] *Loc. cit.*

FIGURE 7: Théophraste Renaudot. By courtesy of the Portrait Collection on the Herzog August Bibliothek, Wolfenbüttel.

(1584–1653).[166] A born Protestant and a physician by profession, Renaudot started his career as a philanthropist. Influenced by Juan Luis Vives (*De subventione pauperum*, 1526) he regarded unemployment as the ultimate cause of poverty. He believed that the poor had to be helped to help themselves.[167] Being a physician, he first aimed to make them fit for work with free medical care.

Through this programme he attracted the attention of Père Joseph, the Capuchin friar who eventually became the "grey eminence" of Cardinal Richelieu and the virtual director of French foreign policy. In 1618 Renaudot, who must have become a Catholic in the meantime, was nominated *Commissionaire Général des Pauvres du Royaume* by the Cardinal. In 1628 he obtained a royal privilege for the establishment of a *Bureau d'adresse*.[168] The *Bureau* was certainly functioning in 1630, and thanks to Renaudot's organizing genius it became an overwhelming success.

Renaudot's basic idea was that post-medieval urbanized society was too intricate for smooth social interaction: "our spirits are puzzled by the crowd and kept busy looking for people and things".[169] What such a society really needed was thus a *Bureau d'adresse & de rencontre de toutes les commoditez de la vie*, a bureau serving as a *lieu public qui soit comme une lunette d'approche, l'abregé & le ralliement* (of the separate parts of society, J.S.), *fournissant des notices generales à nostre esprit, d'especes à la memoire, & d'objets à la volonté.*[170]

The *Bureau* was basically an employment agency combined with an outpatient clinic. Whoever registered there (for 0 to 3 *sous*, according to his means) received free medical treatment and help in finding jobs, cheap clothes, lodgings, and furniture. The *Bureau* also granted its clients small-scale credits on security and helped them in their dealings with government offices and the law. It kept a card index of people looking for service or offering help. It also kept a current price index. Gradually it branched out into an advertising agency, a travel agency, a messenger service, a horse rental and a shop where almost everything could be bought or hired: curios, antiques, domestic animals, houses, estates,

---

[166] On Renaudot cf Bonnefont: 1893; Brown: 1934, 17ff; Yates: 1947, 269ff; Lawn: 1963, 142f; Solomon: 1972.

[167] This same idea was propounded already under Henry IV by Barthélémy de Laffermas, Contrôleur Général du Commerce, a close collaborateur of the Duc de Sully. He planned to improve the social and economic conditions of France by setting up a network of employment agencies, cf Solomon: 1972, 38; Carré: 1980, 206.

[168] Théophraste Renaudot, *Inventaire du Bureau de Recontre, ou chacun peut donner & recevoir avis de toutes les necessitez, & commoditez de la vie & societé humaine......* Paris (Bureau d'adresse) 1630. Renaudot remarks here (4) that he had got an earlier privilege for a *Bureau d'adresse* already on Oct. 14, 1612, which indicates that he had hedged the idea already for a long time.

[169] *nostre espirits s'intriguant par la multitude, & s'occupant en la recherche des personnes & des choses* (*Op. cit.* 9). For this idea, Renaudot refers to Montaigne, *Essais* 34 (10), as Laffermas had already done before him (cf note 167).

[170] Renaudot: 1630, 9. For the metaphor of the telescope cf. Rassem: 1980, 18, 23; see also notes 61, 68, 161, 201, 241.

genealogies, the services of private tutors, funerals.... The *Bureau* arranged marriages, recruited soldiers, found monks for understaffed monasteries and even planned to deal in academic degrees.

This traffic in goods and services naturally also involved the traffic in information. With clients from all walks of life and through a network of correspondents the *Bureau* systematically collected news from home and abroad, which proved very valuable to the government. Indeed, this was the main reason for the continuing protection which it received from Père Joseph and Cardinal Richelieu. They not only skimmed off its information, they also used it to influence public opinion. The oldest French newspaper still in existence, the *Gazette de France*, was founded in 1631 by Renaudot. It also was printed by him, for he eventually owned four print shops. The *Gazette* was much sought after for the news from the whole world which it contained. Père Joseph supplied it with information from the French diplomatic service and the missions of the Capuchins.

Renaudot also made the *Bureau* into a centre of intellectual life. From 1633 on, he organized weekly "conferences" in its rooms on the Ile de St. Louis. As in the earlier Renaissance academies, *quaestiones* were put up for discussion in these meetings which triggered the exchange of opinions, but were not decided by empirical research (e.g. *Quelle est la plus noble partie de nostre corps?*).[171] In other respects these "conferences" were looking towards the scientific societies of the second half of the 17th century: the discussions were held in the vernacular (French, not Latin); it was forbidden to quote "authorities"; religious and political topics had to be avoided. Occasionally even experiments were performed in order to demonstrate some point of discussion. In 1640 Renaudot set up a chemical laboratory. Yet his main interest was not pure science, but its humanitarian and pedagogic application. According to Renaudot's philanthropic principles, the "conferences" were open to everybody who cared and consequently were not considered to be very prestigious among the intellectual élite. Nevertheless, their reports were published by Renaudot and became a success (*Questions traitées et conferences du Bureau d'Adresse*, 5 vols., 1633ff).

If he was no pioneer of scientific research, Renaudot certainly deserves to be mentioned in a history of social research. His brochure *La Presence des Absens, ou facile moyen de rendre présent au médecin l'estat d'un malade absent*[172] was published in 1642, codifying a practice already well-established in

---

171 Théophraste Renaudot, *Seconde Centurie des Questions traitées et conferences du Bureau d'adresse*. Paris (Bureau d'adresse) 1636, 254. Cf also Lawn: 1963, 142f.

172 Théophraste Renaudot, *La Presence des Absens, ou facile moyen de rendre présent au Médecine l'estat d'un malade absent. Dressé par les Docteurs en Médecine Consultans charitablement à Paris pour les pauvres malades*. Paris (Bureau d'adresse) 1642.

the *Bureau*.[173] It was intended for bedridden patients too poor to pay for the visit of a physician. Instead they were required to fill out a form, on the basis of which the diagnosis could be made and the appropriate treatment could be prescribed at the *Bureau*. Renaudot inquires into the symptoms of the most common illnesses and also collects personal data of the patients including the hour of birth, for he apparently also used astrology for his diagnoses. There are special groups of questions for men, for women and for both sexes. Since most of the patients can not have been very articulate, the questions are posed whereever possible in a "closed" form: one only had to underline the right choice in a list of possible answers, or to mark the right spot on a table or chart. *La Presence des Absens* is thus no longer a list of "open" questions like those of the humanists; it is a sophisticated instrument of research which can be compared to the telescope (*lunette d'approche*) mentioned above. This first true questionnaire forms part of the "scientific revolution" of the 17th century.

The *Bureau* was extremely successful for a dozen years, continuously expanding, employing about thirty members of staff, and procuring 5,700 jobs in one year. It was efficiently organized with separate sub-bureaux keeping separate registers for each of its major activities. It also had a branch office in Lyons. The *Bureau d'adresse* seems to have been the first institution systematically documenting its main activities in current indices and can thus be seen as the prototype of the statistical offices of the subsequent centuries. Nevertheless it was not an easy model to imitate. It depended on the organizing genius of one man and on the continuing support of the government. It was easy to foresee what would happen to the *Bureau* without these two essential conditions. Renaudot had made a fortune from his manifold activities but he had offended the professional and business interests of many people in Paris. In order to maintain his position against his enemies he drew even closer to Père Joseph and Richelieu. The *Bureau* turned into something like a government office. For example, from 1639 all vagabonds and unemployed had to register there under the menace of forced labour in the galleys.

Renaudot's most implacable enemies were the medical faculty of the Sorbonne. It is worth considering their arguments. Renaudot and many of his staff had taken their medical degree at Montpelier; they followed their profession in Paris under the privilege of the *Bureau*. Their competitors at the Sorbonne denounced them as a dangerous band of heretics, alchemists and Rosicrucians predicting that their philanthropism would eventually lead to Anabaptism and communism.[174] Even Théophraste Renaudot's name was branded as suspicious — had not Theophrastus Paracelsus been close to the

---

[173] Already in his *Inventaire du Bureau de Rencontre* Renaudot refers to such questionnaires as a current practice in his establishment (Renaudot: 1630, 24).

[174] Solomon: 1972, 43: *d'establir des Bureaux d'Adresse c'est à dire rendre toutes les choses communes, et introduire l'heresie des Anabaptistes.*

Anabaptists and proclaimed communist ideas?[175] Whether through a Paracelsian family tradition or not, Renaudot no doubt belonged to the occultist current of Renaissance philosophy which contributed so much to the "scientific revolution" of the 17th century.[176] With Campanella — who spent his last years in Paris and attended the "conference of the *Bureau d'adresse* - Renaudot believed that the magical relationship between micro and macrocosm, which had been obscured by the Fall, was now about to be re-established through the labours of an élite of Christian philosophers preparing the reunification of mankind and the return of a terrestrial paradise.[177]

In 1638 Père Joseph died and in 1642 Cardinal Richelieu followed. Now Renaudot's enemies gained the upper hand. In 1643 he was forced to discontinue the *Bureau* on charges of usury and the receiving of stolen goods. But he was sensible enough to side with Richelieu's successor Mazarin and was thus allowed to keep the *Gazette* which remained in his family until 1762, eventually becoming the official organ of the Foreign Ministry. Other institutions still existing in Paris, a policlinic, a pawnshop and an auction-house, also date back to Renaudot.[178]

There were many attempts to set up similar *Bureaux* which all failed. They were especially numerous in England, where the ascendency of Puritanism encouraged attempts at socio-intellectual reform.[179] The most portentous *Bureau* was founded by Samuel Hartlib (1595–1662).[180] Coming from a German-English merchant family at Elbing, Pomerania, Hartlib had been educated in Germany and in Cambridge and undergone the influence both of Andreae and Bacon. When Elbing became Catholic in 1628, Hartlib settled permanently in England. A "master of innumerable curiosities, and very communicative",[181] he became "a kind of imaginary institution, of which he represented the proprietors, council and all the officers; the funds too, being wholly his own".[182] He established a network of correspondence, helped Protestant refugees, furthered inventors and scientists, and headed two unsuccessful model schools.

In 1641–42, Hartlib organized the missionary travel of the great educational reformer Johann Amos Comenius (1592–1670) to England. Comenius

---

175 Solomon: 1972, 191. On Paracelsus as a precursor of totalitarian programmes cf Heer: 1959, 261ff. Without being able to prove it, I believe that a main influence besides Paracelsus was Guillaume Postel's *De Orbis terrae concordia*. On Postel (1510-1581) cf Bouwsma: 1957.

176 On Renaudot's occultist leanings see esp. Solomon: 1972, 80ff.

177 Yates: 1947, 285ff; Solomon: 1972, 91f. In Renaudot's *Questions* (see note 171), Lullus, Paracelsus, Postel, Campanella and similar authors are frequently mentioned.

178 Solomon: 1972, 187, 198ff, 216.

179 Brown: 1934, 29f; Turnbull: 1947, 80ff; Solomon: 1972, 217f.

180 On Hartlib see Dircks: 1865; Althaus: 1884; Stimson: 1940; Turnbull: 1947; Trevor-Roper: 1967; Webster: 1970.

181 John Evelyn, *Diary*, 27. Nov. 1655, quoted after Dircks: 1865, 13.

182 Dircks: 1865, 15.

was his fellow pupil under Andreae and a refugee from Bohemia. Influenced by Bruno, Keckermann and Campanella, he hoped to persuade Parliament to support his plan for the collection of all secure and useful knowledge into a *liber librorum* mirroring in its design the invisible order of all visible things. He fervently believed that this focusing of all knowledge would prepare the unification of mankind in a terrestrial paradise.[183] He expounded this programme in his manifesto *Via Lucis*, written in 1641, yet only published in 1668, where he called for the institution of an "order" or "college" of well-intentioned philosophers which should organize the exchange of knowledge between all mankind.[184] In the same year 1641 Hartlib published his own utopian manifesto, called *A description of the famous Kingdome of Macaria*, which he addressed to Parliament, "Macaria" is actually an embellished England, "in which enlightened government and true religion were supported by enlightened promotion of trade, medicine, agriculture, and the mechanic arts".[185] Hartlib put thus his country of adoption in the same position as utopian model polities had had for his predecessors Campanella, Andreae and Bacon.[186]

Yet Parliament, preparing for civil war, "had other things to do than to issue laws for a golden age".[187] In 1642 Comenius left England in despair.[188] Hartlib toned down his utopian plans, but did not abandon them. He had heard of Renaudot's *Bureau* and pursued plans for a similar "public agency" from as early as 1635.[189] Now he questioned his Parisian correspondents more thoroughly about its organization.[190] In 1643 he began to advertise for a news agency which would serve the Protestant cause in a similar way to the Jesuits serving the

---

[183] Johann Amos Comenius, *De rerum humanarum emendatione consultatio catholica*, ed. Academia Scientiarum Bohemoslovaca, Prague 1966, t.2, p. 445, t.1.p. 107. On Comenius see Turnbull: 1947; Trevor-Roper: 1967; Yates: 1972, ch. XII, XIII; Schmidt-Biggemann: ch. 3. IV.

[184] Johann Amos Comenius,*Via Lucis, Vestigata & vestiganda, h.e. Rationabilis disquisitio, quibus modis intellectualis Animorum LUX, SAPIENTIA, per Omnium Hominum mentes, & gentes, jamtandem, sub Mundi vesperam feliciter spargi possit.* Amsterdam 1668. This belated publication is due to the fact that Comenius wanted to claim his share in the foundation of the Royal Society (see below, *Scientific Academies*). In the *Via Lucis*, as published in 1668, he therefore stressed the influence of that society's official "founding father", Bacon, and played down that of Campanella, Andreae and Hartlib, cf Purver: 1967, 193ff.

[185] Boas Hall: 1970-76, vol. VI, 141; cf Samuel Hartlib, *A description of the famous Kingdome of Macaria*. London 1641.

[186] This tendency of taking over one's own country as an "avant garde of mankind", which became characteristic for the American and the French Revolution and for later revolutionary movements, was taken over from the Rosicrucians, cf Péter: 1987, 129. See also ch. VII of the present book.

[187] Yates: 1972, 190.

[188] *Op. cit.*, ch. XIII.

[189] Dircks: 1865, 6.

[190] Turnbull: 1947, 57ff,80, Solomon: 1972, 218. Arnold Boates, Hartlib's Parisian correspondent, writes to him concerning Renaudot: "The Master, viz Renaudot, was a physician, of little practice, no meanes, and no conscience: who by revolting from us to Rome procured for himself leave for erecting the office" (Turnbull: 1947, 124).

Catholic one.[191] In 1647 and 1648 he published two brochures advertising his own "Office of Publick Addresse" with dedications to Parliament, the winning side in the civil war.[192]

He does not mention Renaudot, this traitor to the Protestant cause.[193] Yet he took over his organizational ideas and plagiarized his writings. Hartlib was, however, less of a philanthropist and more of a church politician than his French model. Under Comenius' influence, his "Office" became more lofty and more utopian than Renaudot's *Bureau*.

It was to have two branch offices, one in London , the other in Oxford. The London office, dedicated to "temporal" matters, was a direct copy of Renaudot's *Bureau*. It was to provide information concerning temporal welfare to people submitting their questions by filling in standardized "patterns or forms".[194] The Oxford office, dedicated to "spiritual" matters, was to be a research and documentation centre combined with an international news agency. It was to answer queries on religious, scientific and technical matters and "be Authorized also to negotiate for Spiritual Intelligence; and to maintaine a Correspondency and Learned Trade with all Men of Abilities within and without the Kingdome".[195] Moreover it should publish yearly reports of its activities.[196]

Hartlib had a pronounced interest in registers. This was no doubt a result of his commercial background, but also of the empiricism of the macrocosm-microcosm philosophy, which favoured the collection and interconnection of extant knowledge against the production of new one by means of experiments. His "Office" was to keep minute registers of all its activities. The London branch should "make Inventories, and keep registers of all Commodities, Persons, Employments, Offices, Charges and Things which are Actually in being, and Usefully considerable in the Commonwealth",[197] thereby distinguishing between "perpetual" registers recording socio-politico-cultural facts such as catalogues of libraries, political or legal institutions, or lists of important families, offices, markets, imports and exports, and "Occasional" registers recording transactions between individuals.[198] Taken together, they would make up an inventory of England. The Oxford branch should document its "Stock of Learning" in equally

---

[191] Samuel Hartlib, *A Faithfull and seasonable Advice, or; The necessity of a Correspondencie for the advancement of the Protestant Cause*. London 1643, esp. 2f.

[192] Samuel Hartlib, *Considerations tending To the Happy accomplishment of Englands Reformation in Church and State*. London 1647; *A further Discoverie of The Office of Publick Addresse for Accommodations*. London 1648.

[193] See note 190.

[194] Hartlib: 1648, 28.

[195] Hartlib: 1647, 46.

[196] *Op. cit.*, 50.

[197] *Op. cit.*, 42.

[198] *Op. cit.*, 42f; cf also Hartlib: 1648 8ff.

minute registers[199] which would eventually make up an inventory of the world. The knowledge stored in both branch offices should be, as it were, the working capital of the "Office of Publick Addresse".

There was a hidden dishonesty behind this project which could not have escaped Hartlib: the flow of information was not completely free. The public and the "men of abilities" were expected to inform the "Office" open-heartedly, whereas the latter would withhold some of its knowledge in order to pass it on to the government. This ambiguity between a lofty plan for the redemption of all mankind and a kind of secret service was only precariously concealed by Hartlib's assumption of his own good intentions and those of the government to which he addressed his project.

Like Renaudot, Hartlib was thus forced to lower his sights by seeking alliance with the political power. Unlike Renaudot, he was not a good businessman. His circumstances must have been reduced by his philanthropy and by the civil war. The fact that he published his project instead of merely implementing it, points in this direction. He thereby tried to sell it to Parliament as a kind of "Engine to reduce all into some Order which is confused".[200] Since rational policy-making presupposed "a speciall Insight and Discovery of Affaires neer at hand", the victors of the civil war should "be inabled to look not onely upon the Outward Parts, but as it were, upon the very Anatomy of all the inward bowels of church and State".[201] In compensation for this important service, the "Office" should be financed from the sequestered property of the church of England.[202] If he was an otherworldly enthusiast, Hartlib also had the brutal outspokenness of a puritan. In 1650 the "temporal" branch of his "Office" was actually set up under the superintendence of Hartlib's friend Henry Robinson[203] in Threadneedle Street, London. It was not a success and nothing more was heard of it.[204] The "spiritual" branch, which it seems to have been Hartlib's major concern, never materialized. He nevertheless "continued to act unofficially in accordance with what he thought the superintendent (of such an office, J.S.) should do".[205]

---

[199] Hartlib: 1647, 49.

[200] *Op. cit.*, 45.

[201] *Op. cit.*, 35. Hartlib does not expressly mention here the main auxiliary of the anatomist, the *microscope*. Yet he also uses the light metaphor (cf notes 161,170): through his office, Parliament "will be able upon all occasions to walke, as it were, at noon day in the light, when others will be constrained to doe things but at randome, and grope in difficult Cases, as it were for the wall at midnight" (*ibid.*, 36).

[202] *Op. cit.*, 57.

[203] Henry Robinson (1605-1673?), merchant, printer, philanthropist, member of the East India Company, cf Jordan: 1942, 38ff.

[204] *Op. cit.*, 250ff, see also Henry Robinson, *The office of addresses and encounters: where all people of each rancke and quality may receive direction and advice for the most cheap and speedy way of attaining whatsoever they can lawfully desire....* London 1650.

[205] Turnbull: 1947, 87.

Cromwell awarded Hartlib a pension. In 1657/58 he again came close to opening an "Office of Publick Addresse", this time in Dublin, supported by funds taken away from the vanquished Irish. The restoration took away his last hope. It also stopped his pension. Hartlib died in 1662.

His abortive "Office of Publick Addresse" nevertheless had an important after-effect. Since about 1645, Hartlib had gathered around him "men of abilities" whom he obviously intended as scientific staff in his Office. He is rather elusive about its precise organization, but he seems to have had a semi-secret society in mind, something like the Jesuits. John Wilkins, subsequently Warden of Wadham College, Oxford, belonged to this group along with two young men who had just returned from the continent, the physician William Petty and the chemist Robert Boyle. This society met in Oxford and in London. In London it was closely connected with Gresham College, a foundation for the advancement of mathematics and its practical application. In some of Boyle's letters from 1646 and 1647, the group is referred to as "The Invisible College". It had some members in common with a group which had been meeting in Wilkins' rooms at Wadham College since 1648 to discuss and practice experimental science. This latter group was the nucleus of the "Royal Society for Improving Natural Knowledge", which was founded in 1662.[206]

The Royal Society did not include Hartlib, who died in the same year. Neither did it recognize the spiritual paternity of Comenius, then an impoverished exile in Holland. The time for eschatological enthusiasm was over. The Royal Society included, however, some members of Hartlib's scientific staff who had made their peace with the Restoration. Wilkins, Petty and Boyle were among its most active members, the first eventually becoming its secretary, the second its vice-president, and the third being elected its president, though declining that honour because of religious scruples. Comenius' and Hartlib's share in its origin is still a matter of controversy.[207] Yet the personal links between them and the founding generation of the Royal Society are indubitable. Within the fold of this society dedicated to experimental sciences Petty and Boyle maintained the collecting and registering empiricism connected with the macrocosm-microcosm philosophy.

William Petty (1623–1687) especially carried on Hartlib's endeavours, though he was at the same time a pioneer of modern experimental science.[208] Petty was a selfmade man. The son of a clothier, he went to sea, to a French Jesuit college, and to Dutch universities. Combining broad-ranging scholarship with a gift for applied mathematics and technology resulting from his craftman's and naval background, he was a leading figure in the "scientific revolution". Returning

---

[206] Purver: 1967, 193ff.

[207] *Op. cit.* Cf also Maddison: 1969, and Yates: 1972, ch. XIII.

[208] Cf Strauss: 1954; Rassem-Stagl: 1994, 285ff.

from Holland to France, he served as amanuensis to Thomas Hobbes (who had himself once been amanuensis to Bacon). At that time Hobbes moved in the circle of the learned friar Marin Mersenne, in whom "there was more than in all the universities together". His circle united some of the most advanced thinkers of the day, and far exceeded in prestige the rival circle of Renaudot. Mersenne was a neo-Platonist who attempted to formulate the "harmony of the universe" mathematically. Introduced to this circle by Hobbes, Petty moved in the best intellectual society. Nevertheless in 1646 he discovered his Puritan sympathies and returned to England. Establishing contact with Hartlib, he dedicated his first publication to him. It is called *The Advice of W.P. to Mr. Samuel Hartlib, For the Advancement of some particular parts of learning* (1647/48), and supports Hartlib's project of an "Office of Publick Addresse".[209]

Yet Petty is less interested there in philanthropy than in a sweeping scheme for intellectual reform. He propagates a "generall communication of designes" which shall unite "the wits and endevours of the world" and permit them to survey all human knowledge according to "certaine and well limited Directions". These should serve for the elimination of all useless knowledge. Purified thus of "whatsoever is nice, contentious and meerly phantasticall", the remaining mass of knowledge should then be arranged in "one Booke or great Worke", which should be made accessible to everybody by means of "Artificiall Indices Tables or other Helps for the ready finding, remembering, and well understanding". A learned society — expressly modelled upon the Jesuits — should then keep this work up to date.[210]

Petty then goes on to outline an educational reform in the Spirit of Comenius, whose name, however, is not mentioned. He propagates a scheme for the education of the whole nation, including the children of the poor, focusing on practical knowledge. This reform should culminate in the establishment of a college of technology called *Gymnasium Mechanicum*, a kind of expanded Gresham College. It should be developed into an "Epitome or Abstract of the whole world", including a polyclinic, botanical and zoological gardens and other research institutes, a library containing only useful books, and galleries for "Rarities Naturall and Artificiall", works of art, and "Modells of all great and noble Engines". The most detailed and trend-setting part of the whole scheme is the plan for the organization of the polyclinic. This was apparently the aspect closest to Petty's heart. Curiously enough, this clinic should be less concerned with medical research than with meteorological and statistical observations. One of its officials, skilled in mathematics, bookkeeping and "Judiciall Astrology" should keep a "Journall of all notable Changes of Weather, and fertility of seasons",

---

[209] William Petty, *The Advice of W.P. to Mr. Samuel Hartlib, For the Advancement of some Particular Parts of Learning*. London 1647 (the dedication to Hartlib is dated the 8. January 1647"

[210] *Op. cit.*, 1,2,3,8.

compiling in addition data on the yields of various crops, pest infestation, cattle plagues, and epidemical diseases in man. By comparing these data with the "aspects of the Celestial bodies" he should then be able to "calculate the Events of Diseases, and Prognosticate the Weather".[211] Though pretending to be "not at leisure to frame Utopias",[212] this was precisely what Petty did in his first publication and for the rest of his life he attempted to realize this dream. It was Petty who transformed the humanist research-and-documentation centre into an adumbration of the modern statistical office.

In 1652, abandoning his chair of anatomy at Oxford, Petty went to Ireland as physician-general to the British troops. He had as yet had no connection with that country, but Hartlib and Boyle (the son of an important Anglo-Irish landowner) had been interested in schemes for its colonization. It may also have helped him that his Oxford colleague John Wilkins was Cromwell's brother-in-law. As physician-general, Petty immediately reorganized the British troops' medical service. He also continued his endeavours in applied mathematics. In 1655–56 he carried through the first comprehensive, detailed and representative survey of Ireland.[213] His so-called "Down Survey" was the Irish counter part of the English "Domesday Book" of 1086 and similarly was the consequence of a conquest. Occasioned by the need to assess the lands of the "rebellious" Irish for distribution among the victorious army and the financiers of the war, the "Down Survey" was completed against much Irish resistance and English jealousy in a remarkably short time. Like Renaudot and unlike Hartlib, Petty was an organizational genius. He worked as an independent entrepreneur, employing about a thousand soldiers for the field work whom he thoroughly instructed and closely supervised. The survey, like that for the "Domesday Book", was carried out after the pattern of court sessions with examination of witnesses. Petty insisted on personal interrogation and autopsy as well as a thorough land survey. Petty himself remained at his desk, coordinating the heterogenous parts of this tremendous work.[214]

From his data he also compiled a most accurate map of Ireland and made plans for a census of the country. These geographic and demographic data were to be continuously kept up to date by an office in Dublin. In that context he invited his former protector Hartlib to Ireland. The Restoration foiled this plan. The idea of a statistical office did not become a reality until the French Revolution.[215] The "Down Survey" had enabled Petty to acquire large Irish estates

---

[211] *Op. cit.*, 8,12.

[212] *Op. cit.*, 10.

[213] Goblet: 1930, 154ff.

[214] Sir William Petty, *The History of the Survey of Ireland, commonly called the Down Survey*. Ed. Thomas Aiskew Larcom. Dublin 1851, esp 46-50; Goblet: 1930, 207ff, 241ff.

[215] Cf ch. eight.

which he managed as a model landowner. He continued to prosper under Charles II who knighted him after the Restoration. Sir William Petty became one of the founding members of the Royal Society. Petty's most lasting claim to fame was his foundation (together with his friend John Graunt) of a new scientific discipline which he called "political arithmetic" and defined as "the art of reasoning by figures upon things relating to government".[216] This art actually consisted of two parts: (1) the registration and digestion of relevant data ("political anatomy"), and (2) the calculation of the political forces ("political arithmetic" proper).[217] It combined thus an empiristic and a rationalistic aspect. The first was derived from the registering empirism of Bacon and Hartlib, the second from Mersenne's study of the "harmony of the universe" and Hobbes' related attempt to formulate the laws of political action geometrically.[218] It pretended to exclude all philosophical and theological speculation, yet it had a messianic aspect, like the "scientific revolution" as a whole.[219] By assuming an immutable order behind the apparent chaos of phenomena, it attempted to restitute the lost faith in the meaning of the universe, and to found human welfare on scientific policy-making.

John Graunt (1620–1674) shared these ideas.[220] Like Petty he had belonged to the above-mentioned circle around Gresham College, an institute for adult education controlled by the City of London. A self-educated and prosperous tradesman, Graunt had been able to procure the professorship of music there for Petty. Musical theory was then, like astrology, a recognized branch of mathematics seen as the special expression of the "harmony of the universe". Through his connection with Mersenne, who was also a musical theorist, Petty was well qualified for this chair.[221] Yet while Petty was led by his career to focus on the more practical fields of politics, economics and technology, Graunt remained a shopkeeper and private scholar in London, concentrating on his immediate sphere of life. Stimulated by Bacon's inquiry into longevity, he applied his "shopkeeper's arithmetics" to a set of phenomena which had hitherto been treated merely discursively. He painstakingly collected and compared data on human and animal life cycles, becoming the founder of vital statistics,

---

[216] Sir William Petty, *Political Arithmetick*, London 1690; cf Buck: 1977

[217] Petty: 1690; cf also Sir William Petty, *The Political Anatomy of Ireland*. London 1691.

[218] Buck: 1977, 77f.

[219] Hecht: 1980, 335ff; Horváth: 1983.

[220] On Graunt cf John: 1884, 161-178; Kargon: 1963; Hecht: 1980, 340ff; Rassem-Stagl: 1994, 271ff.

[221] The idea of the "harmony of the universe" goes back to Pythagoras. Its most influential expression was in Plato's *Timaios*. This idea was well known in the Middle Ages and the Renaissance. (Debus: 1968). It had been brilliantly restated in the 17th century by Johannes Kepler (Carrier-Mittelstraß; 1989, 152ff.) and by Marin Mersenne, *Harmonie Universelle*. Paris, 1636, cf. Mandrou: 1973, 144ff.)

an achievement for which he was received into the Royal Society.[222] The old fear of a causal connection between censuses and epidemics revived during the Great Plague in London (1665–66), Graunt being accused of having had a hand in the subsequent Great Fire, through which he actually lost most of his property. Graunt was a lifelong religious seeker, whose spiritual odyssey led from Puritanism to Roman Catholicism. His death was lamented "with tears" by his lifelong friend Sir William Petty.[223]

The further development of political arithmetic confirmed that the time was not yet ripe for a scientific treatment of human fate. The resistance of pre-industrial society proved insuperable. Graunt and Petty have been hailed as the founding fathers of modern scientific statistics,[224] yet the only field where their method could be successfully applied was insurance - then a private undertaking restricted to business circles.[225] Despite his wealth and influence, Petty failed to set up statistical offices first in Dublin and then in London. Political arithmetic had to remain content with data obtained through private researches - which remained sporadic, discontinuous, and insufficient. The manuscripts in which Petty had put together his own researches were published only after his death, when their data had become antiquated (*Political Arithmetick*, written between 1671 and 1676, was published in 1690, *The Political Anatomy of Ireland*, written in 1672 appeared in 1691). The science of political arithmetic was still pursued, albeit with decreasing vigour, by scientific academies until the 18th century. In anticipation of the harmony of the universe with insufficient empirical means it soon developed into a theological justification of divine providence - a development which had already been set in motion with Petty's pious friend Robert Boyle. By the Age of Enlightenment political arithmetic had already become discredited as empty rhetoric.[226]

SCIENTIFIC ACADEMIES

The *Accademia del Cimento*, founded in Florence in 1657, is commonly considered to be the first modern scientific academy. It carried on Galilei's conception of science, with the "Royal Society" in London following suit in 1662 and the *Académie des Sciences* in Paris in 1666. The German equivalent of these foundations was the project of a *Societät in Teutschland zu aufnehmen der Künste und Wißenschafften*, which Gottfried Wilhelm Leibniz propounded in

---

222 John Graunt, *Natural and Political Observations mentioned in a following index and made upon the Bills of Mortality....* London 1662. Cf the critical edition by Eric Vilquin: *Observations naturelles et politiques... faites sur les Bulletins de mortalité...*Paris 1977 and Kern: 1982, 30ff.

223 Cf the article *Graunt* in DNB.

224 Kargon: 1965; Buck: 1977; Schneider: 1980; Plackett: 1988.

225 Schneider: 1980, 56ff.

226 Horváth: 1978, 5ff; Kern: 1982, 27ff; Mackensen: 1983, 485ff.

1669 and 1672.[227] This German project was obviously modelled upon the Royal Society; the intellectual exchange between England and Protestant Germany being especially close in the 17th century. Yet though Leibniz belonged to a younger generation (the generation of Isaac Newton), his project referred not only to the contemporary foundation but also to the earlier circles around Mersenne and Renaudot. All of these would, however, be far surpassed by the German society. It was an utopian project along the lines of Zwinger-Campanella-Andreae-Bacon-Hartlib. Like them, Leibniz strove for a *scientia generalis*, based on an encyclopedic digestion of all useful knowledge, advancing religious unification, rational politics, and the happiness of all mankind.[228]

Though Leibniz mentions Renaudot rather furtively, he took his basic organizational idea from the *Bureau d'adresse*. His project moreover betrays some knowledge of the kindred plans of Hartlib and Petty. Like them he connects philanthropy with social research. Free medical treatment — with help of *exactissima interrogatoria Medica* — should win for his society the confidence of the poor. This confidence should be put to good use by interrogating them on their "knowledge of commonplace things (*simplicien*) which peasants and old women sometimes know better than savants". From the poor this research method should be extended to the common people, to "draw (them) out of their experience in the trades, agriculture, *judicio de meteoris*, etc.", and to the educated classes, for the society should also systematically collect *Manuscripta: relationes, diaria, intineraria, schedas perituras,* useful letters of correspondence, and other *cimelia literaria*. All such information should be entered in a documentation centre (*aerarium scientiarum utilium publicum*). The society should moreover run pharmacies, workhouses for the poor and other philanthropic institutions, schools, and a *theatrum naturae et artis*, and start a "traffic and *commercium* with knowledge". Its treasure of knowledge should thus be constantly augmented, brought up to date, imparted to Germany and hence to the rest of mankind. In order to deepen its empirical knowledge of the people and to make a social science possible it should finally "prompt everybody to write *historiam naturalem* of his own life according to prescribed questionnaires (*interrogatoria*) and make him, as it were, keep a diary".[229]

Though Leibniz was in touch with the intellectual development of all Europe, he gave surprisingly little room to the then modern experimental sciences, favouring instead the collecting, registering type of empiricism. This agrees

---

[227] Gottfried Wilhelm Leibniz, *Grundriß eines Bedenckens von aufrichtung einer Societät in Teutschland zu aufnehmen der Künste und Wißenschafften* (1669); Gottfried Wilhelm Leibniz, *Bedencken von aufrichtung einer Academie oder Societät in Teutschland, zu aufnehmen der Künste und Wißenschaften* (1772), in: *Die Werke von Leibniz, 1. Reihe: Historisch politische und staatswissenschaftliche Schriften,* ed. Onno Klopp, vol 1, Hannover 1864, 111–133; 133–150. See also Brather: 1993.

[228] Schmidt-Biggemann: 1983, ch. III (with further literature).

[229] Leibniz: 1669-1884, 122ff, 125ff.

with contemporary German science, which preferred "a spirit of systematically cataloguing" to "the making of new discoveries".[230] This difference becomes apparent if one compares Graunt's and Petty's "political arithmetic" with the *Notitia rerum publicarum* prepared by Bartholomäus Keckermann in Danzig and inaugurated by Hermann Conring at Helmstädt which was taught from 1660 to future bureaucrats and statesmen at German Protestant universities. As a subject taught to students, this *notitia* was not research-oriented and did not attempt to unveil the secrets of government. It merely digested facts of varying trustworthiness and completeness which were already known.[231] Around 1680, Leibniz outlined a more research-oriented *notitia* in his *Entwurf gewisser Staatstafeln* (Outline of certain state tables) written for the Duke of Hanover. It is the plan for a statistical office, which should use the bureaucracy of enlightened absolutism to make the relevant inquiries and advise the ruler scientifically, informing him at any time "like a telescope" about the real state of his country.[232] This office never came into being, and considering the "totalitarian" aspect of Leibniz's social science, one is tempted to say that this was lucky; like many projects of the great philosopher, and his *scientia generalis* it remained a splendid failure. Yet Leibniz continued to promote his propaganda for scientific societies, and the academies in Berlin (1700), Dresden, Vienna and St. Petersburg refer to his plans, though in reduced scope.

The scientific academies, which continued to be founded in European capitals and even in major provincial cities during the 18th century, bore witness to a *rapprochement* between the "republic of letters" and the state — to the detriment of the churches and church-dominated universities. This opposition subsided well into the 18th century. The academies were the spearheads of the "scientific revolution". They originated from private gatherings of savants — like the circles around Renaudot or Mersenne or Hartlib - which had sought, or on which had been forced, the protection of government. Yet their members remained essentially private persons, free members of the "republic of letters". However, through government protection their research acquired social prestige, financial support, and institutional continuity; theoretical curiosity was thus shielded from ecclesiastic censure.

A certain price had to be paid for these advantages: research in the academies had to avoid politically relevant subjects and focus instead on the "book of nature". This lesson was taught to the founding generation of the academies, e.g. to Petty and Leibniz. The triumphs of the experimental science in

---

[230] Lazarsfeld: 1961, 287.

[231] John: 1884, 52ff, cf also Rassem-Stagl: 1980, 1994, note 57. and ch. one § *Programmes for the improvement of travel.*

[232] Gottfried Wilhelm Leibniz, *Entwurf gewisser Staatstafeln* (1680/85), in *Die Werke von Leibniz*, 1. Reihe: *historisch-politische und staatswissenschaftliche Schriften*, ed Onno Klopp, 5, Hannover 1866; also in Rassem-Stagl: 1994, 321-330.

the late 17th century, the immense prestige of Newton, no doubt had something to do with this taboo. This proved fatal to the dreams of the redemption of mankind through a rational policy directed by scientists.

To a certain extent, however, the governments of "enlightened absolutism" carried on something of that dream themselves. By the end of the 17th century, the more advanced European governments had become infected by a "veritable statistical mania".[233] Inquests by the absolutist governments were numerous and far-reaching; their history has still to be written.[234] They nevertheless contributed little to the progress of the social sciences. Reacting to concrete causes, such inquests were not compared with each other and as secrets of the state they were kept out of public discussion.

Some social research continued to be conducted privately. Originating from opposition among parts of the nobility and bourgeoisie to the absolutist state, it was latently critical of, and suspiciously looked upon by, government.[235] The absolutist state had by its *rapprochement* with the "republic of letters" obtained some control, but not complete control, over the latter. In the second half of the 18th century the educated and upper classes organized themselves into various clubs and circles; patriotic, philanthropic, and agricultural societies, or secret lodges and orders like the Freemasons and Illuminates became common. This international network, the *république des lettres* of the age of Enlightenment, was a revival of the humanist *res publica literaria* which had reasserted itself against confessionalism and absolutism.[236] It also carried on the tradition of utopian meliorism and the collecting, registering type of research connected with it. Following the Inquisition and the influence of the Jesuits, the Freemasons and Illuminates explored their own adherents, interrogating and even spying upon them by means of standardized question lists.[237] This research technique was then employed by the patriotic, philanthropic and agricultural societies, which had many members in common with the secret societies, for the exploration of the living conditions of the poor or common people — a line of research which is considered in the historiography of sociology as the point of departure of modern social research.[238]

---

[233] Esmonin: 1964, 256; cf also Dupâquier-Vilquin: 1978, 85.

[234] Cf however Rassem: 1979.

[235] A good example are the *Tres humbles remonstrances* (Paris 1634) of the lawyer François Guérin. Guérin was a critic of the trade in titles of nobility of the absolutist state. He made inquiries in four communes of Dauphiné and proved with exact data that frequent nobilitations (which implied tax exemption) led to a significant decline in taxable property and in consequence to impoverishment and migration; cf Le Roy Ladurie: 1979, 34ff; cf also Rassem: 1979, 22ff; and Rothkrug: 1965.

[236] Schalk: 1977.

[237] Koselleck: 1959, 49ff.

[238] See ch. six.

There was still one field, however, where collecting and registering re-search with the help of *interrogatoria* could be applied by the scientific academies without endangering secrets of the state. These were the exotic regions. From the foundation of the first scientific academies until the period of the French Revolution, overseas territories, less known areas of Europe and remote corners of western countries were systematically explored under their direction using the traditional information system of the *res publica literaria*. Independent savants gladly cooperated, as it enabled them to achieve political and financial support for their travels, or organization of correspondence networks and, moreover, win fame by publishing their findings in the academy reports — the first scientific periodicals. At least in the field of the remote, the exotic and the quaint, there was no clash of interest between the *res publica literaria*, the state and the churches — for missionary societies and orders continued to work in the same direction. This was another reason for the need of the academies to avoid politically relevant topics: the West became the first great civilization which undertook to explore the whole world systematically to its last nook and cranny.

From its foundation in 1666, the *Académie des Sciences* in Paris es-tablished a far-reaching information system by appointing foreign savants as "corresponding members", a honour much sought after since their names were published annually in the *Almanach Royal*. The *Académie des Sciences* also offered prizes to encourage savants from all regions to submit their works for its judgement.[239] Through its access to the French navy and foreign service, it was able to organize scientific travels on a large scale.[240]

Its rival, the Royal Society in London, went even farther in that direction, especially on the instigation of Petty and Boyle. Its propagandist Thomas Sprat writes:

> "First they require some of their particular Fellows, to examine all Trea-tises, and Descriptions, of the Natural and Artificial Productions of those Countries, in which they would be informed. At the same time, they employ others to discourse with the Seamen, Travellers, Tradesmen, and Merchants, who are likely to give them the best light. Out of this united intelligence from Men and Books, they compose a Body of Questions, concerning all the observable things of those places. These papers being produced in their weekly Assemblies, are augmented, or contracted, as they see occasion. And then the Fellows themselves are wont to undertake their distribution into all Quarters, according as they have the convenience of correspondence."[241]

---

[239] Ornstein: 1963, 139ff; Hahn: 1971, 71; Mandrou: 1973, 207f, 214f.

[240] Faivre: 1966, (with bibliography).

[241] Thomas Sprat, *The History of the Royal Society in London. For the Improving of Natural Knowledge*. London 1667, 155f. Cf also *Op. cit.* 83ff.

Some of these "Bodies of Questions" were published in the *Philosophical Transactions*, the journal of the Royal Society, and thus addressed to the "republic of letters" in general. They concern agriculture, navigation, mining, technology, natural phenomena and geography of little known areas. In the very first issue of the *Philosophical Transactions* (1665), Robert Boyle published *General Heads for a Natural History of a country, great or small*, intended to guide the observations of travellers into such areas. They were re-issued as a small manual in 1692 and became so influential that they were soon plagiarized.[242] Boyle's little book is the first in a long series of manuals for travellers, naturalists and ethnographers written on the instructions of scientific academies which appeared in unbroken succession until the 20th century.[243]

In the generation of Petty and Boyle, the Royal Society was the leader in this kind of research. Thus in 1673 John Ogilby published an *interrogatorium* for a geographical and historical description of England, which was discussed in the Royal Society under the chairmanship of the antiquarian John Aubrey. A comparable questionnaire for Ireland, focusing on the antiquities of that country, was issued in 1684 by William Molyneux on behalf of the "Philosophical Society of Dublin" whose president was Sir William Petty.[244] From 1697, Edward Lhuyd, curator of the Ashmolean Museum and Fellow of the Royal Society, explored the Celtic areas of Wales, Cornwall, the Isle of Man, Ireland, Scotland and Brittany, in person and through correspondence, with the help of question lists aiming at a comprehensive philological-antiquarian description of the Celts.[245]

There were many other comparable researches, on the British Isles and elsewhere, in the 18th century.[246] Yet in the second generation of the scientific academies, the generation of Sir Isaac Newton, they were eclipsed by the rise of the experimental and mathematical sciences. The academies continued, however, to direct and to instruct expeditions into other parts of the world. For European countries, collecting and registering research was carried on by

---

[242] Robert Boyle, *General Heads for a Natural History of a countrey, great or small*, in: *Philosophical Transactions* 1 (1665), 186-189; Robert Boyle, *General Heads for the Natural History of a Country, Great or Small; Drawn out for the use of Travellers and Navigators*. London 1692. Cf Charles-César Baudelot de Dairval, *Mémoire de quelques observations générales, Qu'on peut faire pour ne pas voyager inutilement*. Paris-Bruxelles 1688; Jean-Frédéric Bernard, *Essai d'Instructions Pour Voyager utilement*, in: J.-F. Bernard, *Recueil de voiages au Nord, Contenant divers Mémoirs tres utiles au Commerce & à la Navigation*. 3 vols, Amsterdam 1715-1727, vol. 1, Preface.

[243] See Chapter seven.

[244] Goblet: 1930, 348f.

[245] Edward Lhuyd, *Archaeologia Britannica; an Account of the Languages, Histories, and Customs of Great Britain, from collections and observations in Travels through Wales, Cornwall, Bas-Bretagne, Ireland and Scotland*. London 1707. Cf also Edward Lhuyd, *To promote the work; queries in order to the geography, and antiquities of the country*. Oxford 1691, reprinted in 1961 in *Curiosities of British Archaeology*, compiled by Ronald Jessup, London 1961, 178-179. On Lhuyd (Lhwyd) cf the article in DNB.

[246] Fowler: 1975.

specialized antiquarian academies, such as the *Académie Royale des Inscriptions et Belles-Lettres* in Paris or the Maurists, also in Paris, a congregation of Benedictine monks which was organized as an academy. The Maurists combined their study of the geography, history and institutions of the French regions, which they surveyed by means of "literary tours" and written inquests among the country parsons.[247] This research was, however, in most cases restricted to geography, natural history, antiquities, linguistics, folklore and ethnography, and avoided the social and political aspects.

Yet although public and private research, travels and surveys coordinated by academies or ecclesiastic institutions, were thus imperfectly interconnected, empirical knowledge of European and extra-European countries and peoples advanced slowly but continuously during the early modern period. This advancement was at first hardly visible on the intellectual surface but in the Age of Enlightenment, public and private, academic and ecclesiastic research into cultural, social and political reality began to merge. The time was ripe for a "leap from quantity to quality", for the coming into being of the new disciplines of anthropology, sociology, and political science.

---

[247] Heer: 1938, 1ff, 419; Esmonin: 1964, 279. Cf the questionnaire of Dom Jacques Louis Lenoir, *Mémoire Relatif au Projet d'une Histoire Générale de la Province de Normandie.* Rouen 1760.

CHAPTER THREE

Imagines Mundi: Allegories Of The Continents In The Baroque And The Enlightenment

"They know and do not know, that acting is suffering
And suffering is action. Neither does the actor suffer
Nor the patient act. But both are fixed
In an eternal action, an eternal patience
To which all must consent that it may be willed,
And which all must suffer that they may will it,

That the pattern may subsist..."

(T.S. Eliot: *Murder in the Cathedral*)

IMAGINES MUNDI

Figures of different racial-ethnic type, attired in characteristic garb and carrying telling attributes, were a highly popular theme in early modern art. They served as representations of the continents. Often they were arranged in groups and in their mutual attitudes expressed the relationship between the continents, Europe of course being shown in a privileged position. These allegories of the world and its parts were called "cosmographies" or "*imagines mundi*".[1] So well-known was this theme, that it often was also included in larger allegorical programmes as a standard element. Such "general cosmological programmes", as they have been called,[2] were artistic expressions of the claim to universal domination or universal significance which was raised in early modern times by several powers or institutions in the West, such as the Holy Roman Empire, the Papacy, the missions and scientific academies. They all made use of allegories of the continents in their iconography. Yet when in the late 18th century the West really had achieved world domination, this artistic fashion petered out "with an almost amazing suddenness".[3]

In the following pages, two pictures will be interpreted, whose programmes centre on *imagines mundi*. Both are frontispieces for German travel

---

[1] Cf. these entries in Henkel-Schöne: 1967; cf. also Köllmann-Wirth: 1967 and Schramm: 1928.

[2] Krempel: 1973, 6.

[3] Köllmann-Wirth: 1967, col. 1160.

books.[4] Early modern books often carried allegorical frontispieces which anticipated their basic thoughts like an overture does the basic themes of an opera. The
frontispiece thus *visualized* the structure of the book by means of a conventional
set of imagery which was "principally ambiguous".[5] and could therefore be used
to *condense* thoughts that would need much more space and time if expounded
in the form of a discourse. The frontispiece thus *captivated the attention* of
the reader, like a pleasurable enigma waiting to be solved by him. To the
modern reader, who no longer recognises their imagery, these allegories are
hardly comprehensible. In their juxtaposition of incongruent elements they
appear almost surrealistic. Here the programmes of the said two frontispieces
will be spelt out to the modern reader. This is at the same time a plea to historians
of the social sciences to consider also pictorial sources, something they have been
rather slow to do, probably regarding them as irrelevant.[6]

The first frontispiece dates from 1674, the second from 1745. Between
those two dates, the general conception of the world and its place in the universe
had changed. The accepted conception of the "closed cosmos", which had been
adopted by Christianity from the science of antiquity and which saw the universe
as a self-contained, majestic edifice in which man also had his proper place,
had been replaced in the minds of the educated by the conception of an "open
universe". In this conception, also rooted in antiquity and propagated by early
modern science, nothing was forever fixed and man had a marginal position.[7]
After this had become common lore, an intellectual crisis set in; relativistic doubt
was cast on the foundations of Western culture and society.[8] In order to master
this crisis, the educated public looked to science as the new guiding star; from
now on science had to give intellectual *and* moral direction to mankind.[9] The
Age of Enlightenment had set in.

The two frontispieces, representing general cosmological programmes,
are thus convenient examples of the old and new conception of the world. They
are, however, in other respects remarkably similar and they obviously belong to
the same artistic tradition. These similarities as well as the differences make their
comparison rewarding. However a word of caution has to be raised in advance.
In the following interpretation, the second frontispiece will be treated as if it
were directly dependent on the first and had, so to speak, only adapted it to
the changed mentality. This assumption cannot be proven, but is supported by

---

[4] Found whilst I was looking through German travel literature at the Herzog August Bibliothek
Wolfenbüttel. I thank the Herzog August Bibliothek for permission to reproduce them.

[5] Klemm: 1979, 151.

[6] The only other comparable interpretation of an allegorical frontispiece in the social sciences I
know of is Certeau: 1985.

[7] Koyré: 1957. See also Blumenberg: 1975.

[8] Hazard: 1961.

[9] Tenbruck: 1989, part II, 9.

the fact that the two *imagines mundi*, though dating from different periods, were contemporary on the German book market, the first even being re-engraved eight years after the appearance of the second.[10] The similarity between both allegories could also be explained by their belonging to a common artistic tradition. Which explanation is more plausible is a question to be decided by an art historian. The treatment of the two pictures by a historian of the social sciences as *examples* of intellectual tendencies is not directly affected by it.

AN *IMAGO MUNDI* OF THE BAROQUE

The first frontispiece, dating from 1674, adorns a book of travel called *Welt-Beschauung* ("Inspection of the World"). The author, Georg Christoph von Neitzschitz, was a Saxonian nobleman who had toured the Ottoman Empire between 1630 and 1637. He died soon after his return to Saxonia, leaving behind a manuscript describing his travels. This manuscript was edited 25 years later, on behalf of Neitschitz's brother, by Christoph Jäger, a learned clergyman. The first edition, which appeared in 1663, was an immediate success; the book was re-edited several times until 1753. This was when the frontispiece was re-engraved.[11]

Originally, the frontispiece of the *Welt-Beschauung* was much simpler than represented here, containing only the allegory within the central circle and above it. The present form was reached in an edition from 1674 in Nürnberg, when the allegory of the continents was added and some changes were made to the central allegory in order to include it in a general cosmological programme. It was retained in this form in all subsequent editions. It is a rather impressive, well considered work of art, and looks as if it had always existed as one piece. Unfortunately the artist is unknown. It is reproduced here from the re-engraving for the 1753 edition by Johann Gottfried Krügner jnr., a well-known draughtsman from Leipzig.[12]

---

[10] Cf. note 12.

[11] There exists no study on Neitzschitz and his *Welt-Beschauung*. For the author see Beckmann: 1807, vol. I, 234; Zedler's *Universal-Lexicon*, vol. 23, col. 1667–1670; Jöcher-Rotermund: *Gelehrten-Lexico*, vol. 23, col. 471. The bibliography of the book is not completely clear. Röhricht: 1963, mentions a first edition which he says appeared in Bautzen 1663, which he, however, has not seen himself and which I too could not trace. I could not examine the 2nd (or 1st) ed. Bautzen 1666 either. I did, however, examine the 3rd (or 2nd) ed. (*Des weilant Hoch Edlen Herrn Georgen Christophs von Neitzschitz Sieben Jährige und gefährliche WELT-BESCHAUUNG. Also beschrieben und in Druck gegeben von M. Christoph Jägern zu S. Afra und der Churf. S. berühmten Landschul daselbst Past. Prim.* Bautzen 1673, 4 to) and all subsequent editions. These are: Nürnberg 1674, Würzburg 1678, Nürnberg 1686 and Magdeburg 1753.

[12] Johann Gottfried Krügner jnr. (1714–1782) was employed by Leipzig publishers as an engraver of writing, notes and vignettes. Cf. Thieme-Becker, vol. 27, 1.

FIGURE 8: Frontispiece of Georg Christoph von Neitzschitz: *Welt-Beschauung*, Magdeburg 1753. By courtesy of the Herzog August Bibliothek, Wolfenbüttel.

There are three levels in this picture: (1) the foreground, (2) the circle in the centre as "picture in the picture" and (3) suspended above it, the view of a city. Three male figures are contained in the foreground. They represent the three continents visited by the author during his travels; Europe, Asia, and Africa. The printed title of the book[13] is included in the frontispiece; it is not very conspicuous but is referred to by the imagery on all three levels.

The globe is supported by an Atlas-like figure. He is Negroid, draped with strings of coral beads, but otherwise naked with the exception of a loin-cloth. By his side crouches a lion and below him is a banderole carrying the following motto, "*Ich, als Barbar halt mich schlecht*" ("I, as a barbarian, have a bad posture"). Under the burden of the world he carries, he almost sinks down. Left and right, or rather east and west of this world, two other figures are standing, balancing it with their hands, as if they were taking possession of it. These are the Sultan and the Holy Roman Emperor, the two monarchs claiming universal domination in Asia and in Europe. In contrast to the black Atlas, they have no attributive animal, but instead are richly dressed, armoured and carrying their regalia. Thus they embody civilization and political order in contrast to the state of nature displayed in primitive man.[14]

The Sultan wears a caftan and a turban with tufts of heron's feathers and wields a scimitar (these were Ottoman regalia). The Emperor wears armour, ermine, the Golden Fleece and the old crown of the Holy Roman Empire. He carries a sceptre and a sword. It is strange that among the imperial regalia which should have been familiar to an artist in the ancient imperial city of Nürnberg, where they actually were preserved, the orb is lacking. On closer examination, however, one realizes that the whole world, with the superimposed view of the heavenly city, can be seen as an orb, which the Emperor holds in his hand, but to which the Sultan also lays claim. This is indeed an ingenious artistic solution. *Both* emperors claim world-domination with equal force, but only for *one* of them, the Holy Roman Emperor, is it rightfully a part of his regalia. Hence there is an inequality hidden behind the strict axial symmetry of the foreground which is strikingly apparent.

In the composition, the scimitar of the Sultan (a weapon) corresponds exactly to the sceptre of the Emperor (a symbol of peaceful domination). Equally, the mottos of the two emperors written on banderoles placed above them,

---

[13] In many early modern books, the basic idea was expressed simultaneously on three levels: (1) the printed title (which was often elaborate and a typographical work of art), (2) the allegorical frontispiece and (3) the discursive text. One could compare them to three stages of growth: seed, embryo, full-grown form.

[14] Since classical times, Africa was personified by a scantily dressed Black figure adorned with coral beads and accompanied by a lion. Asia and Europe were more richly dressed. In early modern cosmographies, Africa is shown in a subservient attitude, Asia and Europe in a dominating attitude. Cf. Köllmann-Wirth: 1967, col. 1174 and the entries *Africa* and *Asia* in *Lexicon Iconographicum Mythologiae Classicae*. (1981ff), vol. I, 250–255, vol. II, 857–859.

correspond. Moreover, they rhyme in German with each other and with the motto of the black Atlas. The Sultan's motto says *"Wen ich zwing mach ich zum Knecht"* (Whoever I conquer shall be my slave); that of the Emperor says: *"Mir gebühret sie mit Recht"* (To me the world belongs by right).

In these mottos, a theory is tersely expressed, which had influenced Western political thought since Herodotus and Aristotle: the theory of oriental despotism. This theory opposes the oriental polities, where the rulers are absolute masters and the ruled are slaves, to the occidental polities, where domination is based on the higher principle of a common law binding rulers and ruled alike.[15] This theory was very prevalent during the 16th and 17th centuries, when the West was severely menaced by the Ottoman empire.[16] It was still topical when the present frontispiece was contrived. Only nine years later, in 1683, a Turkish army again besieged Vienna, the Imperial capital. Orient and Occident, Sultan and Emperor, are therefore shown as opponents of equal rank struggling for the possession of the world, a world in which the black Atlas, representing the barbarian peoples without proper institutions, is condemned to everlasting slavery.

These three figures carry or hold the central globe from the outside. Its circle sharply demarcates another sphere of meaning. It is not brutal force that governs herein, but morality. Here we observe an allegory of human toil and salvation. Here the life of man on earth is represented as a pilgrimage. In a landscape adorned with churches and castles a man struggles toilsomely uphill. He carries no symbols of social status, but instead wears a pilgrim's garb and leans on a pilgrim's staff. He is not just a man, he is Man himself, the allegorical representative of mankind, weighed down by the burden of misery and sin. From the west a soldier is aiming at him with his rifle, from the east a horned and cloven-hoofed devil is watching him intently. These figures convey the impression of lurking danger. Warrior and tempter personify the corporal and the mental threats to Man during his earthly pilgrimage, whereas castles and churches symbolize the temporal and the spiritual powers protecting and supporting him.

This toilsome and terrible world has, however, an exit at its top. The path of the pilgrim leads upwards after all, and it leads in the direction of the house of God. High up, just at the exit of the circle, Man is shown for a second time, this time as the human soul after death. Depicted as a naked, innocent child, the soul soars between the hands of God, reaching from the clouds to present it with the palm of victory and the crown of life towards the transfigured Christ and upwards into heavenly Jerusalem. Two pairs of banderoles accompany and explain its ascent. They are arranged in the form of a cross. Their messages again

---

[15] Aristotle, *Politics* I (1225b). Cf. Richter: 1973 and Introduction § *Empiricism versus Science*.

[16] Bohnstedt: 1968; Göllner: 1978.

rhyme in German. They are: *Von der Last – Zu der Rast* (From burden to rest) and *Diss zum Lohn – Sammt der Kron* ["This (the palm of victory) as a reward — together with the crown (of life)"]. The palm of victory and the crown of life are traditional emblems of merit and grace. They refer to the well-known biblical passage: "Blessed is the man that endureth temptation: for when he is tried, he shall receive the crown of life" (James 1, 12 cf. also 2 Tim. 4, 8 and Revelation 2, 10).[17] The figure of Christ comes from an illuminated city poised in the air. This is heavenly Jerusalem, whose bastions are guarded by angels. In its center, Christ is also shown for a second time, as the lamb of God who takes away the sins of the world standing on a hill amidst an aureola.

This politico-theological imagery is a striking example of the so-called "Protestant inwardness". Access to the kingdom of heaven is open to everybody individually, not mediated through the church, but through Christ. The drama of temptation and salvation thus takes place inside every man. Thus, the interior of the globe also represents the interior of the human soul. But this demarcated

---

[17] For the special motifs of this allegory, such as life as a pilgrimage, palm of victory, crown of life, hand from the clouds, tempter, and heavenly Jerusalem, cf. Henkel and Schöne 1967 under the respective entries. On the pilgrimage of life see Ladnev: 1967. This moral allegory was the main theme of the original frontispiece. It showed the circle of the world and the heavenly city above. Allegorical Man is shown as a pilgrim in a landscape, on whose way snakes and scorpions are strewn by a horned, tailed, winged and cloven-hoofed devil. There are no castles and no warriors and only one church. Then Man is shown again after death, as an adult, dressed man, but without burden or a pilgrim's staff, soaring up to heaven. One hand from the clouds offers him the crown of life. There are two banderoles, one below, saying *Von Mühe* (from toil), the other above, saying *Zur Ruhe* (to rest). The printed title is also contained on a banderole underneath the circle of the world. This allegory is explained by a poem:

Erklärung des Kupffer-Titul-Blats.

Diss Leben gleichet sich der Wanderschafft auf Erden/ Die Müh und ungemach/Gefahr und voll Beschwerden. Wer Himmel-auf gedenckt/der muss durch Dornen gehn Und unters Teuffels-Bruth von Ungezieffer stehn. Wer selig stirbt/der geht und schreitet aus dem Leiden Mit breitem sichern Fuss dort auf den Pfad der Freuden/ Geht hin auf Rosen fort zur Himmels-Freuden-Stadt/ Da Gott ihm Ehr und Cron lägst beygeleget hat. Drumb fort; nur hurtig fort von überhäuffter Mühe Hinauff geschritten fort zur ewig stoltzen Ruhe/Da Christi Mittler-hand nimmt auf und weiset ein. Es muss ein saurer Tritt darnach gewaget seyn.

There is no doubt that this poem – which does not belong to the summits of German Baroque lyric – is from the pen of the editor Christoph Jäger, to whom the programme of this moral allegory is also to be attributed. Jäger thus reinterprets the voyage of G. Chr. v. Neitzschitz, which had also included a pilgrimage to Jerusalem, in an edifying way as the pilgrimage of Man's life. Later editors have retained Jäger's *Erklärung*, although it no longer really corresponded to this enlarged allegory of the frontispiece. Only Gottfried Vetter in Magdeburg, the last publisher of the "*Welt-Beschauung*" (1753), dispensed with this poem, which was no doubt no longer in keeping with the prevailing taste, and instead added maps and further illustrations to the book, making it thus look more "scientific". The new version of the frontispiece appeared with the edition Nürnberg 1674 (cf. note 11). It differs from the old one on the following points: (1) the parallelism between spiritual and temporal power is elaborated; (2) in connection with this, the composition has gained symmetry; (3) the devil has become less conspicuous, most probably because he could thus be contrasted with the newly appeared warrior; (4) the soul of man has been changed from an adult man into a child; (5) the cruciform structure of the four banderoles above the circle of the world has been added; and (6) Emperor, Sultan and black Atlas have been added to personify the three continents visited by Neitzschitz. Generally speaking, this new version reinterprets Jäger's morally edifying allegory of the pilgrimage of life again as a description of a real voyage.

FIGURE 9: Frontispiece of *Der reisende Deutsche*, s.l. 1745. By courtesy of the Herzog August Bibliothek, Wolfenbüttel.

sphere of moral meaning is surrounded by physical space, where not the law of God, but the laws of nature, that is laws of brutal force, are effective. The moral sphere is, moreover, placed precisely at the intersection of the two axes of physical space. The horizontal axis represents the to and fro of the struggle for political power. Here the emperors of the east and the west confront each other over the head of the powerless barbarian. The vertical axis represents the history of salvation, which, in contrast to political history, is a story of continuous ascent. It starts with the heathen barbarian, who does not know the word of God, though Christ had died for him too (aptly symbolized by his being the only figure in the foreground who reaches with his head into the inner, moral world). This line of ascent then leads, through countless dangers and temptations, to the mediator figure of Christ, who beckons Man into heavenly Jerusalem, where there is everlasting rest. Though sharply demarcated in the lower two thirds of the picture, the physical and the moral sphere converge in the upper third in order to give way to the religious sphere.

AN *IMAGO MUNDI* OF THE ENLIGHTENMENT

The second frontispiece inaugurated a yearbook with the title *Der reisende Deutsche* ("The Travelling German"). This periodical aimed to extract the most curious and interesting facts from the travel literature each year in order to present them to an enlightened public. The idea was roughly the same as that of a "Reader's Digest." But in spite of that, this yearbook was not a success. Even an introduction from the pen of the well-known historian and statistician, Martin Schmeitzel,[18] was of no avail. A second volume of "The Travelling German" never appeared.

The first and only volume, together with its frontispiece, was published in 1745. The engraver was Friedrich Schönemann of Leipzig, who is now regarded as a "very mediocre craftsman".[19] A closer look at the picture confirms this judgement. Not only the draughtsmanship, but also the design are decidedly inferior to those of the first frontispiece (the engraver, however, was in most cases not responsible for the design). The pictorial programme, on the other hand, is well considered and certainly allows comparison with that of the first frontispiece.

---

[18] The full title is *"Der reisende Deutsche im Jahre 1744, welcher Länder und Städte beschreibt, auch die alten und neuen Städte-Begebenheiten bekannt macht. Mit einer Vorrede Herrn Martin Schmeitzels"*. s.l. 1745, 8vo. Martin Schmeitzel, a native of Transsylvania, was professor of public law and history at Jena and Halle and one of the prominent representatives of German "university statistics". Cf. Hiller: 1937, 136ff. Schmeitzel could well have been responsible for the programme of this frontispiece.

[19] *Er gehört zu den ganz mittelmäßigen Arbeitern.* (Georg Kaspar Nagler, *Künstler-Lexikon*, vol. 15, 468. Cf. also Thieme-Becker, vol. 30, 225.

The composition, the personnel and the inventory in both are almost the same, but the overall impression is very different. One could almost think that the elements of the first frontispiece had been jumbled up and been differently put together. Only the central circle representing the earth has remained in the same place. The main explanation for the different overall impression is a rotation of the two axes of the picture. These no longer run horizontally and vertically, but diagonally; forming no longer a cross, but an X. The solemn symmetrical arrangement has disappeared too, as have the explanations through mottos and banderoles. The Baroque has been transformed into Rococo.

The allegorical figures have stepped out of their hierarchically arranged places and have dispersed agreeably over the foreground of the picture. There are neither emperors nor slaves, but rather citizens of the world. The European is dressed à la mode, wearing justaucorps, escarpins and lace cuffs. The exoticism of the Turk has been toned down, in order to make him appear more pleasant. He now looks almost as if he came from an opera by Mozart. In place of the one barbarian, we now have two savages. The African has been joined by an American, who wears lip pegs, a poncho and a feather crown. These are the conventional attributes of America in the iconography of the continents.[20] Compared to the European and the Turk, these two noble savages are somewhat more scantily and informally dressed. They are deeply involved in a discussion. What could their discussion be about? Most probably on the great theme of the blessing and curse of civilization, a theme which at that time had been dealt with brilliantly by Montesquieu.[21] The Asiatic points gracefully with his forefinger to the circle of the earth, which the European touches with both hands apparently less to dominate it than to explore it.

The circle of the earth is empty. The allegory of human temptation and salvation has disappeared from its interior, as indeed has everything pictorial. To make up for that, it has been transformed from a circle into a globe. In other words, what in the first frontispiece had been the *world* has now become the *earth*. On this globe are inscribed the names of the four continents: from top to bottom these are Europe, Asia, Africa and America. Is this mere coincidence or is it a ranking list?

Has the allegory of man as a pilgrim on earth completely disappeared? I think not. Most probably it has only changed its appearance and its place in the picture. In the second frontispiece, allegorical Man has left the moral-religious sphere and stepped out into the physical world in order to join the representatives of the four continents. Now he sits in the foreground of the picture, in the guise of a secretary, half covering the Asiatic. With powdered

---

[20] Köllmann-Wirth: 1967, col. 1177ff.

[21] Charles-Louis de Secondat, Baron de Montesquieu, *Lettres Persanes*. Amsterdam 1721 (originally anonymous). Cf. Hazard: 1961, 11ff.

hair and modestly clad in black, he is ready to note down eagerly with his quill the investigations and conversations of the four gentlemen. Various scientific utensils are scattered, in picturesque disarray, around him: books, compasses, a set square, a telescope and a celestial globe. While all these are traditional attributes of Europe,[22] here they are related to all continents alike. The new aim in life, which the Enlightenment assigned to all mankind, is that Science replace Salvation.

The emptiness noticeable in the circle of the earth is even more obvious in the heaven above. The most striking impression of this picture is indeed the emptiness of its upper third. Where might heavenly Jerusalem, which occupied the heavens in the earlier frontispiece, have gone? Again, it has not completely disappeared. Like allegorical Man, it has merely come down in the order of being and in the composition of the picture, for on the upper left side of the foreground there looms a fortified city.[23] The emptiness of the heaven is indeed so awkward, that for merely aesthetic reasons the title of the book had to be put in its centre. Thus where in the earlier frontispiece heavenly Jerusalem with its towers guarded by angels had shone, we now read the three very prosaic words "The Travelling German".

However, emptying the moral-religious sphere has not altogether abolished the allegory. It has, as it were, gone underground, hiding behind a secular screen. The three levels distinguished in the earlier frontispiece, foreground, central globe, and heaven above, are also present in this one. The heaven is empty, but this too conveys a message. As before, the globe is sharply demarcated, but this does not represent the dualism between the inner, moral, and the outward, physical nature of man. Rather, all men on this picture confront the globe from the outside, as subjects confront objects, in order to explore and to dominate them.

No doubt these philosophical citizens of the world do not carry arms. But this does not mean that arms have disappeared from the picture. On the contrary: in the left foreground there is a stack of cannon-balls and, on the right, mingled among the scientific utensils, one can see pieces of armour. Higher up, under the walls of the fortified city that were probably once was heavenly Jerusalem, two battles are raging; to the left, on land, to the right, on sea. The two diagonal axes, that give the composition of this picture its basic structure, lead precisely from the parts of armour to the land battle and from the cannon-balls to the sea battle.

---

[22] Köllmann-Wirth: 1967, col. 1177ff.

[23] The interpretation of this city as the secularized new Jerusalem depends of course on the assumption that the second frontispiece directly varies the first. This cannot be proven. So whoever does not share this assumption is free to see just a walled city in it. But would not in this case a mere battle on land have wholly sufficed to parallel the battle at sea on the right hand side? Why should it have to take place under the walls of a city, for which there is no other explanation? Mere chance? Just thoughtlessness of the draughtsman? I cannot bring myself to believe in these alternatives.

This pell-mell of knowledge and war is by no means fortuitous, for the exploration and domination of the world are linked.[24] Knowledge here is paralleled with physical force, just as in the earlier picture spiritual power had been with temporal power. But it is significant that, in the younger picture, this interdependence is located in the world of things, not of man. War, knowledge, and indeed the mutual relationship of the four continents have evolved into a self-regulating system, which is beyond the control of all participants. Since all men, actors and sufferers alike, have become involved in the dynamics of this system, they have become principally *equal*. If there are hierarchies, they are only temporary. In 1745, Europe is the most powerful and enlightened continent. Previously it had been Asia. But the globe will continue to rotate, and the ranked list of the continents inscribed on it could thereby become inverted. Could America, now the last on the list, thereby become the first?[25] The Asian is pointing, probably intentionally, with his finger to the name America.

The change of positions in the personifications of the continents between the first and the second frontispiece is not fortuitous. Now it is Africa-America and Asia, who are standing to the left and to the right of the globe. This means that the Turk, the most formidable rival of the European until 70 years before, is now put by the latter on an equal footing with the savages. The decline of Ottoman power, and the ascent of the West to world domination, could not be more strikingly expressed. The European is now shown in a singular, privileged position against these exotic figures: it is he who has taken over the position of the Atlas, who, however, does not carry the world, but seizes it.

CONCLUSION

What does all this prove? Strictly speaking it proves nothing at all. It is just an interpretation of two pictures which might or might not have had a historical connection. But they are convenient examples of the change which took place in the self-conception of Europe *vis-à-vis* the other parts of the world in connection with the supersedence of the old Christian conception "closed cosmos" by the new scientific[26] conception "open universe". Somewhat surprising in this respect is the rather early date of the second picture. At a time when the West was asserting its world domination and Western science was marching from triumph to triumph, it announced the principal equality of all men and expressed scepticism whether European supremacy would be durable. This might have had something to do with its nature as a German picture, Germany

---

[24] See the preceding chapters of this book.

[25] The idea that civilization travels from East to West following the course of the sun (*ex oriente lux!*) was well known in Europe at least since Otto von Freising, cf. Thyssen, 1960, 20.

[26] See note 7.

being at that time marginal to the dynamics of Western culture and too divided to undertake serious colonial ventures.

It would be presumptuous to draw a definite inference from the discussion of only two examples, but it is probably worthwhile to attach a few loosely connected thoughts:

EUROPE AS A CONTINENT

The most basic concept of a continent seems to be that of a land mass having a particular climate, natural products and inhabitants, and demarcated by natural boundaries. The inhabitants, however different among themselves, are thought to be similar enough to set them off in physique, manners and customs, religion and political organization from those of other continents. Thus bridging nature and culture, the concept of the continents is a convenient device to pre-structure experience of the world and to classify pertaining observations.

This is a very old concept, dating back to the first millennium BC or beyond and stemming from the eastern Mediterranean. Biblical, Phoenician and Greek geography knew a *tripartition* of the *oikouméne* corresponding to the southern, eastern and northern shores of the Mediterranean and their hinterlands. The Greeks symbolized it by three mythological-allegorical figures, Europe, Asia and Libye (later called Africa by the Romans).[27] In the course of three millennia, the hinterlands of these three shores, and the conceptions of *continents* applied to them, were extended until they reached their boundaries in the Atlantic, the Indian and the Pacific oceans.

In the course of this extension, the natural-cultural boundary between Asia and Africa proved to be continuous, whereas that between Asia and Europe behind the Black Sea was indeterminate. So why was the traditional tripartition carried on? What reasons were there to oppose the eastern and western parts of the great Eurasiatic land mass as a separate continent?

The reason was obviously historical. "Europe" distinguished itself from "Asia" on the basis of its common Greek-Christian-Roman heritage.[28] "Asia" being thus negatively defined as a residual category. Thus, Europe is actually a self-invented continent. The subsequent inclusion of the eastern and southern parts

---

[27] Europe, Asia and Libye are juxtaposed on equal footing for the first time in Pindar (Pyth. IX, 8); cf. Thomson: 1948, 21. The first geographers making use of this tripartition were Hecataeus of Miletus and Herodotus of Halicarnassus (who both considered the Nile, and not the Red Sea, to be the frontier between Asia and Africa). Cf the entries *Africa, Asia, Europe* and *Libye* in RE; cf. also Fritz: 1971, 28f. This tripartition seems to go back to the Ancient Near East. The chart of the peoples of the *oikouméne* in the Old Testament is arranged according to the three stocks of Shem, Japhet and Ham, which obviously correspond to the three continents Asia, Europe, and Africa (I. Mose 5:32, 6:10). The geographical thinking of the Greeks was deeply influenced by the Ancient Near East. The names *Europe* and *Asia* have Phoenician origins (Müller: 1972-80, vol. I, 48, 55.

[28] Jaeckle: 1988; Braudel: 1988; Isensee: 1993.

of the ancient Mediterranean *oikouméne* into the world of Islam emphasized European singularity even further with regard to Asia and Africa.

The traditional tripartition was finally globalized by the "European miracle".[29] From the 15th century onwards, the Western *oikouméne* continuously expanded until it had absorbed all other *oikouménes*. It was then that the concept of the continents gained new importance: it allowed the West to digest its experiences of hitherto unknown parts of the world. The assimilation of culture to nature, which is contained in the idea of the continents, was used in the theory of the "climates," prominently expounded by Bodin and Montesquieu, to explain human variability.[30] The idea of the particular nature of all inhabitants of one continent was condensed into the idea of "race," the races being identified by the highly symbolic characteristic of skin colour[31] which was also used in pictorial art. The importance of the continents for early modern thought explains why allegorical representations of them loomed so large in early modern art.

Due to the European expansion "new" continents had to be added to the three traditional ones. The concept of the continents proved to be expandable too. After some discussion, the inhabited land mass discovered to the west of Europe was recognized in around 1500 as a separate continent. It was named *America*, after one of the geographers participating in this discussion. This new continent also acquired symbolical attributes. Hence four continents appear on most early modern *imagines mundi*.[32] There are comparatively few of them showing five continents, *Australia* only being recognized as a separate continent around 1770, by which time this artistic fashion was already in decline[33] and the continents were beginning to be conceived in a more scientific way. *Australia* was named, not after a mythological or historical person, but after an abstract principle; its position in the southern half of the globe.

The naming of the continents is also significant in a further aspect. America and Australia are placed by means of alliteration on the same footing as Asia and Africa. Europe, the only continent not beginning with the letter A, stands out conspicuously among them. The self-invented continent thereby stressed its singularity. The concept of the continents bridges nature and culture, but in Asia, Africa, America and Australia it was nature that prevailed, in Europe it was culture.

COSMOS AND SYSTEM

The idea of the continents also implies that of the *world*. Continents can only be conceived in *contrastive relationships* to one another. Together they

---

[29] Jones: 1981.

[30] Zacharasiewicz: 1977.

[31] Poliakov: 1974.

[32] Köllmann-Wirth: 1967, col. 1177ff.

[33] *Loc. cit.*

form a *cosmos*, a whole made up by the continuous interplay of divergent parts in conformity with immutable laws.[34] The concept of the cosmos, which Babylonian science passed on to the Greeks and Greek science passed on to Western science, is clearly connected with the social realities of an *oikouméne* made up of different political-cultural units locked in permanent confrontation with each other. The conditions of an *oikouméne* also occasioned the emergence of the concept of *mankind*.[35]

Although known to ancient geography and, since Polybios, ancient historiography, the idea of the cosmos did not loom large in ancient art. There are apparently no *groups*, showing representatives of the continents in interaction. The evolution of cosmographies in early modern times clearly demonstrates that the feeling that the world was one regardless of natural and cultural boundaries was becoming part of the contemporary mentality stimulated by the rise of the West. However different in their programme, the majority of early modern cosmographies expressed the world view of the closed cosmos. Much rarer, and later, were cosmographies hinting at the infinite universe. Our second frontispiece is an early example of this "open" view.

During the 17th century, the concept of the cosmos was gradually replaced by the concept of the system.[36] Both refer to wholes composed of interacting parts, but in the case of the cosmos, the static (or repetitive) *structure* is stressed, while in the case of the system it is the dynamic (or entropic) *functioning*. The concept of the system meant a decentralization of the traditional cosmos. This had been *one* majestic edifice, in which every thing had its appropriate place according either to the immutable law of nature or to the equally immutable will of God. This is why allegorical thinking so closely corresponded to the world view of the closed cosmos. In allegory, things exist not only as themselves, but also have *meanings*, that is a structural reference to certain other aspects of reality. This is why allegories of the infinite universe are scarce: both concepts are intrinsically opposed to one another. An infinite universe comprises an indeterminate number of systems developing according to their own laws, forever drawing closer to or farther from each other. Hence, the allegory has to be replaced by a systems theory.[37]

THE NATURALIZATION OF THE ALLEGORY

It was this transition from cosmos to system which made allegorical thinking wither. The transition was slow and was finally achieved only at the turn of the 19th century. It found its expression in what may be called the naturalization

---

[34] Kranz: 1939. Cf also Introduction § *The Ancient Near East*.

[35] Tenbruck: 1989.

[36] Cf. note 7.

[37] Jonas: 1981, vol. 1.

of the allegory. From the Baroque to the Enlightenment, naturalistic description came to the fore in allegories. The world of symbolic meanings was receding and the "world of things" advancing.[38] Meaning was still there, but it was increasingly hidden behind things pretending to be just themselves. In allegories of the continents attributes that were deemed characteristic for each continent from all three realms of nature — minerals, plants and animals - as well as from the realm of culture — apparel, adornment, weapons and other ethnographica - were lovingly depicted in arrangements resembling the contemporary "chambers of curiosities."[39]

Our second frontispiece exemplifies this tendency rather modestly. It better exemplifies the related tendency for the allegory to go "underground". This was the last stage of a time-honoured tradition. At the end of the 18th century, allegorical frontispieces began to appear fatuous to the public, their splendid imagery being considered irrelevant to scientific truth. Imagery was relegated from the world of knowledge to the world of art. The typical 19th century frontispiece became a portrait of the author, accompanied with a facsimile of his signature. These were irreproachably objective representations, but at the same time hidden allegories of the mind and the hand that had created the book. A later stage still was the choice of one illustration deemed to be "characteristic" of the book as a frontispiece. All this now seems old-fashioned to us and contemporary scholarly or scientific works no longer display frontispieces.

---

[38] *Vordringen der Dingwelt weit über das attributiv Notwendige hinaus* (Klemm: 1979, 151).

[39] Hodgen: 1964, 111ff. See also notes 65 and 70 to ch. two of the present book.

CHAPTER FOUR

The Man Who Called Himself George Psalmanazar or: The Problem of the Authenticity of Ethnographic Description

"C'est le charme des êtres nouveaux que cet espoir de transformer pour eux, en le niant, un passé que l'ou eût voulu plus heureux"

André Maurois, *Climats* I, 1

"quid rides? mutato nomine de te fabula narratur..."

(Q. Horatius Flaccus, Serm I 1, 69—70).[1]

A DESCRIPTION OF FORMOSA

The island of Formosa was almost unheard of in Europe in the early years of the 18th century. The Dutch had gained a footing there but had been driven out again by the Chinese. A short ethnographic description by Georgius Candidius, pastor to the Dutch garrison, was all that was known to the reading public of Formosa's inhabitants.[2] Yet in 1704 a book called *An Historical and Geographical Description of Formosa, An Island Subject to the Emperor of Japan. Giving an Account of the Religion, Customs, Manners etc of the Inhabitant* was published in London. Its author bore the unusual name George Psalmanaazaar, "a native of that island".[3]

---

[1] I had already placed this motto in front of the first draft of this chapter when I discovered that Psalmanazar himself had used it in his *Dialogue between a Japanese and a Formosan* (see note 27).

[2] For the history of Formosa in the 17th century and European knowledge of the island cf. Imbault-Huard: 1893, XIXff and Campbell: 1903. Candidius' report is from 1628. It was printed under the title "*Kurtze beschreibung der Insel Formosa*" in Hulsius: 1649, 33–47. An English translation appeared in 1704 (*An Account of the Island of Formosa*, in Churchill: 1704, vol. I, 526–553). This English translation came too late to have influenced Psalmanazar's plan to pose as a Formosan; he had, however, to take issue with it when he published his imaginary description of Formosa, as will be shown below.

[3] In the title he is called "A Native of the said Island, now in London".

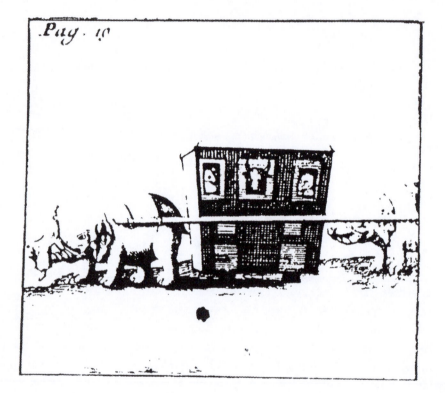

FIGURE 10: "'Formosan' sedan chair, carried by elephants. From: George Psalmanazar: *Description de l'isle Formosa*....., Amsterdam 1705. By courtesy of the British Library, London.

Though presenting a comprehensive ethnography of the island, covering history, government, religion and rituals, manners and customs, physical appearance, clothes, habitations, commodities, weights and measures, food, natural produce, language, writing, education, weapons, musical instruments, liberal and mechanical arts, the text focuses on the religion of the Formosans. This religion is said originally to have consisted simply of the worship of heavenly bodies, connected with maxims of natural law. But a prophet, on whom the people bestowed the honorific name "Psalmanaazaar", meaning "creator of peace", developed this paganism further into monotheism. The religion instituted by this prophet with its Holy Writ, its temple containing altars of the sun, the moon and the stars, its powerful priesthood and its complex rituals, is thoroughly described and visualized in accompanying engravings. The cult is one of baroque splendour, but also of exquisite atrocity. In some respects, the Formosans are well-mannered and sensible, even exemplary. They have an excellent educational and social system and therefore know neither beggars nor vagabonds. The losses suffered by the population through the mass sacrifice of 18,000 boys every year are made good by the institution of polygyny. There is much else that is disquieting in Formosa. Persons of quality travel in sedan chairs as large as houses, carried by elephants whose drivers squat not on the back, but on the trunk of the animals, as an engraving clearly shows. Roots and vegetables are mostly eaten raw. The same applies to human flesh, which, contrary to the meat of most animals, is subject to no food taboo. The flesh of persons sacrificed or executed is even publicly distributed for that purpose.

Besides the religion, customs and manners of the Formosans, their language and writing is also worthy of study. The particular style of writing was also introduced by the prophet Psalmanaazaar. It is written like Hebrew from right to left, and consists of an alphabet of twenty signs, which are recorded with their designation and phonetic value on a folding table. Interlinear translations of the Lord's Prayer, the Creed and the Ten Commandments are given as samples for the language.

This language is, as the author explains, the true, unadulterated original Japanese. Formosa does not belong politically, as is often erroneously believed in the West, to the Chinese but to the Japanese empire. The Formosan-Japanese language was introduced long ago on the islands east of China by a resolution of the people: a singular event in history which the author cannot explain but can only describe with amazement. It is related to no other idiom. Its structure, however, vaguely resembles that of many European languages, but is simpler and more regular. Also in its vocabulary are some analogies with Spanish, Greek, Italian and Hebrew. There are other surprising analogies between Formosan and European nature and culture: a kind of rice liqueur, for example, is called *ar-magnok*; flora and fauna are dominated by the common European species.

Page 17.   *Fig. 11*

Alphabet de la Langue des Formosans

Nom	Valeur			Figure			Nom
Aũ	A	a	ao				
Mem	M	m̃	m				
Neñ	N	ñ	n				
Taph	T	th	t				
Lamdo	L	ll	l				
Samdo	S	ch	s				
Vomera	V	w	v				
Bagdo	B	b	b				
Hamno	H	kh	h				
Pedlo	P	pp	p				
Kaphi	K	k	x				
Omda	O	o	c				
Ilda	I	y	i				
Xatara	X	xh	x				
Dam	D	th	d				
Zamphi	Z	tf	z				
Epfi	E	ε	η				
Fandem	F	ph	f				
Raw	R	rh	r				
Gomera	G	g	j				

FIGURE 11: The "Formosan" alphabet. From: George Psalmanazar: *Description de l'isle Formosa....., Amsterdam 1705. By courtesy of the Herzog August Bibliothek Wolfenbüttel.

Dragons, unicorns and griffins, on the other hand, do not occur in Formosa, as the author slyly declares.

This ethnographic description forms about one half of the book. The other half is aptly summarized by its subtitle, which has not been mentioned so far: *Together with a Relation of what happen'd to the Author in his Travels; particularly his Conferences with the Jesuits, and others in several parts of Europe. Also the History and Reasons of his Conversion to Christianity, with his Objections against it (in defence of Paganism) and their answers.*

Obviously, the author was fascinated by the order of the Jesuits. He imputes to them a systematic striving after world domination, obscured by propaganda and covered by skilful adaptation to local conditions. Why, for example, did the Japanese wipe out Christianity with fire and sword in their dominion?.... Because they had realized that the missionary activity of the Jesuits must necessarily lead to a conspiracy of the Christians and the assumption of power by this order. But, as the author declares, the Jesuits never accept a defeat as final. From their Asian headquarters in Goa a secret missionary activity continues to spread. These missionaries are excellently trained in the language and customs of their destined country. In Japan they live underground, passing themselves off as natives of distant provinces, following ordinary occupations and recognizing each other by means of secret signs. Their motives are "ambition, profit, curiosity, vanity".[4]

Such a missionary — and here the personal narrative of the author sets in — worked in Formosa in the disguise of a private tutor and tempted the son of the family into fleeing from his home.[5] The Jesuit intended thereby to present in Europe a native converted to Catholicism in order to increase his own reputation and that of his order; the youth (who incidentally bore the name of the prophet Psalmanaazaar) allowed himself to be led astray by curiosity and a fondness for travelling. The odd pair were turned into accomplices having stolen from the father of one and the master of the other for the benefit of their travel purse. Then the Jesuit led his pupil across half the globe to Avignon, where he finally disclosed himself as a missionary. The author's account of his stay in Avignon is vague and inconsistent. He says that he lived in the convent of the Jesuits where he took part in religious discussions, which all amounted to his refusal to recognize a principal difference between the mixture of paganism and natural law in which he himself believed and Catholicism as interpreted by the Jesuits.

---

[4] According to the French Edition, 224. I could not find this quotation in the English Edition (on the different editions, see note 28).

[5] In the first English editions (1704) this report precedes the description of Formosa. This arrangement was apparently caused by an unauthorized (and wrong) decision by the editor or publisher. It is contradicted by the whole conception of the book as well as by its title. In all other editions that I could get at, the original arrangement of the author is followed however. Cf. note 24.

The Jesuits gave him an astonishing freedom. They even permitted him to live outside the convent. But the spiritual pressures which they exerted on him forced him into constant dissimulation and caused him fits of melancholy. For weeks he roamed through the environs of the town "to soothe the bitterness of the sorrow that tore him up".[6] Nevertheless the Jesuits allowed him a pilgrimage to Rome, where, however, the splendour of the Papal cult failed to make the desired impression on him. This finally caused the Jesuits to hand him over to the Inquisition. The youth fled from Avignon. On foot and without any money he wandered to Protestant Germany.

From now on the narrative becomes more concrete. Several times the author was enlisted as a solider and set free again. Still a pagan, he discussed religion with Catholic, Lutheran and Calvinistic clergy. Even the latter, who appealed more to him then the Catholics could not move him to baptism, since they did not succeed in making their doctrines of the Communion and of predestination credible to his naturally unsophisticated intellect. It was left to the chaplain of a Scottish regiment stationed in Sluys in the Netherlands, by the name of Innes, to finally acquaint him with the milder doctrine of predestination of the Anglican Church and thereby to dispose of his last objections against Christianity and lead him solemnly to baptism. The commander of the regiment stood godfather to him and bestowed on the noble savage his own Christian name, George. Thus, furnished with the best recommendations, the former Pagan travelled together with his converters to London at the invitation of the bishop. There, in a dispute in front of the assembled Royal Society, he defeated a Jesuit missionary recently arrived from China.[7] At the end of his narrative he is preparing himself to go to Oxford for the study of theology.

The final three chapters of this strange story demonstrate that George Psalmanaazaar no longer stood in need of theological study. With self-assurance and even a certain mastery he expounds by means of definitions, postulates, axioms and propositions a systematic outline of Christianity in its Anglican interpretation as the only one which could be made credible to the intellect of a pagan of his calibre. He then disposes of all the arguments still possible against that system from the point of view of paganism and of natural reason in the question-and-answer form of a catechism, and ultimately directs the exhortation towards himself to remain true to his discovery of "the right way". The last word of his book is a confirmingly resounding AMEN.

---

[6] French ed., (as in note 4), 256.

[7] This dispute is the main theme of the preface to the first English edition and is referred to also in the other editions (cf. note 28).

FIGURE 12: Mr. George Psalmanazar. From: George Psalmanazar: *Memoirs* ..... London 1764. By courtesy of the British Library, London.

FROM THE CONFESSIONS OF AN IMPOSTER

When the man who called himself George Psalmanazar closed his eyes sixty years later in 1763, a confessional work was found among his papers publicised under the title *Memoirs of * * * * Commonly known by the Name of George Psalmanazar; A Reputed Native of Formosa. Written by Himself In Order to be Published After his Death*. Therein he gives an account of his life, his wanderings and his literary hoax from the standpoint of a repentant sinner. These *Memoirs* are the only independent source on the early part of his life. It is a difficult question how far they can be trusted.[8] In the following account they are used cautiously according to the criteria of inner consistency and psychological plausibility.

The author's real name remains unknown to this day. It seems he was born in around 1680 somewhere in the south of France to an "old but decayed family".[9] The father had absconded to Germany, the mother, a pious woman, cherished great hopes for him. He went to school first with the Franciscans, then with the Jesuits, than with the Dominicans, and finally for a short time to a university. He was a precocious boy and a model pupil. But with the onset of puberty he began to loaf around. This did not attract attention immediately because of his former achievements, his quick wit and his excellent memory. He broke off his study of theology, and tried his hand at private tutoring, but without success. He lost all self discipline and simply roamed. His mother had entered into a new relationship and the youth, who realized that he had disappointed family expectations and that he now belonged nowhere, relinquished respectable society. He went on the road.

He was inclined to melancholy; his wandering urge was connected with this, as he himself observed. Unsure of himself and very much dependent on the opinion of others, he was prone to dissimulation. He regarded "vanity" as his main fault, the need to arrogate to himself merits that he did not possess. This was

---

[8] This book revived the interest of the public in Psalmanazar. There were three editions: London 1764, London 1765 and Dublin 1765. Their texts are identical. The second edition had the subtitle: *Containing an Account of his Education, Travels, Adventures, Connections, Literary Productions, and pretended Conversion from heathenism to Christianity; which last proved the Occasion of his being brought over into this Kingdom, and passing for a Proselyte, and a Member of the Church of England.* Detailed summaries appeared in the leading British journals (*The Gentleman's Magazine XXXIV* (1764), 503–508, 573–576, 623–629, and *XXXV* (1765), 9–14; and *The Annual Register* 1763, Characters, 43–46, and 1764, Characters, 66–71). A subsequent letter to the editor in *The Gentleman's Magazine XXXV* (1765), 78–80, contains interesting biographical information. On the question of the trustworthiness of the *Memoirs* see Needham: 1985, 80.

[9] Psalmanazar's chronological information is deliberately unreliable and contradictory. Generally, 1679 is given as his year of birth. His testament, printed at the beginning of his *Memoirs* (1-9), allows for 1679 or 1680. But according to what he tells in this book, he must have been somewhat younger. On this question cf. also Sergeant: 1925, 203. Most people who knew him had no doubts that Psalmanazar came from the south of France (see, however, note 21). There were rumours that he was a Jew (Needham: 1985, 81), but this might have had something to do with his Hebrew scholarship.

apparently compulsive. Otherwise he attributed his misbehaviour to seduction by persons of authority and to a lack of supervision.[10] There was also something amiss in his relationships with the opposite sex. Women fascinated him, but he remained morbidly self-conscious towards them, and thereby virtuous in outward appearance if not in thought. A topic he often and gladly dwelt upon was the debauchee he could have become if Providence had not prevented it by means of his timidity. In his favour he had intelligence, a gift for languages, and a special inclination and talent for theological controversy. He was moderate in his habits, endowed with knowledge and ingratiating manners, speaking Latin fluently. Thereby he easily gained the sympathy of superiors.

What could he do? His craving for recognition drove him into the "shameful pretence to be something like a martyr for the sake of religion".[11] He posed first as a converted Protestant and then as a Catholic refugee from Ireland. He donned a pilgrim's garb which he had found hanging in some chapel, and thus strutted solemnly along. He succeeded in acquiring a passport which identified him as an Irish pilgrim on his way to Rome. But he turned to Germany. It was not so much the Holy Father whom he was drawn to but his own, unholy father. When he finally found him, his father had no money and no use for him. From that moment the family definitely disappeared from his sight. He was on the road again. He had now degenerated into a true vagabond. He developed a frightful skin eruption, was almost hung as a spy in Landau, became a coffee-house waiter in Aix-la-Chapelle and then a soldier in Bonn, only to be dismissed again on account of his feeble condition. While his feet carried him on, his mind was occupied elsewhere. The play with mirrors and masks, the mystification of the world and of himself had become his second nature. As a pupil he had learned from the Jesuits something of the cultures of the Far East, the "antipodes" of the West in almost everything, religion, custom, manners, garb, etc., and thus appropriate symbols of "otherness".[12] He had also realized that the knowledge of these cultures in the West rested on very narrow foundations, with the Jesuits almost monopolizing that knowledge.

Like many youths he amused himself by confabulating an artificial world. This he called "Japan". Himself a nobody and almost a shadow on earth, he reconstructed in his dreams the remote island country with its inhabitants, their manners and customs, garb and calendar, religion and writing. This writing he practised until he was able to perform it effortlessly. He started a copy-book with idols of the sun, the moon and the stars and "verses and prose in a kind of gibberish, written in my invented scripture which I murmured or rattled off at fancy".[13] He thereby created a stir which flattered him. He disclaimed his

---

[10] Psalmanazar: 1764, 92, 101.

[11] *Op. cit.*, 116.

[12] *Op. cit.*, 135; cf. also Stewart: 1989.

baptism, posed as a pagan and thereby had the opportunity to utter sarcasms and paradoxes against the Christian faith with impunity. He falsified the passport designating him as an Irishman into that of a Japanese and invented a new biography. The identities of the drop-out student, whom nobody knew any more, and of the noble young pagan abduced into Europe began to merge. The new personality resulting from this fusion was given the euphoniously exotic and vaguely old-testament name "Salmanazar". He kept this name, alienated at the zenith of his career into "Psalmanaazaar" and later simplified into "Psalmanazar", for the rest of his life. From now on this is what I will call him.

In this way his two books were also brought together. The rest occurred as reported in the *Description of Formosa*, though with a slight difference. The chaplain of the Scottish regiment had seen through the imposture of the youth, and proved it by making him translate the same passage of Cicero's *De natura deorum* twice into "Japanese". Only about half of the words were the same, and the youth proved unable to construe the sentences. The chaplain had, however, found it expedient not to expose him, as a Japanese converted to the Church of England could be admirably used in achieving the goals of Mr Alexander Innes.[14] These goals can be summarized in one word: career. Though " an unscrupulous rascal and a disgrace to his cloth"[15] Innes was no fool. Since he was aware that something was known about Japan in England, he recommended another, less known country of origin to the young man. Formosa was the obvious choice. The young man with his inventive mind immediately worked out a theory of Formosa's affiliation to the Japanese empire and the kinship of both languages. The two men marvellously complemented one another; they became accomplices.

Whoever takes delight in Psalmanazar's phantasmagoria has to recognize Alexander Innes as its co-author. He knew exactly what he wanted and it is he who brought a definite goal and a system to Psalmanazar's imposture. It is he who forced the latter to truly work out a "Japanese" language and to memorize it so well that he was able to speak it consistently and fluently. Innes also made him

---

[13] *Op. cit.*, 172

[14] The first name - and thus the identity - of this clergyman still remains a mystery. Psalmanazar only mentions his family name; in his *Memoirs* he even makes an attempt to cover this up. The family name Innes is certainly the right one since the *Description of Formosa* appeared shortly after these events and was never corrected in this respect. There existed one Dr. Alexander Innes, who made himself ingloriously renowned by another literary hoax in 1728, which helped him to a rich living. This identification was already made by Boswell (*Life of Johnson*, vol. I, 359, cf. note 31). There are also footnotes supporting it in Psalmanazar's *Memoirs* (178, 180). But it might be that these notes were introduced by Johnson himself, who most probably had his finger in the edition of *Memoirs*, and also gave this hint to Boswell. The entry on Alexander Innes in DNB, however, in no other way supports the identification of our chaplain Innes with this undistinguished theologian and miscellaneous writer besides the fact that both were involved in literary hoaxes. Sir Sidney Lee in his well-informed entry on Psalmanazar in DNB gives Innes the first name William; Adams: 1962, 93ff, calls him George: both for unstated reasons. Since I have never heard of either William or George Innes I will stick with Alexander.

[15] Winnett: 1971, 15.

translate the catechism of the Church of England into this "Japanese ", a language which, almost a kind of Esperanto, fed upon all languages which Psalmanazar had experienced.[16] It was, however, so rich, logical and well-constructed that even true scholars were taken in by it.[17] Artificial languages were a common feature of 17th century Utopian literature. They succeded as it were, the sacred languages of the Christian tradition. For example, Denis Vairasse in his travel romance *Histoire des Sérérambes* (1677–79) presents a detailed grammar of the language of that imaginary people. This corresponded with the striving of contemporary logicians and linguists, such as John Wilkins or Leibniz, to construct an ideal, universal language designating the true essence of all things.[18] Psalmanazar was apparently the first man who actually *spoke* an artificial language. His imposture in that respect was successful, since the rational, systematic character of language was over-emphasized in his time. If he wanted to pass off an artificial language for a genuine one today, he would have to enrich it with irregularities, as he did in his ethnography.

Apparently it was also Innes who urged Psalmanazar to eat only herbs, roots and raw meat and thus to impersonate a true savage. The wily chaplain sent a report about the sensational conversion and baptism of this pagan to the Bishop of London. By invitation of his Lordship this odd pair came to England in 1703.

There Psalmanazar immediately became fashionable as a "noble savage". He was finally the centre of attention. Even the Royal Society invited him for dinner on the instigation of its secretary, Sir Hans Sloane. In his dispute with the Jesuit missionary Jean de Fontaney,[19] he mastered the situation with brazen lies, even turning the tables on the Jesuit: how could the Père de Fontaney prove that it was not himself and the whole order of Jesuits who were systematically lying? The Jesuit-hating audience applauded. The "noble savage" was not slow to point out to the crowd those close parallels between England and Japan, both island countries menaced by Catholic conspiracies. He was invited to "every great table of the kingdom".[20]

---

[16] Chevalley: 1936, 212.

[17] "Psalmanazar invented even a language, sufficiently original, copious, and regular, to impose upon men of very exclusive learning" (Richardson: 1778, 237).

[18] Cornelius: 1965; Knowlson: 1965; Buijnsters: 1969. According to Needham: 1985, 104f, Knowlson adduces "no particular evidence" for an influence of the "universal and Ideal-language planners" on Psalmanazar. Needham considers such an influence "most improbable". Yet considering the frequency of this motive around 1700 I doubt this improbability.

[19] Jean de Fontaney (1643–1710), a well known astronomer and linguist, afterwards rector of the college of La Flèche; cf. *Dictionnaire de Biographie Français*, 332. If Psalmanazar really got the better of Fontaney, as he tells us, he owed it mainly to anti-Jesuit feelings in the Royal Society. A few years before Psalmanazar, a false Chinese princess was exposed by the Jesuit Sinologist Louis Le Comte (Stewart: 1989, 51); a few years later a true Chinaman in Paris was examined by Montesquieu by means of a Sinological questionnaire (Moravia: 1970, 112ff).

[20] *The Gentleman's Magazine* XXXV (1765), 78.

142   DESCRIPTION

Du SEIGNEUR L'ORAISON.

KORIAKIA VOMERA.

Nôtre Pere qui dans Ciel es,
Amy Pornio dan chin Orhnio viey,

fanctifié foit ton nom, vienne ton
Gnayjorhe fas lory, effodere fai

Roiaume , faite foit ta volonté
Bagalin , Jorhe fai domion

comme dans Ciel , &
apo chin Orhnio , kay

dans terre auffi , nôtre Pain
chin Badi eyen , amy Khatfads

quotidien donne nous aujourd'hui ,
nadakchion toye ant naday,

& pardonne nous nos offenfes ,
kay radonaye ant amy fochm ,

comme nous pardonnons nos
apo ant radonem amy

offenfeurs , induy nous pas en
fochiakhin , bagne ant kau chin

                              ten-

DE L'ILE FORMOSA.   143

tentation , mais délivre nous du
malaoork; ali abinaye ant tuen

mal, car tien eft Royaume ,
broskaey, kens fai vie Bagalin ,

& Gloire , & toute Puiffance
kay Fary , kay Barhaniaan

à tous Gécles. Amen.
shinania fendabey. Amien.

LA CHRETIENNE CROYANCE.

AI KRISTIAN NOSKIAYEY.

Je croi en Dieu tout Puiffant
Jerh noskion chin Pagot Barhanian

Pere , Cieateur du Ciel & de la
Pornio, Chorhe tuen Orhnio kay tuen

Terre, & en Jefus-Chrift fon
Bads, kay chin Jefu-Chrifto ande

bien aimé fils nôtre Seigneur ,
ebdoulaman bot amy Koriam ,

qui conceu fut du Saint Efprit,
dan vienen jorch tuen gnay Pichos,

                              né

144   DESCRIPTION

né de Marie Vierge , fouffert
ziesken tuen Maria Boiy , lakchen

fous Ponce Pilate , été crucifié,
bard Pontio Pilato , jorh carokhen,

mort & enfeveli , defcendu dans
bosken kay badakhen , mal-fion chin

infernales places , troifiéme jour
xana khie , charhy nade

refufcité des morts , monté dans
jandafien tuen bosken, kan-fien chin

Ciel , affis à droite main de
Orhnio , xaken chin teftar-olab tuen

Dieu fon Pere tout Puiffant , qui
Pagot ande Pornio Barhanian , dan

viendra juger vivans & morts.
foder banaar tonien kay bosken.

Je croi dans Saint Efprit ,
Jerh noskion chin Gnay Pichos ,

Sainte Catholique Eglife ,
Gnay Ardanay, Chflae ,

Communion des Saints, remiffion
Ardian tuen Gnayij, radonayun
                              des

DE L'ILE FORMOSA.   145

des péchés , refurrction de chair,
tuen fochin , jandafiond tuen krikin,

vie éternelle. Amen.
ledum chalmmajey. Amien.

LES DIX COMMANDEMENS DE DIEU.
OS KON BELOSTOS TUEN PAGOT.

Ecoute ô Ifraël , je fuis le
Giftaye ô Ifraël , jerh vie oi

Seigneur ton Dieu.
Korian fai Pagot.

I.

N' auras autre Dieu devant moi.
Kau zexe apin Pagot oyio jenrh.

II.

Ne feras te ftatuë, ni image
Kau gnadey fen Tandatou, Kau adiato

femblable aux chofes qui dans
bfekoy oros day chin

Ciel font , ou dans terre , ou
Orhnio vien , ey chin badi , ey
                 G   fous

FIGURE 13: Samples of the "Formosan" language: From: George Psalmanazar: *Description de l'isle Formosa* ...., Amsterdam 1705. By courtesy of the Herzog August Bibliothek Wolfenbüttel.

To the astonishment of a society addicted to drinking he refused liquor of any kind. Herbs and roots had to be put before him raw, accompanied by just a small piece of raw meat. According to the eyewitness report of Jean de Fontaney he was "a youth of about twenty-two years with blonde hair and a white, fresh complexion, who spoke the European languages without any Asiatic accent and seemed to be a Fleming or Dutchman".[21] He used a gibberish constructed of different idioms and accents in order to disguise his true origins so successfully that even the Frenchman Fontaney could not discover the ruse. His suspiciously light complexion he justified with his noble lineage. On the whole he was a subtle master of disguise.

A letter of 1704 conveys an impression of how Psalmanazar entertained a company at table. In Formosa, so he brags, the men have absolute power over their wives and are permitted to kill and eat them on the mere suspicion of adultery. "Barbarous!" a shocked lady exclaims. Barbarous indeed, he concedes, when the accusation was false. With regard to the consumption of human flesh, however, he could not consider this a sin, although he had to admit it was slightly unmannerly. His grandfather, incidentally, had prolonged his life by sucking the blood of a viper every morning. In this way he had reached 117 years of age, and there had been no choice but to kill him. The Formosans, he continued, had pet snakes of great affection, which their masters wound several times round their waists in order to keep themselves cool during travel. These snakes protected their masters better than bulldogs; he sorely missed these "sweet animals" while in England. English snakes were not suited for this purpose. When the famous bishop Burnet asked him to prove that he was Formosan and not Chinese, Japanese or something else, he replied: "The manner of my flight did not allow me to take letters of credence with me. But I pray your lordship to imagine you were in Formosa and told there that you were an Englishman. Could not a Formosan answer this with the same right: 'You are telling that you are an Englishman, but what proof can you supply that you do not come from another country, since you are resembling a Dutchman as surely as any who had ever traded with Formosa?'". His Lordship was silenced.[22]

---

[21] Fontaney: 1705, 589. This review of the *Description of Formosa* in the Jesuit *Journal de Trévoux* is anonymous, yet no doubt inspired, if not written, by Fontaney. A letter reprinted in *The Gentleman's Magazine* XXXV (1765), 78 describes Psalmanazar as "a middle-sized, well-proportioned man with a light complexion".

[22] This letter by an unknown author was reprinted in *The Gentleman's Magazine* XXXV (1765), 78–80, no doubt as a sequel to the publication of the *Memoirs* (cf. note 8). S.R. Maitland has shown that this letter was also used in an anonymous letter novel, *Pylades and Corinna* (London 1731–32), and implies that the letter could have been written by Daniel Defoe (S.R. Maitland in *Notes and Queries* 7 (1853), 479–480). He also thinks that Defoe could have had something to do with the publication of the *Description of Formosa*. In his answer to Maitland, James Crossley (*Notes and Queries* 7 (1853), 551) disproves Defoe's authorship in both cases and shows that *Pylades and Corinna* (actually by Richard Gwinnett and Elizabeth Thomas, cf. the bibliography in Needham: 1985, 233f), included many genuine letters from this time. Crossley considers the report on Psalmanazar authentic. It refers to the latter's period at

No wonder that the hosts scrambled for such an entertaining guest. Psalmanazar had made it his principle never to retract anything he had once said. After he had allowed the astonishing tale of the yearly sacrifice of 18,000 boys to escape from his lips, he stuck with and justified it by the further spinning out of his phantastic ethnography. "Alas, for me — he declares — my fancy was but too fertile and ready for all such things, when I set about them, and when any question had been started on a sudden, about matters I was ever so unprepared for, I seldom found myself at a loss for a quick answer, which, if satisfactory, I stored up in my retentive memory".[23] Thus his phantasmagoria grew and rounded itself off in constant feedback with the expectations of his audience. In the background Alexander Innes continued to pull the strings. The "noble savage" had now shone enough in high society; it was time to allow those who were not asked to the great tables of the kingdom to profit from his tales. The *Description of Formosa* was written in great haste and for trifling royalties within two months or so says Psalmanazar.[24] It was originally written in Latin and translated into English by a Scottish clergyman called Oswald, otherwise unknown, who is probably Innes himself.[25] A certain N.F.D.B.R. published a parallel French edition in Amsterdam. According to a later communication by Psalmanazar,[26] these initials stand for a certain "Nicolas François Du Bois Refugié". This latter contributed his own foreword to the French edition, in which he fiercely attacks the Jesuits. Both translations take considerable liberties with the manuscript.[27] The *Description of Formosa* was apparently a great success; it was immediately re-edited and also translated into French, Dutch and German.[28]

Oxford and shows his skill at adapting to any table company. In view of these examples, it is astonishing that Sergeant: 1925, 201ff attributes to Psalmanazar "no sense of humour". The latter was certainly a practitioner of black humour.

[23] Psalmanazar: 1764, 115.

[24] *Op. cit.*, 182f.

[25] In the preface to the first English edition, a "Mr. Oswald" is said to have been the translator (XIII). In the preface to the first French edition, he is even called "Dr. Oswald" and designated as a Scottish clergyman who had already written other works under a *nom de plume* (XIV). In his *Memoirs*, Psalmanazar reports that Innes had acquired a doctoral degree of a Scottish university (Saint Andrews?) shortly after his return from Holland (Psalmanazar: 1764, 178). This strengthens my tentative identification of that clergyman with Dr. Alexander Innes (see note 14). "Dr. Oswald" continued the role played by Chaplain Innes in pointing out many "improbabilities" in the manuscript (Psalmanazar: 1764, 216f).

[26] George Psalmanazar, *L'Eclercisseur Eclercy, or an Answer To a Book Entitled Eclercissments Sur ce que, etc. By Isaac d'Amalvy, Minister of the French Church of Sluice*, in Psalmanazar: 1710?.

[27] Cf. note 4.

[28] I was able to trace the following editions: English: *An Historical and Geographical Description of Formosa* ... 1st ed. London 1704, 2nd ed. London 1705. French: *Description de l'isle Formosa en Asie* ... 1st ed. Amsterdam 1705, 2nd ed. Amsterdam 1708, 3rd ed. Amsterdam 1712, 4th ed. (*Description dressée sur les mémoires du sieur George Psalmanazar*) Paris 1739. Dutch: *Beschryvinge van het eyland Formosa in Asia* ... Rotterdam 1708 (of which an extract was reprinted in John Toland, *Van den oorspronk en de kracht der Vooroordelen* ...

But this success also gave the sceptics an incentive. It was now possible for the Père de Fontaney to get his revenge. In the *Journal de Trévoux* he published a brilliantly written review which pulled the *Description* to shreds and convinced even the most prejudiced members of the Royal Society of its lack of substance. It closes with the sentence: "With regard to the author... he is a passable declamator, well supplied with commonplaces, strongly biased against the Roman Church, and apt enough to become a country parson".[29]

But this was never to be. While at Christ Church, Oxford, he busied himself with leisurely pastimes, music and numismatics, making himself interesting with feigned illnesses.[30] The Bishop of London had commissioned him to teach the "Formosan" language to aspiring missionaries. What came of this is not known. He also prepared a second, definitive edition of the *"Description"*, in which he included new information which he had "remembered" during his table conversations, such as for example on snakes. As a matter of course the second edition expatiates on those peculiarities of "Formosa" which especially fascinated the British public, such as cannibalism. It also contains an author's preface in which the objections directed against the first edition are catalogued and ingeniously refuted.[31] Unfortunately Psalmanazar does not explain why he returned to London after only six months at Oxford. Here a bitter disappointment was in store for him: Alexander Innes had disappeared. This man of God had decided to dissociate himself from his protégé before he became exposed or made himself ridiculous. He had for some time coveted the post of Chaplain General to the British troops in Portugal and had duly secured it. Without a wire-puller of his calibre, the "noble savage" found it increasingly hard to sustain his role.

He tried to make himself remembered with the publication of two further works. One is a dialogue between a Japanese and a Formosan, in which natural reason is defended against the mystifications of the priests; the other is a systematic discussion of the arguments brought forward against the *Description of Formosa*".[32] Both are more thoroughly written and more elegantly printed

---

Amsterdam 1710). German: *Historische und Geographische Beschreibung der Insul Formosa.* I have not seen the Dutch and German translations. There has never been a critical study of these editions.

[29] Fontaney: 1705, 253.

[30] I could find no proof of Psalmanazar's enrollment in Oxford. Thomas Hearns: 1885, vol. I, 271, quoted after Needham: 1985, 85, says that after contemporary reports Psalmanazar stayed at Christ Church where his protector Henry Compton, the Bishop of London, had been a canon.

[31] For bibliography see note 28.

[32] *A Dialogue Between A Japanese and A Formosan, About Some Points of the Religion of the Time.* By G.P.–m–r. London 1707. *An Enquiry into the objections against George Psalmanaazaar of Formosa.. to which is added G. Psalmanaazaar's answer to M. d'Amalvy of Sluice.* London s.a. (1710). Isaac d'Amalvi was a Calvinist preacher with whom Psalmanazar had disputed in Holland and who in order to justify himself against the latter's misrepresentation had published a brochure: *Eclaircissements nécessaires pour bien entendre ce que le S.N.F.D.B.R. dit.... par rapport à la conversion de Mr. G. Psalmanazar Japonais, dans son*

than the *Description*. The dialogue is a rather conventional piece of free thinking, but the justification with its brilliant sophisms, its spurious documents and its imputation that the trustworthiness of the Church of England was dependent on the trustworthiness of Psalmanazar, is indeed a superb piece of pseudo-science. Considered purely as a work of art, it is even superior to the *Description*, yet it failed in its purpose. The situation was hopeless: Psalmanazar's sands had run out, the public had ceased to believe him, and sneering voices intermingled with the choir of sceptical ones. The *coup de grâce* was the following announcement in the *Spectator* of Friday, 16. May 1711:

> "On the 1st of April in the theatre on the Haymarket an opera will be performed with the title "The Cruelty of Atreus". N.B. The scene in which Thyestes eats his own children will be played by the famous Mr. Psalmanazar, recently arrived from Formosa; the whole meal will be accompanied by kettle-drums."

Psalmanazar continued to uphold his claim to be a Formosan, but allowed himself to sink quietly into obscurity. He lived a low life in the London Bohemia, intermittently trying his hand as a teacher of languages that he himself had only partly mastered, as a propagator of "Formosan" lacquer work, quack doctor, regimental clerk, painter of fans ... continuing to accept financial aid from pious people who suspected nothing of his conduct. He was evidently about to return socially from where he came.

But after his fortyieth year in England there was an unexpected change. His conscience had never been quiet. Now he seriously began to reform himself, supporting himself by honest work, making translations and working for booksellers. This anonymous, poorly paid hack-work he was to pursue till to the end of his days. It suited his delicate social position and his penchant for the mask. He led a frugal but busy life, spending twelve hours at his desk every day. He autodidactically made up for the education he had missed, learning Hebrew and becoming an authority on the Old Testament. At the end of his *Memoirs* he no longer speaks as a repentant sinner, but as an expert scholar. Psalmanazar was a principal collaborator of the monumental *Universal History* (1736–65), the "first world history which to at least some degree merits its name".[33] In it he treats the history of Jewry from Moses down to his own times as well as the archaic ages and the "barbarian" peoples of Classical Antiquity. After a dangerous illness —

---

livre intitulé Description de l'isle Formosa. Den Haag 1706. N.F.D.B.R. was the editor of the French ed. of the *Description* (see also note 26). Needham: 1985, 87 seems to think that *An Enquiry into the objections against George Psalmanazar* was written by a "group of investigators" independent of Psalmanazar, but does not reveal for what reasons.

[33] According to the opinion of Fueter: 1936, 322. Butterfield: 1955, 47 even says that thanks to it "for a short period it seemed that the English held the leadership in historical scholarship". The title of this monumental work is *An Universal History, from the earliest account of time to the present compiled from the original authors.* 23 vols., London 1736–65. German ed. by D.F.E. Boysen: *Die allgemeine Welthistorie.* 37 vols. Halle 1769–90. See also ch. VI of the present book.

he was now approaching his fifties — he was converted to a mystically tainted kind of private piety somewhat resembling Methodism.[34] He now felt obliged to confess his guilt. He wrote his *Memoirs*, which he, so he says, stored away to be printed only after his death, in order to expose or to disappoint no-one. In his article on Formosa in a geographical handbook, he makes a somewhat veiled, but nevertheless public avowal of his imposture.[35] After he had passed his seventies, this one-time free thinker published a justification of the miracles in the Old Testament against the objection of scepticism.[36] The last remaining vice which he indulged was an economical, strictly controlled consumption of opium.[37]

When Dr. Samuel Johnson sought his acquaintance, George Psalmanazar, a dignified old man, lived at Ironmonger Row, Old Street, Clerkenwell. He was venerated there because of his piety, unpretentiousness and charity; "scarce any person, even children, passed him without showing him the usual signs of respect". His rich, idiomatic English had acquired a distinctly Cockney accent. He studiously avoided the topic of Formosa... From time to time, in a tavern close by, he presided at the table where Dr. Johnson and some friends, among them a "metaphysical tailor", used to gather. Johnson at that time was already a famous writer, but he would no more have thought of contradicting Psalmanazar than, for example, a bishop. He later told this to his biographer Boswell, and added that Psalmanazar had been the best man whom he had ever got to know. This peculiar and touching friendship helped the old imposter after all to a modest apotheosis. His death, after the "pious and patient endurance of a tedious

---

[34] At that time (1728) he read, among other devotional works, William Law's *Serious Call*, "the book which profoundly influenced the young John Wesley, and which proved 'quite an over match' for young Samuel Johnson at Oxford and was 'the first occasion of thinking in earnest of religion'" (Winnett: 1971, 19ff).

[35] George Psalmanazar, Entry *Formosa* in Emanuel Bowen, *A Complete System of Geography. Being a description of all the countries of the known world*. 2 vols. London 1747, vol. II, p. 251. It cannot be denied that this avowal was made rather late, that is, 20 years after Psalmanazar's conversion, and that it was moreover made, as Psalmanazar: 1764, 339 admits, "so to say from third hand". He even there throws a shadow on Candidius' excellent and sober ethnographic report (cf. note 2). Incidentally this also shows that the *Memoirs* were revised after 1747.

[36] "*Essays on the Following Subjects: I. On the Reality and Evidence of Miracles.... , II. On the Extraordinary Adventure of Balaam.... , III. On the Surprising March and final Victory, gained by Joshua over Jabin, King of Hazor... IV. On the Religious War of the Israelitish Tribes.... , V. On the Amazing speedy Relief which Saul.... Brought to the besieged Inhabitants of Jabesh-Gilead... Wherein the most considerable Objections raised against each respective subject, are fully answered; The difficulties removed; and each of these remarcable Transactions accounted for, in a rational Way. Written some Years since, and at the Desire, and for the Use of, a young Clergyman in the Country, by a Layman in Town.*" London 1753. This interesting piece of argumentation in his tendency to reconcile the rational and the miraculous is characteristic of Psalmanazar. It is his last independent work, and testifies to his Old Testamental scholarship. He there shows remarkable insight in the sociological and military aspects of the Ancient Israelitic federation.

[37] *Memoirs* (as in note 8), 56ff. He also reports on the dosage and on his personal experiences with the drug. In this he is a predecessor of Thomas de Quincey, with whom he also has other personality traits in common.

illness", was exemplary. Johnson expressed the wish that his own death some day would resemble this one.[38]

At the beginning of the *Memoirs* Psalmanazar's will is printed.[39] In it he again solemnly retracts his imposture, bequeaths his modest possession to the woman he had apparently lived with already for a considerable time, and asks to be buried without further circumstances "in an obscure corner"[40] of the cemetery in the cheapest grave. He took his mask with him into this grave. His true name, "the name which would locate him in time, space and genealogy"[41] remains a mystery.

AN ANALYSIS OF THE *DESCRIPTION OF FORMOSA*

The bipartition of his biography into an "interesting" and a "respectable" half contributes significantly to the charm of the man Psalmanazar. The light of this knowledge of his person will be now reflected in his *Description of Formosa*. I will analyze this work according to its three principal objectives: (1) as a false book of travels, (2) as a satire on religion and (3) as an autobiography.

THE FALSE BOOK OF TRAVELS

The *Description of Formosa* claims to describe the island and its inhabitants as they really are. This claim is validated by the personal knowledge which the author pretends to have of them. With the same claim to objectivity, the "experiences" of the author after his flight from "Formosa" are described. This claim is made unjustly and the *Description* therefore belongs to the subspecies of books of travels which are *false*. The theoretical problems connected with them will be dealt with below. Among the many false books of travels published in the early modern period, the *Description of Formosa* shows a further peculiarity. Other authors of false books of travels (called "fireside travels" by Percy G. Adams)[42] have also pretended that their reports were based on personal experience and have become imposters by this pretence. But in these cases the book is primary, the imposture secondary. In Psalmanazar's case the situation was reversed. His book was part of a system of imposture, which was first *lived* and only subsequently codified and expanded through the printing press.[43]

Psalmanazar's original objectives were modest. He merely wanted to amaze his contemporaries and earn his livelihood. Long-term objectives and a systematic form were only introduced into his imposture by Alexander Innes.

---

[38] Hill: 1934–50, vol. III, 443–49, appendix A, *George Psalmanazar*, where the relevant passages are compiled. Cf. also Winnett: 1971, 6.

[39] Cf. note 9.

[40] Psalmanazar: 1764, 4.

[41] Stewart: 1989, 70.

[42] Adams: 1962.

[43] Chevalley: 1936, 200.

But whereas the chaplain kept himself under cover, the "noble savage" acted in the limelight; he could be seen and heard and talked to. For this public role both co-authors of this system of imposture had competently selected those features which had the greatest effect on the fantasy of the public: the unexpected appearance out of nowhere,[44] the association with the closed microcosm of the island,[45] cannibalism,[46] the preference of the raw to the cooked,[47] and rational, virtuous paganism.[48] In connection with Psalmanazar's talent for play-acting and his smoothness of speech, his penchant for cultural-relativistic paradoxes had an almost irresistible effect on the public.

The written book merely had the additional function of enhancing Psalmanazar's notoriety and authenticating his imposture with the authority of the printed word. It gave to Psalmanazar's fleeting appearance before the public a more durable background — in the words of Susan Stewart a "context" or "tangible social world"[49] to which he could always refer. In order to achieve this, the *Description* had to make a distinct claim to objectivity and therefore had to satisfy two conditions: (a) to do justice to the sources and (b) to contain no contradictions. The first condition did not cause any particular trouble for Psalmanazar. He opted for the Island of Formosa precisely because almost no sources existed on it. What he needed was a white spot on the map which he could fill in with his phantasmagoria. He wanted to give the public something "wholly new and surprising";[50] the principal source, Candidius, he only quotes in order to dispose of it.[51] The local colour, on the other hand, he obtained from Bernhard Varenius' *Descriptio regni Japoniae*, which of course does not deal with Formosa.[52] But above all he adapted the knowledge on extra-European

---

[44] He thus had, no "context", as Stewart emphasizes: "Without a context, without a tangible social world, any visitor could be an imposter: any pauper a prince; any author a god, to put it positively, or a forger, to put it negatively" (1989, 51).

[45] Islands, as closed microcosmoi, have always been the abodes of utopias, cf. Brunner: 1967.

[46] Cf. Pagden: 1982, 81f; Stewart: 1989, 60ff.

[47] The opposition raw/cooked, a universal symbol for the opposition nature/culture. (Lévi-Strauss: 1964), corresponded in Psalmanazar's case also to his audience's "antipodal expectations" (Stewart: 1989, 60.

[48] At the turn of the 17/18 centuries, the "noble savage" was frequently used to bolster the arguments for Deism. (Hazard: 1961, 234ff). John Toland, the Deist (cf. also *op. cit.*, 135ff), reprinted even an extract of Psalmanazar's *Description* in one of his books (see note 28).

[49] See note 44.

[50] Psalmanazar: 1764, 217.

[51] *Loc. cit.* Actually, Candidius gives in a short space an excellent ethnographical description, which refers, as he conscientiously remarks, only to eight villages near the fort where he was stationed (cf. note 2). This gives Psalmanazar the opportunity to dispose of his report as dealing with a bunch of unimportant savages at the periphery of Formosa . Cf. Psalmanazar: 1710, 3ff. See also note 35.

[52] Bernhard Varenius: *Descriptio regni Japoniae...* Amsterdam 1649. Varenius was still the leading authority on Japan in Psalmanazar's time, though his compilation was somewhat outdated. Psalmanazar also follows Varenius to a certain extent in the distribution of his subject matter.

civilizations which he shared with his reader. The influence of the Old Testament on the *Description of Formosa* is obvious. The prophetic foundation of Islam — and the Christian polemic against it — also shines through as a pattern. But apparently Psalmanazar was most impressed by the reports on ancient American civilizations with their sanguinary rituals and their state-managed social and educational systems.   Compared to the mass sacrifices of human beings in Ancient Mexico, the annual sacrifice of 18,000 boys in *Formosa* does not look so fantastic.[53] In the illustrations of the *Description* the "Formosans" look almost like American Indians. Yet not only the content but also the literary form of the *Description* is compatible with the sources. Ethnographic descriptions of early modern times renounced stylistic brilliance; they pretended to be nothing other than compendia of sober facts.[54] One would do an obvious injustice to Psalmanazar by objecting to the dry, enumerating style of his text.[55] He was far too clever to arouse the suspicion in his readers that he was writing fiction by showing off those literary gifts, which he so clearly possessed.[56]

While he treated the question of sources flippantly, Psalmanazar fulfilled the condition of consistency with great bravura. Extravagant and shocking as they might appear, his tales are consistent in themselves; his numerical data can be checked. It is precisely this systematic playfulness which distinguishes Psalmanazar and almost raises him to the rank of an artist. In this respect he is compared by Abel Chevalley to those eccentrics who amuse themselves by working out imaginary railway timetables.[57] Chevalley's study on Psalmanazar, the first serious one, appeared during the heyday of surrealism, which re-evaluated the art production of the eccentrics. It considers the *Description* from the point of view of the *l'art pour l'art* and disregards its fraudulent objective as far as is possible. Chevalley extols Psalmanazar as the "greatest artist whom geography and sociology have produced".[58] This compliment was no doubt well

---

[53] Cf. Adams: 1962, where relevant sources are mentioned.

[54] See ch. I, §*Travel Reports* of the present book.

[55] As does Hill: 1934–50. Needham rightly states that Psalmanazar used this enumerative style as a protection against being found out: "So long as Psalmanazar sticks to the mere accumulation of exotic cultural particulars, avoiding the postulation of systematic relationship among them, he is fairly safe" (1985, 112f). The "imaginary travels" of the 18th century oriented their style on authentic travel reports of the 17th century (Buijnsters: 1969).

[56] In his *Enquiry into the objections against George Psalmanazar* he even ironically comments on this question: "We are plebeians, and the highest state of our education has been restricted to the grammar school. If there is any logic at all (in our arguments), it is purely natural, and what concerns rhetoric, we lay not the slightest claim to it" (Psalmanazar: 1710, 51).

[57] Chevalley: 1936, 212.

[58] *Ibidem.*

FIGURE 14: "Formosan" national costumes. From: George Psalmanazar: *Description de l'isle Formosa*....., Amsterdam 1705. By courtesy of the British Library, London.

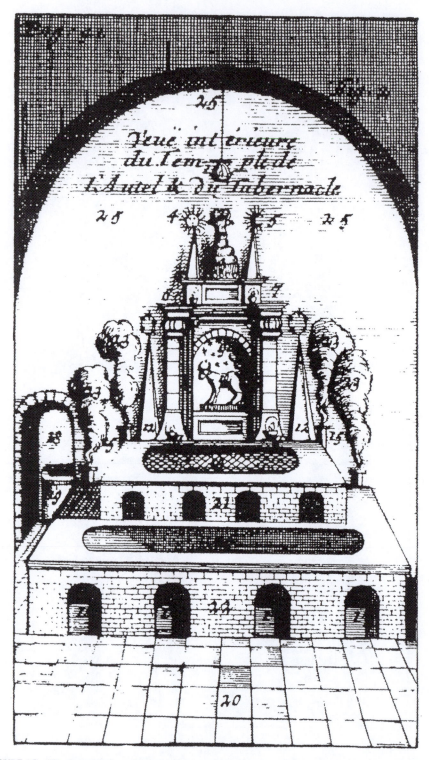

FIGURE 15: "Formosan" altar, destined for the annual sacrifice of boys. From: George Psalmanazar: *Description de l'isle Formosa*....., Amsterdam 1705. By courtesy of the British Library, London.

meant. But the spurious Formosan would have been extremely displeased to hear somebody referring to his product as a work of art. His main objective was to allow no doubt as to its claim of objectivity. Those literary problems which resulted from this situation will be considered now.

THE SATIRE ON RELIGION

As merely a false book of travels the *Description* could never have attracted so much attention. Its recipe for success was rather the combination of literary exotism with religious satire. This echoed Psalmanazar's basic idea of posing as a "noble savage". The "noble savage" is a living objection to his surroundings. He challenges them to constant self-justification. In a somewhat unfair manner the "noble savage" saddles others with the burden of proof, his role being only to ask and that of others being to supply the answers. Such ostensible "children of nature" began to obtrude themselves in early eighteenth century literature.[59] This undoubtedly corresponded to a need for self-examination in public. The popularity of books of travel furthered a tendency to emphasize alien points of view and to distance one's own.[60] The Jesuits in their highly sympathetic ethnographic reports were the main proponents of this tendency. They also nourished the myth of the "noble savage".[61] In this, Psalmanazar was their docile, though unorthodox pupil.

It is quite possible that in posing as a "noble savage" he had originally intended to attack Christianity itself. Psalmanazar came from the south of France, a region with strong heretic traditions. Before starting his wanderings, he had come into contact with "Libertines"; Crypto-Protestants, who through their technique of dissimulation and by ridiculing outward religiosity had deeply impressed him.[62] After having lost the faith of his childhood, he had obviously become something like a Deist, venerating natural reason and the belief in a non-specific deity.[63] However, he lacked the mental equipment as well as the courage to attack Christianity directly. Hence his attack is a indirect one, in accordance with his penchant for masks and paradoxes.

On his wanderings, posing as a "noble savage", he had apparently engaged in religious disputes with clergymen of various denominations. He reports these disputes with palpable self-satisfaction. Once he asked a Calvinist whose God was more cruel, the Formosan one, who every year required the sacrifice of so many

---

[59] van Wijingaarden: 1952.

[60] Cf. Atkinson: 1924; Hazard: 1961; Bitterli: 1976.

[61] Chevalley: 1936, 200. Cf. also Gonnard: 1946.

[62] Psalmanazar: 1764, 109.

[63] See note 48.

FIGURE 16: "Formosan" deity, the recipient of the annual sacrifice of boys. From: George Psalmanazar: *Description de l'isle Formosa*....., Amsterdam 1705. By courtesy of the British Library, London.

boys, or the God of Calvin, who pulls out millions of souls from nothingness, only to deliver them to everlasting damnation?[64] His tale of the consumption of the flesh of the sacrificed boys by priests and laymen must surely be taken as a deliberate travesty of the Holy Communion? The distortion of natural religion by theologians and priests was the original target of Psalmanazar's religious satire.[65]

This approach, however, posed him with two problems. It could not be carried out with reference only to "noble savages". It required a sophisticated civilization subdivided into laymen and priests. Psalmanazar solves this problem rather skilfully by introducing a pointed contrast between the natural religion and the revealed religion of the "Formosans". According to him their religion consists of two layers, the first being worship of the heavenly bodies, probably a metaphor for the worship of the laws of nature, connected with natural reason and morality. On this is grafted as a second layer the gruesome parody of the prophetically instituted worship of a personal God. This syncretism, which is codified in a Holy Writ inaccessible to the people, is administered by a selfish clergy in the name (and at the expense) of an ignorant laity. Psalmanazar, alledgedly having left the island as a youth not yet initiated into all its religious secrets, claimed an ignorance of the revealed religion of the Formosans which allowed him to retain his cherished and profitable pose as a "noble savage".

But this was precisely the reason why he could never go so far with his satire that it became recognizable as such. This was his other problem, and he solved it with his accustomed skill. He narrowed down its original anticlerical tendency into a mere pamphlet against Catholicism and Jesuitism, and, in a milder form, also against Lutheranism and Calvinism. That gave him the opportunity to shift the bulk of his religious polemics from the ethnography of Formosa to the narration of his wanderings in Europe. It also allowed him to mobilize the prejudices of his public.

This strategy proved successful, but to a reader of our present age this religious satire, which is perverted and almost suffocated by the requirements of an imposter's role, leaves an unpleasant impression. Its underhand exploitation of the fears of a Jesuit world conspiracy put it close to concoctions like the *Protocols of the Sages of Zion*. One would like to blame the less attractive figure of the chaplain Innes for this, were it not for the fact that Psalmanazar had identified himself from his early youth with the Japanese, the enemies and persecutors of his former teacher, the Jesuits.

---

[64] Psalmanazar: 1704, 33f.

[65] This becomes palpable in a "notable story" told in Psalmanazar: 1704, 223: A countryman exposed a hoax by a priest. The "Pope" of the Formosans then condemned the priest to perpetual imprisonment, the countryman, however, to death "for not yielding due reverence and submission to the Priest".

THE AUTOBIOGRAPHY

Like many an imposter,[66] Psalmanazar was an exhibitionist. He has no choice, he himself must offer us the evidence for his exposure, if we would only take the trouble to have a closer look at him. Was it necessary to call this rice liqueur *ar-magnok*? Why did he tell the reader that the cult as well as writing of the "Formosans" had been introduced by a man called Psalmanazar? Could Innes not have recognized himself in the missionary who deceived his master and led the young pagan astray, thus finding himself compared to a Jesuit? These private jokes and half-hidden derisions were by no means without danger. It is easy to imagine that Psalmanazar in the progress of his impostor's career wrested from his original timidity an increasing and triumphant impertinence, thereby anticipating his exposure in a mixture of dread, shame, and lust. Both of his major works are autobiographies. In different ways both mirror the personal drama of their author.[67] What he is really interested in is self-examination and self-justification. The rest is insignificant. Through insinuations, as hidden wish-fulfilling, the *Description* tells us the same story as that which the *Memoirs* tell directly in autobiographical retrospective and not without the exultation of a convert.

Psalmanazar became aware of his singularity very early in life — a singularity which he later expressed by means of his artificial name and his artificial biography.[68] The traumas of his early childhood are not known; he has covered his tracks here even more thoroughly than elsewhere.[69] In any case he appears as a deeply disturbed personality. In order to make sure of himself, he constantly reflected himself in the eyes of others. This reflection he accepted for a while as his true ego. He had a tendency to slip into the skin of others who were stronger than himself: were not the motives he ascribed to the Jesuits working undercover in Japan, "ambition, profit, curiosity, vanity",[70] in fact his own? Perhaps at school he had sometimes toyed with the idea of becoming a Jesuit and going to Japan?

We know that he was also sexually disturbed with fears about potency[71] and macabre inclinations. A horror story which he relates somewhat unneces-

---

[66] Greenacre: 1953; case studies in Sergeant: 1925.

[67] Anthropologists frequently repeat their objectivistic ethnographic descriptions on another level in personal memoirs. (Pratt: 1986). Psalmanazar anticipated this tendency by the sequence of his two major works, the *Description* and the *Memoirs*. Susan Stewart observes: "we might hypothezise that we find in these later complementary rhetories the ghost of anthropology's missionary connections" (1989, 67).

[68] Psalmanazar: 1764, 57. This artificial name and biography severed him from his unsatisfactory background and early life and thus from his "context"; cf. note 44.

[69] See note 9. Hill: 1934–50 has shown that Psalmanazar's indications concerning his place of birth are contradictory. He explains this by Psalmanazar's basic insincerity (*op. cit.*, 444). I prefer to think that Psalmanazar deliberately veiled his origins.

[70] Cf. note 4.

[71] This is at least the opinion of Chevalley: 1936, 217f. Greenacre: 1953, 373 states that potency problems are frequent with imposters.

sarily in the *Description* is apparently a daydream: a stranger who usurps the Japanese throne first kills the empress who had made eyes at him and then commits an assault on her body, only then too is the emperor killed.[72] Had the discussion of human sacrifices something to do with this necrophile streak? Psalmanazar had been destined for an ecclesiastical career by his mother. Did he see himself as one of the boys who had been sacrificed to a cruel God and a corrupt Church? Whatever the case, the drop-out student who trod the road like François Villon before him, like Arthur Rimbaud after him, had himself experienced *Une Saison en Enfer.* Like those *poètes maudits* he had created a vice out of his necessity. Knowing that he was intrinsically destined for something better, this *savant maudit* had given himself over to wickedness, cynicism and imposture.

The depiction of the re-ascent of this fallen angel from hell follows the pattern of the pilgrimage of life (*peregrinatio vitae*).[73] Again the bold and skilful grasp with which Psalmanazar adapts the events and experiences of his wanderings to this age-worn model is to be admired. He makes his odyssey appear as a logically consistent rise from paganism via Catholicism, Lutheranism and Calvinism to Anglicanism. The light of faith, which in the initial darkness had only dimly shone before his natural reason, becomes ever clearer and brighter as he proceeds on his path, finally to outshine the powers of darkness in the shape of the Church of England. Now the redemption of this sinner could be sealed by his baptism. The "savage" who in the small garrisons of the Lower Rhine attracted the attention of his superiors has been turned into a symbol of humanity and a guide for his fellow men. What had started as a sensational book of travels ends as a religious allegory. However, it is all too beautiful to be true.

The shift from a satire on religion to an apology to the Church of England corresponded only too well to the interest of Psalmanazar, of the worthy chaplain Innes who had led him to baptism, and of the Church of England whom both had the honour of serving. This Church, which had grown out of self-interest and compromise, laboured under an uneasy conscience and had too little self-assurance for missionary work. A noble pagan therefore, who, following only the light of his reason, asked for admission into its fold, could become a propaganda success not to be undervalued. And propaganda meant much in the "confessional age". The play of interests behind this conversion story was already examined by the Père de Fontenay, who sarcastically congratulated the Church of England

---

[72] Psalmanazar: 1704, ch. II. In ch. XXVII of the 2nd ed. a further horror story is added, which, however, seems rather an example of Psalmanazar's tendency to minister to the need of his public for being shocked: "a tall, well-shaped, rather fat virgin" is crucified for some crime and kept alive by the hangman by means of drugs for six days, in order to make her flesh more tender and savoury. It thus found a ready market with substantial customers. This second story was parodied by Swift, see note 83.

[73] See ch. three, § *An Imago Mundi of the Baroque.*

on its new acquisition.[74] But Psalmanazar himself was not deceived. He knew that his skilfully constructed religious allegory was in fact part of a system of imposture, and was therefore already rotten in its roots. He really wanted to believe and thereby become a new man, as his entreaty at the end of the *Description* shows. But a confession made half-heartedly and for selfish reasons will never have the stabilizing effect which one expects of a true confession.[75]

The seventeenth and eighteenth centuries were the fitting period for an adventurer like Psalmanazar, who provided some entertainment for a civilized society slightly bored by its own smooth functioning. But Psalmanazar was not just one of these colourful, albeit insignificant figures. As Abel Chevalley rightly points out,[76] he was a harbinger of some ideological tendencies which only came to the surface in the nineteenth and twentieth centuries. Does he not look like an early "hippie" with his enthusiasm for Asia, his raw diet, his drugs, his gentle cheekiness, his long blond hair and his penchant for music? Is he not already one of the "free-floating intellectuals" who allow themselves to be employed for the justification of causes which are not theirs? And does he not resemble in his life, cast of mind and confessional urge the initiator of the "age of ideology", the one generation younger Jean-Jacques Rousseau?

When the short hour of his glory had expired and he retired into the obscurity of his garret, Psalmanazar ceased to be a symptom of his time interesting only to the sociologist, and regained the dignity of a personal biography. But whether his second confession was more sincere than the first is a difficult question to determine. In tone, style and a certain calculated vagueness the *Memoirs* closely resemble the *Description*; both books are obviously written by the same man. And both books fulfilled the same function, viz. to give a durable background, in the absence of a family and of a social context, to a social role played by this isolated man. But in *Memoirs* his despair as well as his playfulness have given way to a laboriously acquired self-confidence. In other words, more respectable, but less interesting. It is to be hoped, however, that the piety towards which he had so laboriously struggled was genuine.

THE PROBLEM OF THE AUTHENTICITY OF ETHNOGRAPHIC DESCRIPTION

Where does this combination of biography, history of ideas and literary criticism lead to? It apparently has some general relevance for anthropology. *Mutato nomine de te fabula narratur.*[77] Among other things, George Psalmanazar

---

[74] Cf. note 21.

[75] Cf. Hahn: 1982.

[76] Chevalley: 1936, 195.

[77] See note 1.

was a harbinger of a type not uncommon, but complacently overlooked these days: the fake ethnographer.

FALSE BOOKS OF TRAVEL

Travel literature reached the height of its influence on Western culture in the period from the sixteenth to the eighteenth century, with its largest ever share of the book market. This boundless desire of the public to enter vicariously into other regions of the world was no doubt a symptom of the mentality which called forth the West to world domination. This public was, however, rather indiscriminate in its reading habits. It approached travel literature with a mixture of genuine interest, a need for entertainment, and sceptical reserve, but without looking too intently for a factual basis to the information given.[78] Indeed, its expectations were sometimes better served when facts were mingled with fantasy, as for example with colonial or missionary propaganda, or light reading, where one could identify with the hero and the setting. Travel literature reached the absolute summit of its popularity in England at the turn of the 17th century as a result of England's isolation from other centres of civilization, its commercial and colonial ventures overseas, and also its social and intellectual history. The English public which greedily devoured both true and fantastic books of travels had been educated by Puritanism to despise poetry and theatre as amoral pastimes, and to be interested only in reason, truth, and fact. But it would swallow poetry when it was presented in the guise of reason, truth and fact. The early 18th century in England was a period when the borderline between poetry and knowledge was blurred. This has been referred to as the "retaliation of proscribed fantasy".[79]

This was the time, and the public, to which Psalmanazar, cleverly stage-managed by the Reverend Innes, directed his appearance as a "noble savage" and his imaginary book of travels. And his was by no means the only "fireside travel" of that time. The spoliation of true travel reports, resetting their debris into false ones, became a flourishing trade sponsored by many publishers.[80]

What exactly is a true book of travel? There are apparently shades of meaning between pure truth and outright falsehood, otherwise the public would not be taken in so easily. Travel reports have (1) an objective, (2) a subjective and (3) a literary dimension, since they (a) tell something about some other region of the world, (b) do this from the perspective of one particular person and (c) present the information in a literary form which follows its own laws as well as adhering to the expectations of the public. Though these three dimensions are present in every travel report, they exist in different proportions. A travel report focusing on the objective dimension could be called *true*, one focusing on the

---

[78] Cf. Adams: 1962.

[79] Chevalley: 1936, 200. Cf. also Fraser: 1930, 161ff, 172ff; Frantz: 1934; Hazard: 1961, 315ff, 335ff; Moravia: 1967, 943ff.

[80] Chevalley: 1936, 220.

subjective dimension *sentimental*, and one focusing on the literary form *untrue*. This latter category could be further subdivided, according to whether it makes claims to authenticity or not, into *false* and *fictive* travel reports.[81]

The concept of *authenticity* relates to the idea of the *experienced world*, and also to the notion of *sincerity*. It means being sincere towards some kind of experienced world. Since travelling connects different experienced worlds, those through which the traveller passes and those from which he came and to which he returns, much depends on his sincerity. He must be sincere towards the worlds he visits as well as the world to which he reports, otherwise his report will not be authentic and will be of no independent objective value. The cornerstone of authenticity of a travel report is of course the fact of the traveller's actually having been there.[82]

A true travel report is *authentic* because the author is sincere towards the other experienced worlds he visited. A *sentimental* one is authentic too, but here the author is more sincere towards his own inner experiences than to their external causes. In a *fictive* report the question of authenticity is not raised; illusion takes over. It is only the *false* travel reports which claim authenticity where in fact there is none, or at least much less than alleged. In false travel reports, the traveller has not been where he tells us, or he has been there only in another capacity and under other conditions, or he has not seen or experienced what he refers to. The way of authenticity is simple and straight; the ways of the false report are manifold and slippery.

Travellers always had to contend with the issue of authenticity. In order to prove the sincerity of their own reports, they had to resort to certain strategies of authentification. The most important thing was to convince their public that they actually had been where they said they had. Once this was established, they had won a great advantage over their public who had not been there themselves: to a certain degree they escaped its control. In order to prove the other points, they had to develop more subtle strategies. It is worth recalling Psalmanazar's strategies of authentication. He pretended not just to have *been* there, but to *come* from there, that is, to be a *native*. He supported this pretension with bizarre behaviour, which neatly fitted Western expectations, and by his alleged inability to follow Western customs and to share Western beliefs. He screened himself against discovery with his gibberish and his sophisms. Once he had established his claim to be a native, thanks to the support of some important persons whose opinion others followed, he scored his greatest victory. He could now *monopolize* the knowledge available on Formosa, because nobody else had been there. As long

---

[81] A similar classification is made by Buijnsters: 1969, who, following Adams: 1962, differentiates between "authentic", "imaginary", and "pseudo-authentic" travel reports, omitting thus merely my category "sentimental'.

[82] I have elaborated this in Stagl: 1985 and Stagl: 1993a. See also Needham: 1985, 75ff.

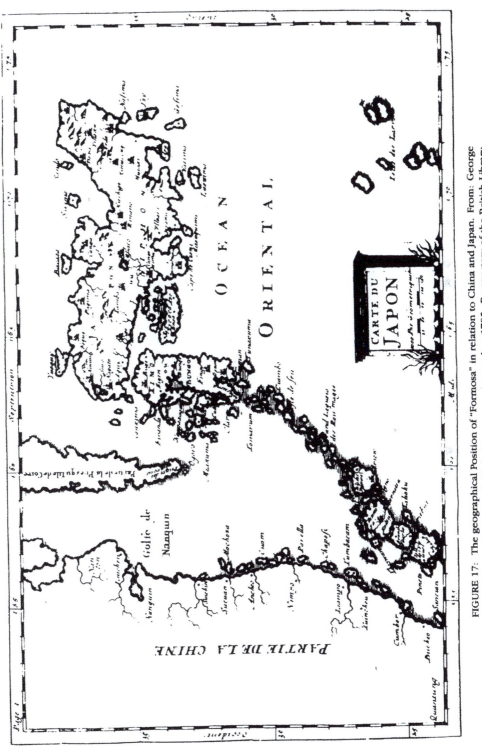

FIGURE 17: The geographical Position of "Formosa" in relation to China and Japan. From: George Psalmanazar: *Description de l'isle Formosa.....*, Amsterdam 1705. By courtesy of the British Library, London.

as he followed the two conditions specified above, source-adequateness and consistency in his stories, nothing serious could happen to his pretension.

There are two fictive books of travel of the same period and addressed to the same public that have since become famous. These are Daniel Defoe's *Robinson Crusoe* (1719) and Jonathan Swift's *Gulliver's Travels* (1725). Defoe takes his background material from contemporary books of travel for a story told in such realistic detail that it was often believed to be true. Swift is even more pseudo-exact. He moors the scenes of his action by means of slightly falsified maps in known space, and the action itself by means of precise dates in known time. Moreover he makes his hero Gulliver write an author's introduction wherein he points to a contemporary travel report as the pattern for his plain, candid style and where he (Gulliver) claims to be the cousin of its author.[83] Whereas the *Description of Formosa* was a pseudo-scientific fake that, in the consistency of its phantasmagoria, almost became a work of art, *Robinson* and *Gulliver* were works of art which, to enhance the illusion (and in the latter case also for parodistic reason) assumed a pseudo-scientific character. There is also another crucial difference: the two novels were written from the perspective of reasonable men bearing such commonplace names as Robinson or Gulliver, an ordinariness which authenticated their experiences on unnamed or scurrilously named islands leading them to borderlines of the human condition. In Psalmanazar's case, the island bears a true name and is to be found on maps,[84] whereas the author is a romantic figure with a scurrilous name, who appears in person before a public to whom Puritanism had denied the joys of the theatre. Both the similarities and the differences between these three books of travel are connected with the fact that *Robinson* and *Gulliver* are fictive ones and the *Description* is a false one. Whether a book claims to be factually true or a work of art is not as unimportant as Abel Chevalley makes it appear.[85] It has been shown that it was an artistic handicap for Psalmanazar to be forced to keep up the appearance of authenticity. Authenticity is a quality which is not restricted to the experienced world. It extends from there to the worlds of art and of knowledge. Where authenticity is concerned, no clear dividing line between these three worlds can be drawn. It is a moral as well as an aesthetic and cognitive issue.

---

[83] Adams: 1962, VI, 80f. This ironic handling of strategies of authentication is peculiar to Swift. He also refers to Psalmanazar in this context. In *A Modest Proposal for Preventing the Children of Poor People from becoming a Burden to their Parents or the Country* (1729) he refers to the "famous Psalmanazar" as an acquaintance of one of his friends and as the leading authority on the taste of human flesh. See also note 72. For the fictive books of travels in general cf. Gove: 1961.

[84] A very similar pseudo-map was, however, added by Psalmanazar to the 2nd ed. of the *Description*. Formosa there appears in its true geographical position, but as an archipelago consisting of five islands. This is in conformity with the text.

[85] Chevalley's in other respects admirable study shows an "artistic" disregard for factual truth and moral sincerity which, however, certainly mattered to Psalmanazar himself. Chevalley thus gives an early example of the "post modernist" view on literary creations.

FALSE ETHNOGRAPHY

The ethnographic description is a variant of the travel report. It also tells of foreign regions of the world, but it uses a different literary form. Travel reports follow the itinerary of a traveller and are thus arranged chronologically; in ethnographies the material is arranged synchronously, following some conventional pattern of description. In the former case, the organizing centre is the person of the traveller, in the latter case, some abstract scheme. Ethnographies in the modern sense of the term (ethnographic monographs) are thought to correspond to comprehensive (holistic) fieldwork and thus to be an achievement of the twentieth century. But already in early modern times there existed the distinction between a chronological (*iter, peregrinatio*) and a synchronous arrangement of information on foreign countries and peoples (*descriptio, relatio, status*).[86] It should be remembered that Psalmanazar's book was in its first part a *descriptio* and in his second part a *peregrinatio*.

In a synchronous exposition, singular experiences are generalized for a whole single unit of observation. This is justified by the author's claim that he knows this unit well and had grasped its intrinsic order. This allows him to step back as it were, to envisage the sum of his experiences, and rearrange them according to the scheme he thinks appropriate. Instead of a tale, he thereby gets a summary. "Subjectivity" is turned into "objectivity".

The ethnographic description thus poses special problems of authentification. In the travel report, the traveller's person had been in the foreground. The public could follow him, duplicate his experiences, and draw its own conclusions. In an ethnography, the author disappears backstage and thus escapes the control of the reader. He draws all the conclusions himself, and makes them appear as authentic as his own experience. In an ethnography, authenticity is generalized; it is a sort of "package deal". The authenticity of ethnographies is indeed a tricky problem. In order to be accepted wholesale, the claim of the ethnographer to sincerity and to a grasp of the total situation must be made to appear very strong indeed "there is probably no ethnographic statement that an outsider can confidently accept as it stands, but the one thing that we should not be able to call into question is the ethnographer's trustworthiness" (Rodney Needham).[87] Nowadays, ethnographers belong to a profession guided by rigorous scholarly ethics, firmly established in academia, and exerting control over its members, a profession whose trustworthiness is a guarantee for its individual members. The mutual control of the ethnographers and the growing interconnection of ethnographic knowledge serve thus as an authentificating system. But no such system existed in Psalmanazar's time.

---

[86] See ch. one.

[87] Needham: 1985, 76.

Being thus in a position to depict a whole foreign experienced world by means of one text which is to be accepted as authentic in its entirety, means that one intellectually disposes of this other world. It is a highly privileged, almost God-like position which invites misuse and has been misused. The classification provided above for travel literature also applies to ethnography. There are *true*, *sentimental*, *fictive* and *false* ethnographic descriptions.

Ethnographic descriptions also have their objective, subjective and literary dimensions, which can be stressed differently. True descriptions, sincerely and objectively depicting other experienced worlds according to the ability of the author, form the vast bulk of this genre, but the other three categories are allowed to sponge on them. A sentimental ethnography is for example Lévi-Strauss' *Tristes Tropiques*,[88] a fictive one H.G. Wells' *Time Machine*.[89] But these categories will not be dealt further with here. What is of interest at this point is the false ethnography. A false ethnography is a holistic depiction of a foreign experienced world which claims to be objective but in fact is not. The author either knows the world he depicts and its intrinsic order far less than he pretends, is less competent than he makes himself appear, has been there in another capacity than he tell us, or even has not been there at all. In all these cases, the objective knowledge that is lacking is covered up by falsehood. The author behaves insincerely.

It is not so easy today to produce a major ethnographic fake like Psalmanazar's. The world is too well known for that. Psalmanazar's fake is a reflection of the "Age of Discoveries", when whole new civilizations became known to the West. To "discover" means to "take notice for the first time of a piece of the surface of the earth for one civilization" (Hanno Beck).[90] It thus establishes a bridge between two regions hitherto separate. The discovery of the whole globe by the West meant that social bridges were established between all regions and that their inclusion into one social system ("one world") was prepared.

Whoever came to build a bridge into one particular region first, thereby established for himself a monopoly of access to it and therefore also a monopoly of disposition over it. He could use it for political, commercial, religious and, by describing this region, even for cognitive goals. In the latter case he would become the "leading authority" on that region. He now only could be dethroned by other authorities contradicting his and appearing more credible to the public.

We have the example of Marco Polo. He was the leading authority on China in the West for many centuries. But from the fourteenth century until today, there have been sceptics who have considered his book *Il Miglione* a fake.[91] It was

---

[88] Lévi-Strauss: 1955.

[89] Wells: 1895.

[90] Beck: 1955, 197.

[91] Reichert: 1988; Harth: 1992.

dethroned as a leading authoritative work in the seventeenth century only by the reports of the Jesuits.

Psalmanazar is a Marco Polo in miniature. His report had always been impugned by sceptics, especially the Jesuits. Nevertheless, it was the dishonest and fantastic Psalmanazar and not the honest, sober Candidius who was the leading authority on Formosa in the West during the first third of the eighteenth century. The *Description* continued to be re-edited until 1739 and even found adherents after the public recantation of its author in 1747.[92] This is all the more strange since Psalmanazar had never been on the island on which he had established his intellectual monopoly of access. He owed this to his daring and original strategy of authentification by posing as a native. In order to make a comparable fake today, one would have to pretend to have had access to one of the remaining "white spots" on the map. The white spots have decreased in size since Marco Polo's and Psalmanazar's days, but such a feat can still be achieved. This is proved by the recent "discovery" of a so-called untouched Stone-Age people, the Tasaday, on the Philippines.[93]

In the meantime, false ethnography has also become a theme for literary fiction. There is a novel called *Krippendorf's Tribe* whose author, Frank Parkin, is a sociologist and so presumably knows what he is writing about. Its hero, Krippendorf, an unemployed and henpecked ethnographer, improves his situation by describing a new tribe of his own invention which is dominated by women.[94]

Even after all existing civilisations and ethnic groups have been duly registered by ethnography, new discoveries can be made. In the same measure in which the horizon separating the familiar from the alien recedes, there are new phenomena to be discovered and thereby to be included in the expanding sphere of the familiar.[95] When no more new people can be discovered, there are still new aspects of the already known groups. Ethnography advances. This opens up a whole new field to fake ethnography. Examples abound.[96] The best known contemporary case is that of Carlos Castaneda, who has reaped more success than even Psalmanazar could dream of. He describes in five volumes the extraordinary experiences and insights imparted to him by one Don Juan, a shaman of the Yaqui Indians. These books have become cult-books of the hippie generation. Castaneda states his profession as "anthropologist". He states that his initiation by Don Juan into the secret lore of the Yaqui took place as a part of his fieldwork. He thus claims for his texts, which would never have had a major impact as a fictive or as a sentimental ethnography, the status of true ethnography

---

[92] Cf. note 28. Boucher de la Richarderie: 1808, 289ff still considers Psalmanazar as an authority on Formosa.

[93] Nance: 1975.

[94] Parkin: 1986.

[95] I have discussed this in Stagl: 1980b and Stagl: 1981b.

[96] Cf. Clifford-Marcus: 1986; Duerr: 1987 and my review of the latter book (Stagl: 1989a).

(just as Duchamp made a bottle rack into a work of art by simply removing if from the life-world to the world of art, thereby multiplying its value). It is difficult to prove or to disprove the authenticity of Castaneda's experience, since it relies on the authority of one single informant, whom nobody else knows, and on the authority of an anthropologist who is extremely difficult to meet, although he seems to be able to give taped interviews and to deal with his publishers. The kindest view of Castaneda not coming from an adept is that he is a "trickster".[97]

The great success of more or less false ethnographies, relates to the strategy of authentification of the anthropological profession as a whole. Since the early twentieth century, anthropology has made field work its holy cow. Nobody can be a proper anthropologist without having done fieldwork. The inverted conclusion is near at hand: whoever has done "fieldwork" is a proper anthropologist. This is no doubt faulty logic, but having personally been "there" is sufficient to imprint the hallmark of authenticity on field-reports, not only in the eyes of the general public, but also in those of many anthropologists, as long as these reports keep to the two basic requirements of source-adequateness and inner consistency.

False ethnographies seem to be written mainly for the three following reasons: (1) to cover up for lacunae in one's research, (2) to supply evidence for some extremist stance, and (3) to minister to a craving of the public for imaginary worlds that are opposed to its own life-world (idylls, thrilling or miraculous adventures, secret knowledge, visions of horror). These motives are perfectly understandable; they had also been those of Psalmanazar. But beneath these purposely rational motives there is also the deeper psychological motive of self-assertion which Psalmanazar also displayed. Who are the fake ethnographers? This question is related to another: Who are the true ethnographers?

It has often been observed that ethnographers (just as travellers) show some traits of social peripherality: having mixed ethnical origins, coming from frontier areas, belonging to minority groups labouring under status inconsistency, or being in some other comparable way maladjusted to society.[98] It is easy to see that such persons will tend to have deeper identity problems than the rest, but will also tend to be more attentive to socio-cultural diversity. Travelling abroad can mean for them escaping alienation at home. They can choose travel to escape a place in the world which has been defined for them by a society to which they feel maladjusted. To prove one's personal worth by confronting a wider world on one's own can be a means of regeneration.[99] By bridging different experienced worlds, insecure individuals can feel that everything now depends on them.

---

[97] Personal communication to the author by Hans Peter Duerr.

[98] Stagl: 1981a, Part II, where also further literature is quoted.

[99] Günter Wallraff in *Die Zeit* 33 (11. VIII. 1989, 34). — Wallraff is a quite well known German writer whose method consists in working in some enterprise under an assumed identity, in order to later expose the malpractices of the management. In recent times the authenticity of some of his finding has been impugned.

This is an outline of the personality type exemplified by George Psalmanazar. He has written a fake ethnography. But it seems that the fake ethnographer bears a closer resemblance to the true ethnographer than the latter would care to admit, like the criminal and the policeman having something in common. It is probably circumstances that make a true into a false ethnographer. "Given the opportunity, what a marvellous genuine ethnographer he (Psalmanazar, J.S.) could have been", exclaims a genuine ethnographer, Rodney Needham.[100] Yet there can also come into play an inherent criminal disrespect for truth and common decency, or a pathological compulsion in a disturbed personality which enjoys the privilege of a creator to make unreal things real and thereby to convince himself of his own reality.

In the face of the danger of falsification inherent in ethnographic work, anthropologists will do well not to cover up these things with respectful silence only to be annoyed at their exposure. Rather, they should confront them openly and try to meet them with stricter source criticism. This would mean more self-awareness and also more objectivity. As the examples discussed show, sincerity is not just a personal virtue, but also a basic requirement of scholarly method.

Let the last word be given to Psalmanazar's great contemporary, Jonathan Swift:

> "...the greatest liar has his believers, as well as the basest writer his readers; and it often happens that a lie only needs to be believed for an hour, in order to reach its purpose... Falseness flies, and truth limps behind; thus when men realize the deception, it is already too late: the hit has already gone home, and the lie has achieved its effect".[101]

---

[100] Needham: 1985, 115.

[101] Jonathan Swift: *The Examiner and other Pieces Written in 1710–11*. Ed. Herbet Davis. Oxford 1957. Here: *The Examiner* No. 14, 9. XI. 1710.

CHAPTER FIVE

Josephinism and Social Research: The *Patriotic Traveller* of Count Leopold Berchtold

"Ein wahrer Patriot ist derjenige gottselige, redliche, standhafte, gedultige, beherzte und weise Mann, welcher mit einer gründliche Kenntnis der Gesetze und Verfassung, der Quellen der Wohlfahrt und der Gebrechen seines Vaterlands den aufrichtigen Willen verbindet, die sicherste Rettungs -, gelindeste Hülfs- und dauerhafteste Verbesserungs- Mittel ausfindig zu machen, und von wahrer Menschenliebe entzündet, ohne Ansehen einer Parthie oder Person, und mit Verläugnung seines eigenen Nutzens oder Schadens sie bekannt und nach aller Mölichkeit geltend zu machen sucht."

(Friedrich Carl von Moser: *Beherzigungen* (1761))

PATRIOTISM, PIETISM, PHILANTHROPISM, JOSEPHINISM

"Patriotism" was very much in vogue all over Europe during the second half of the 18th century, but more especially in Germany. Between 1760 and 1820 around sixty "patriotic societies" were founded in the German speaking countries.[1] They were frequented by an élite of enlightened noblemen and upper middle-class citizens and interconnected by a network of multiple membership, thus creating an organization uniting a politically divided Germany. Such wide-ranging memberships also linked patriotic with philanthropic, agricultural, learned, and secret societies (such as Freemasons or Illuminates) extending from Germany all over Europe. Within this network, the ideas of Enlightenment circulated across political, social and religious boundaries.[2]

A modern historian has defined late 18th century patriotism as "a middling virtue determined by altruism, goodwill, discernment and uprightness", linked to a "community-related moral-political attitude" and intended to "organize and preserve one's own native country as a place of life fit for human beings and protected by law" (Rudolf Vierhaus).[3]

---

[1] Kopitzsch: 1980, 71.

[2] Bourde: 1953, 179ff; Kroker: 1971; Wurzbacher: 1972; Balázs: 1979; van Dülmen: 1986.

[3] Vierhaus: 1980, 12, 25. Cf. also Krauss: 1963, 313ff and Belcher: 1978, 104ff.

It was a "middling virtue" because it did not lay claim to a heroism inaccessible to the common man. The "patriot" was not a revolutionary. He did not want to change man, but rather to pursue his programme under the given circumstances. He wanted, however, to improve these circumstances, to give an example to the vast majority, to induce it to follow in his steps. The renunciation to moral heroism was thus no effect of modesty, but of the élitism of the social reformer, who had chosen the immature majority as the object of his work. Patriotism was founded on "discernment" because social reformers have to know given circumstances in order to improve them. This discernment likewise had to be a "middling" one, because it had to stand open not only to extraordinary minds, but to general common sense, and also because it was justified not by its theoretical truth, but by its practical applicability. In this respect patriotism appeared as a demanding set of ideals since everybody was bound by insights which were accessible to everybody.

"Philanthropism" was related to patriotism but was more radical and also more internationally oriented. Its programme for social reform consisted of a fundamental re-orientation of Christian charity. Philanthropism saw the customary praxis of almsgiving as a well-meant but unsystematic activity, enticing its objects to dependence on the help of others and thereby only augmenting misery. Instead it called for a preventive welfare policy. The symptom of social evils should not be attenuated but rather extirpated at their roots.

Philanthropism thus worked towards a terrestrial paradise. Its systematic programme of social policy required as supporting measures appropriate population, education, employment and health policies. Patriotism thus subordinated the singular case to the system and the individual to the collective. It was closely related, especially through the activities of the elder Mirabeau, to the physiocratic school of political economy. In its comprehensive programme for social change and its strict separation between goals and means it already foreshadowed the revolutionary mentality of the times to come.[4]

But for the time being, patriotism and philanthropism were not clearly distinct movements; one could easily belong to both (multiple membership!). At first glance, both appear to have been typical products of the Enlightenment. While both were concerned with the terrestrial world they also had a religious background. In their frame of mind, their motivation and their social structure (the élitist, sectarian penchant to form conventicles) they were derived from Pietism; a "transference of structure" having taken place between the religious and the secular context.[5] Pietistic motives were for example "unselfish charity", the "mortification of self-will", the call to set an example and the "perfectionistic

---

[4] Im Hof: 1967, 223ff; Ahrbeck-Wothge: 1971; Rassem: 1992.

[5] Kaiser: 1961, 97.

conception of man and the world".[6] Pietism had also had a programme of social reform: "By means of a systematical awakening of kings, statesmen, teachers, subjects, in short of all estates" it wanted to create "Christian states with a minimum of social problems. The kingdom of God (was) something to be realized in this world". Such was, for example, the policy of the Prussian government in the first half of the 18th century.[7]

A common denominator for all these intellectual movements was Leibnizian optimism. In his influential *Théodicee*, Leibniz had equated "real piety" with "true happiness" and this with an "enlightened love for GOD", where "zeal has to be linked with discernment". A really pious man thus works "with all his intents for the public interest, which is not distinct from the glory of GOD".[8] The ultimate purpose of good works was for the followers of Leibniz "not only practical, useful help, but the perfection of man and culture".[9]

The intellectual movements mentioned sofar originated in Protestant Germany. However, they soon made their way into the Catholic territories under Habsburg rule. By the middle of the 18th century Austria was locked in a protracted struggle for existence with the leading Protestant power, Prussia. A programme of social reform and political centralization, similar to the Prussian example, was felt by the Austrian government to be necessary.[10] The concomitant ideas were eagerly seized and Austria thereby adopted Enlightenment "in its early, theist form".[11] Leibnizianism became the Austrian state philosophy. This alliance between theistic Enlightenment and Austrian state interest is called Josephinism.[12]

Josephinism wanted to broaden the basis of national consensus by enlisting, besides the nobility and gentry, the support of the middle classes and the peasantry. To this end it relied on reason and Christianity, though to be common — at least in their elementary forms — to all classes. "Unreason" and "abuses" thus had to be fought in both church and state. Josephinism was not irreligious. Although in practice it turned out to be the "bureaucratic variety of enlightened absolutism",[13] it did not regard the polity as an end in itself. Religion had to be its foundation, and human perfection its aim. "Imbued with the dignity of man, Josephinism required of government to be subservient to it".[14]

---

[6] *Op. cit.*, 9, 14.

[7] Hinrichs: 1943, 528f.

[8] Leibniz: 1726, 7f.

[9] Rassem: 1992, 616; cf. also Winter: 1968, 22.

[10] Redlich: 1920, vol. I, 27f; cf. also Winter: 1962.

[11] Valjavec: 1945, 9, 34.

[12] Cf. Valjavec: 1945; Winter: 1962; Beloff: 1966, 116ff; Hanke: 1974.

[13] Valjavec: 1945, 133.

[14] *Op. cit.*, 127.

Among all Habsburg territories ("crown lands") German theistic Enlightenment, flowing in via neighbouring Saxony, gained the first and strongest foothold
in the lands of the Bohemian crown (Bohemia, Moravia, and Silesia). This
became "the classical country of Josephinism"[15], most probably because these
ideas were here directly adopted rather than imposed from Vienna. By the
middle of the 18th century powerful members of the local nobility and gentry
had made them their own. In 1769, Bohemian nobles constituted a "patriotic-
economic society", in 1770 their Moravian and Silesian compeers followed suit
with "agricultural societies". Such gatherings — which were also established in
other crown lands, served as semi-official organs of Josephinism, destined to
stimulate technological innovations and economic activity and thereby to combat
Austria's backwardness.[16]

The lands of the Bohemian crown were characterized by large estates
which induced their owners to become entrepreneurs as well as landowners; a
system referred to as "feudal capitalism".[17] This system procured for them the
manoeuvrability necessary for private social reforms. In the latter half of the
18th century, many large estates were turned into "experimental theatres and
model farms of Josephinism",[18] displaying examples of private educational and
welfare systems.[19] The Kreisämter (rural district offices), run by members of the
same class, also became "pinions of Josephinism".[20] Aristocrats and bureaucrats
collaborated in realizing the Leibnizian dream of the prestabilized harmony
between individual, polity and the human race.

Enlightened social reformism created an intellectual climate favourable
for social research. Pietism, Josephinism, patriotism and philanthropism made
the whole nation into the object of their reformatory activity, thus giving a new
perspective to social research: its heuristic interest shifted from the curious,
conspicuous or momentarily important to the massive, typical and permanent
phenomena. The benefactors of the people had to truly know their subjects. A
systematic taking stock of social reality was sought. The collective thus became
more important than the individual. Domains of social reality which had previously been inconspicuous or deliberately hidden from the eye of the observer,
such as poverty, crime or marginality, were expressly brought into view.

Among the self-imposed tasks of patriotic and agricultural societies was
the awakening of civic virtue and the exploration of the fatherland. Both tasks

---

[15] Winter: 1962, 208.

[16] Thienen-Adlerflycht: 1967, 69.   On agricultural societies in Austria see Dinklage: 1965;
Schindler-Bonß: 1980, 263ff.

[17] Stark: 1934.

[18] Thienen-Adlerflycht: 1967, 42.

[19] Op. cit., 41ff, cf. also Winter: 1962, 179ff.

[20] Thienen-Adlerflycht: 1967, 42.

were held to be intimately linked. These societies thus furthered the establishment of elementary education and practical schools for agriculture, industry and housekeeping together with the statistical-topographical stock taking of their native country; their aim was a comprehensive description of every crown land (*Landesbeschreibungen*).[21] They also inquired into regional geography and history, working for the establishment of historical-technological-folkloristic museums. The most famous establishment among many of this kind was the *Joanneum*, founded by Archduke Johann in 1811 for the crown land Styria. In such establishments

> "the utilitarian, practical and didactical penchant of old patriotism made itself felt in the collection of works of art and of culture of the past, in order to convey an impression of the creative life of the people in town and country. Not the extraordinary, but the normal and average should become visible. The sense of home and fatherland should thus be preserved and renewed in a time of change and of shattered traditions".[22]

The same connection between patriotism and social research can be found in the travels, circular tours and surveys undertaken by Josephinistic government and church officials in their respective areas of responsibility in order to come to know their real social, cultural and economic conditions. Here belonged the "*Landes- und Kreisbereisungen*" (land- and district-tours) expected of government officials.[23], the "*Commerzreisen*" (tours devoted to the study of economic life) of Josephinistic statesmen.[24], and ultimately also the travels which Emperor Joseph II himself undertook under the alias "Count Falkenstein" in order "to know reality" beyond the bounds of court etiquette.[25] Bishop Hay, a Josephinistic prelate, inquired into the social and religious conditions in some Protestant pockets in Moravia, before he attempted to reconvert them in 1777, not by the usual force but by persuasion and good example.[26]

Social research in the period of Josephinism, and in the Age of Enlightenment in general, still rested on the three age-old basic methods of research represented in the Introduction to the present book, travel, the survey, and systematic documentation. There had been no significant methodological advance in the early modern period.[27] Yet with the perceptible intensification and extension of

---

[21] Schindler-Bonß: 1980, 275.

[22] Vierhaus: 1980, 26.

[23] Cf. Kropatschek: 1799.

[24] Wandruszka: 1963, vol. I, 161.

[25] Winter: 1962, 102.

[26] *Op. cit.*, 168ff.

[27] With two exceptions which cannot be discussed here: (1) the beginning quantification of socio-political data and application of probability calculus to them ("political arithmetic", cf. notes 216–226 to ch. two), and (2) the loving description of popular culture, furthered especially by anti-dogmatic, mystically tainted religious movements, such as Pietism; cf. Kluckhohn: 1934; Kaiser: 1961, 100ff, 180ff.

K.R.v.Siegl.

FIGURE 18: Leopold Berchtold. By courtesy of the Porträtsammlung, Nationalbibliothek, Vienna.

social, cultural and political research in the second half of the 18th century, and its shift of interest from the individual and extraordinary to the collective and average, such an advance did seem imminent. One Josephinistic philanthropist played a significant role in this period of transition.

A JOSEPHINISTIC PHILANTHROPIST

Count Leopold Berchtold, baron of Ungarschitz, Fratting and Pullitz, was born at Platz in Moravia on July 16, 1759. After the early death of his mother, he was educated by her unmarried sister, an enlightened landowner. This formidable aunt entrusted her nephew to a private tutor of the Piarist order (a Catholic order active in education and historical research, not to be confused with the Pietists). Later he frequented schools for nobles in Olmütz and Vienna. Originally destined for a military career, he chose to join the civil service, and at the age of twenty became deputy head of the *Kreisamt* at Iglau. But his fondness for travel made him leave his native province. His birth and his "uncommon knowledge of commerce and trade routes"[28] facilitated his transfer to the board of trade (*Commerzbehörde*) at Triest.

There he assiduously studied geography, politics and languages. He was employed by several business houses "and thereby gained not inconsiderable sums"[29] enabling him to exercise his penchant for charity. Endowed with 50,000 guilder, he set out on his great journey in September 1780, finally returning seventeen years later.[30] The chronology of his travels is unclear. Berchtold first went to Italy, Dalmatia, and then toured the whole Mediterranean area, including the Turkish empire and the Barbaresque states spending a great deal of time in Tuscany. Ruled by Grand Duke Leopold, brother of Joseph II and father of Archduke Johann, Tuscany was famous for its enlightened legislation and efficient administration. The Grand Duke as well as his minsters belonged

---

[28] Pluskal: 1859, 18. If not otherwise indicated, I follow Pluskal in my précis of Berchtold's life. Cf. also note 30.

[29] *Op. cit.*, 18.

[30] A biography of Berchtold in manuscript by Cajetan Haschke, his steward and confidant, supplemented by Heinrich Rziha, tutor to his sons, was kept together with his papers in the archive of the Berchtold family in Buchlau. Pluskal (cf. note 28) draws on this manuscript. His biography is written under the instructions of Berchtold's younger brother Friedrich, and thus is somewhat embellished. The Berchtold papers are said to be now at the communal archive of Brünn (Brno). Since I have not consulted them, this biographical sketch is only preliminary. Berchtold was the great-grandfather of another Leopold Berchtold, foreign minister of the Austrian-Hungarian monarchy at the beginning of World War I. The younger Berchtold has written a history of the domain Buchlau (*Berchtold*: 1893). For the account of the life of his great-grandfather, he completely relies on Pluskal (179ff). There is a short biography of the elder Berchtold in Hantsch: 1963, 31f. Hantsch, however, relies completely on the younger Berchtold, and does not even take the trouble to consult Pluskal. In addition, there are biographical sketches of Berchtold in Ersch-Gruber: *Allgemeine Encyclopädie der Wissenschaft und Künste*; C.v. Wurzbach: *Biographisches Lexikon des Kaiserthums Österreich*, and *Biographie Universelle*, Nouv. éd.

to the "European party of the Physiocrats".[31] His court became something like a finishing school for Berchtold, whom the Grand Duke held in great esteem, elevating him to the rank of a Knight of the military order of St. Stephen.

He also gained access to the enlightened salons of Europe. During his travels, he met many famous or highly placed men, but did not disdain the more modest gatherings of middle-class social reformers, like the "Royal Humane Society" in London, founded and led by Dr. William Hawes, and devoted to the resuscitation of the drowned and the apparently dead. He made it his principle, to associate with all classes of people. A typical Josephinist, he was not interested in knowledge for its own sake. He did not share with the radical Enlightenment in Western Europe the desire to replace the personal God of Christianity by an abstract "supreme being". Instead he strove to better the lot of men in this world, but for religious motives. His Oriental travels had included a pilgrimage to Jerusalem. There, in the chapel of the tomb of Christ, the Austrian count had solemnly vowed to dedicate his life to the alleviation of human suffering.[32] He remained true to this vow till his death. A later biographer even implied that Berchtold had undertaken all his travels in order "to come to know human happiness and misery in various degrees of culture and unculture".[33]

Berchtold had a gift for languages. Besides the current European languages and Czech, he also spoke Spanish, Portuguese, Greek, and Turkish and understood Arabic, Persian and Hebrew. Wherever he stayed, he had booklets printed in the national language and distributed free wherein useful inventions for the prevention or alleviation of human suffering were described. As an active member of the "moral International" of Enlightenment[34], he considered the distribution of useful harm-preventing inventions from one nation to the other as the main objective of travel. He recommended to the Spaniards a special bed for babies, called *arcuccio* and previously used in Tuscany. In Portugal he publicly opposed bullfights. He never lacked courage in his philanthropic endeavours. In Algiers he collected life-histories of Christians who had fallen into captivity among the Barbaresques hoping that the publication of such "slave tidings" would arouse pity for them and raise money for their redemption. Sadly the only result of his efforts was to force up the slave prices and therefore it had to be abandoned - a dearly bought insight into the social effects of social research.[35]

In Alexandria, Berchtold came under the influence of the merchant and British Consul General George Baldwin. Baldwin, a religious enthusiast and mystical writer, had developed a method of preventing the plague by rubbing

---

[31] Wandruszka: 1963, vol. I, 261ff.

[32] Pluskal: 1859, 32.

[33] Entry *Berchtold* in *Biographie Universelle*, nouv. éd.

[34] Koselleck: 1959, 64.

[35] Pluskal: 1859, 30.

the body regularly with olive oil. Berchtold checked the efficaciousness of this method by working as a male nurse in a plague hospital in Smyrna - an experience he luckily survived and afterwards documented in German, Turkish, Italian and Croatian.[36] Berchtold wrote booklets on many topics including: the resuscitation of the apparently dead and prevention of premature burials; a floating light for the rescue of persons gone overboard; an emergency rudder made from materials present on every ship; new machines for the prevention of professional illnesses of artisans; a successfully tried remedy for dog-bites; instructions for taking precautions against dangers to life at sea and on land; remedies against professional illnesses common to seamen; a method to learn swimming and diving; an essay to extend the limits of charity to animals and men.[37]

From 1788 to '89 Berchtold stayed in England, becoming friendly with Arthur Young, the physiocratic model farmer and travel writer. He also published his only book, the "Patriotic Traveller" (1789)[38] which carried a dedication to Young. Shortly afterwards he went to Germany in order to prepare for his Oriental travel. He established contacts with the circle of Orientalists around the university of Göttingen, where he also found a German translator for his book in the person

---

[36] *Op. cit.*, 33. For bibliography see the following note. — Baldwin, who died in poverty in 1818, was like Berchtold an opponent of the slave trade. He could have induced Berchtold to collect his "slave tidings". According to the entry on Baldwin in DNB he also published a mystical work in bad Italian, called *"La Prima Musa"*, which I could not get hold of and which the said entry dismisses as the product of a lunatic.

[37] Considering Berchtold's way of distributing his booklets it is difficult to establish a complete bibliography. A first attempt was made by Pluskal: 1859, 20ff. I have consulted the following booklets by Berchtold not mentioned there: *Projet pour prévenir les dangers très-fréquens des inhumations précipitées; présenté à l'Assemblée Nationale par le Comte L.B. Paris 1791; Projet d'une méthode sure et aisée D'approfondir les vértiables causes des maladies des gens de mer, et trouver la meilleure manière de les guérir, avec des observations sur la nécessité d'amettre l'art de nager et de plonger dans l'éducation nationale. Présenté à l'Assemblée nationale par le Comte Léopold de Berchtold.* Paris 1791; *Kurt Kurzgefasste Methode alle Arten von Scheinbartodten wiederzubeleben...* Wien, 1791; *Ensaio de varios meios Comque se intenta salvar, e conservar a vida dos homens em diversos perigos, a que diriamente se acháo expostos... Parase distribuir gratuitamente a bem da humanidade.* Lissabon 1792; *Ensaio sobre a extensão dos limites da beneficencia a respito, assim dos homens, como dos mesmos animaes... para se distribuir gratuitamente a bem da humanidade.* Lissabon 1793; *(Versuch die Gränzen der Wohlthätigkeit gegen Menschen und Thiere zu erweitern.* Wien 1800); *Nachricht von dem im St. Antons-Spitale in Smirna mit dem allerbesten Erfolg gebrauchten einfachen Mittel, die Pest zu heilen, und sich selber zu bewahren, welche im Lande selbst gesammelt worden ist...* Wien 1797 *(Descrizione del nuovo rimedio curativo e preservativo contro la peste..* Wien 1797, 2 Aufl. Ital. and Croat. Zara 1810); *Kurzgefasste Naturgeschichte der schädlichsten Waldinsekten, nebst ihrer Oekonomie und einigen bewährt gefundenen Wehr- und Rettungsmitteln ...s.l.* 1800. *Noth- und Hiefstabellen für die, so lange zu leben wünschen.* s.l. 1802.

[38] Leopold Berchtold, *An Essay to direct and extend the inquiries of patriotic travellers; with further Observations on the Means of preserving the Life, Health and Property of the unexperienced in their Journies by Land and Sea. Also a Series of Questions interesting to Society and Humanity, necessary to be proposed for Solution to Men of all ranks and Employments, and of all Nations and Governments, comprising the most serious Points relative to the Objects of all Travels. To which is annexed a List of English and foreign Works, intended for the Instruction and Benefit of Travellers, and a Catalogue of the most interesting European Travels, which have been published in different Languages from the earliest Times, down to September 8th 1787.* By Count Leopold Berchtold, Knights of the military Order of St. Stephen of Tuscany etc. etc. 2 vols, London 1789. 8 vo.

of the Orientalist and librarian Paul Jakob Bruns. The German edition entitled *"Anweisungen für Reisende"*, appeared in 1791 at Brunswick.[39] Meanwhile the French Revolution had begun. Postponing his Oriental plans, Berchtold hastened to Paris. He frequented radical circles critical to the régime, where he met many influential figures including the Orientalists Volney and Langlès.[40] He even dedicated a French version of his method for resuscitation of the apparently dead to the *Assemblée constituante*.[41] But his revolutionary sympathies — like Arthur Young's — soon cooled. His Austrian biographers tell with some emphasis the moving story of how he had to leave Paris at some speed because he had publicly given vent to his abhorrence for the execution of the King.[42]

Berchtold spent some time on the Iberian peninsula and in Switzerland, where he tried to establish a genealogical link between his house and the ducal house of Bade. In 1794 he departed on his postponed tour of the Turkish empire. In 1797 the French edition of his book, *"Essai pour diriger et étendre les recherches des voyageurs qui se proposent l'utilité de leur patrie"* appeared in Paris. The translator was the citoyen (and former comte) Charles-Philibert de Lasteyrie, brother-in-law to Lafayette, physiocratic author and liberal politician.[43] During this time Berchtold returned to Austria, after an absence of seventeen years, in order to take over his aunt's possession, the domain of Buchlau in Moravia.

In the same year he married and started to develop Buchlau into an agricultural-industrial-philanthropic model enterprise. He introduced new methods, machines, cultivated plants and breeding stock, such as Merino sheep from Spain.[44] The park was deforested and converted into farmland. Tree nurseries were laid out. He encouraged agricultural improvements and charitable actions among his serfs with offers of premiums. The poor were granted cheap

---

[39] Cf. note 75.

[40] Cf. ch. seven, § *The Making of a Traveller.*

[41] *Projet pour prévinir les dangers très- fréquens des inhumations précipitées; présenté à l'Assemblée Nationale par le Comte L.B.* Paris 1791.

[42] Pluskal: 1859, 20f. Pluskal is followed almost verbatim by the younger Berchtold and even by the prominent historian Hantsch (cf. note 30). Yet the story is much too beautiful to be true. Since the King was executed in 1793 (Jan. 21), Berchtold must have returned to France in that year, which does not seem likely. Yet, notwithstanding his pronounced Austrian patriotism in his later years, Berchtold retained some of his early revolutionary sympathies. In 1806/7 he was one of the very few who had the courage to visit Andreas Riedl, one of the Austrian "Jacobins", whom he had known as mathematics tutor to the sons of Grand Duke Leopold in Florence, in his prison. (Körner: 1977, 333).

[43] For the full title of this French version cf note 75. Lasteyrie (1759–1849) contributed to it an interesting *Discours préliminaire du traductueur* (IX–XIV).

[44] Berchtold's French translator Charles-Philibert de Lasteyrie (cf. the preceding note) was one of the propagators of Merino breeding. So were the family of Berchtold's wife, the counts Magnis, whom Lasteyrie also knew. The cloth and cashmere factories which Berchtold later established on his domain (see below) served the local manufacturing of the wool. Cf. Lasteyrie: 1802; Bourde: 1967, vol II, 814f 873ff.

FIGURE 19: The new castle of Buchlau in Moravia. By courtesy of the Porträtsammlung, Nationalbibliothek, Vienna.

loans and the opportunity to buy basic food cheaply. Midwives were engaged. In order to create new jobs, Berchtold erected a cloth and cashmere factory, and, in order to improve the working force, five schools, where he held the exams in person. Finally he built a mortuary for the resuscitation of the apparently dead.

In order to work undisturbed in his study, he rose at four in the summer and at five in the winter. He dedicated the time from breakfast at nine to dinner at six to his various enterprises. Then he worked again in his study until midnight, never eating supper. The dressing-gown he called the "livery of laziness".[45] He demanded the same energy and dedication from those around him, family and serfs. At the boundaries of the domain of Buchlau, notices were posted in German and Czech that every sick person would find gratuitous and friendly care within. If one of these visitors recovered, he had to promise the count that he himself would take pity on the first helplessly sick person that he met. Berchtold himself was directly involved with the sick, making smallpox vaccinations and distributing trusses. His château at Zerawitz was converted into a hospital for infirm old people, prescribing a schedule for the day containing much praying and spinning. He often served them their meals personally. He finally converted his castle at Buchlau into a hospital, whereby it became permanently disfigured.

He himself had declared: "Individual men or charitable societies have to induce the government to admit humaneness into its budget, thereby making private endeavours superfluous".[46] This is no doubt in the spirit of 18th century patriotism. But there was a radicalism in Berchtold's measures coming close to self-sacrifice. This was ultimately founded in his personality, but was also a direct reaction to Austria's desperate situation in the Napoleonic wars, where regular poor relief had broken down and a patriotic philanthropist like himself must have felt the need to step in for the government.[47]

Nevertheless, the count was no starry-eyed dreamer. He always set great store on a sound economic foundation. Only after his enterprises flourished and became lucrative did he extend the circle of his activities. He founded a Humane Society for Moravia following the example of Dr Hawes. He offered rewards for the invention of life-saving machines or for a sound answer to the question of how Austria's underpopulation could be resolved. He reserved a years savings to help an "outstanding man held down by poverty".[48] In Brünn (Brno), Prague and Vienna he set up institutions for the rescue of the drowning. With the Vienna

---

[45] Pluskal: 1859, 74.

[46] Op. cit., 79.

[47] Cf. Winter: 1962, 189.

[48] Pluskal: 1859, 53f.

institution he planned to connect "an exhibition containing the most important life-saving machines" and a chair for philanthropy.[49]

He addressed many well-documented petitions for social reforms to Emperor Francis, e.g. against animal-baiting in Prague, for the dispensation of cheap medicine to the country folk, premiums for "sleeping talents", relief for destitute clergy of all confessions, the establishment of military swimming schools, routine checks of soldiers for syphilis, a soup of bone-gelatine for the army, premiums for the salvation and resuscitation of the drowning, and the establishment of mortuaries all over the monarchy.[50] He also continued to publish booklets, such as macrobiotic instructions in German and Czech, or a natural history of forest pests together with remedies. His last publication was "Contributions to the improvement of the Austrian militiaman, by a patriot (1809).[51]

Among his papers the following manuscripts were found: (1) On charity; (2) Miscellaneous maxims (mainly of religious nature); (3) Truly useful remarks on travel (among others on how to treat the Moors, precautions on drinking, scorpions and remedies against their sting, health rules for travels in Barbary, trade interests, remarks on antiques, gems and old coins in the Orient.[52] These are obviously material for a second book on travel announced in the *Patriotic Traveller*. Did Berchtold ever attempt to describe his own seventeen year-long voyage? We do not know.

In his last years, prompted by the war, Berchtold sought a public sphere of activity. He became interested in the militia. He co-organized the quelling of a famine in the Riesengebirge. In 1808 the commander-in-chief, Archduke Karl, nominated Berchtold lieutenant colonel of the militia and commander of the military hospitals of the Hradschin rural district. After the battle of Aspern, searching the corpses on the battlefield for apparently dead, Berchtold was infected with typhus, to which he succumbed on July 26, 1809.

A SERIES OF QUESTIONS FOR A
PATRIOTIC TRAVELLER

The full title of Berchtold's main work reads: *"An Essay to direct and extend the Inquiries of Patriotic Travellers; with further Observations on the Means of preserving the Life, Health, & Property of the unexperienced in their Journies by Land and Sea. Also a Series of Questions, interesting to Society and Humanity, necessary to be proposed for Solution to Men of all ranks, & Employments, & of all Nations and Governments, comprising the most serious*

---

[49] Loc. cit.

[50] Op. cit. 56.

[51] *Beiträge zur Veredlung des österreichischen Landwehrmanns, von einem Patrioten.* s.l. 1809.

[52] Pluskal: 1859, 76ff.

Points relative to the Objects of all Travels. To which is annexed a List of English and foreign Works, intended for the Instruction and Benefit of Travellers, & a Catalogue of the most interesting European Travels, which have been publish'd in different Languages from the earliest Times, down to September 8th, 1787. By Count Leopold Berchtold, Knight of the Military Order of St. Stephen of Tuscany, &c. &c." [2 Vols., London 1789]. The two words *Patriotic Travellers* are printed in bold type; they will serve as a short title for the book[53] which is no doubt one of the most curious works to have appeared in that portentous year.

As a *grandseigneur*, Berchtold did not covet the fame of an author. His sincere concern was the distribution of useful knowledge and thus he wanted to impart to like-minded travellers the experiences which he himself had so dearly bought during his long travels.[54]

As a treatise on the method of travelling, Berchtold's book is one of the very last works of the *ars apodemica*.[55] Yet the author imbues this time-honoured model with the spirit of the patriotic-philanthropistic-physiocratic milieu in which he moved. The book is dedicated to the physiocratic writer and model farmer Arthur Young,[56] who had just returned from his travels in pre-revolutionary France when Berchtold visited him in Bury St. Edmunds. Young was for him the model traveller. A second name that looms in this book is that of the physician William Hawes,[57] who in 1774 had founded a society in London for the rescue and resuscitation of the drowned and apparently dead. Berchtold asks all travellers to propogate the goals of this group, which had been granted the honorific name "The Royal Humane Society", wherever they went.

There is a series of questions rather similar to Berchtold's, though much smaller in scope, in the "*Ami des Hommes*" (1759/60) of the elder Mirabeau[58], which he must have known, although he does not mention it. However, he does mention as one of his models (and even reprints as an addendum to his book) the questions used to ascertain the relative wealth or poverty of any town or country, taken from the *Instructions for Travellers* (1757) of Josiah Tucker, Dean of Gloucester, and economic writer close to the Physiocrats.[59] As a second source of his inspirations Berchtold points out *The Naturalist's and Traveller's Companion* (1772) of the Quaker physician John Coakley Lettsom, co-founder of the Royal Humane Society and a personal acquaintance. This is a guide for exploring

---

[53] Subsequently quoted as PT.

[54] PT, *Dedication*.

[55] Cf. ch. one, § *Further Developments*.

[56] PT, *Dedication*. Cf. Young: 1792. On Arthur Young cf. Schnapper-Arndt: 1908, 373ff and Gazley: 1973.

[57] Cf. Hawes: 1794; on William Hawes see the enteries in DNB and in Chalmers, *The General Biographical Dictionary*, new ed. Cf. also Abraham: 1933, 138ff and Owen: 1965, 60f.

[58] Mirabeau: 1759/60, vol. IV, 251–276; cf. Gaulmier: 1951, 321ff and Confino: 1962.

[59] Tucker: 1757. Cf. VI, X and appendix. On Tucker (1712–1799) cf. the entry in DNB.

expeditions.[60] Berchtold must also have been familiar with the famous series of questions which the Göttingen Orientalist Johann David Michaelis had devised for the Arabian journey of Carsten Niebuhr, since he himself was something of an Orientalist and was personally acquainted with Niebuhr.[61] The *Patriotic Traveller* forms two volumes. The second does not concern us here; it contains bibliographies which are in no way remarkable, being based on Gottlieb Heinrich Stuck's well known German bibliography of works of travel.[62] The first volume is divided into two parts: (1) reflections on travel in the form of numbered aphorisms organized into 12 "sections", and (2) a monumental series of 2443 questions organized into 37 "sections". This questions were intended as a travel aid to guide the attention of travellers and enable them to describe the countries which they toured.

The book is addressed to the "youthful Traveller"[63], who is apparently an *alter ego* of the author. Though well-placed and well-off, he nevertheless does not travel for his own pleasure or advantage, but rather for the acquisition of useful knowledge - useful for his country as well as for humanity in general. Steeped in the Leibnizian way of thinking, Berchtold is firmly convinced that the interest of the individual, his country and of mankind coincide, and on all three levels consist in a "general spirit of improvement" to be furthered by the extension of knowledge.[64] A good traveller is one, who "... looks upon his country as a sick friend, for whose relief he asks advice of the whole world".[65]

Berchtold's apodemic counsels are rather commonplace but are curiously interlaced with the author's personal experiences, methodological observations and humanitarian appeals. The manner of presentation is thus rather erratic. Berchtold seems to have been aware of this fact, and that aphorisms, even if numbered, are not exactly the correct form in which to present such an extensive subject matter. He therefore promises to the reader another, more systematic treatise on travel, which alas never appeared. True to the apodemic tradition, Berchtold considers a journey that is not well-prepared to be useless. He thus urges the traveller to acquire by means of conversation and reading a sound knowledge of humanity in general and of the country to be toured in particular.

His journey will become even more profitable when he knows his father-land, perhaps by having completed an "Economical and Commercial Tour" there

---

[60] Lettsom: 1772. This useful guide was re-issued in 1773 and 1799 and translated into French 1775. Cf. PT VI. Cf. also Abraham: 1933, 118ff.

[61] On Michaelis' questions see ch. seven. Cf. Niebuhr: 1774–1834. Berchtold had visited Niebuhr in his native place; the latter had helped him to find a translator for the PT; cf. Pluskal: 1859, 20 and note 75.

[62] Stuck: 1784/5. Cf. also note 28 to ch. six.

[63] PT, *Dedication*.

[64] PT, 1.19, 28f.

[65] PT, 85.

before going abroad.[66] Necessary in addition are courses in applied sciences, from jurisprudence to medicine, languages, and practical skills like swimming or drawing; useful, for amusement, is the ability to play a portable instrument, such as the flute.

A traveller with this preparatory training will show comprehensive interests. What should he investigate? Fundamentally, everything is worth knowing, if not in equal measure. A patriotic traveller, however, will focus on that which is useful to his country as well as to mankind, such as techniques of life-saving, methods for poor relief, the living conditions of rural labourers, the educational systems of different countries and the national characters produced by them, improvements in agriculture, manufacture and trade, patriotic, philanthropic and agricultural societies, who help to exchange useful innovations, or the administration of justice, which is, for example, handled in exemplary fashion by the Grand Duke of Tuscany, "one of the wisest and most humane legislators".[67]

The well-instructed and well-intentioned traveller should rely as much as possible on autopsy and as little as possible on hearsay. He should be everywhere and look into everything. Only in areas of specialized knowledge will he turn to questioning the experts which should be done with caution, since experts can be incompetent or prejudiced. The common man, however, is the best expert on himself. Areas of common knowledge, such as manners and customs or the spirit of the nation[68] can be best learned from him, sometimes indirectly, e.g. by listening to court sessions. In his dealings with the lower classes, the traveller must disguise his rank in order to encourage communication. This kind of verbal information garnering is more unspoilt in the remote provinces than in the capital.

For Berchtold every truly interesting phenomenon has two aspects: its present condition and its history. The traveller should investigate both, and therefore must also frequent archives and libraries. He must set up a list of men of outstanding merit with whom he must make friends in order to gain correspondents who will keep him informed about the country on his return home. Hardly less important is a second list "of such persons as are reputed as eccentric geniuses and extraordinary men", for these often have valuable, if neglected ideas.[69] The traveller should also look out for unpublished manuscripts of possible use to humanity.

How does the traveller make notes? On the spot, in shorthand, and if possible furtively, since he does not want to become conspicuous or to be thought of as a spy. To each set of notes he should add the time and place

---

[66] PT, 15.

[67] PT, 32.

[68] PT, 38.

[69] Ibidem.

where he obtained the information and if possible the name and profession of the informant. In the evenings these notes should be transferred in cypher into a diary, or rather two diaries, for one can easily get lost during travel. Periodically, the most important facts from the diary - only positive facts, no assumptions - must be transferred into a ledger already organized into chapters which will form the basis for a subsequent description of the country. The facts, at first collected pell mell, are thus arranged first chronologically and then systematically, during which they are gradually sorted out and woven together.

To this methodological advice is linked practical advice for the traveller's dealings with fellow travellers, contact persons, landlords and servants, for the use of letters of recommendation, exchanges and luggage, and for special forms of travel, such as on sea or in hot lands. This advice is given with the authority of first-hand experience, and much of it is valid even today. But the author cannot refrain from introducing two of his humanitarian projects into its midst: instructions for the resuscitation of the apparently dead by Dr. Hawes and an appeal for help for the Christian slaves of the Barbaresques — since it is the privilege of reason to lead our sensibility beyond those phenomena immediately before our eyes. Thus closes the first section of the *Patriotic Traveller*.

Its second section, given even greater emphasis, in space as well as in importance, comprises the series of questions. It is a curious mixture of perspicacity and naivety. Berchtold presumes that the country to be described is completely unknown: "Which are the chief sea-ports?" "Which are the most celebrated mountains?"[70] Such questions could be useful when applied to recently discovered countries, but not for the well-known great Western nations on their way to industrialization. However, Berchtold's monster survey manages to cover them all. Some of his questions are rhetorical; their object is to point out abuses: "Are there not some great abuses in religion which are great hindrances to agriculture? too many holidays? too frequent processions? rural devotions? pilgrimages? confraternities? & c. & c."[71] As this example shows, one question can contain a whole nest of further questions. Not all questions are precise, some are repeated in different contexts. But in general, Berchtold is very competent in most areas of social, economic and political life. Sometimes his questions show a methodological genius anticipating later developments in social research. The question "In what do commonly the possessions of a peasant of this country consist?" A question which is repeated for his food and his daily expenses[72], anticipate the school of Frédéric Le Play in the late 19th century.

Berchtold's questions begin with the physical features of the country, its population, its professional structure and demographic movements and with

---

[70] PT, 97ff.

[71] PT, 170.

[72] PT, 121.

the class most important to the author, the agricultural labourers. He moves on to examine then agriculture, cattle breeding, forestry, mining, manufacturing (section XI contains a list of questions for the description of any manufacturing processes), internal and external trade (several lists of very precise and detailed questions after the economic forces of the country and their legal-political regulation, among these also the slave trade and trade agreements with the Barbaresque states), colonies and their importance for the mother country, inland and open sea navigation (with a list of questions for the description of any seaport), shipyards and fisheries.

The survey continues with civil and criminal jurisdiction (the plan for a "Philanthropic Society" is included at this point: this society should contribute to the prevention of crimes, the resocialization of criminals and should also have the power to remove children from incorrigible felons "in order to train these embryo robbers and nuisances, to useful purposes in life; and thus to draw riches and strength to the state...".[73] Berchtold then turns his attention to the police, market prices, with a table where movements in prices of the most important consumer goods can be inserted and a table for the costs of an average household in the capital, charitable institutions (e.g. for the resuscitation of the drowned, hanged, poisoned by gas or frozen to death, asylums, workhouses, pawnshops, employment agencies) and the educational system (from child care to schools and universities and to a list of famous men).

The final section contains questions on manners and customs, the origins and the spirit of the nation, the physical characteristics of the population, the effects of the climate and nutrition on the same, the life conditions of women, religion and clergy (here again there are polemical questions, especially regarding the mendicant orders), the nobility, system of government, taxes, finances, army and navy. The ultimate questions concern the person of the sovereign, his role, his character and his household.

Though he has so much to say on observation, questioning and notation, Berchtold remains curiously silent on what to do with all of the information. He assumes that, being an addition to knowledge, this information will have a use, but he does not tell the traveller how to process and to present his data in a literary form. Like many methodologists, he seems to be more concerned with the thoroughness of his instructions than with their effects. It is not easy to study his book without becoming infected by his mania for numbering and listing. The book thereby has a superficially systematic appearance, though it is actually something of a hotchpotch. After reading it carefully, one gets a feeling of unreality. All the statements are reasonable and every question makes sense but their sheer quantity and lack of coordination have a disquieting effect. The author overwhelms his reader with good advice and makes high demands on

---

[73] PT, 368.

him, without telling him how his individual interest coincides with that of his country and of humanity. These interests only coincide if the reader is as selflessly concerned with the welfare of his fellow-men as the author apparently was - if he is, in short, a patriotic traveller.

This failure to state a true and realistic objective of his book explains why no description of any country was ever made as a result of it, not even by the author himself. The *Patriotic Traveller* was a methodological *tour de force*, almost a monstrosity in which early modern social research had reached its utmost limit. No further development was possible in this direction, only reorientation.

A POINT OF NO RETURN

The *Patriotic Traveller* treated two of the basic methods of early modern social research, travel and the survey, for the first and last time as correlated methods of equal importance. This was made possible by a re-evaluation of travel which already foreshadowed future developments. Because he was not interested in travel for the sake of amusement, prestige, collecting, profit or education, but only for information, Berchtold does not prepare his addressee for a professional or educational journey nor for a Grand Tour, but for an expedition of exploration with humanitarian aims. The *Patriotic Traveller* is thus the first true methodology of travel as a means of social research. Thoroughly integrated into that methodology is his survey intended as an aid for the exploration and description of all countries, the most extensive and comprehensive survey hitherto published.

The *Patriotic Traveller* received an ample and very favourable review in the leading London periodical, *The Gentleman's Magazine* (59/2, 1789) immediately upon publication. The reviewer summarizes somewhat enthusiastically:

> "The brilliant and well-wishing author has extended his considerations to any object that could be interesting to a traveller and to any situation in which he probably could find himself. His book could have been aptly called 'The Traveller's Catechism' ".

But then he apprehensively concludes:

> "We sincerely wish, that such a capable traveller does not leave the world without obliging it with the results of his own observations".[74]

Berchtold did his best to propagate his book after such an auspicious start. Through his international connections he found competent translators

---

[74] Anonymous review of the PT in *The Gentleman's Magazine* 59/2 (1789), 1016f.

in Göttingen and in Paris for the German and French editions.[75] Nevertheless, the *Patriotic Traveller* was not a success and is rarely mentioned in subsequent literature.

Besides its domestic difficulties Berchtold's book appeared in an ominous year, the last year of the *ancien régime*. After the French Revolution had destroyed the optimistic intellectual climate which Berchtold had taken for granted, his book must have made a naive and old-fashioned impression. The German (1791) and French edition (1797) thus came too late (though the French edition had some impact on the further development of social research via Volney; this story will be told in chapter seven). The main significance of the *Patriotic Traveller* was a negative one. It marked a point of no return in an epoch of transition. Berchtold's *Patriotic Traveller* was one of the two last great books of the *ars apodemica*.[76] The other one was incidentally written by a Bohemian, Franz Posselt (*Apodemik oder die Kunst zu reisen*, 2 vols., Leipzig 1795).[77] Why did the *ars apodemica* have its last flourish in Habsburg Austria of all countries?

One reason is the influence which the University of Göttingen exerted on the Josephinists. Many of them had been there, some such as Franz Posselt had even attended the lectures on travel given by the famous August Ludwig Schlözer.[78] Another is the generally conservative intellectual climate in Austria. Here the *ancien régime*, strengthened by a controlled adoption of Enlightenment in the shape of Josephinism, weathered the storms of the revolutionary movement. Thus its traditional techniques for inquiring into social reality also survived for some time. The custom among the upper classes of travelling abroad declined, however, in consequence of the wars of the French Revolution. The young gentlemen who would have travelled in more peaceful

---

[75] *Anweisungen für Reisende, nebst einer systematischen Sammlung zweckmäißger und nützlicher Fragen.* Transl. Paul Jakob Bruns. Brunswick 1791; *Essai pour diriger et étendre les recherches des voyageurs qui se proposent l'utilité de leur patrie, avec des observations pour préserver la vie, la santé et ses effets...* Transl. Charles-Philibert Lasteyrie. Paris An V (1797). On Lasteyrie cf. notes 43 and 44. Bruns (1743–1814), librarian in Helmstedt, was an Old Testament scholar with a special interest in geographical questions. He belonged to the Göttingen school of Michaelis and had been recommended to Berchtold by Niebuhr (cf. note 61). Bruns translated only vol. I of PT; vol. II being based on the well-known German bibliography of Stuck (cf. note 62). He calls himself in his preface a "German patriot" and tells us that he had only revised a translation made by somebody else. This anonymous translation apparently had not found Berchtold's approval. Bruns complains that "instructions for reasonable travel" had gone out of fashion; therefore he had taken the trouble to present Berchtold's book to the German reader. He nevertheless has some qualms about the number of Berchtold's questions; but tries to get out of it by recommending to the traveller to extract from these "a catalogue of what is actually *incognitum*" for every country (preface).

[76] See ch. one, § *Further Developments*.

[77] Franz Posselt: *Apodemik oder die Kunst zu reisen. Ein systematischer Versuch zum Gebrauch junger Reisenden (sic!) aus den gebildeten Ständen überhaupt und angehender Gelehrter und Künstler insbesondere.* 2 vols., Leipzig 1795. Posselt was librarian in Prague. Cf. on him the entry in Wurzbach, *Biographisches Lexicon des Kaiserthums Österreich*.

[78] See ch. six.

times now entered the army. Thus the *ars apodemica* withered; these were no longer times for a sophisticated art of travel.

Josephinism must be understood as a transitional stage between princely absolutism and the new movement towards sovereignty of the people, a transitional stage which in view of the special conditions of the Austrian monarchy lasted for several decades. It is thus not fortuitous that the Austrian intellectual climate was favourable to phenomena of transition. Berchtold's *Patriotic Traveller* was one of these phenomena. It not only epitomizes the old forms of social research, it also prepares the new ones.

Firmly rooted in the old order, this *grandseigneur* nevertheless extends his interest and sympathy to the phenomena peripheral to that order, such as the country provinces, eccentrics, slaves or the apparently dead. As a social reformer, he also focuses on inconspicuous or unpleasant phenomena, such as poverty, illness, crime, or religious abuses, if only in order to eradicate them. No longer a gentleman on his Grand Tour and not yet an explorer, he is something like an independent bureaucrat on a tour of inspection. A leather belt with compartments for his papers around his waist[79], a love of mankind in his heart, he discretely, watchfully and solitarily moves among all nations.

Leopold Berchtold embodied the cosmopolitan aspect of Josephinism, an aspect which was never very pronounced and which disappeared during the wars of the French Revolution. However Josephinism did retain a supranational orientation within the Austrian monarchy. Its loyalty went to historical-political, not to ethnic units. Nevertheless, it involuntarily prepared the nationalistic movements which would ultimately destroy the Austrian monarchy.[80] In conclusion, something must be said regarding the nationalistic aspect of Josephinism and social research. For Josephinism not only aimed at knowing the people and doing good for them, but also at "awakening" them into self-reliance.[81] This word sounds decidedly Pietistic but the subject to be "awakened" was no more the individual conscience, but a mystical collective, "the people". The Josephinists were, however, still prevented from displaying that irrationalist devotion to "the people" later to be shown by revolutionaries as well as romantic nationalists, by their insistence on individual reason and virtue.

In the lands of the Bohemian crown, a national consciousness arose towards the end of the 18th century which was historical-political rather than ethnic, and thus comprised both the German and the Czech element.[82] The attempts of the patriotic and agricultural societies to describe and document the particular features and achievements of these crown lands had significantly

---

[79] PT, 49f.

[80] Lemberg: 1950, 173ff; Lemberg: 1961; Winter: 1968.

[81] Thienen-Adlerflycht: 1967, 69.

[82] Winter: 1962, 65ff.

contributed to this "Bohemian" consciousness. After peace had finally returned to the Austrian empire, these patriotic endeavours culminated in 1818 in the foundation of a "Museum of the Kingdom of Bohemia" (*Museum des Königreichs Böhmen*). Intended as a centre for documentation and research stimulating patriotic feelings and disseminating useful innovations, it was modelled on Archduke Johann's Styrian *"Joanneum"* and planned and financed by the local nobility, with some help (and control) from Vienna. As its founding programme said with a neo-Platonic metaphor, this museum should "combine all patriotic endeavours in a mirror for the purpose of the self-knowledge" of the Bohemian people.[83]

As has been shown earlier, since the Renaissance such centres of documentation and research had been connected with societies based on the models of Plato's or Aristotle's academies.[84] Such societies of independent notables, protected — and remotely controlled — by the government, were the characteristic early modern solution to the problem of the logistics of extensive research. A reflection on their functions for social research would have completed Berchtold's methodological observations on travel and the survey. That he did not offer this reflection — although he had spent much of his life in the orbit of such societies — is a serious shortcoming of his book. But there is no doubt that — had he lived — he would have collaborated enthusiastically in the establishment of the Museum of the Kingdom of Bohemia. As it happened, Leopold Berchtold had an indirect influence on this establishment through his younger half-brother, who had been deeply influenced by his example. Count Friedrich Berchtold (1780–1876) had taken a medical degree — an exceptional step for a nobleman — and had become both a botanist and an explorer. He also became one of the principal planners of the Bohemian museum.[85] The history of that institution was a splendid if not a happy one.[86] It became for some time the world centre for the study of Slavic languages and folklore but it was shaken and ultimately immobilized by the rise of German and Czech national passions which coincided with the slow decline of the "Bohemian" national consciousness.

Whereas Leopold Berchtold had still called Germany his "native Country"[87], Friedrich Berchtold, like many a representative of late Josephinism in Bohemia, had become an "Austroslavist", who united an identification with the Slavonic

---

[83] Nebesky: 1868, 2. On the metaphor of the mirror see note 68 to ch. two.

[84] Cf. Ch. two, § *Treasure Houses for Knowledge*.

[85] Nebesky: 1968, 65, 116, 142, 306; Entry *Berchtold* in Sturm: 1979. Pluskal had dedicated his biography of Leopold Berchtold to his brother Friedrich Berchtold with the following words: "The nestor of the physicians of his fatherland; the meritorious botanical author; the felicitous investigator into the specific curative effects of plants; the undefatigable explorer; the ready and selfless physician of the poor, & c" (Pluskal: 1859, *Dedication*).

[86] Cf. Nebesky: 1868; Kohn: 1953, 11ff.

[87] PT, *Dedication*.

people with a Bohemian local patriotism and a loyalty to the Habsburg dynasty. This Austroslavist position proved abortive in the end, just as Friedrich Berchtold's noble-minded conciliatory attitude in the quarrels of the museum proved to be ineffectual; he soon lost his influence there.[88] There is no reason to assume that his brother Leopold would have been pleased by an atmosphere of nationalist struggle either. These aristocratic Josephinists were pushed aside by a development which they themselves had helped to prepare.

Josephinism had once again opposed the ideal of the *whole man* to the specialization and alienation of the coming industrial society — not as a utopian dream or romantic nostalgia, but as a concrete possibility to be realised immediately through responsible action. They refused to recognize the "Manichaean" rift between lofty ideals and cruel practice, to which their revolutionary and romantic successors resigned themselves.[89] A figure such as Leopold Berchtold was like a Renaissance *uomo universale* transferred to the epoch of the French Revolution. He felt the coming of a new age but tried to master it with the old methods. This was only possible by the utmost personal exertion. No wonder that he tried to understand and to know everything, wanted to direct and to control everything, posed thousands of questions and was incessantly alert and active from daybreak to midnight. Berchtold's methodical and tense lifestyle leaves us with a bleak and dreary impression of the man himself, yet it cannot be denied that he embodied a noble-mindedness, which is not to be found in escapism but only in proving one's worth.

---

[88] Cf. note 85. On "Austroslavism" see Plaschka: 1955.

[89] Thienen-Adlerflycht: 1967, 59.

CHAPTER SIX

August Ludwig Schlözer and the Study of Mankind According to Peoples

It can be said that Schlözer was the first who was inspired with the idea of one great whole, a unity formed by all times and peoples. He wanted to comprise the whole world, everything alive, at a glance. It was, so to speak, as if he yearned to possess one hundred Argus-eyes in order to see everything that happened, even in the remotest countries of the globe, at the same time. His style is *like lightening* illuminating the objects almost simultaneously, if only for a moment, yet with dazzling clearness........His terms are curiously fiery, pert; they seem to be the fruit of a happy moment, a sudden inspiration, and are full of evident truth.

Nikolai Gogol: *Schlözer, Herder, Müller.*

ON THE EARLY HISTORY OF "ETHNOGRAPHY", "ETHNOLOGY" AND RELATED DISCIPLINAL NAMES

The study of man has been called "anthropology" (*anthropologia*) since 1501.[1] This name was coined in Germany and remained restricted to German speaking areas until the late 18th century. *Anthropologia* meant a theory of man under his dual aspect; corporal and mental. Like its name, this theory was a creation of Humanism; it aimed at the emancipation of the study of man from the realms of theology in order to found it on positive knowledge. *Anthropologia (Anthropologie)* remained a recognized branch of German philosophy during the early modern period, reaching its peak in Kant's *Anthropologie in pragmatischer Hinsicht* (1798).[2] At that time in Western Europe, a "science of man" (*science de l'homme*) had developed combining the physiology of the human species with the history of the progress of mankind

---

[1] Diem: 1962; Marquard: 1971.

[2] Immanuel Kant: *Anthropologie in pragmatischer Hinsicht*. Königsberg [1]1798, [2]1800. This book is derived from a lecture which Kant regularly held from the winter semester 1772/73 on.

233

towards civilization.[3] Scholars like the German-born cosmopolitan Georg Forster (1754–1794)[4] equated this "new Science" with *anthropologia* and thereby introduced that term to Western Europe, where it became deeply fixed, whereas in Germany it was increasingly restricted to the study of the corporal aspect of man and became a natural science.[5]

This restriction of the term "anthropology" can be explained by the fact that in the last quarter of the 18th century a bunch of new disciplinal names gained currency in Germany, which instead of coming from the idea of *ánthropos*, "man", were derived from *éthnos*, "people". Instead of the abstract concept of "human nature" and consequently the unity of mankind these new names emphasized the concrete life of human groups in space and time and consequently the diversity of mankind. The disciplinal names derived from "man" had implied an orientation towards the natural sciences, psychology and philosophy; the names derived from "people" meant a reorientation towards geography, history and the philologies. The coinage of these new names was closely linked to the upsurge of historical scholarship in late 18th century Germany and its accompanying attitude of "historism".[6] Like Ernst Cassirer, who thought that names are not just arbitrary signs but express something of the thing itself by emphasizing some of its properties and disregarding others,[7] I find it impossible to "separate in the 'genealogy' of ethnography the factual issue from the issue of names" (as Arno Seifert would have it).[8] I maintain that the history of its names leads right into the heart of a discipline. This chapter deals with the early history of the *éthnos*-names.

These names, "ethnography", "ethnology", *Völkerkunde* and *Volkskunde*, which were all coined in Germany between 1771 and 1783, have been in use since that time, and spread into the main European languages in the 19th century. There was possibly an independent coinage of "ethnology" in French Switzerland in 1787 (see below) and the 19th century English offshoot "folklore", which certainly follow the German pattern (see below). The history of all these names and the context in which they occurred is only imperfectly known, despite the

---

[3] Moravia: 1973; Meek: 1976; cf. also ch. seven.

[4] Rupp-Eisenreich: 1984, 101ff.

[5] Marquard: 1965, 214ff.

[6] Troeltsch: 1925; Antoni: 1951; Butterfield: 1955; Eisermann: 1956, 20ff; Meinecke: 1965; Szalay: 1985.

[7] Cassirer: 1972, 132ff.

[8] Seifert: 1980, 242.

studies of Möller,[9] Fischer,[10] Lutz,[11] myself,[12] Kutter,[13] Rupp-Eisenreich[14] and Könekamp,[15] who all focused on individual names, but not on their entirety. This was first done by a Dutch scholar, H.F. Vermeulen, in his master's thesis at Leiden 1988.[16] In the following pages I reopen the issue and discuss their findings.

The first terms to appear were "ethnography" and *Völkerkunde*, which both meant the same, the one being the Greek, the other the German equivalent of "knowledge of peoples". Fischer summarizes: "In the 1780s a great number of book titles and titles of journals (containing *Völkerkunde*, J.S.) are found which have two things in common: they all come from the North German area, especially from Göttingen, and they are either textbooks of geography or collections of travel reports. It is difficult to spot the very earliest reference among this profusion. In all likelihood, the word was coined in the seventies and immediately taken up by a great number of authors".[17] But who could have coined the word? Möller[18] and Fischer[19] point to the Göttingen historian Johann Christoph Gatterer (1727–1799). Gatterer wrote a series of textbooks on those sciences which were subsidiary to history, whose titles all begin with *Abriss* (outline). Among these was also an *Abriss der Geographie* (Göttingen 1775), in which the names *Ethnographia* and *Völkerkunde* can be found. This book is known to historians of geography since it attempted to emancipate that discipline from the subservient position of a science supporting history. The rapid increase of knowledge on the surface of the earth in the second half of the 18th century had upgraded geography, and Gatterer made allowances for this development. He instead linked geography closely with *Statistik*, the collection, classification and enumeration of empirical information on countries, peoples and constitutions, also called *Staatenkunde*, a speciality of German universities, and foremost of Göttingen.[20]

In his *Abriss der Geographie*, Gatterer distinguishes between the empirical knowledge of countries (*Länderkunde, Staatenkunde*) and that of peoples (*Völkerkunde* or *Ethnographia*). Both are subdisciplines of geography dealing

---

[9] Möller: 1964.

[10] Fischer: 1970.

[11] Lutz: 1973.

[12] Stagl: 1974b.

[13] Kutter: 1978.

[14] Rupp-Eisenreich: 1984.

[15] Könekamp: 1988.

[16] Vermeulen: 1988; cf. also Vermeulen: 1992a and b.

[17] Fischer: 1970, 170.

[18] Möller: 1964, 220.

[19] Fischer: 1970, 170f.

[20] Beck: 1973, 159ff; Rassem: 1980; Seifert: 1980; Lutz: 1980, 255ff; Beck: 1980; Kern: 1982, 19ff; Rupp-Eisenreich: 1984; Kaufhold-Sachse: 1987, 72ff.

with the inhabitants of the earth considered as social bodies, whereas the study
of man, regardless of the spatial distribution of mankind, is called by Gatterer
Menschenkunde or *Anthropographia*. He tells us that all these terms are his
own coinages.[21] Were they? As shown in my own study of the subject, Gatterer
had been preceded in the coinage of *Völkerkunde* and *Ethnographie* by August
Ludwig Schlözer (1735–1809). Schlözer was Gatterer's colleague and rival in
Göttingen, and both habitually refused to quote each other. But the fact remains
that both terms were used by Schlözer already in his *Vorstellung seiner Universal-
Historie*, which appeared in 1772.[22] Vermeulen discovered a still earlier use of
both terms in the *Allgemeine nordische Geschichte* of the same author, published
already in 1771. Gatterer too had used *Völkerkunde* (if not *Ethnographie*) already
in 1771 in his *Einleitung in die synchronistische Universalhistorie*.[23] Schlözer's
claim to priority, and the relative chronology of these works, which is more
involved than appears at the first glance, will be discussed below. Meanwhile
something still remains to be said on the other *éthnos*-names.

  After "ethnography" and *Völkerkunde* were once known, the coinage of
new terms after the same pattern was very likely, and apparently did indeed
occur several times. According to present knowledge, "ethnology" (*ethnologia*)
appears for the first time in a treatise on Hungarian constitutional law by the great
Slovak historian and Orientalist Adam Frantisek Kollár (Adam Franz Kollár von
Keresztén, 1723–1783), which was published posthumously in 1783 (*Historiae
iurisque publici regni Ungariae amoenitates*).[24] This is an example for the
influence of the University of Göttingen on Austrian Josephinism.[25] Kollár was
head of the imperial library in Vienna and stood in personal contact with his
fellow-orientalist Schlözer; both worked on the same problem: the origins of
nations.[26] Kollár defines *ethnologia* as "*notitia gentium populorumque, sive ...
doctorum hominum studium, quo in variarum gentium origines, idiomata,
mores, atque instituta, ac denique patriam vetustasque sedes eo consilio in-
quirunt, ut de gentibus populisque sui aevi rectius iudicium ferre possint.*"[27]
Ethnologie was used again in 1787 by two authors who seem to have written

---

[21] Gatterer: 1775, 4f.

[22] Cf. Stagl: 1974b.

[23] Vermeulen: 1988, XIVff, 23ff. The titles of Gatterer's and Schlözer's works are: Johann
Christoph Gatterer: *Einleitung in die synchronistische Universalhistorie, Und Erläuterung
seiner synchronistischen Tabellen*. 2 vols., Göttingen 1771; August Ludwig Schlözer: *Allgemeine Nordische Geschichte (Allgemeine Welthistorie XXXI. Theil, Historie der Neuern Zeiten
13. Theil (Fortsetzung erster Theil)*. Halle 1771.

[24] I owe this information to Vermeulen: 1988. Cf. Tibenský: 1978; Tibenský: 1983; Belay: 1989.

[25] See note 80 to ch. five.

[26] Vermeulen: 1988, 6.

[27] Kollár: 1783, 80.

independently of each other and of Kollár, Johann Ernst Fabri and Alexandre César (de) Chavannes.

Fabri (1755–1824), who came from the University of Halle, at that time taught geography and *Statistik* in Jena. He had also been in Göttingen for some time, where he was especially close to Gatterer, Schlözer and Blumenbach. He used *Ethnologie* for the first time in his annotations to the second part of Gottlob Heinrich Stuck's *Verzeichnis von Aeltern und Neuern Land- und Reisebeschreibungen*,[28] a well-known bibliography of regional descriptions and travel reports. He used it indiscriminately together with *Ethnographie* and treats both terms as self-evident. In a later work (1808), however, Fabri gives a systematic outline of *Ethnologie* as an independent cultural science midway between geography and *Statistik*. In his rather clumsy Latin, he defines its object as "*Notitia, s(eu) doctrina de moribus et ritibus gentium, s(eu) de cultura vitae, morum, ingeniorum gentium et hominum*", to which he adds in French: "*Science, ou Connaissance des moeurs et des coutumes*".[29]

Chavannes (1731–1800), Professor of Theology at the Academy of Lausanne, published in 1787 his *Essai sur l'Education Intellectuelle avec le Projet d'une Science Nouvelle*.[30] Therein he gives a classification of the sciences in the spirit of the encyclopaedists as the basis for a reorganization of higher learning. He defines *ethnologie* as that part of the general science of man (*anthropologie*) that considers mankind as "one species distributed over the surface of the globe and subdivided into different corporate bodies whose individual members act in view of a common interest".[31]

Most authors writing on that subject connect the coinage of the term ethnology with the French speech area.[32] To me this seems extremely doubtful and another deplorable example of the tendency among anthropologists to cling to national traditions, insofar as their own history is concerned, and thus to disregard the international exchange of ideas. After all, Kollár, a scholar of international repute, had preceded Chavannes in Austria, and Fabri had used the term in Germany also in 1787, and he and other German authors had continued to use it, whereas Chavannes is considered as a "precocious curiosity".[33] To my

---

[28] Gottlob Heinrich Stuck: *Verzeichnis von Aeltern und Neuern Land- und Reisebeschreibungen. Ein Versuch eines Hauptstücks der geographischen Litteratur mit einem vollstaendigen Realregister, und einer Vorrede von M. Johann Ernst Fabri*. Part I Halle 1784, Supplement Halle 1785, Part II Halle 1787, References for *Ethnologie* are to be found in Part II, 34, 43, 65, 90, 128, 147.

[29] Johann Ernst Fabri: *Encyclopädie der Historischen Haupt-Wissenschaften und deren Hülfs-Doctrinen*. Erlangen 1808, 89ff, 351ff, 353f; cf. Lutz: 1973, 33ff.

[30] Alexandre César Chavannes: *Essai sur l'Education Intellectuelle avec le Projet d'une Science Nouvelle*. Lausanne 1787, (*Nouv. éd.* Paris 1886).

[31] *Op. cit.*, 98.

[32] Cf. Fischer: 1970, 176 (with further literature).

[33] Rupp-Eisenreich: 1984, 98.

knowledge, nobody spoke of *ethnologie* in France for the next forty years.[34] Could this neologism thus be better understood in a German than a French context? This is a suspicion first voiced by Britta Rupp-Eisenreich.[35]

No doubt Chavannes' book introduces itself into French intellectual history. Its debt to the encyclopaedists has already been pointed out. There is another debt to the physiocrats, who insisted that social bodies united by common interests were like great individuals, following their own quasi-natural laws of development.[36] Members of this school, like the great Turgot, applied this principle to the history of civilizations, sketching through all their vicissitudes the progress of the human mind from darkness to light.[37] Chavannes was their faithful pupil. It should be remembered that Chavannes was also a Swiss and a Calvinist theologian. He thus belonged to a nation which had discovered its particular cultural identity in the 18th century and served as a "cultural broker" between its French and German neighbours.[38] As a Calvinist theologian, he was more in touch with intellectual life in Protestant, Northern European countries than in Catholic France. He had been a minister in the Germanophone town of Basel from 1759–1766, where he had known the town clerk Isaak Iselin (1728–1782), who was a doctor of the University of Göttingen, a leading German physiocrat and philanthropist, and author of a widely read *History of Mankind* (1764,1770).[39] If seen in this context, Chavannes is less of a "curiosity" than has been assumed.

Could it be that this German orientation explains why his coinage of *ethnologie* had so little success in France? On the other hand, Chavannes was one of those Germanophone scholars who, like Georg Forster, introduced the term anthropology into Western Europe. We have already seen that he used it for *science de l'homme*. In 1788 he followed up his *Essai sur l'Education* with a systematic work, *Anthropologie, ou Science Générale de l'Homme,*[40] which has not as yet been studied by historians of that subject, although a late 19th century encyclopedia calls him "the founder of anthropology"[41] as a result of this work.

---

[34] Rohan-Csermak: 1967; Rohan-Csermak: 1970; cf. also Fischer: 1970, 178f and Lutz: 1973, 20. According to Rohan-Csermak the first one to use *ethnologie* again in France was André-Marie Ampère in his classification of the sciences (1829–34), where he assigns to it a place among the "*sciences anthropologiques*".

[35] Rupp-Eisenreich: 1984, 98f. cf. also Vermeulen: 1988, 6.

[36] Zorn: 1967.

[37] Meek: 1973; Meek: 1976, 68ff.

[38] Antoni: 1951, 9ff.

[39] Isaak Iselin: *Über die Geschichte der Menschheit*. 2 vols., Frankfurt 1764, Zürich 1770, Basel [4]1779, [5]1787; cf. Im Hof: 1767; cf. also Rupp-Eisenreich: 1984, 98f.

[40] Alexandre César Chavannes: *Anthropologie, ou Science Générale de l'Homme*. Lausanne 1788.

[41] Meyers *Konversations-Lexikon*. Leipzig-Wien [5]1897, vol. III, 1038.

Ethnology stands linguistically between ethnography and anthropology. It could have originated from both. Kollár and Fabri most probably took ethnography as their starting point. Fabri originally used both terms more or less synonymously, though he later distinguished between them as descriptive and comparative knowledge of peoples, as one still does today in the German speaking area. Chavannes seems to have started from the other direction. He opposed a diversifying *ethnologie* to a unifying *anthropologie* in exactly the same way in which Gatterer had contrasted his *ethnographia* and *anthropographia*.

A second term which probably came into being after *ethnographie* and *Völkerkunde* had once been coined was *Völkskunde*, appearing in the eighties. The first reference was spotted by U. Kutter in 1782. It is to be found in a popular journal *Der Reisende* ("The Traveller") edited by Friedrich Ekkard (1744-1819), who was at that time librarian at Göttingen and amanuensis to August Ludwig Schlözer. Kutter assumes that it was Ekkard himself who wrote the anonymous passage containing *Volkskunde*. It appears there together with *Völkerkunde* as its singular form. The author asks the travellers in this passage to describe popular festivities instead of the splendid festivities at courts.[42]

With the possible exception of Chavannes, the *éthnos*-names remained a speciality of the German language area (including Switzerland, the Austrian Empire and Scandinavia) for the next generation. According to Vermeulen more than 40 publication (books and journals) appeared in German between 1771 and 1791 where the terms *Ethnographie, Ethnologie, Völkerkunde* and *Volkskunde* were used and whose authors were mostly in some way or other connected with Göttingen.[43] Though the Northern, Protestant part of Germany remained leading, Austria soon followed suit. We have seen that the term *Ethnologie* was for the first time used (and probably coined) there in 1783. The second known reference to *Volkskunde* appears 1787 in the title of work on the *Statistik* of Bohemia.[44] The Bohemian Josef Dobrovský, the founder of the study of Slavonic languages and literatures, who had been a student of Michaelis in Göttingen, used *Völkerkunde* in 1789.[45] It is noticeable that in all three cases the use of these neologisms had something to do with non-German peoples of the monarchy, and we will see below that their emergence in Göttingen was also occasioned by the study of non-German, especially Slavonic peoples. (About 1820, *ethnos*-terms were adopted by other languages of the Austrian Empire, thus in 1821 *národpis* (ethnography) in Czech and in 1822 *Ethnográphiai* in

---

[42] Kutter: 1978; cf. also Möller: 1964, 220f; Narr-Bausinger: 1964; Könekamp: 1988, 7ff.

[43] Vermeulen: 1988, 218ff; Vermeulen, 1992b, 5f.

[44] J. Mader: *Verzeichniss einiger gedruckten Hilfsmittel einer Programmatischen Landes- Volks- und Staatskunde Böhmens*, in J. A. v. Riegger (ed): *Materialien zur alten und neuen Statistik von Böhmen I*. Prag 1787.

[45] Krbec-Michálková: 1959, 12.

Hungarian).[46] The apparently isolated case of Charvannes' *ethnologie* (1787, the second known reference for that term) in French Switzerland points also towards Göttingen, as has been shown above. In the Netherlands, which had close intellectual contacts with Northern Germany, an *éthnos*-term surfaces for the first time in 1794 (*volkenkunde*).[47]

Göttingen was thus certainly the center of diffusion, and through the fame of that university, the *éthnos*-terms spread first to the German language area and its fringes and then, after a long delay probably due to the Napoleonic Wars, to the other European nations. Though they became known abroad especially through the translations of the great synthetic works of two Göttingen professors, the philosopher Christoph Meiners (1747–1811)[48] and the anatomist Johann Friedrich Blumenbach (1752–1840),[49] they only began to enter French and English usage from around 1820. *Ethnographie* was introduced into the French language in the twenties by Adriano Balbi (1782–1848), another cosmopolitan scholar. Born in Venice, he had taught geography and *Statistik* in Venice which at that time belonged to the Austrian Empire, before going via Portugal to France, where in 1826 he published his *Atlas Ethnographique du Globe* (Paris 1826),[50] a geographical representation of language groups. In his *Introduction*, probably published separately already in 1822,[51] he says that he uses *ethnographie* in order to avoid another German neologism which had proved distasteful to the French, *linguistique (Linguistik)*.[52] Now *ethnographie* was immediately accepted, though retaining its linguistic connotations for a long time.[53] It apparently paved the way for the reappearance of *ethnologie* in 1839, simultaneously in a monograph on Egypt[54] and in the name of a learned society, the famous *Société Ethnologique*.[55]

The main influence for the introduction of ethnology and ethnography

---

[46] Vermeulen: 1992b, 10.

[47] *Op. cit.*, 8.

[48] Rupp-Eisenreich: 1983.

[49] Plischke: 1937; Rupp-Eisenreich: 1983, 162ff.

[50] Adriano Balbi: *Atlas Ethnographique du Globe, ou Classification des Peuples Anciens et Modernes d'après Leurs Langues ...* Paris 1826.

[51] Adriano Balbi: *Introduction à l'Atlas Ethnographique du Globe Contenant un Discours sur l'Utilité et l'Importance de l'Étude des Langues*, t. 1. Paris 1826. This theoretical introduction was published separately of the *Atlas Ethnographique*. Only vol. 1 appeared. Some catalogues mention also an edition of 1822, which I could not verify.

[52] *Op. cit.*, 61. Balbi refers here (via the geographer Malte-Brun?) to F.J. Bertuch – J.S. Vater: *Allgemeines Archiv für Ethnographie und Linguistik*. Weimar 1808.

[53] Fischer: 1970, 177; Vermeulen: 1992b, 8ff.

[54] M. Jomard: *Appendice*, in Félix Mengin: *Historie sommarie d'Egypte sous le Gouvernement de Mohammed-Aly. Troisième Partie: Etudes Géographiques et Historiques sur l'Arabie*. Paris 1839. Cf. Fischer: 1970, 178; Vermeulen: 1992b, 9f.

[55] Cf. *Mémoires de la Société Ethnologique*, t. 1–2. Paris 1841–45.

into English in the thirties[56] was the most important British anthropologist of the first half of the 19th century, James Cowley Prichard (1786–1848).[57] Prichard had been deeply influenced in his youth by Blumenbach's theory that mankind, despite its observed diversity, belonged to one species (monogenism); his doctoral dissertation (*De Generis Humani Varietate*, Edinburgh 1808) used the same title as Blumenbach's (Göttingen 1775). It is thus very probable that he got the names ethnology and ethnography directly from the source in Göttingen. However, they carried a new significance in English.

In land-locked, colony-free Germany, the *éthnos*-names had originally been applied to all peoples, regardless of their skin colour or degree of civilization. Even the physical anthropologist Blumenbach had followed this usage,[58] which had also been introduced, as we have seen, in France by Balbi. In around 1800, however, a dichotomy arose between the disciplines dealing with peoples living in "civil society" (*Statistik*, political geography) and those dealing with less organized and civilized peoples (*Völkerkunde*, ethnography, ethnology).[59] This dichotomy, going back to Gatterer,[60] was elaborated by Prichard and his colleagues in England, for whom ethnology came to mean "the study of linguistic, physical and cultural characteristics of dark-skinned, non-European, 'uncivilized' peoples" (G.W. Stocking).[61] Ethnography somewhat later was also given a racial connotation.[62]

This new English usage mainly found its way into the French language through the activities of the *Société Ethnologique*. This learned society was founded in 1839 by another cultural mediator, William Frederic Edwards (1777–1842), a British naturalist living in Paris and writing in French. The society's object was "the study of the human races according to the historical traditions, the languages and the physical and moral traits of each people".[63] When the "common people" were upgraded by the romantic movement at the beginning of the 19th century, a new discipline arose dealing with those white-skinned

---

[56] In the USA, "ethnology" appears much earlier than in England. In 1802 a survey for a research expedition (Lewis and Clarke) requires "Ethnological Information"; the term was accepted for Noah Webster's *An American Dictionary of the English Language*. New York 1828. Cf. Vermeulen: 1992b, 11.

[57] Stocking: 1973; Stocking: 1987, 46ff.

[58] Plischke: 1937, 78ff.

[59] Möller: 1964, 227; Könekamp: 1988, 13.

[60] Vermeulen: 1988, 212ff.

[61] Stocking: 1987, 47.

[62] Prichard defines "ethnography" as "a survey of the different races of men, an investigation of the physical history" (J.C. Prichard: *Researches into the Physical History of Man*. London ³1836, 110). Another British author of that time, Luke Burke, calls it "the Natural History of Man" (L. Burke: *Outlines of the Fundamental Doctrines of Ethnology; Or, The Science of Human Races*, in *The Ethnological Journal* 1 (1848), 1–8, 129–141, 235–239, here 1. Cf. Fischer: 1970, 177.

[63] *Bulletin de la Société Ethnologique*, in: *Mémoires de la Société Ethnologique*, vol. 1. Paris 1841, II. Cf. also Edwards: 1841.

Europeans who did not belong to the politically relevant classes.   Another *éthnos*-name, *Volkskunde*, had stood ready for this development since 1782.[64] After about 1810, the references to *Volkskunde* multiply, though it became a recognized discipline in Germany only in the fifties.[65]

The vogue of *Volkskunde* even led to the coinage of a new disciplinal name in English. In 1846, William John Thoms (1803–1885) invoked *folklore* as a more Germanic sounding equivalent for what so far had been called "popular antiquities".   The new term comprised "the traditional beliefs, legends and customs current among the common people, manners and customs, observances, superstitions, ballads and proverbs".[66] This concept of folklore, which focuses on cultural "survivals" of the past but avoids race and the social problems of the present, achieved immediate success in England and subsequently also in France.[67]

The winding paths of all these *éthnos*-names ultimately leads back to one period, (the 1770s and 1780s), one place (the University of Göttingen) and as I will attempt to show one man, (August Ludwig Schlözer).

THE UNIVERSITY OF GÖTTINGEN

Adam Smith writes in *The Wealth of Nations*:

> "In general the richest and best endowed universities have been the slowest in adopting (intellectual innovations, J.S.), and the most averse to permit any considerable change in the established plan of education.   Those improvements were more easily introduced into some of the poorer universities, in which the teachers, depending upon their reputation for the greater part of their subsistence, were obliged to pay more attention to the current opinions of the world".[68]

The history of the *Georgia Augusta* in Göttingen is an apt illustration for this.[69] It was founded in 1734 by the electorate of Hanover with the intention to rival Halle in Prussia, at that time the most progressive university in Germany. Like the founders of Halle a generation earlier, those of Göttingen were influenced by Leibniz's idea of a modern, practically oriented educational institution free from medieval scholastic traditions. Both universities were established in poor and remote provincial cities, but whereas Halle specialized in the education of theologians, Göttingen was especially destined for the education of civil servants.

---

[64] See note 42.

[65] Bach: 1960, 33f; Möller: 1964, 218ff.

[66] Ambrose Merton (William John Thoms) in *Athenaeum 982* (1846), 862f.

[67] Varagnac: 1938; Schulze: 1949; Dorson: 1968.

[68] Smith: 1933, vol. II, 256 (originally 1776).

[69] Selle: 1937; Srbik: 1950, vol. I, 122ff; Antoni: 1951, 159–199; McClelland: 1980; Costas: 1987, 127ff.

It soon became crowded by sons of the higher bourgeoisie, the gentry and the nobility.

The progressiveness of this new university rested in its "perfect adaptation to the requirements of the bureaucratic-mercantilistic state".[70] But there was still something more: the electorate of Hanover was linked by personal union with the kingdom of Great Britain, and thus became that part of Germany where British empiricism and scepticism most easily laid roots. These attitudes became an official policy in Göttingen. Tolerance was its guiding principle. Unlike in Halle, the centre of Pietism, religious disputes and "enthusiasm" were resolutely suppressed by Baron Gerlach Adolf von Münchhausen, for many years curator of the university. If any single man was responsible for the success of Göttingen, it was Münchhausen (1688–1770), who in 1765 also became First Minister of Hanover. He was an autocrat who was wise enough to give some degree of freedom to his subordinates, and he was a good judge of human character. Many of the celebrated Göttingen professors had been very young and gifted men, whom Münchhausen had attracted from all parts of Germany by high salaries and special privileges. They were only bound to a somewhat shallow official Protestantism, but otherwise were assured that they could say and write whatever they thought fit. A much coveted privilege was the exemption from postal charges which furthered the exchange of ideas and information in an otherwise quite provincial university. In exchange, the professors at Göttingen had to be assiduous. Their income depended to a large extent on their lectures, which were, however, well paid. They were also required to write textbooks — another source of income.

These scholars soon came to form an intellectual oligarchy closely united by common interests and kinship, even if torn by jealousy and rivalry. They were not exactly a "school", though often called so. Nevertheless, their scholarly attitudes were remarkably similar.[71] The Göttingen scholars preferred description to speculation, and applied a down-to-earth, commonsensical approach even in philosophy, theology and the moral sciences. They thus turned from dogmatic quarrels to critical, historical and philological research. Therefore those sciences supplementary to history flourished especially in Göttingen. This prepared the famous upsurge of historical scholarship in 19th century Germany.[72] Generally, the heavy teaching load and the obligation to write textbooks did not impair the productivity of the Göttingen scholars, but gave it a didactic, systematical feel. Thus in the heyday of the *Georgia Augusta* - from its foundation up to the French Revolution — many new disciplines were founded there, such as "ecclesiastical historiography, *Statistik* as a historical and empirical political

---

[70] Antoni: 1951, 159.

[71] Srbik: 1950, 122ff.

[72] Wesendonck: 1876; Dilthey: 1962; Meinecke: 1965, 285ff.

science, and archaeology as the historical science of antiquity" (Carlo Antoni).[73] We could also add the study of mankind according to peoples.

THE PORTRAIT OF A GÖTTINGEN SCHOLAR:
AUGUST LUDWIG SCHLÖZER

August Ludwig Schlözer was born in Gaggstatt (Gaggstedt) in the county of Hohenlohe-Kirchberg, one of the many small constituent states of the Holy Roman Empire. His father, a minister, died young, leaving the family in poor circumstances. The forebears on both sides had been Protestant ministers for many generations. True to that tradition, August Ludwig Schlözer first read theology at Wittenberg, but in 1754 he went to Göttingen where he was enrolled *gratis ob paupertatem*. He depended on small scholarships and later on his own remarkable successful exertions as a teacher of languages for a meagre income.

He had been attracted to Göttingen by the growing fame of Johann David Michaelis (1717–1791), the Old Testament scholar, who applied the historical-critical method to the Bible as to any other text from antiquity and attempted to explain it through the geographical and social conditions of the Ancient Near East. Michaelis was moreover Baron Münchhausen's closest ally at the university. He took an interest in the young man, made him study Oriental languages, and acquainted him with the work of Montesquieu, which had an enormous influence on Schlözer's thought. It led him to the study of history and politics.

Schlözer now prepared himself for Oriental travel by the additional study of medicine, natural sciences and history (the last as a pupil of Gatterer). In 1755, giving way to his fondness for travel, he accepted a position as private tutor in Sweden, where he remained for three years. He rapidly mastered the language and entered into relations with Swedish scholars, among them the great Linnaeus (1707–1778) and the astronomer and statistician Pehr Wargentin (1717–1783), whose classificatory approaches to empirical reality Schlözer made his own. He returned to Göttingen in 1759 continuing his encyclopedic studies and hoping to be appointed to the Danish expedition to Araby, whose scientific preparation lay in the hands of Michaelis.[74] When this expedition finally left without Schlözer in 1761, it was the greatest disappointment in his life. Most probably Michaelis had not recommended Schlözer because of his stubborn and egocentric character.

Schlözer now planned to return to Sweden. Still feeling responsible for him, Michaelis procured for him the position of adjunct to the geographer and historian Gerhard Friedrich Müller (1705–1783) at the Academy of Sciences at St. Petersburg. Schlözer stayed in Russia from 1761–1767, with the exception of one year's leave which he spent again at Göttingen. After he had learned the language in a surprisingly short time, he set out to apply his historical-critical scholarship

---

[73] Antoni: 1951, 166.

[74] See ch. seven.

FIGURE 20: August Ludwig Schlözer. By courtesy of the Porträtsammlung, Nationalbibliothek, Vienna.

to the earliest documents of Russian history. Today he is considered to be the founder of scientific historiography in Russia. The poet Nikolai Gogol, for some time reader of history at St. Petersburg university, two generations later still had great admiration for Schlözer as echoed in this chapter's opening quotation.[75]

Schlözer rapidly climbed the career ladder at the Academy of Sciences, where his arrogance nevertheless caused resentment among his colleagues. Embittered by the subsequent quarrels, Schlözer applied for leave to Germany, taking his manuscripts and documents with him as a precaution. This proved to be a wise decision. In 1769, through the good offices of Michaelis and Münchhausen, he was appointed to a chair of history at Göttingen. Marrying the daughter of a Göttingen professor, he settled down there for the rest of his life. Schlözer turned out to be an outstanding success as a scholar, a publicist and a teacher. A few words have to be said on him in each of these capacities.

As a scholar, he was a polyhistor rather than a specialist. He wrote on linguistics, statistics (qualitative and quantitative), politics, pedagogics and history (ancient, medieval and modern). He focused on economic, social and cultural history, on peoples marginal to the main European nations, such as the Scandinavians, Slavs, Balts, Germans living abroad and non-European peoples, on the philosophy and methodology of history and the edition of historical sources (his monumental achievement being his edition of the Russian annalist Nestor where the critical-philological method was for the first time applied to a medieval author).[76] He was, however, less interested in history for its own sake than in its bearing on the present, thus in its "utility". His guiding principle was the idea of a socio-cultural progress, or self-emancipation of mankind from barbarism and tyranny, which he had taken over from Montesquieu and Voltaire. Contrary to most of his Göttingen colleagues, Schlözer looked more towards France than to England. This adherence to the French Enlightenment later led to his being accused of "shallow cosmopolitanism" (Robert von Mohl).[77] As a practically oriented historian, Schlözer wanted to put historical knowledge to the service of a comparative science of human organization, which he called *Metapolitik* and which today would be called sociology.[78] Another basis for *Metapolitik* would have to be the cognizance of the present state of all countries and peoples, and thus the discipline which was called *Statistik*.[79] When the founder of Göttingen *Statistik* and Schlözer's former teacher, Gottfried Achenwall (1719–1772) died, Schlözer gladly took over his courses and eventually emerged as a leading figure of German statistics. He applied the principles of

---

[75] Gogol: 1832, quoted after L.v. Schlözer: 1923, 9f.

[76] Schlözer: 1802–09; cf. Winter: 1961.

[77] Mohl: 1856, vol. II, 446.

[78] Cf. Warlich: 1972, 190ff; Saage: 1987.

[79] Cf. note 20.

historical scholarship, such as the criticism of sources, to the evaluation of travel reports, the periodical press and private correspondence, by which the basic data for *Statistik* were furnished, and has therefore been hailed as a pioneer of modern empirical social research.[80]

Important and seminal as Schlözer's scholarly work was, it only made up the lesser part of his reputation in his time. He rapidly achieved national fame through his activity as a publicist. Like many scholars of early modern times, Schlözer had used his travels (he later also went to France, 1773–74, and Italy, 1781–82) to create a network of foreign correspondents which he cultivated and extended by assiduous letter writing, making use of his privilege of exemption from postal charges. In 1775 he began to publish parts of this correspondence as *Briefwechsel*,[81] which of course attracted further correspondents even in the higher echelons of politics and bureaucracy, who leaked semi-official or secret materials into his hands. He continued with his *Staatsanzeigen* (18 vols., 1782–93),[82] the leading journal of its kind in Germany. It took the stance of enlightened reformism ("patriotism").[83] Schlözer believed that facts speak for themselves. He only occasionally edited the contributions of his correspondents, sometimes providing them with short, sarcastic comments. The *Staatsanzeigen* have been aptly called the "complaints book of the German nation".[84]

Schlözer's lecture room was always crowded, sometimes attracting more than half of the students present in Göttingen. Many came with a craving for sensation, listening to the famous man's outspoken political comments. But Schlözer also attracted the intellectual élite. His lectures were well structured, forceful, and often witty. They were inspiring because they offered outlines rather than predigested intellectual food. His *cursus politicus*, aimed at educating enlightened servants of state and society, consisted of lectures on metapolitics, history and *Statistik*, including the art of travel and the art of using the periodical press, which were constantly brought up to date. Schlözer also vented his didactical bent by publishing children's books which popularized historical knowledge in an enlightened and patriotic spirit. His literary output is tremendous but of uneven quality. He wrote hastily and without regard for style, a practice which he had become accustomed to when writing for money in his youth. It gave him the confidence to write in Swedish, Russian and French — besides Latin, like most other German scholars of his time. He would have regarded polishing

---

[80] Kern: 1987.

[81] A.L. Schlözer: *Briefwechsel meist statistischen Inhalts. Gesammlet, und zum Versuch herausgegeben.* Göttingen 1775. A.L. Schlözer: *Briefwechsel meist historischen und politischen Inhalts.* 10 parts, Göttingen 1776–82.

[82] A.L. Schlözer: *Stats-Anzeigen/Gesammelt und zum Druck befördert.* 18 vols., Göttingen 1782–93. Cf. Zelger: 1953; Winbauer: 1971; Saage: 1987, 13ff.

[83] See ch. five.

[84] Warlich: 1972, 94.

his texts as beneath the dignity of a serious scholar and upright man. This is rather a pity, since his style has its own merits, as Gogol has shown. It is clear and vigorous, with a marked tendency to epigrammatic intensification and to telling neologisms. Of these, apart from *Völkerkunde* and *Ethnographie*, which still have to be discussed in the context of his thought, also "semitic languages" and *Justizmord* (judicial murder) have entered current usage.[85] The rugged self-reliance which characterizes the man and his style are also expressed in a peculiar orthography considered whimsical even by his contemporaries.[86]

The peak of Schlözer's creativity came to an end with the French Revolution. He had greeted it enthusiastically at first as the realization of Montesquieu's ideas but he very soon became sceptical and disillusioned. The last volumes of the *Staatsanzeigen* are remarkably reticent and he seems to have been rather relieved when the government of Hanover forbade further publication in 1793.[87] Like many "patriots" of the 18th century, Schlözer was disappointed by the Revolution. The disappointed reformist lost his influence on the new generation which considered him first a reactionary and later an old-fashioned relic. Never very popular with his Göttingen colleagues, Schlözer became a lonely man. But his acquired wealth gave him independence and he was still productive. He finished two long-cherished projects. His *Theory of Statistics* (1804), an influential summary which significantly contributed to the spread of the word "statistics" into the other European languages,[88] and his great edition of Nestor, his "most important scholarly work"[89] (5 vols., Göttingen 1802–09). A final triumph came about when he was ennobled by Tsar Alexander I for his work in the field of Russian historiography. Schlözer died in 1809 in Göttingen, the founder of a family well-known in German intellectual life.[90] Wilhelm Dilthey's portrait of Schlözer is probably the best summary:

> A character through and through, rough and bluff, self-assured and domineering, again and again striving for political activity and manly struggle for the thoughts of Enlightenment, against princely despotism, class rule, and domination of the priests, against lie and stupidity in every form. A boundless drive to come to know countries and peoples, the remoter and more steeped in legend the better, led him early into the wide world. The

[85] Fürst: 1928, 17, 75f, 186f.

[86] A striking example is Schlözer's idiosyncratic spelling of *Staat* (state) as *Stat* (cf. note 82). The true title of his famous journal is thus *Stats-Anzeigen*.

[87] Saage: 1987, 47ff.

[88] A.L. Schlözer: *Theorie der Statistik. Nebst Ideen über das Studium der Politik überhaupt. Erstes Heft. Einleitung.* Göttingen 1804. (French ed. Donnant: 1805; Dutch ed. Tijdeman: 1807, 1814). For the introduction of the term "statistics" into French and English see note 60 to ch. VII of the present book.

[89] Entry *Schlözer* in ADB, vol. 31, 589.

[90] On Schlözer's life and work see the literature indicated in notes 16, 59, 62, 64, 65, 67, 72 and 89. Cf. moreover Chr. v. Schlözer: 1828; Karle: 1972; Becher: 1980; Hennies: 1985.

Orient was his goal. He only saw Sweden and Russia, and at thirty-four already he came to rest in the quiet sphere of a German university. Here he now indefatigably collected every piece of historical and statistical material he could get from his reading or the correspondence "with the malcontents in the whole world." His interests and studies embraced all peoples and all times; he thus arrived at his own accord at universal history.[91]

UNIVERSAL HISTORY

After Schlözer had taken over his chair in Göttingen, he immediately made his presence felt. This caused bad feeling, especially with Johann Christoph Gatterer, the colleague whose range of interest was closest to his own. It has been mentioned that Gatterer had been one of Schlözer's teachers and that he wrote a series of textbooks on the sciences supplementary to history. He also founded a research centre for the critical edition of the sources of German history.[92] Gatterer is not known for any great historical work of his own, but has been credited by Herbert Butterfield with a "programmatic character" of his thinking and the "attempt to map out the further development in historiography".[93] His main achievement was in the sciences auxiliary to history, and especially geography.[94] He was also interested in contemporary history and *Statistik*. After Achenwall's death in 1772 there was some rivalry between Gatterer and Schlözer as to who should step into his shoes, a contest that Schlözer won. The main issue between them was, however, the related subject of "universal history". In 1769, Schlözer had already announced a course on the "general history of the world", which he then repeated every year. This was clearly a trespass into Gatterer's field, and Schlözer, being the better lecturer, took away most of Gatterer's students. This led to a protracted quarrel which embittered them both,[95] but also led to the coinage of the first *éthnos*-names.

"Universal history" was another German speciality. Thanks to the influence of Melanchthon, it had been taught at German Protestant universities since the 16th century.[96] Universal history meant the subdivision of the principal events of history into periods for a better understanding of the Bible and the history of the church. It led to the conception of all history as one system, to which events without regard to the history of salvation could also be subordinated. It has been said that it was this conception which saved German historical scholarship from

---

[91] Dilthey: 1962, 263.

[92] On Gatterer see Wesendonck: 1876 and Reill: 1980.

[93] Butterfield: 1955, 42.

[94] Vermeulen: 1988, 192ff.

[95] Fürst: 1928, 49ff; Vermeulen: 1988, 13ff.

[96] Srbik: 1950, vol. I, 70.

a tendency to fragmentation likely in an empire with several hundred constituent states.[97] This tension between "particularistic-folkish traditionalism on the one hand and a speculative striving for the whole on the other" (Erich Auerbach) remained characteristic for German historiography even in its classical period.[98] Before being revived at Göttingen by Gatterer and Schlözer, universal history had however "froze(n) into routine in a way that is only too common with a teaching syllabus".[99] Schlözer contemptuously spoke of "a congeries of some historical dates which the theologian needed for the understanding of the Bible, and the philologist for the explanation of ancient Greek and Roman authors and monuments" which was thus "nothing else but an auxiliary science to biblical and profane philology".[100]

The rebirth of universal history in Göttingen was due to a synthesis of German critical scholarship with French schemas of world history — in terms of a history of salvation (Bossuet, Rollin) or of progress (Montesquieu, Voltaire, Turgot) — and with British empiricism employed in a world-wide perspective (*A Universal History from the Earliest Account of Time to the Present Compiled from the Original Authors*, 23 vols., London 1736–65). This later monumental co-operative work has been mentioned in ch. four of the present book, since one of its principle collaborators had been George Psalmanazar. There also the historian of historiography Eduard Fueter was quoted, who called it the "first world history which at least to some degree merits its name",[101] even if it was only "a rambling and discursive compilation" by poor hack writers "needing much annotation and amendment when it made its appearance on the continent".[102] The German edition began to appear at Halle, the rival university of Göttingen, in 1744, but was discontinued after its severe criticism by Gatterer, Schlözer and other Göttingen scholars in 1765/66, only to be resumed in 1771 by a new team which included those same Göttingen critics.[103]

His study of these questions led Gatterer to write a *Handbuch der Universalhistorie* ("Handbook of Universal History"), whose first (of eight) edition appeared in 1761. It was followed by a *Synopsis historiae universalis* (1765) and an *Einleitung in die synchronistische Universalhistorie* (1771).[104] This

---

[97] Butterfield: 1955, 46. Butterfield here ascribes this observation to "somebody" whom he does not care to name.

[98] Auerbach: 1946, 392.

[99] Butterfield: 1955, 47.

[100] Schlözer: 1785–89, 1 (cf. note 109).

[101] See note 33 to ch. four of the present book.

[102] Butterfield: 1955, 47.

[103] Wesendonck: 1876, 112; Butterfield: 1955, 47f (with bibliographical references); Vermeulen: 1988, 7ff.

[104] J. Chr. Gatterer: *Handbuch der Universalhistorie, nach ihrem gesamten Umfange von Erschaffung der Welt bis zum Ursprunge der meisten heutigen Reiche und Staaten*. Göttingen

trilogy was immediately acclaimed as "epoch making":[105] "He widened the horizon of a subject which had hitherto kept close to Europe; he introduced an unprecedented amount of cultural history; and he showed skill in his diagnosis and discussion of the turning-points in history".[106] Thus Gatterer could feel secure in his position as leader in this field, when he was suddenly challenged in 1769 by Schlözer's course on the history of the world, which was followed in 1772 by Schlözer's own handbook, called *Vorstellung seiner Universal-Historie* ("Introduction to his Universal History", Göttingen and Gotha).

This is the text where the terms *Ethnographie* and *Völkerkunde* appeared for the first time in print. I pointed this out in my paper on Schlözer in 1974.[107] H.F. Vermeulen was later able to show that they were also used in Schlözer's *Allgemeine Nordische Geschichte*, and *Völkerkunde*, moreover in Gatterer's above-mentioned *Einleitung*, which both appeared in 1771.[108] In order to disentangle these complicated questions of priority, some words have to be said about the chronology of these works. Schlözer's *Vorstellung* came out early in 1772; the preface is dated from the 4th January of that year.[109] His *Allgemeine Nordische Geschichte* preceded it by some months, its preface being dated from 9th October 1771.[110] This was certainly too late to have influenced Gatterer's *Einleitung* of the same year 1771, where the term *Völkerkunde* is used. Vermeulen thinks that Gatterer adopted that term from Schlözer's teaching or personal communication.[111] This assumption is, however, not necessary. In the preface to his *Vorstellung* Schlözer tells us, that the first six of its sixteen sheets had already been printed in June 1771, in order to be distributed by the author among his acquaintances for comments.[112] It is most likely that Gatterer got the term *Völkerkunde* from there. Insofar as print is concerned, the priority belongs evidently to the *Vorstellung*. Yet this work and the ANG form part of the same context of ideas, as Vermeulen has shown. Schlözer worked on them

---

[1]1761, [2]1765 (I have seen the 2nd ed); J. Chr. Gatterer: *Synopsis historiae universalis.* Göttingen [1]1765, [2]1769; J. Chr. Gatterer: *Einleitung in die synchronistische Universalhistorie, Und Erläuterung seiner synchronistischen Tabellen.* 2 vols. Göttingen 1771; cf. Vermeulen: 1988, 153ff.

[105] Wesendonck: 1876, 207.

[106] Butterfield: 1955, 49.

[107] Cf. note 12.

[108] Vermeulen: 1988, 1ff.

[109] For bibliographical details see Warlich: 1972, Bibliography. The 1st ed. was translated into Russian, Dutch and Latin, thus contributing to the spread of the *éthnos*-concepts. Schlözer also published an edition for children, *Vorbereitung zur Weltgeschichte für Kinder*. Göttingen 1779, which was re-edited five times and translated into French, Russian, Latin, Hungarian, Danish and Polish.

[110] The full title of the Allgemeine Nordische Geschichte (from now on referred to as ANG) is given in note 23.

[111] Vermeulen: 1988, 3.

[112] Schlözer: 1772, Preface (pages not numbered).

concurrently at least since 1766. Vermeulen assigns the priority to the ANG on the strength of the relative frequency of the *éthnos*-concepts, which appear six times in the *Vorstellung* and eighteen times in the ANG.[113] Yet this is hardly convincing, since the latter work has three times the size of the former. A discussion of the introduction of the *éthnos*-concepts has certainly to consider both works.

Because of its formal priority I turn to the *Vorstellung* first. Like Gatterer's *Handbuch der Universalhistorie*, with which it competed, Schlözer's *Vorstellung* served as a textbook for the author's students, and was re-issued several times. The most important editions, which deserve to be mentioned here, are (a) the private printing of the first six sheets, which appeared in June 1771; (b) the 1st edition, which appeared under the title: August Ludwig Schlözers Prof. in Göttingen: *Vorstellung seiner Universal-Historie*, Göttingen and Gotha 1772; (c) a second, revised edition ("*Zwote, veränderte Auflage*") under the same title, Göttingen 1775; (d) a much enlarged edition appeared under a new title *WeltGeschichte, nach ihren Haupt Theilen im Auszug und Zusammenhange* in 2 vols., Göttingen 1785 and 1789; (e) A 4th and 5th edition of the *WeltGeschichte* were published in 1792 respectively in 1801.[114]

The first edition of 1772 is a smallish booklet containing two parts, a theoretical introduction called *Ideal einer Weltgeschichte* ("idea of a world history", pp. 1–112) and a series of chronological tables called *Summarien der Weltgeschichte* ("summaries of world history" pp. 113–224). These tables, listing the principal events of the "history of mankind" from Adam to the present, do not concern us here. In the following pages, I only discuss Schlözer's "idea of a world history". According to this "idea", world history is an ongoing process intertwining the "individual histories" of separate cities and countries as well as the "special histories" of separate peoples into one coherent whole called "universal history". Curiously enough, Schlözer refers for this conception not to the Christian authors Bossuet and Rollin, but to the Pagan Polybius (I,3), whom he quotes extensively in Greek. Yet the reference system for the arrangement of the data of universal history is for Schlözer no longer the Christian West, and not even classical antiquity, but "the earth and the human race".[115] He thus secularized universal history[116] following a trend of his time, which has already been exemplified by the "Imago mundi of the Enlightenment" in ch. three (an allegorical representation of the history of the world most probably conceived by Martin Schmeitzel, the teacher of Schlözer's teacher Achenwall).[117] For his

---

[113] Vermeulen: 1988, 35.

[114] See note 109.

[115] Schlözer: 1772, 3.

[116] Butterfield: 1955, 49ff.

[117] Cf. ch. three, § *An Imago Mundi of the Enlightenment*.

universalistic conception of history Schlözer refers, albeit critically, in the very first sentence of his book to the British *Universal History*.[118]

Nevertheless, the history of the world for him still begins with one couple, Adam and Eve, from which the human race descends, spreading in the intervening 6000 years over all parts of the globe (Schlözer is thus, like his Göttingen colleagues Meiners and Blumenbach, a "monogenist"). The variability of mankind, as it is presently found, presupposes therefore a high degree of malleability in man: "By nature man is nothing, but he can become everything by conjunctures".[119] This principle has led to the formation of very different units called "peoples" and "stages of culture".[120]

Schlözer thus fills the empty shell of the Biblical chronology with a theory of his own combining the idea of progress (and decadence) with environmentalism. For this theory he depends of course on Montesquieu, Voltaire, Turgot and Iselin.[121] Like them, he does not see the "matter of world history" in the reigns of princes or in wars, but in the great "revolutions of mankind and the earth" such as the introduction of cultivated plants, the spread of diseases, the propagation of inventions or the foundation of religions.[122] It is the task of universal history to give a form to this matter. Two main forms are imaginable. Schlözer calls them "aggregate" and "system". An aggregate consists of a mere addition of individual and special histories ("*Völkergeschichten*" such as the British *Universal History* had attempted to give). A system requires the integration of these "separate parts" into "a living idea of the whole". This idea Schlözer believed he had found in "the general look embracing the whole ... which appraises the peoples only according to their relation to the great revolutions of the world".[123] By it, "all political bodies of the globe" are reduced "to one single unit, the human race".[124]

How is a system of universal history possible? Its smallest units are called the "facts" or "events". Not the facts "the Psalmanazars are searching for", names of kings, years of wars, places of battles, but those which "the Voltaires" are interested in, that "disclose the course of mankind in a nation".[125] Such facts are either linked by their being contemporaneous (*Zeitzusammenhang*) or by relations of cause and effect (*Realzusammenhang*). There are thus two ways to construct a system of universal history (this division is taken over from

---

[118] Schlözer: 1772, Preface.

[119] *Op. cit.*, 6

[120] *Op. cit.*, 7.

[121] Warlich: 1972, 122ff, 130ff.

[122] Schlözer: 1772, 13.

[123] *Op. cit.*, 19.

[124] *Loc. cit.*

[125] *Op. cit.*, 43f, 44f.

Gatterer[126] whose name however is not mentioned): either "synchronistically", according to ages, or "synthetically", according to peoples. In the former the facts are divided into periods and represented by chronological tables. The latter is the more demanding way. Different authors have tried to use it in different forms, but altogether four methods of a synthetic arrangement of the facts of the universal history are imaginable: (1)The *chronological* method, which forms the transition between a synchronistic and a synthetic arrangement of the facts. It isolates certain epochs, e.g. centuries, and enumerates the "world events" falling into these, (2) The *technographical* method, by means of which the "arts" and "inventions" of mankind "are duly classified, their histories according to various countries and epochs are coherently described, and all other world events are arranged as direct or indirect causes, or immediate or mediate effects, of these inventions",[127] (3) The *geographical* method, which subdivides the globe into continents and countries and "relates the fates of each of these separately, but nevertheless systematically intertwined",[128] and finally (4) The *ethnographic* method: "The inhabitants of the globe are subdivided into greater or smaller clusters (*Haufen*), according to certain more or less fortuitous similarities, which are shared by a certain multitude of men. Because of this similarity, the whole multitude is considered as a unit, and is called One People".[129]

Schlözer resumes: "Now, according to the 4th method, peoples are the main pigeonholes for the events, to the 3rd countries, to the 2nd inventions, and to the 1st centuries or other divisions of time".[130]

THE CONCEPT OF "PEOPLE"

The new term "ethnographic" is introduced by Schlözer in a prominent place. Being "the Linnaean, that is, the most unconstrained, most comprehensible and most useful" one, the ethnographic method is for him best suited for a presentation of universal history in a textbook for beginners.[131] Moreover, it is the most appropriate method for a synthetic system of universal history, whose main units are, after all, peoples.[132] But what exactly are "peoples"? Schlözer's terminology is not very consistent. It will have been remarked that he designates the main units of a synchronistic system alternately as "ages",

---

[126] Gatterer: 1765, 4. Vermeulen: 1988, 178ff gives a penetrating discussion of the dilemma connected with this opposition.

[127] Schlözer: 1772, 98.

[128] *Loc. cit.*

[129] *Loc. cit.*

[130] *Loc. cit.*

[131] *Op. cit.*, 96.

[132] *Loc. cit.*

"epochs" and "centuries", those of a synthetic system as "peoples", "countries", "nations" or "political bodies". In this latter case, Schlözer senses the ambiguity and tries to amend it. He distinguishes between three principal meanings of the concept "people": (1) geographical (inhabitants of the same country), (2) genetic (human beings having the same origin, which in most cases means that they speak the same language), and (3) political (human beings standing under the same sovereign).

"All these meanings, even if sounding strange in individual cases, have been abstracted from everyday language, whose obstinacy history can overcome no more than philology, against whose errors and confusions it can however take precautions by making distinctions".[133]

Schlözer did not completely succeed in overcoming the "obstinacy" of this concept. Though always reckoning with its geographical and genetic (or linguistic) meanings, Schlözer in most cases focuses on its political meaning, thus for practical reasons identifying "clusters" kept together by common features and by human sociability with "states" integrated by "common actions and a common fate". He substantiates this choice as follows: "Political association is the mother of mankind, and without the state men would never have become men".[134] As a political scientist by profession and authoritarian by temperament, Schlözer was not tempted to idealize a pre-political stage of human society, and thus to oppose "people" and "state", as his antagonist Herder did.[135] Instead, he subscribed to Pufendorf's theory of human self-domestication by political institutions.[136] Nevertheless, the distinction between "people" (later also called "society") and "state" remained fundamental for Schlözer's thought. In this he showed his transitional position between bureaucratic absolutism and the emerging liberalism.[137]

The unresolved tension between his concepts of "people" and "state" is reflected in a tension between "universal history" (*Universalgeschichte*) and "history of the world" (*Weltgeschichte*). In the first and second editions of the *Vorstellung* (1772 and 1775) both concepts are used synonymously, although there is a tendency to equate the "history of the world" with a "general history of the states", which can serve as a convenient system of coordinates for its data,[138] and to use it for the description of actual events and "universal history" in contrast

---

[133] *Op. cit.*, 103f.

[134] *Op. cit.*, 15.

[135] Cf. below.

[136] On Schlözer's dependence on Pufendorf cf. Warlich: 1972, 199ff. On Pufendorf's concept of culture – the first truly scientific one – cf. Sobrevilla: 1971, 31ff.

[137] Saage: 1987, 34f, following Jellinek: 1914, 85. Georg Jellinek credits Schlözer as having been the first German author who systematically distinguished between "state" (*civitas*) and "society" (*societas civilis*).

[138] Schlözer: 1772, 105.

to that for comments on these events.[139] This tendency is recognized in the third edition (1785–89), where Schlözer distinguishes between "history of the world" as the subject matter and "universal history" as its theory, namely "the systematical collection of all factual propositions by means of which the present state of the earth and the human race may be understood in terms of causes and effects",[140] a theory which would be called sociological in modern parlance. Since the third edition contains more detailed and better arranged historical facts than the two preceding ones, but no more theoretical innovations, Schlözer consequently changed its title into *WeltGeschichte*.[141]

If the history of the world is oriented by a general history of states, it must obviously be distinguished from universal history, since there are peoples without a state. In some cases they have survived their state, such as the Jews, whereas other races never succeeded in developing an all-inclusive state, such as the Greeks, the Germans or the Slavs. "People" is thus the more fundamental concept and "state" the more tangible one. Generally, for ancient and medieval history and the extra-European continents Schlözer prefers to speak of "peoples", for Europe and the modern period of "states". Nevertheless, an unresolved tension between both concepts remains in his thought. It no doubt reflected the fact that the Holy Roman Empire was a medieval political structure that had never become a nation state.[142] But we need not feel superior to Schlözer even today. Sociologists or ethnologists who depend on statistical data collected for political instead of social or ethnic units are exposed to the same sort of tension. And Schlözer was also, after all, a statistician who had to make use of the data he gathered.

Peoples are classified by Schlözer as follows: "considerable" peoples, who substantially contributed to the great revolutions of mankind, and "inconsiderable" peoples, who did not, or whose contribution is unknown. Only the first class belongs in the systematic form of world history, whereas all peoples, considerable and inconsiderable alike, together make up its aggregate form. The "considerable" peoples are further subdivided into (1) "conquering" (e.g. Persians or Mongols), (2) "important" (e.g. Egyptians, Phoenicians, Hebrews or Greeks, who have "embellished the earth without great conquests") and (3) "principal" peoples (who have done both, e.g. Romans or Britons).[143] This subdivision he complements by (4) "classes of peoples" (who are inconsiderable

---

[139] *Op. cit.*, 7f. One could say that "history of the world" is the field of "the Psalmanazars" and "universal history" the field of "the Voltaires"; cf note 125.

[140] Schlözer: 1785–89, vol. I, 4.

[141] Cf. note 109.

[142] In the second edition of his *Vorstellung* Schlözer added the following revealing footnote: "Actually, between a system and an aggregate of world history there is hardly more of a difference than between the history of the German Empire and the history of its separate constituent states" (1775, 238).

[143] Schlözer: 1772, 20, 106f.

separately, but considerable all together, e.g. the Slavs),[144] (5) "additional" and (6) "emerging peoples"; the last two categories being added in the 2nd edition (1775) under the influence of Gatterer's *Ideal einer Allgemeinen Weltstatistik*,[145] which Schlözer again does not care to mention.[146]

The ethnographic method describes all peoples "with loving care and deliberation..... in their details", if always with regard to a system of universal history: "From the jumble of information under which the history of an important people is frequently buried, it selects only those which make it characteristically known; only really great actions, together with their mainsprings ... All the rest is cinders for it".[147] The concept of "mainsprings" (*ressorts*) is taken from Montesquieu and Voltaire.[148] According to Schlözer they consist for any people "partly in the condition of its country and the number of its inhabitants, partly in its constitution, its legislation extending to all branches of policy, its culture in customs, religion and sciences, and its industry in agriculture, trade and manufactures".[149]

Schlözer adds a schema for the description of a people, which he expressly calls "provisory", thereby underlining the novelty of his *Völkerkunde*. He proposes that:

"1. The extension of the people should be determined and those additional peoples included which either form part of the principal people or are methodically reckoned with it.

2. The dignity of the people and its concatenation with the greater history of the world, on account of which it goes by the name of a principal people, have to be expounded shortly; and

3. The sources for its history have to be commented on generally and impartially.

Subsequently the people itself is described:

4. geographically, according to the boundaries of its countries, the natural features which are memorable in these, and whatever art and industry have reshaped in them;

5. historically according to its principal internal and external events, whose interconnection can and must be preserved by means of a suitable distribution into measured periods; and finally

---

144 *Op. cit.*, 108.

145 Gatterer: 1773, 36ff.

146 Schlözer: 1775, 298ff.

147 Schlözer: 1772, 21f.

148 Warlich: 1972, 136, 245ff.

149 Schlözer: 1772, 21f.

6.   statistically, according to all branches of its constitution, legislation, culture and industry, so far as relevant information can be gathered".[150]

This schema reappears, slightly extended, in the second edition (1775) and in the *Weltgeschichte* (1785–89).[151] We certainly can say that this is the programme for a new science. If this was not immediately recognised even by Schlözer himself — this is due to the fact that he still considered it as an auxiliary science to univeral hisory. The "culture" he refers to in the quotations above is culture in the singular, the process of the cultivation of all mankind. A true *Völkerkunde* in the sense of cultural anthropology uses culture also in the plural ("cultures"), thus underscoring the uniqueness of the cultural synthesis arrived at by every people. The originator of this approach was not the enlightened Schlözer but the great precursor of romanticism, Johann Gottfried Herder (1744-1803).

THE QUARREL WITH HERDER

We have a precious piece of evidence from Herder no less, that Schlözer's new term "ethnographic" was seen as new and ugly by contemporaries. It is not a pleasant story. In 1771/72 there was some talk that Herder should be offered a chair at Göttingen. His candidacy was furthered by a set of Schlözer's enemies there, including Gatterer, and was opposed by Schlözer and Michaelis. Almost immediately after Schlözer had published his book a review of it by Herder appeared in the *Frankfurter Gelehrte Anzeigen* (June 28, 1772). This critique was obviously written in bad faith and because of its underhanded, conceited and forcedly jocular style it is almost painful to read, even today. Herder's critique is to a certain degree justified, coming from an organic, relativistic point of view. He objects to Schlözer's rationalistic, mechanistic conception of universal history, in which he can see nothing more than an apery of Linnaeus' *Systema Naturae*, and he correctly remarks that Schlözer's confident synopsis is only made possible by his idea of progress, which he naively takes for granted and which gives him a standpoint outside of history. He goes on to say however that everything in Schlözer's book is either commonplace or plagiarised.[152]

Concerning Schlözer's ethnographic method he says:

> The little fable of the fox hanging his tail in retracing his steps is well known, and whatever *Herr Schlötzer* (sic!) here reclaims as his own regarding the spirit, the plan, the idea of history (treatment of all history as a great whole, "synchronistic", "ethnographic" or how all these hard words are called for which we know no whetstone), actually hides achievements which have already been made (by others, J.S.).[153]

---

[150]   *Op. cit.*, 111f.

[151]   Schlözer: 1775, 301f; Schlözer: 1785–89, vol. I, 118f.

[152]   Herder: 1891 (originally 1772).

[153]   *Op. cit.*, 437f.

This was obviously a hatchet job. Johann Gottfried Herder had sold his pen to further his own ambitions in Göttingen by catering to the resentment of his friends there.[154] Schlözer was furious. He immediately sat down to write a reply to Herder, explaining and defending his conception of universal history. It grew into a whole book, and was added to Schlözer's *Vorstellung seiner Universal-Historie* as Part Two (1773).[155] In it he says:

> Herr Herder calls my words synchronistic, ethnographic and others hard words, for which he knows no whetstone. But 1. synchronistic certainly is not new (this is less than ingenuous, since the term is actually Gatterer's, J.S.); whether ethnographic be new I do not know. 2. If it were new, it is not hard, but analogic (to already existing terms, J.S.) e.g. geo-, cosmo-, hydrographic. 3. If it were new and hard the question remains: is it not necessary?... 4. If it is new and hard, but necessary, Herr H. might provide me with a softer one. 5. If he does not have one, and moreover no whetstone for his manners as a reviewer: he may keep them as well.[156]

Herder was silenced by Schlözer's deployment of polemic, method and erudition. He might have felt ashamed for himself; it is also said that his friend Johann Georg Hamann advised him not to reply — the same Hamann who wrote a short but venomous review of Schlözer's book.[157] Herder did not get his chair. This whole sordid affair does not concern us further here, especially since both protagonists later made their peace with each other and Herder made amends with a highly positive review of Schlözer's *WeltGeschichte*.[158]

Schlözer was proved right in the end regarding the "new hard words". The spread of the *éthnos*-names in the seventies and eighties shows that the time was ripe for them. Schlözer was the first one to have found "ethnographic" and, as an authoritarian innovator in matters of language also, he immediately had it printed. He seems to have considered the term originally as self-evident, and only claimed his intellectual copyright when he was attacked for it by Herder.

THE "*GENERAL HISTORY OF THE NORTH*"

In 1766, Schlözer had published scathing reviews of parts 29 and 30 of the German edition of the *Universal History*, dealing with the eastern and northern

---

154   Cf. Wesendonck: 1876, 128ff; Haym: 1958, vol. I, 634ff; Warlich: 1972, 80ff.

155   August Ludwig Schlözer's, Prof. in Göttingen: *Vorstellung seiner Universal-Historie. Zweeter Teil. Göttingen and Gotha 1773: Hrn. Johann Gottfried Herders, Gräfl. Schaumburg-Lippischen Consistorial-Raths zu Bückeburg Beurteilung der Schlözerischen Universalhistorie in den Frankfurter Gel. Anzeig. St. 60, 1772, mit August Ludwig Schlözers Anmerkungen über die Kunst, Universalhistorien zu beurteilen* (the pagination goes on from vol. I (cf. note 109), and thus begins with p. 225.

156   *Op. cit.*, 235f.

157   Warlich: 1972, 81; cf. Hamann: 1952, vol. IV, 381–382.

158   Haym: 1958, vol. I, 643f.

European countries.[159] He had suggested to the editor to stop translating the worthless compilations of the British authors and to continue the series with new, original works. This had led to his being commissioned to deal with these countries himself, a most congenial task since he knew Russia and Sweden well and had studied Scandinavian and Slavonic languages. His *Allgemeine Nordische Geschichte* (ANG) appeared in 1771 as part 13 of the new series of that monumental work.[160]

Vermeulen has given a thorough analysis of the ANG; I can thus afford to be short on it. Its conception of history is close to that of the *Vorstellung*. Though less known than this popular text book, the ANG is highly original in its method and contains some seminal ideas. Schlözer treats the north and the east from Island to Kamchatka as *one* area, whose true history begins only with the introduction of writing due to the spread of Christianity. Though it is currently dominated and drawn into the history of the world by the Russian Empire, the acting units in this area are "peoples" rather than "states". The special histories of the northern states have thus to be preceded by a general history of the north. In order to understand the dynamics of that area, one has to identify its most important peoples and to trace their interrelations. This object of cognition Schlözer calls a "*systema populorum*" or "*Völkersystem*".[161] He is aware that he is doing pioneer work here which could make his name famous.

The first thing to establish this *systema populorum* is to clear away the pseudo-knowledge existing on that area and its peoples. The east and the north are outside the scope of biblical and classical history and geography. They thus do not fit into the scheme handed down by traditional universal history, but have to be treated completely afresh. This state of affairs is obscured by the tenacious persistence of classical *names*. In succession to the ancient historiographers and geographers, the humanists had continued to use such names as "Scythians". This name, which originally designated a people or cluster of peoples with similar ways of life, was also applied to the area where it lived, its successors in that area, and to its hinterland, so that "Scythia" finally came to stand for southern Russia, or even for all Russia. Certainly such a name was worse than useless; it was misleading. The same applies to other such names frequently used in European history, such as "Germans" and "Celts". (Unfortunately for him, it was George Psalmanazar of all people who had written the parts on the "Scythians", the "Germans" and the "Celts" in the *Universal History* and thus advanced to being Schlözer *bête noire*.[162]) The continuing identity of such "peoples" was a historical myth, just

---

[159] *Göttingische Anzeigen von gelehrten Sachen*, 27 January 1766: 90f; 12 April 1766: 340–348.

[160] See note 23.

[161] Schlözer: 1771, 211, 324.

[162] See note 125. For Psalmanazar's contributions to the *Universal History* cf. Psalmanazar: 1764, 321f.

as the presumed descent of all Germanic tribes from Odin or, come to that, from Noah's son Japhet. The task of critical scholarship was to explode such myths and to prepare the ground for true, solid knowledge.

Notwithstanding its universal point of view, and its decomposition of all history into histories of singular peoples (*Völkergeschichten*), the British *Universal History* was a backwards looking work. Due to its method of compilation, and with the explosive growth of available knowledge, it had swollen to an unmanageable size and marks a point of no return for humanist historiography. A fresh start had to be found. It was found in the critical-phylogenetic method of the school of Göttingen.

Schlözer aimed to arrive at his *Völkersystem* by an undubitable, "natural" method. His guiding stars were Leibniz and Linné. In connection with his theory of language Gottfried Wilhelm Leibniz had postulated that in the absence of written documents history can still be written by a systematic comparison of words. (For this he collected translations of the Lord's Prayer in as many languages as possible.) The origins and original homelands of all peoples could be found out by a *historia etymologica* (which would be called today "historical linguistics").[163] Schlözer combined this method with Linné's method of systematic classification. He envisages a "*Systema Populorum in Classes et Ordines, Genera et Species redactum*": here *languages* could be the same to the historian as *stamens* are to the botanist. Yet beforehand a *philosophia ethnographica* would be necessary. ...[164] This *systema populorum* Vermeulen aptly calls "a revising of Leibniz's programme in Linnaean's terms".[165] Schlözer applied this method brilliantly, arriving by it, among other things, at a classification of the Slavonic and Baltic languages which is basically still valid today.[166]

As has been mentioned *éthnos*-terms appear eighteen times in the ANG.[167] Schlözer's "*philosophia ethnographica*" is no chance hit, but a well-considered concept designating a new discipline which he thought necessary for the progress of human knowledge. Schlözerian "ethnography" was not intended as a comprehensive description of peoples according to their own culture. Though it included data on language, culture and social organisations, it was primarily intended as a method for critically ascertaining the kinship and interrelations of the peoples in a certain area (which would be called today "ethnohistory"). It thus still formed part of "universal history", whose theory Schlözer provided in his concurrently written *Vorstellung*.

---

[163] Vermeulen: 1988, 84ff.

[164] Schlözer: 1771, 210f.

[165] Vermeulen: 1988, 88.

[166] Winter: 1961, 26; Mühlmann: 1968, 42.

[167] References in Vermeulen: 1988, 43.

A DISCUSSION OF SCHLÖZER'S NEW TERMS

In the *Vorstellung* and in the ANG Schlözer was apparently the first to use the adjectival form *ethnographisch* ("ethnographic") its substantival forms *Völkerkunde* and *Ethnographie* and its derivation *Ethnograph* (ethnographer). These are the archetypes of all subsequent *éthnos*-names. The *Vorstellung* remained in print until 1801 and was translated into Russian, Dutch and Latin.[168] The corresponding course in universal history was taught by Schlözer for over thirty years and was attended by an élite of students from Germany and abroad. The ANG, though well received at its publication, had less direct after-effect because its subject-matter was more specialised and because it appeared not as an independent work, but as a part in a series. Schlözer's new terms were, however, immediately adopted by his competitor Gatterer and also spread by him. Schlözer's and Gatterer's writing and oral teaching are thus to be seen as the centre of the diffusion of these names into German and other European languages. Thus it is worth looking closely at the employment of these terms in the context of Schlözer's and Gatterer's work:

THE QUESTION OF PRIORITY

After all that has been said, the question of whether Gatterer or Schlözer originally coined these terms seems to be decided in favour of Schlözer. According to Vermeulen's analysis[169] the parts of the ANG containing them were written in 1770 and 1771. The same can be said for the first part of the *Vorstellung*, which was printed in June 1771. It is quite possible that Schlözer used the terms from the same time, or even earlier, in his lectures. Gatterer's *Einleitung in die synchronistische Universalhistorie* appeared, as we have seen, very late in 1771, and thus late enough to make use of Schlözer's preprint. Gatterer's *Abriss der Geographie*, where *Ethnographie* and *Völkerkunde* are used synonymously, though dated 1775, appeared according to its preface only in 1778.[170] Gatterer may, however, also have used the terms earlier in the lecture room. In his *Einleitung* Gatterer also spoke of *Bevölkerungskunde* (knowledge of the population),[171] but although this could serve as a linguistic bridge to *Völkerkunde*, it meant something different, namely population statistics or historical demography, the German equivalent of the English "political arithmetic". Gatterer is generally considered as the originator of the term *Bevölkerungskunde*, which was used from the seventies by many German authors, including Schlözer.[172] However, it could only have been a remote stimulus for *Völkerkunde* and related terms,

---

[168] Cf. note 109.

[169] Vermeulen: 1988, 42f.

[170] Gatterer: 1775, Preface.

[171] Gatterer: 1771, 64, 67, 70; cf. also Möller: 1964, 220.

[172] Könekamp: 1988, 8ff.

which we still must attribute to Schlözer while bearing in mind that both men taught at the same university and used their respective ideas without mentioning each other.

THE TERM "ETHNOGRAPHIC"

This occurs only three times in the *Vorstellung*, if I have counted correctly, and in all cases in the expression "ethnographic method".[173] As shown, Schlözer introduces it in a list together with chrono-, techno-, and geographic. It forms a consonance with these — a mnemotechnic device well suited to a textbook. I think that this was Schlözer's original coinage, at which he arrived by the bridge of geographic (chrono- and technographic being apparently Schlözerian neologisms too). Even if the ethnographic method was only one of four methods of arriving at a synthetic system of universal history, it was the one preferred by Schlözer himself.   In the ANG "ethnographic" appears three times: (1) in the preface as *"ethnographische Vorstellung"* (ethnographic notion); (2) in ch. two as *"ethnographische Grundsätze"* (ethnographic principles); (3) in the important note to the same chapter quoted above in its Latin form (*"Philosophia ethnographica"*).[174] This adjectival use is thus always closely connected with methodological considerations central to Schlözer's thought.   For him, like Gatterer, Herder and many other German authors of that time, "people" was an important concept.   Being politically, religiously and socially fragmented, settling in the centre of Europe with almost all other European peoples as direct neighbours, the Germans first and foremost saw themselves as a "people" and therefore as a "unity".   This concept thus acquired a highly symbolical and emotional quality in the last decades of the Holy Roman Empire. German authors preferred the term "peoples" when referring to what contemporary Western authors called "races" or "nations".[175]

THE TERM *"VÖLKERKUNDE"*:

This is used only once in the *Vorstellung*. It appears in the discussion of the concept "people". I have already quoted the passage, where Schlözer comments upon the obstinacy of that concept, which forces him to distinguish between its geographical, genetic and political meanings.[176] He then goes on: "It is hardly believable how fruitful and important these distinctions become in the criticism of ancient ethnography (*Kritik der alten Völkerkunde*)".[177] In the ANG however, *Völkerkunde* is used no less than twelve times. All these references appear in

---

[173] Schlözer: 1772, 99, 101.

[174] Schlözer: 1771, 6, 211.

[175] Kluckhohn: 1934; Bach: 1960, 32ff; Mühlmann: 1968, 52ff.

[176] Cf. note 133.

[177] Schlözer: 1772, 104.

ch. two, where Schlözer deals with the "ethnohistory" of northern and eastern Europe and the critique of its classical and biblical sources. Half of them refer to ancient, the other half to modern ethnography or to history in general. This use of a noun instead of an adjective is by no means a trifling event. A new method is thereby reified into a new discipline. It is for Schlözer a discipline still auxiliary to history, or, to be precise, to history before the appearance of nation-states, where statistical data are almost completely lacking, where the equation "people" — "state" is most difficult to sustain, and where, therefore, the geographical and genetic meanings of "people" are relatively more important. In this context, a comparison between the three editions of Schlözer's *Vorstellung* is especially rewarding. Already in the 2nd edition (1775) he uses *Völkerkunde* in the same passage without the qualification "ancient"; he thereby extends the auxiliary function of *Völkerkunde* from ancient history to history in general.[178] Concurrently, he draws away from the traditional system of coordinates which still focused universal history on classical antiquity and the Christian West: "For southern Europeans the Romans may well be the principal people, but not for citizens of the world. I fear that the great concept of world history is contracted and degraded, if one people or another is taken as a general basis".[179] In the third edition (1785–89) he then makes the decisive step already discussed to distinguish between "universal history" and "history of the world",[180] the former being a philosophical and thus cosmopolitan undertaking, the latter actually a history of mankind according to peoples which are equivalent on principle. This stressing of the uniqueness of each "people" was another form of secularization of Protestant thought. With the Reformation, the Protestant parts of Christendom had become institutionally severed from Rome. Intellectually and emotionally, however, Rome remained its centre of gravitation as the focus of the classical and Christian tradition of the West — a somewhat awkward situation for the Protestant nations. The conception of a basic equivalence of all peoples — the logical precondition of the *éthnos*-disciplines — also meant a spiritual severance from Rome. It is certainly not fortuitous that this decisive step was made on the occasion of the encounter between the Germanic and the Slavonic world.

THE TERM "ETHNOGRAPHY":

This also appears once in the first edition (1772) of the *Vorstellung*, namely in Schlözer's discussion of the aggregate form of universal history. There are two ways to make such aggregates, he says. The first is to study individual peoples

---

[178] Schlözer: 1775, 297f. Vermeulen: 1988, 172 draws the same conclusion.

[179] Schlözer: 1775, 285f. In congruence with this changed view, Schlözer also changed his chronology. In the 2nd. ed. the "Ancient World" no longer begins with the mythical Romulus (753 B.C.), but with the historical Cyrus, the founder of the Persian Empire (558 B.C.) cf. *op. cit.*, 14ff, 88, 276.

[180] Schlözer: 1785–89, vol. I, 4, 114.

separately "from their origin to their death", the second to collect "all peoples of the earth into measured periods"; and he comments:

> There (the history of the world, J.S.) was ethnography, here it is chrono-graphy; there it makes its pupil read the book of the fates of the world by length, here by breadth".[181]

Although this is the very first mention of an *éthnos*-name in the book (the other two only being introduced at the end of the theoretical introduction), I think that it is here a derivative of "ethnographic method". It again forms a consonance with chronography, which also appears as a noun in this passage. An additional mention of ethnography is found in the second part of the *Vorstellung*, viz. the polemic against Herder (1773):

> "Individual human beings have biographies. Those descending from the same line have genealogies. Those belonging to the same state have ethnographies. The history of all human beings according to their general fates is called universal history: it is the History of the Most Serene House of Adam".[182]

In the ANG the term ethnography is used twice; once in the preface where it is opposed to "chronology", secondly in ch. two, where Schlözer speaks of "Leibniz's method in ethnography" (*Leibnizens Methode in der Ethnographie*).[183] I think that these references confirm the opinion that this noun is a derivative of "ethnographic method".

THE TERM "ETHNOGRAPHER"

In ch. two of the ANG Schlözer complains how difficult and unrewarding the comparison of languages is: "till today it was not fashionable to study ethnography in this way (*die Völkerkunde auf diese Art zu studiren*), since it is arduous to investigate unknown languages in such a way that they purvey fruitful propositions to the ethnographer (*dass sie dem Ethnographen-fruchtbare Sätze liefern*)". The ethnographer is thus someone who studies *Völkerkunde*. A few pages earlier, Schlözer had called such a man "a classifying historical investigator in ethnography "(*ordnenden Geschichtsforscher in der Völkerkunde*)".[184] This is an apt definition for Schlözer himself.

DISCUSSION OF THESE TERMS

These passages show that Schlözerian ethnography considered the peoples of the world not only systematically or "statistically" ("by breadth"), but

---

[181] Schlözer: 1772, 22; Schlözer: 1775, 237.

[182] Schlözer: 1773, 220f.

[183] Schlözer: 1771, 3, 288.

[184] *Op. cit.*, 288, 271.

also historically ("by length", or from birth to death like living organisms — a perspective close to Herder's). This spatial-cum-temporal concept of "people", makes ethnography a part of the history of the world.

Originally, Schlözer thought of ethnography only as of one possible method to construct a system of universal history. The step to consider it as a separate discipline he took only hesitatingly. Yet he was led into this by the "obstinacy" of the concept "people", which he had chosen as a basis for his universal history. This "obstinacy" also blurred his initial distinction between aggregate and system and is the cause for a principal weakness of his *Vorstellung*: he has to repeat most of his ideas on the aggregate form (where he speaks of ethnography) in his discussion of a synthetic system of universal history "according to peoples" (where he speaks of ethnographic method and of *Völkerkunde*). An aggregate becomes a system for him only by the "general look embracing the whole", a personal quality of the historian, but certainly not the property of the historical material itself. But whether universal history is seen as an aggregate consisting of all peoples or as a synthetic system "according to peoples" makes no great difference, for in both cases the material is essentially arranged spatially, whereas a synchronistic system "according to ages" give it an essentially temporal arrangement. (It will also have been remarked that Schlözer opposes the ethnographic to the chronographic method.) Now he connects - probably inadvertently — the adjectival use ("ethnographic method") with the systematic form and the substantival use (*Ethnographie, Völkerkunde*) with the aggregate form of universal history. This latter one is approximately the same as we today would call ethnology or cultural anthropology.

A last question remains: *how* did Schlözer arrive at his new term. Obviously by making analogies and oppositions with already existing ones. Some of these I have mentioned and Vermeulen discusses some more.[185] *Which* of these exactly led Schlözer to his neologisms (if it was a single one) I dare not say. I suppose that he formed them inconsciously, regarding them as self-evident. However, I disagree with Vermeulen about how they were formed in his mind. In my earlier paper on Schlözer[186] and also in the preceding pages I have speculated that he arrived via their adjectival at their substantival use. Vermeulen thinks the reverse to have been the case. His argument certainly appears strong, since he discovered these terms in the ANG, where the substantival form occurs fourteen times and the adjectival one only three times. Yet I am not wholly convinced. The quantitative consideration must be supplemented by a qualitative one. For the adjective form appears in the ANG, like in the *Vorstellung*, in methodological propositions central to Schlözer's thought. I leave this question open. Less strong is Vermeulen's claim that Schlözer found first the German form *Völkerkunde* and

---

[185] Vermeulen, 1988, 136ff, 184ff.

[186] Stagl: 1974b, 79.

only then its Greek equivalent *Ethnographie*. He bases it on the observation that the Enlightenment preferred the vernaculars to the classical languages. Yet this premise is somewhat general for such a concrete conclusion. German *Kunde* ("information", "knowledge") was quite frequently used in Schlözer's time for the Greek suffix *-graphia*, (e.g. *Erdkunde*-geography, *Weltkunde*-cosmography). Here the Greek terms no doubt precede the German ones. The literal equivalent of *-graphia* is, however, *Beschreibung* ("description"). Vermeulen weakens his own argument by another discovery he has made: G.F. Müller (who has been mentioned as Schlözer's superior in St. Petersburg) used already in 1740 the term *Völkerbeschreibung* ("description of peoples") in a written instruction for J.E. Fischer, member of an expedition to Kamchatka (whose findings were later utilized by Schlözer in the ANG).[187] The expression *Völkerbeschreibung* seems to have been current in German scientific circles in Russia.[188] If Schlözer had translated it literally into Greek, he would have arrived at *Ethnographie*, whereas the correct Greek rendering of *Völkerkunde* would have been *Ethnologie*, as Vermeulen himself observes.[189] Now Schlözer does not yet use *Ethnologie*. I think it thus much more probable that he first coined the Greek terms *ethnographisch* and *Ethnographie* in analogy to the other well-established disciplinary names, and that he chose the German equivalent *Völkerkunde* because he especially dealt with *ancient* peoples - *Kunde*, knowledge, does after all not presuppose such a comprehensive experience of its objects as *-graphia*, description.

CONCLUSION

Fischer's statement that the *éthnos*-names first occur in collections of travel reports and textbooks of geography connected with the University of Göttingen has to be substantiated as follows: the original context in which these names were coined was history, and especially the sciences auxiliary to it, to which geography and *Statistik* also belonged (travel reports being raw material for both). Universal history, in a textbook on which the first three of these names were printed for the first time, had also initially been one of these auxiliary sciences, but was developed by the Göttingen scholars into a super-discipline, integrating geographical and statistical material with the historical under the guidance of a "proto-sociological" theory. This super-discipline was actually conceived as too grandiose and all-embracing to be of practical value, but it provided the characteristic combination of the careful description of singularities with a "speculative striving for the whole" (Auerbach) in which the new disciplines

---

[187] Vermeulen: 1992b, 11.

[188] It was also used by Schlözer's "old friend", the explorer Peter Simon Pallas (*loc. cit.*). Cf. Pallas: 1771–76.

[189] Vermeulen: 1988, 220.

could originate whose object was the *éthnos*. As I have shown previously, the remaining *éthnos*-terms originated in the same context. In Kollár's and Fabri's coinage of ethnology this is obvious, and Chavannes' possibly independent coinage of the same name was very likely influenced by the renewed universal history. Though *Volkskunde* (itself the root of folklore) was apparently also coined several times, and also in the different context of political arithmetic or *Bevölkerungskunde*,[190] the very earliest reference (1782) also occurs in the context of travel reports and leads back through personal connections to August Ludwig Schlözer. To him is due the honour of having launched the *éthnos*-names, thereby giving *anthropology* a stronger anchoring in space, time and particularistic folkishness than it would otherwise have had.

---

[190] Könekamp: 1988, 6ff. Könekamp mentions Kutter's discovery of the hitherto earliest reference to *Volkskunde* (Kutter: 1978), but avoids discussing it, regarding it as "almost fortuitous" (Könekamp: 1988, 10).

CHAPTER SEVEN

From the Private to the Sponsored Traveller: Volney's Reform of Travel Instruction and the French Revolution

"Une verité est un don éternel à l'humanité"

(Constantin-François Volney: *Questions de statistique à l'usage des voyageurs*, 7)

THE MAKING OF A TRAVELLER

Constantin-François Chasseboeuf was born in 1757 at Craon, Anjou, into an old and wealthy *bourgeois* family with aspirations to nobility. In order to get rid of the somewhat ridiculously sounding name Chasseboeuf, his father, a wealthy lawyer and landowner, bestowed on him the name Boisgirais after a family property. His father intended him for the legal profession and hence ensured that he received a good education. At 17, however, Boisgirais inherited a substantial annuity from his mother. He used it to establish his independence from his father and went to Paris to become a man of letters.

Once in Paris he soon moved in the *salons* of the radical Enlightenment, such as those of the Baron d'Holbach, Helvétius' widow or the Marquis de Condorcet. Deeply influenced by the philosophy of the encyclopaedists, he conceived the great project of his life: to apply the methods of science to the world of human thoughts and actions and, thereby, to found a "science of man" (*science de l'homme*). The obvious empirical foundation of such a science was travelling, and Boisgirais educated himself to become a scientist and a traveller by studying medicine and Oriental languages and by physical training.[1]

---

[1] For Volney's biography cf. Gaulmier: 1951 and Gaulmier: 1959a. In recounting it I follow Gaulmier, if not otherwise indicated. On the *science de l'homme* cf. Moravia: 1982.

One of the main targets of the Enlightenment was the exploration of the Near East. This was, after all, the cradle of Christianity. Through the thorough exploration of the conditions of its origins, Christianity could be made understandable, i.e. forced to submit to reason and scientific method. There were also the more mundane interests of the rising colonial powers of the West, stimulated by the decay of the Turkish empire. The Danish expedition to Araby (1761–67) served as a model for this Enlightened Oriental travel, as described by its sole survivor, Carsten Niebuhr.[2]

This voyage had been thoroughly prepared at the University of Göttingen. It had no commercial or political, but only scientific targets, and has been called the first true exploratory expedition, its hero, Carsten Niebuhr, acting as the "impersonal collecting organ of European science".[3] Like his companions, he had been precisely instructed at Göttingen what to look for and to describe. After the deaths of his companions he had also taken over some of their tasks. This expedition had, moreover, been supplied with a survey constructed by a commission of Göttingen scholars under the direction of the Orientalist Johann David Michaelis, which came too late to be of practical use for its explorations, but had rather the goal to enable the public to follow the progress of the expedition. This task it certainly fulfilled: Michaelis's survey became a European success, being speedily translated into French and Dutch. It taught scientific travellers to look for precisely indicated pieces of new information.[4]

These were certainly important innovations in the art of travel. Boisgirais became acquainted with them through his teacher of Arabic. He was so deeply impressed that he resolved to imitate and, if possible, to surpass Niebuhr.[5]

Prior to his departure he assumed another name. No satisfactory explanation of the name Volney has been given but it is most probably contracted from "Voltaire" and "Ferney." Boisgirais was as elegant a name as Volney, and it would have certainly sufficed in order to get away from Chasseboeuf, but the name Volney was his own invention, not bestowed on him by his father. Now he was his own father, a self-made man like the great Voltaire. The play with names and identities is not uncommon with travellers and ethnographers and relates to

---

[2] Niebuhr: 1772; Niebuhr: 1774–1837; cf. Kommers: 1982, 17f.

[3] Osterhammel: 1989, 244. Cf. also Beck: 1971.

[4] Johann David Michaelis: *Fragen an eine Gesellschaft Gelehrter Männer, die auf Befehl Ihro Majestät des Königs von Dännemark* (sic) *nach Arabien reisen.* Frankfurt am Main 1762. French translations: *Les Voyageurs Savant et Curieux*....London 1768; *Recueil de Questions, Proposées à une Société de Savants*....Amsterdam 1774; Dutch translation: *Vragen an een Gezelschap van Geleerde Mannen*....Amsterdam – Utrecht 1774. It was in the French translation that Volney, who did not read German, became acquainted with Michaelis' survey and its important methodological preface (Gaulmier: 1951, 33f). Cf. also Selle: 1937, 88, 144).

[5] Gaulmier: 1959b; Gaulmier: 1959a, 6f.

FIGURE 21: Le Comte de Volney. By courtesy of the Porträtarchiv, Nationalbibliothek, Vienna.

the nature of their endeavour.[6] From now on he was Volney, and he intended to make this name famous.

In 1783 Volney left France for Egypt. Most probably the 6,000 gold guldens he carried with him in his leatherbelt were his own, but there can be little doubt that he was also a secret agent of the minister Vergennes, a former ambassador to Constantinople and a friend of Turkey. Volney enjoyed secret missions. He was a man with a mask, secretive and temperamental, whose true personality is difficult to assess. In the Near East he remained as inconspicuous as possible, but kept his eyes and his notebook open. He returned in 1785 and in 1787 published his *Voyage en Egypte et en Syrie pendant les années 1783, 1784 et 1785* (2 vols., Paris). It was immediately acclaimed as a masterpiece.

In concurrence with the literary conventions of the travel report, Volney tells us as little as possible of his personal adventures. Instead, he gives an encyclopaedic description of the countries visited. It is organized, for Egypt as well as for Syria, in two great parts: "natural" and "political" conditions of the country. We will see that he retained this organizational principle in later publications. Volney is clearly more interested in the political (including social, ethnic, linguistic and religious) conditions, but he tries to derive these wherever possible from the natural elements, such as geography, climate, soil and diet. He shows himself to be a disciple of the school of Holbach and Helvétius; his personal observations are precise and shrewd, confirming his hatred of despotism. After the death of his patron Vergennes he published a sequel to his travels entitled *Considérations sur la Guerre Actuelle des Turcs* (1788), in which he demonstrates the weakness of the over-extended, despotically ruled Turkish empire, but advises against the French conquest of Egypt, much discussed at that time.[7]

His clear and forceful language and his newly discovered talent for agitation made him a highly successful pamphleteer. Having found a new patron in Necker, he went to Bretagne, to campaign for his programme of centralization. In his widely read polemics against the class egoism of the Breton nobility, he appeared as a convinced egalitarian who equated Oriental despotism with the abuse of paternal power and the present condition of the French monarchy. He was among the first to consider the idea of a "general strike"[8] and his political journalism led to his nomination as director of agriculture of Corsica and his election as representative of the third estate for Anjou to the States General (1789).

There he played a very active role. Not being an orator, he preferred the work of committees and backstage intrigue, where he could exert his gift

---

[6] See ch. four.

[7] Charles-Roux: 1910.

[8] Dommanget: 1963.

for convincing argument. He relied for broader appeal on his alliance with the great orator Mirabeau. Like Mirabeau, he became frightened by the excess of revolutionary fervour after the assembly had moved from Versailles to Paris and he gradually withdrew from its sessions.

Volney never became a full-time politician. He continued to see himself as a *philosophe*. This partly explains his failure as a revolutionary leader. In 1790–91 most of his time was spent on the writing of his masterpiece, *Les Ruines, ou méditations sur les révolutions des empires* (1791). It is a poem in prose with learned annotations expounding his philosophy of history. Like his friend Condorcet a few years later, he depicts the progress of the human mind from error to truth, from metaphysics to science. The ruins that cover the face of the earth are the vestiges of past errors, religious (including Christianity) and imperialistic, which can both be attributed at the most basic level to the abuse of authority.

Having lost most of his political influence, Volney found it expedient to take up the office in Corsica to which he had been appointed under Necker. Under the vague title of director of agriculture, he was to report to the *Assemblée Législative* on the implementation of revolutionary ideas on that remote island which had only recently been incorporated into France. He even acquired an estate which he planned to convert into a model farm for Oriental crops and an idyllic retreat worthy of a philosopher. But his endeavours ended in disaster. He was resented as an intruder, a French spy and — because of his *Ruines* — an atheist. Eventually he was forced to leave the island thereby incurring the loss of his property. But in the meantime he had made friends with the Bonaparte family.

As an intellectual of international repute, Volney was constantly visited by distinguished foreigners. Among these was Leopold Berchtold, who had most probably been introduced to him by their common friend Arthur Young.[9] Berchtold is known to have been in Volney's company in the summer of 1790[10] and the consequences of this visit are more important than previously imagined. Among the many interests which the two men shared were the techniques of travel and the survey as methods of social research; despite having the clearer mind and being the greater scholar of the two, Volney was deeply influenced by the Austrian count.

TRAVEL AND THE QUESTIONNAIRE
DURING THE REVOLUTION

When Volney returned from Corsica in February 1793, the political climate had already changed. The King had been executed in January and this had es-

---

[9] Gaulmier: 1951, 195. Cf. also ch. five.

[10] *Loc. cit.* Gaulmier only mentions Berchtold by chance. He apparently does not know who he was.

tranged many former sympathizers of the Revolution, such as Young or Berchtold. The revolutionaries became marked men and had to sustain continuous wars against the rest of Europe. This stage of siege forced France to rationalize and centralize its internal structure.[11]

Volney managed to maintain an uneasy balance between the moderates and the radicals as he had friends among both parties. Among his regicide friends was Dominique Joseph Garat (1749–1833), a man of letters turned politician like himself. In March, 1793, Garat was nominated Minister of the Interior. In April, the *Comité de Salut Public* passed a decree by which special functionaries called *Commissaires observateurs* were appointed under the auspices of the Minister of the Interior. In May, Garat organized for them, with the collaboration of Volney, an office called *Bureau de renseignements*.

In a report to his superiors, the *Conseil exécutif*, Garat wrote:

> "The correspondence of the Ministry has to be made more active, detailed, vigilant; it has to be conveyed to one single centre, where the rays emanating from all places of the Republic are to focus; intelligent, discreet, well-intentioned men, true republicans, have to proceed to these different places in order to watch and to observe whatever happens round them, to study conditions and men, to scrutinize persons in high office and simple citizens as well as the customs and the feelings of the people, and to ascertain the effects produced by new laws, so that the Minister of the Interior, charged with the receipt and analysis of this correspondence, may point out to the *Comité de Salut Public* and the *Conseil exécutif* at any time the true state of France."[12]

Each *Commissaire observateur* was provided with a salary of republican modesty, a questionnaire drawn up by Garat and Volney after the model of Berchtold's, and, at the instigation of Volney, a copy of Arthur Young's recently published *Travels in France*,[13] as a model of how to travel and how to observe. Volney himself was one of these commissioners. He had the instinct for survival indispensable in revolutionary periods, and this instinct suggested that he should remove himself from the Committee of Public welfare without giving the impression of counter-revolutionary haste. He departed for his native province in May. It would seem that this was not a moment too soon. On 2 June the moderate members of the Congress were arrested and the reign of terror began. Garat, who was not trusted among the radicals, was impeached in August. The charge against him related to his plan to assess the true state of France, with his

---

[11] Brinton: 1948, 206ff.

[12] Quoted after Gaulmier: 1951, 265f.

[13] Arthur Young: *Travels, during the years 1787–89. Undertaken more particularly with a view of ascertaining the cultivation, wealth, resources, and national prosperity of the Kingdom of France.* 2 vols., Bury St. Edmunds 1792. Cf. also note 56 to ch. five.

questionnaire serving as evidence. Its technical, value-free questions aiming at objective answers were considered to be counter-revolutionary propaganda.[14] Volney meanwhile tried to win time, studying agricultural conditions in Anjou and writing *La loi naturelle ou catéchisme du citoyen*, an ethic based on the principle of enlightened self-preservation. If he wrote a report to the *Bureau de renseignements*, it has not been preserved. Gaulmier suspects that he found means to make it disappear under Napoleon.[15] It is quite possible that other *Commissaires observateurs* were also more interested in weathering the storm of terror than in committing possibly dangerous denunciations to paper. Nevertheless, some of their reports survive. They have been edited by Caron.[16]

In September, when he could no longer linger safely in Anjou, Volney returned to Paris. He tried to secure a position in the Foreign Service, which was another way of disappearing discreetly from the centre of terror, and through the good offices of Garat, he was entrusted with a scientific expedition to the USA. Although he speedily prepared his departure, he was arrested in November and spent the rest of the reign of terror in prison. He only escaped the guillotine by the overthrow of the radicals. But Volney was not so easily discouraged. A traveller has to be persistent. If his scheme of mass observation through the Ministry of the Interior had proved a failure, he was convinced it would work under the auspices of the Foreign Service. Since the days of Vergennes he had enjoyed good connections there. In November 1794 he was put in charge of official correspondence with the Turkish empire. In that position he conceived the grandiose idea of an inquiry covering the whole world.[17]

In his attempt to systematize and to intensify the information being submitted by French diplomats all over the world he was following the well-known tendency of the Revolution to unify and standardize. For that purpose he adapted his questionnaire of 1793 and had it distributed to all French consuls. Gaulmier calls this new questionnaire of 1794 "simply the précis of the *Voyage en Egypte et en Syrie*",[18] but since he does not know the *Patriotic Traveller*, its obvious influence on Volney's questionnaire escapes him. By making them answer his questions, Volney wanted to transform the consuls into "*voyageurs diplomatiques*".[19]

---

14 Garat: 1862, 283ff.

15 Gaulmier: 1951, 269.

16 Caron: 1913.

17 He had had a predecessor in the economist André Morellet (1727–1819) who, under Vergennes, had launched an inquiry among the French consuls and ambassadors on the trade of all countries. As he reports in his *Mémoires* (Paris 1821, vol. I, pp. 182f), he had formulated his questions "with method and precision so that it was in most cases possible to answer them with yes or no, or by giving sums or quantities." Nevertheless his experiences were as discouraging as Volney's: he got not a single response (Gaulmier: 1951, 321, 323f).

18 Gaulmier: 1951, 323.

19 Volney: 1813, 1.

In his instructions he gave them a concise and elegant definition of social research ("*économie publique*") that holds true even today:

> "The Ministry has decided to collect facts concerning the important science of *économie publique* in sufficient numbers to deduce from them by careful comparison either new truths, or the confirmation of old truths, or finally the refutation of current errors".[20]

A committee chaired by Volney was formed for the evaluation of the returns. But no returns came. No consul took the trouble to carry out Volney's instructions.[21] The world-wide inquiry never got off the ground just as the national survey had been an utter failure. Why? The organizers of sociological inquiries habitually overestimate the willingness of others to supply information. As practical men, the consuls might have had an anti-intellectual prejudice. They obviously felt no urge either to document the superficiality of their knowledge or to embark on painstaking research just for the greater glory of Volney's *économie publique*. When the *citoyen* (and former *comte*) de Lasteyrie published his French translation of Berchtold's *Patriotic Traveller* in 1797,[22] he seems to allude in his *Discours préliminaire* to Volney's projects of systematic research by means of travel:

> "Convinced that travels greatly contribute to the increase of knowledge and of national welfare, the legislative body has decreed that a certain number of scholars are to be dispatched every year to different regions in order to conduct investigations and observations there. France can call itself lucky on account of such a wise law, all the more since thereby a first example deserving to be followed by other nations has been given."[23]

Lasteyrie is being deliberately vague. He does not specify the decree; he equates the "increase of knowledge'" with "national welfare" and thus ennobles the rather dubious goals of the *Commissaires observateurs* and *Voyageurs diplomatiques* by a reminiscence of Bacon's "New Atlantis".[24] Nor does he explain whether the "different regions" where these "scholars" are to be sent are inside or outside France. It is also possible that he had already referred to the nationwide inquiry which the Ministry of the Interior resumed in 1797 and which will be discussed below.

After his two failures Volney apparently became disillusioned with research by government agencies. As he had done before the Revolution, he again

---

[20] *Ibidem.*

[21] With one partial exception: Félix, the consul in Saloniki, answered Volney's meteorological questions. But Félix was himself a travel writer (Gaulmier: 1951, 324; Gaulmier: 1959a, 146ff).

[22] See note 75 to ch. five.

[23] Lasteyrie: 1797, Xf.

[24] Cf. ch. two, § *Utopian Research and Documentation Centres.*

appealed to enlightened public opinion through his own publications. What the *Commissaires observateurs* and *Voyageurs diplomatiques* had failed to do, private travellers of good intentions and independent means were called upon to achieve. He revised his survey again and published it under the title *Questions d'économie publique* (1795).[25] As has been said, these questions cover the same ground as Berchtold's. But Volney had reduced the confusing maze of the *Patriotic Traveller* to 135 precisely formulated questions. These he arranged, as he had done in his *Voyage en Egypte et en Syrie*, under two headings called "*état physique*" and "*état politique*". The former consists of 44 questions on the geographical conditions, climate, soil and agricultural products with the latter heading comprising 91 questions on the population (physical characteristics, activities, nutrition, health, moral qualities, demographic data), agriculture, trade and industry and on government and administration (including jurisdiction, taxation and socio-cultural conditions). The *état politique* is considered to be the product of the *état physique*. As a good pupil of the physiocrats, Volney considered agriculture to be the most important human activity, and devoted many detailed questions to it.

The survey was reissued in 1813 as a separate brochure under the new title, *Questions de Statistique à l'usage des Voyageurs*.[26] In his preface, Volney indicates his debt of gratitude to German social science, and especially to Berchtold's *Patriotic Traveller*.[27] This is the last mention of that book which I could find in literature. Apparently it had fulfilled its purpose.

FROM THE ART OF TRAVEL TO ETHNOGRAPHIC METHODOLOGY

At the end of the 18th century, travel reports were increasingly criticised for their inaccuracy, conventionality and repetitiveness. They were felt to lag behind the progress of the exact sciences:[28] Since the facts reported in them depended ultimately on the authority of one person, the traveller, through whose eyes they were seen, they were considered more or less personal documents. The traditional art of travel had tried to achieve a synthesis between the personal

---

[25] "Questions d'économie publique par le citoyen Volney". in: *Magasin Encylopédique* I, an III (1795),pp. 352–362. The questionnaire distributed to the consuls in 1794 does not seem to have been preserved. Gaulmier (cf. note 1) always refers to this printed text. This text Volney seems to have revised for publication. He e.g. speaks of a "Ministry" (cf. note 19), whereas actually at the time of his inquiry a *Commission exécutive des Relations Extérieures* existed, the title of Minister having been abolished under the reign of terror as unworthy of true republicans.

[26] Constantin-François Volney: *Questions de Statistique à l'usage des Voyageurs*. Paris 1813. Cf. also Volney: 1860, 748–752 and Broc: 1974, 486–489.

[27] Volney: 1813, 1f. Volney stresses here the German example, but forgets to mention that of the Frenchman Morellet (cf. note 17).

[28] Moravia: 1967; Stewart: 1978.

education of the traveller and his gathering of useful knowledge. In order to get a picture of social reality, the public had to rely on the common sense or wit of the travellers.[29] The individual traveller was autonomous. There were no self-evident criteria for judging the validity of a traveller's observations. Volney was one of the critics of that practice. His books abound with sarcasms regarding the "pompous descriptions" and "prejudices" of the "*voyageurs romanciers*".[30] Instead, he wanted to make travel into a sound method of observation appropriate for a "science of man". He had been deeply impressed by the progress made in the methodology of travel at the University of Göttingen. In order to make any further progress, he had to develop and expand on these achievements.

Both Volney and the school of Göttingen attempted to augment the travel reports by improving the education of the traveller as well as the practice of travel itself but they chose to work in different directions. In Göttingen the schema for observation and description of the traditional *ars apodemica* was extended and refined. August Ludwig Schlözer, the unquestioned authority on travel at the University of Göttingen for a generation had already done this in his course on travel and in his methodological publications,[31] Berchtold and Posselt in their great books on the *ars apodemica*.[32] However, these sources gave the travellers only more detailed rules for observation but no clearly defined standards for what was worth observing. This choice was still left to the common sense of the travellers.[33] Thus many who were influenced by the revival of the *ars apodemica* in late 18th century Germany chose to report whatever caught their fancy, and their books became so detailed and voluminous that public interest waned. A good example is Friedrich Nicolai's *Beschreibung einer Reise durch Deutschland und die Schweiz im Jahre 1781*, which appeared in 12 volumes between 1783 and 1796 and was at first greeted enthusiastically, but had eventually to be discontinued because of increasingly hostile reviews and dwindling sales.[34] Famous travel reports like Niebuhr's *Beschreibung von Arabien* owed much of their success to the fact that the author had had the common sense to disregard much of the advice of the methodologists.[35] Other solutions to the dilemma produced by this encyclopaedic ideal of travel were to publish the reports of

---

[29] Lepenies: 1976, 55f.

[30] Cf. Gaulmier: 1951, 99, 465.

[31] August Ludwig Schlözer: *Vorlesungen über Land- und Seereisen, nach dem Kollegheft des stud. jur. E.F. Haupt* (ed. Wilhelm Ebel). Göttingen 1962; August Ludwig Schlözer: *Entwurf zu einem Reise–Collegio.....nebst einer Anzeige seines Zeitungs–Collegii*. Göttingen 1777. On Schlözer see ch. six.

[32] See ch. one, § *Further Developments*, and ch. five.

[33] Stewart: 1978, ch. 2; Jäger: 1989.

[34] Bürgi: 1989, 43ff.

[35] Cf. notes 2 and 3.

travellers piecemeal in periodicals like Schlözer's *Staatsanzeigen*.[36] or to make works of art of them as Georg Forster did in his *Ansichten vom Niederrhein* (1791–94).[37]

The obvious way of preventing travel reports from becoming overloaded with trivial details or private effusions was to give precise instructions to the travellers instead of trusting their common sense. A first step in that direction was made by Lasteyrie in the *Discours préliminaire* to his translation of the *Patriotic Traveller*. There he states, somewhat defensively, that Berchtold's questions are indeed too numerous and unspecific for most readers. He advised the average traveller to make an "organizational plan" of his travels which would include an appropriate list of specific questions.[38] Nevertheless this meant not the extension and refinement, but rather the *concentration* and *standardization* of the traditional schema of observation. The final decision of what to observe and to report, was still left to the individual traveller.

Volney went one step further: He believed that travellers had to execute organizational plans made by somebody else. Of course this did not concern his own person. He, Constantin-François Volney, still travelled by means of his own wit: he set himself up as an *example* of how to travel and to write travel reports. Those travellers coming after him had only to follow his example and his directions in order to do their bit for the "science of man". This can be called the principle of the *heteronomy of the traveller*.

Yet Volney had not completely freed himself from the old conception of travel. If his means were modern, his ends were still old-fashioned. He aimed at the exploration and documentation of all natural and socio-cultural facts in one country relevant to a science of man. His goal was thus an *encyclopedic* one, and he strived for a completeness of information. He knew that individual travellers could meet these requirements only for very limited areas. Thus he encouraged them to become specialists for these areas but to leave the choice of what to observe and the comparison of information to a higher organisation. This organisation he envisaged as a centre of documentation in connection with an academy consisting of the most important "scientists of man". During the Revolution he had shared the Platonic-Baconian illusion of a scientifically administered ideal society, and thus tried to identify this documentation centre-cum-academy with the government of revolutionary France. He wanted to subject travel, which had been an all-round, though dilettantic, activity to the division of labour and professionalization. This meant the relegation of the traveller from

---

[36] Herbst: 1973, 115ff; cf. also notes 81 and 82 to ch. six.

[37] Cf. Michéa: 1945; Wuthenow: 1980; Berg: 1982; Griep–Jäger: 1983; Meier: 1989.

[38] Lasteyrie: 1797, XIV.

an independent, self-reliant gentleman to an unpaid functionary collaborating in a large-scale project.

The realization that acquiring knowledge for self-improvement and for the public good were two different things heralded the demise of the old *ars apodemica*. It became evident that the experiences of the travellers belonged to different levels of actuality. Thus Berchtold's *Patriotic Traveller*, though conveying a homogeneous impression by the serial ordering and numbering of its questions, is actually heterogeneous in that respect. Questions after the most important mountains or seaports of a country, its national character or its constitutional-features which do not change over a long time have to be asked only *once*. Questions after new laws or inventions have to be *repeated* from time to time in order to keep abreast of new developments, those after demographic movements have to be asked *more often*, and those after the movements of the market prices of consumer goods *still more often*; in order to discover regularities behind demographic or economic movements, the two last categories of questions are best asked periodically.[39] The consequence of all this is clear: once a basic stock of information on a country has been accumulated, the travellers need not explore this country anew independently of each other. The more general and constant information can be sedimented in geographical handbooks, whereas the more specialized and variable information, which is more important politically and thus in greater need of actualization, has to be renewed periodically and then be stored for comparison. Quantitative data lend themselves most easily to that procedure. Although systematic attempts to collect such data at periodical intervals and to document them have been made since the mid 17th century,[40] this was not seriously put into practice until around 1800. The first nation to achieve this was France, thanks to the unifying and standardizing tendencies of the Revolution. Quantitative statistics thus became a "symbol of Napoleonic rule",[41] although it was soon emulated by other European powers.[42]

It is obvious that this development made the old *ars apodemica* superfluous. From the 16th century, the *ars apodemica* had helped Western societies to accumulate a basic stock of knowledge on most European countries and regions and some overseas countries. But the more the information accessible through the *ars apodemica* approached completeness, the more it began to outlive itself. The dignity of travel thereby declined. Having saturated its basic demands for information, the public became fastidious and critical of the travel reports.[43]

---

[39] See ch. five.

[40] Schneider: 1980; Kern: 1982, 19ff.

[41] Kern: 1987, 68; cf. also Stigler: 1975, 503ff.

[42] John: 1884, 316ff; Meitzen: 1903, 24ff.

[43] Moravia: 1973, 133ff.

This loss of dignity also meant a liberation for the travellers. Relieved of the task of gathering encyclopaedic knowledge, they could finally specialize. Some of them could become scientific travellers and nothing else, focusing on the type of research for which they were best suited: the collections of qualitative information of a middling degree of relevance on countries or regions still insufficiently known.

TRAVEL AND THE QUESTIONNAIRE
DURING THE DIRECTORY

Besides publishing his *Questions d'économie publique* in 1795, Volney also gave a series of lectures at the *Ecole Normale* in the same year, their subject being the theory of history. This offered him the chance to expound his thoughts on empirical research and documentation. "History" was for Volney an empirical socio-cultural science embracing all peoples and all ages. For this conception he expressly referred to Herodotus, the "father of history".[44] Herodotus had used the term *historia* for any systematic inquiry presented in a narrative form.[45] Yet his conception of history as a science of man closely corresponds to the programme of "universal history", which had emerged one generation ago at the University of Göttingen. Volney's conception of history like that of the Göttingen scholars goes back to Montesquieu and Voltaire.[46] He was thus interested in nations and peoples and the progress of civilization, but not in kings, treaties and battles. History according to Volney "studies a political body in all its parts, which means that by considering peoples or nations like identical individuals it follows them step by step through their whole physical and moral existence... It is as it were the biographical history of a people and the physiological study of the laws of increase and decrease of its social body".[47] In thus viewing peoples as organisms of a higher order, Volney shows himself a true disciple of the Physiocrats.[48] The parallel between this passage and the definition of "universal history" given by Schlözer in his polemic against Herder will not have escaped the reader.[49] Like other authors of their period[50] Volney and Schlözer see the whole human race

---

[44] Herodotus had impressed Volney during his Oriental travels as the most reliable writer on the ancient Near East. He later wrote a special monograph to defend him against the customary reproach of mendacity (C.-F. Volney: *Chronologie d'Hérodote*. Paris 1809).

[45] Herodotus I 1. See the Introduction, § *Empiricism versus science*.

[46] Cf. ch. six, § *Universal History*.

[47] C.-F. Volney: *Leçons d'histoire prononcées à l'Ecole Normale, en l'an III de la République Française* (1795), in Volney: 1825, vol. V, 107f.

[48] Zorn: 1967.

[49] Schlözer: 1773, 220f. See ch. six, § *The Term "Ethnography"*.

[50] Cf. Fueter: 1936, 334ff; Butterfield: 1955, 32ff.

as a kind of super-organism following its own laws of development, the laws of *progress*. Yet Schlözer views the development of mankind as a historian, and Volney as a physiologist. Volney wanted to make history an *empirical science*, founded on travels and surveys rather than on the criticism of sources. The writing of history had to rest for him on an *"enquête des faits"*.[51] He aimed thus not at a "system" of universal history, but instead proposed a world-wide stocktaking of social bodies by means of empirical research which today would be called sociological or ethnological:

> "Travels undertaken and executed under this point of view would yield the best materials for history we could wish, not only for the present time, but also for past times; for they would serve for the collection and verification of a wealth of dispersed facts that are living monuments of antiquity: and such monuments are more abundant than one thinks; for besides the debris, ruins, inscriptions and medals there are also the customs, manners, rites, religions".[52]

Volney here takes up the argument of his *Ruines*. Like other contemporary "universal historians", as e.g. Gatterer and Schlözer, and Michaelis and Leibniz before them, he wants to explore time via the exploration of space. This necessarily leads to the doctrine of "survivals" and to the intensive search for these in all, even the remotest, parts of the earth.[53] What Volney first called "ruins" and later "living monuments" is obviously the same concept as E.B. Tylor's "survivals". Connected with that concept is the comparative method and the evolutionary perspective.[54]

This programme of research clearly surpassed the working capacity of any private individual so Volney proposed to organize it through scientific societies. He imagined two types of academies dividing that task between themselves. The academies of the European nations should concentrate on their respective countries (exploring them, as might be inferred, by correspondents resident in the provinces and by travelling researchers like the *Commissaires observateurs*). The endeavours of these national academies should, however, be integrated by an international super-academy dedicated to the human race as such, in all its epochs and peoples, and especially to the less civilized nations which did not possess national academies. Volney does not say where he wanted to locate this super-academy, but it may be safely assumed that he thought of Paris. Did not revolutionary France march at the head of civilization, a model to all other nations? Like Hartlib, Bacon and the Rosicrucians in the 17th century,

---

[51] Volney: 1852, vol. V. 10.

[51] *Op. cit.*, 110f.

[53] Teggart: 1925, 99ff; Hodgen: 1936.

[54] Désirat Hordé: 1984.

he thus identifies his own nation with all mankind as the trail-blazer of human development.[55]

In planning this super-academy, Volney nevertheless made a step away from the Platonic-Baconian dream of an ideal state organizing social research. He did not think of this super-academy as an office of the French Government, but apparently reckoned with the voluntary cooperation of enlightened persons of all nations, for whose benefit he also had published his *Questions d'économie publique*. The events of the Revolution had taught him at least one thing, namely that an indissoluble contrast exists between the requirements of objective research and the inherent necessities of power politics. This lesson had also been learned by his successors Saint-Simon and Comte; it underlies their projected separation of the "spiritual power" of science from the "temporal power" of the state.[56] Though fundamentally indissoluble this contrast does not exclude cooperation between both powers, but it makes the establishment of special, autonomous institutions for scientific research desirable.

If Volney had become somewhat disillusioned with government operated social research, the French Ministry of the Interior continued his and Garat's project of a nationwide inquiry. Two Ministers, François de Neufchâteau under the Directory (in office 1797–99) and Chaptal, incidentally a personal friend of Volney, under the Consulate (in office 1799–1804) administered question-naires to the prefects of the departments in order to prepare a *Statistique générale de la France*.[57] This attempt at a national stocktaking was no "pure", value-free research. Like the kindred endeavours of Archduke Johann or the Bohemian-Moravian estates in Austria it still breathed the spirit of late 18th century "Patriotism".[58] The aim of the ministers was "to get to know France in all respects" in order "to construct the nation, to forge its unity".[59]

The prefects were more successful than the *Commissaires observateurs* had been. Conditions were more stable by now and the government, more firmly established, could reckon with the cooperation of patriotic local nota-bles belonging to the provincial academies. The returns were numerous and generally of good quality, some of them were published. For these reports the term "statistics" was used, which, emanating from the University of Göttingen had suddenly become fashionable in Western Europe around 1800.[60] Like the

---

[55] In 1790 Volney had already addressed his colleagues in the *Assemblée constituante* as follows: "Till this moment you have deliberated in France and for France; today you will deliberate for the universe and in the universe. You will, I dare say it, convoke the assembly of nations" (18.V.1790). Quoted after Lemay: 1984, 129.

[56] Emge: 1987, 99ff.

[57] J. Peuchet: *Essai d'une Statistique Générale de France*. Paris, an IX (1801); cf. Perrot: 1978.

[58] Cf. ch. five.

[59] Bourguet: 1984, 260f.

[60] Cf. Elesh: 1972; Hilts: 1978; Rupp-Eisenreich: 1984.

Göttingen statisticians the prefects still followed an encyclopaedic ideal; they collected quantitative and qualitative data. Chaptal's survey, no doubt in some remote way influenced by Volney's, was divided into five sections: topography, population, living conditions of the citizens, agriculture, and industry/commerce. The prefects and their local friends were, moreover, encouraged to submit detailed monographs on manners and customs, especially for the less well-known border districts.[61]

But this procedure of data collection was so cumbersome and so time consuming that the data lost their interest for the government. In the course of time, Napoleonic administration relinquished its pretensions for encyclopaedic research and focused on *quantifying* statistics. Great progress was made at that time in mathematical statistics, especially through the efforts of Pierre Simon Laplace, who for a short time in 1799, had also been Minister of the Interior.[62] The *Statistique générale de la France*, however, remained a magnificent remnant. In 1812, the *Bureau de statistique*, which had been concerned with its coordination, was closed down.[63]

With this story, I have already hurried ahead in Napoleon's reign but there remains something still to be said on social research and on Volney's role during the Directory. For besides making inquiries among resident informants, the Directory also dispatched travelling observers, and one of these was Volney. As previously mentioned, he had been nominated by the Foreign Service for travel to the USA before his arrest in 1793. After the closure of the first *Ecole Normale* in summer 1795 he returned to this offer. He was at that time rather short of money and disillusioned with the lukewarm revolutionary spirit of the Directory. He thus decided to execute his own programme again and thereby to offer an example to others. The USA was of special interest to him as a country where a revolution had been successful. He departed immediately on his "*voyage d'observation*"[64] and stayed in the USA till 1798. Volney was less successful in America than he had been in the Near East. His experiences rather resembled those in Corsica. Again he was hampered by local opposition (including that of the official representative of the French Republic), attacked as an atheist and a spy and was finally forced to leave the country. Considering his reputation as a *voyageur observateur* and the current French-American rivalry over Louisiana, this attitude is quite understandable. But Volney had not wasted his time. He

---

[61] Bourguet: 1984, 620ff; cf. also Bourguet: 1976.

[62] The history of quantifying statistics is much better known than the history of verbal-descriptive statistics; cf. Hilts–Cohen: 1981; Perrot–Woolf: 1984; Tankard: 1984; Stigler: 1986; Pearson–Kendall: 1978; Kendall–Plackett: 1987; Hald: 1990.

[63] Perrot: 1978; Perrot–Woolf: 1984.

[64] Gaulmier: 1951, 350.

had seen much, questioned people of all ranks, collected specimina of natural history.

His *Tableau du climat et du sol des États-Unis d'Amérique* appeared in 1803 (2 vols., Paris). As its title indicates, it only realizes the first part of Volney's programme of observation.[65] But this description of the *état physique* of the USA is a much more mature and systematic work than his Oriental travel had been. It is, however, more austere and thus has been less successful. It also contains some fragments on the *état politque of the USA*, especially on the American Indians, obtained by the methodical questioning of a native informant, which has been hailed as an early attempt at scientific ethnography.[66] He also proposed the establishment of a research centre for Indian languages. It is quite characteristic that Volney should have written something on the aborigines, but nothing on the white Americans. He pleaded his bad state of health as an excuse, for his missing study of the *état politique* of the USA, but this was only part of the story. In discussing *état politique*, Volney would have had to measure his actual observations of American society and politics against his ideal of an enlightened, post-revolutionary society, and to mention the bad reception he had met in the USA together with its causes. He would have had to do this in the face of a public that, quite contrary to the Near Eastern one, would *read* him. This was of course incompatible with the position of a senator of France which he held at the time of the publication of the *Tableau*. So he remained till the end entangled in the web of contradictions into which his deliberate confusion between pure research and intelligence work had led him. What could have been his most original work therefore remained unwritten.

Volney had returned from the USA too late to join the greatest political-scientific mission undertaken by the Directory, the expedition to Egypt (1798–1801). Its commander Napoleon Bonaparte was accompanied, besides his army, by a staff of 167 scholars, scientists and artists. As the most sober and factual description of the country extant, Volney's *Voyage en Egypte et en Syrie* turned out to be extremely useful to that expedition. Volney also turned out to have been right when he had counselled against the imperialistic overstretch of such an expedition. However, he took a lively interest in its scientific part. During his stay in the USA he had been elected to the newly established *Institut de France*. This put him in a position to correspond officially with Napoleon's scientific staff, which meanwhile had been constituted into an *Institut d'Egypte*. This could be seen as a partial realisation of Volney's dream of an international super-academy coordinating the research of national academies. He sent one of his inevitable questionnaires to Cairo, which he had worked out together with his colleagues at the *Institut*, such as the Orientalist Langlès and the linguist Grégoire, in order

---

[65] As presented in his *Questions d'économie publique* (cf. note 25).

[66] Volney: 1803, vol. II, 474ff; cf. Moravia: 1973, 133ff.

to collect information on the languages, sects, ethnic groups and local conditions of Egypt.[67] The *Institut dÈgypte* was too short-lived and overworked to answer these questions, but it used similar research techniques. Its vice-president, Napoleon Bonaparte, twice honored it by submitting to it his own questionnaires on Egypt. The *Institut d'Egypte* also formed a permanent commission intended to coordinate the research of travellers with special regard to the geography, antiquities, agriculture and commerce of the country.[68] Although its endeavours were cut short by the capitulation of the French army in 1801, it had collected huge masses of information which was published under the title *Description d'Egypte* in 23 volumes between 1809 and 1823, inaugurating the new discipline of Egyptology.[69] Unlike the contemproary *Statisque générale de la France*, this gigantic work was actually completed because it was a prestige project that compensated for the military disaster of the Egyptian expedition. After it had lost its politcal importance for France, Egypt could the better become an object of scientific curiosity.

TRAVEL AND THE QUESTIONNAIRE DURING THE CONSULATE AND EMPIRE

Volney's relations with Bonaparte were uneasy. They resumed their friendship after the latter's return from Egypt; Volney took part in the coup d'état of 1799 and was rewarded with a senatorship. The First Consul flattered Volney's author's vanity and the *philosophe* hoped to be able to become the mentor of his younger friend the dictator. Their illusion was a mutual one. Volney expected the First Consul to become a president in the manner of George Washington; Bonaparte hoped to control public opinion and thus to pave his way to autocracy by "buying" the leading revolutionary intellectuals. But Volney, though prudent, was not exactly a pliant character. The two men soon fell out with each other. There is even a story that Napoleon, well-known for his bad manners, kicked Volney in the abdomen. Volney, a wealthy landowner since the death of his father, wished to retire into a private life. But this was not acceptable to Napoleon's plans. He had to remain a hostage to the Napoleonic government till the end. After the establishment of the empire he was even created a count. In the senate he guarded a haughty silence and his personal relations with the Emperor were icy.

---

[67] Langlès was also an acquaintance of Berchtold, whom he seems to have brought together with Volney; cf. Gaulmier: 1951, 195. Henri Grégoire (1750–1831), Constitutional Bishop of Loir-et-Cher, co-founder of the *Institut* and Volney's friend and colleague in the senate, had organized under the directory a survey of the French dialects; cf. Certeau, *et al.*: 1975.

[68] Charles–Roux: 1935, 181, 347f.

[69] *Description de l'Égypte, ou recueil des observations et des recherches qui ont été faites en Égypte pendant l'expedient de l'armée français.* 9 vols. + 14 vols. of plates. Paris 1809–1823.

Volney was a prominent member of that group of intellectuals which Napoleon, after initially having courted their favour, used derisively to call the "*Idéologues*".[70] Confirmed republicans, they traced their intellectual descent via the encyclopaedists to Leibniz and to Bacon (and could have traced it further to Ramus). Their aim was a "science of man" (*science de l'homme*, sometimes also called *anthropologie* or even *ethnologie*) oriented on the methods of the natural sciences. They were called *idéologues* because by a rigorous analysis of human ideas and sense perceptions they hoped to reduce all empirically observable manifestation of mankind to their pure and natural elements and thereby also to reduce the "moral" to the "physical" dimension of human existence. The radicalism with which they applied this programme to the whole range of knowledge was no doubt connected with the fundamental rupture of tradition by the Revolution and with revolutionary internationalism.[71] After having won power in the Revolution, the *Idéologues* used it to reorganize French higher learning under the Directory and the Consulate. But after Napoleon's *rapprochement* with the Church, which he needed to restore national unity, their influence declined. They became a grudgingly tolerated opposition, increasingly critical of the regime. In 1803 Napoleon reorganized the *Insitut* and under that pretext abolished the *Classe des Sciences morales and politiques*, to which Volney also belonged, for "being above all the academy of the Revolution".[72] The short duration of their actual power explains why so many grandiose projects of the *Idéologues* did not find time to ripen. Under Napoleon's rule many of the prominent *Idéologues* joined two scientific gatherings which attempted to organize social research by the systematic deployment of travel and the survey. The *Société des Observateurs de l'Homme* existed from 1799 to 1805[73] and the *Académie Celtique* from 1804 to 1813.[74] They coincided almost exactly with the two main periods of Napoleon's rule, the Consulate and the Empire. Their sad story illustrates the ambiguities of social research under an authoritarian regime.

The basic idea of Volney's super-academy of 1795, which was only incompletely realized in the *Insititut de France*, was continued by these two gatherings. One could say that they attempted to organize all those aspects of social research not covered by Napoleonic statistics. Though close to the government, especially at the beginning, they attempted this research on a private basis, appealing to the curiosity and desire for fame of individual travellers or local correspondents. Both applied the comparative method, strongly advocated by Volney as the

---

[70] Moravia: 1973; Moravia: 1974; Gusdorf: 1978; Moravia: 1982.

[71] Cf. Billington; 1980, 179.

[72] Simon: 1885, quoted after Gaulmier: 1951, 462.

[73] On the *Société des Observateurs de l'Homme* cf. Moore: 1969; Moravia: 1973, 171ff; Gusdorf: 1978; Copans–Jamin: 1978; Jamin: 1979; Stocking: 1982.

[74] On the *Académie Celtique* cf. Durry: 1929; Moravia: 1973, 158ff; Ozouf: 1980.

equivalent in the science of man to the experiment in the natural sciences.[75] The membership lists of these gatherings, which partly overlap, contain many great names of French intellectual life of the day, such as Volney or his life-long friend Cabanis, the main propagator of the "science of man"; other men mentioned here, Langlès, Grégoire and Lasteyrie, also belonged. They were all interested in social and educational reform, many of them had experience in intelligence work. Volney was active in both gatherings. By their means, he hoped to collect the basic data for his greatest project, the study of comparative linguistics. This endeavour met with the least response, and even with ridicule, during his lifetime and after. In it Volney followed the philosophy of language and the comparative method of Leibniz.[76] He wanted to "simplify" the existing languages by reducing them to a more "reasonable", simple grammar and to a generally applicable system of writing. By their comparison and classification, he wanted moreover to shed light on the evolution of human ideas. Since he also considered the empirical use of language in its socio-cultural context, linguistics meant to him, at the same time, ethnography.[77]

Of the two gatherings, the *Société des Observateurs de l'Homme*, though more ephemeral, is much better known thanks to the research of Gusdorf, Stocking, Moravia and Jamin. Its foundation in 1799 was greeted enthusiastically; the *Idéologues* still being powerful and self-assured.   The most spectacular among their manifold activities was the scientific preparation of Captain Nicholas-Thomas Baudin's expedition to Australia (1800–02).

The captain had been tactful enough to ask the *Institut* for advice, alluding to Volney's research programme: "History and political economy need more detailed information on the peoples living in these climates and details on their population, customs, forms of government as well as on the trade relationships to assume with them".[78] The *Institut* thereupon had formed a commission, heavily filled with *Idéologues*, who handed this request on to the *Observateurs de l'Homme*, who had already announced their intention to give an "anthropological education" to travellers.[79] As shown by Rupp-Eisenreich,[80] their programme for research was profoundly influenced by the encyclopaedic empiricism of the school of Göttingen, especially by the *Völkerkunde* of Christoph Meiners and the *Statistik* of August Ludwig Schlözer. The *Observateurs de l'Homme* thus hoped to assume the same function for the French expeditions which the University of Göttingen had fulfilled for the Danish expedition to Araby.

---

[75] Volney: 1787, 399.

[76] Cf. Aarsleff: 1982.

[77] Gaulmier: 1951, 313ff; Désirat–Hordé: 1984.

[78] Quoted after Moore: 1969, 10.

[79] Jamin: 1979, 321.

[80] Rupp-Eisenreich: 1983; Rupp-Eisenreich: 1984.

A rising young star among the *Idéologues*, the citizen Degérando, was entrusted by the *Société* with the drawing up of an instruction for ethnographic research for Captain Baudin as well as for the African traveller Levaillant. Joseph-Marie Degérando (before and after the Revolution called de Gérando) had spent some years as an emigrant in Germany and like his protectress, Mme de Staël, had become a cultural mediator between France and Germany. He had made his way back to Paris by writing a book on Garat's theory of signs and the psychology of Cabanis which had won a prize of the *Insititut*.[81] With the help of Necker's daughter, in 1799 he had entered the Ministry of the Interior, then under François de Neufchâteau, where he was to make a splendid career.[82] Degérando's *Considérations sur les méthodes à suivre dans les observations des Peuples Sauvages*, published in 1800, are now regarded as the first methodology for anthropological field work.[83] Leaning heavily on Meiners for his encyclopaedic schema of description,[84] he showed himself in his conscientious and rigorous methods for observation on site to be a true disciple of the *Idéologues*. His dependence on them, and in this case especially on Volney, is evident in the devastating critique of the contemporary practice of travel by which he introduces his *Considérations*. Instead of the usual dilettantish and superficial observers, he calls, as he already had done in his prize-winning essay,[85] for a *voyageur philosophe* especially interested in the *état moral* (languages and socio-cultural conditions) of primitive peoples. This kind of knowledge he regarded as equally important for the *science de l'homme* as the physiological study of the human body. Echoing Volney (and not quite tactfully playing off the Australian expedition against the Egyptian) he hails ethnography as the key to universal history:

> "The *voyageur philosophe* who sails till the end of the world actually travels in time; he explores the past; every step he makes corresponds to the course of an age. These unknown islands which he reaches are for him the cradle of human society. These people, which our ignorant vanity despises, open up before him as old and majestic monuments of the origin of times; monuments which are infinitely more worthy of our admiration and respect than those famous pyramids with which the Banks of the Nile boast".[86]

---

[81] J.-M. Degérando: *Des signes et de l'art de penser dans leurs rapports mutuels*. Paris, An VIII (1800). (Degérando: 1800a).

[82] Cf. Gérando: 1880; Trénard: 1958, 703ff; Trénard, Entry *Gérando* in *Dictionaire de Biographie Française*.

[83] J.-M. Degérando: *Considérations sur les diverses méthodes à suivre dans l'observation des peuples savages...* s.l.s.a. (Paris 1800). Cf. Moore: 1969 and Moravia: 1973, 219–251. (Degérando: 1800b).

[84] Rupp-Eisenreich: 1986.

[85] Degérando: 1800a, 478f.

[86] Degérando: 1800b, Introduction.

After these methodological reflections follows the instruction for ethno-graphic observations in the already familiar form of a series of questions, which need no further discussion here. Degérando no doubt had a brilliant mind, but he was no practical traveller. Because of their comprehensive, detailed and systematic character, his questions were more apt to please an academy than be answered under the difficult conditions of contemporary overseas travelling. Generally speaking, Baudin's Australian expedition was not a success. It was oversupplied with enthusiastic, inexperienced and egocentric scientists. Despite the heroic efforts of the captain, who died *en route*, it ended in disaster. Nobody really made an effort to answer Degérando's questions. The ethnographer of the expedition, François Péron, was, however, among those who returned. He published his findings, but he could not realize the over ambitious standards of the first methodology for field work.[87] Neither did Levaillant respond, his main interest having turned to exotic birds.

After its first glorious year the *Société des Observateurs de l'Homme* began to wither. The bad news arriving from Baudin's expedition and Napoleon's falling out with the *Idéologues* deprived it of its prestige. The reorganization of the *Institut* in 1803 was a decisive blow. The *Société* split over Napoleon's proclamation of the empire in 1804 and quietly expired in 1805. Many members joined the newly founded *Académie Celtique*, others the *Société Philanthropique*.

The *Académie Celtique* had a similar fate, but it is less known to historians of ideas because its range of interest was more restricted. Nevertheless, "Celtic" in 1800 meant much more than it means today. It was a dazzling concept. It stood for archaic times and thus also for nature. It stood for the common identity of the Western and Northern European peoples without regard to the Christian and classical heritage, which had hitherto guaranteed the unity of the West. In the years before the Revolution, "Celtomania" had raged among intellectuals, who had been avid readers of Ossian — the young Bonaparte among them.[88] Linguists like Volney[89] considered "Celtic" to have been the original language of the principal peoples of Europe, including the Germans, and at the same time a model language for all others. Induced by his personal connections with Bretagne, he saw in the dialects, legends and customs of that Celtic-speaking province a series of "living monuments" equally relevant for universal history as those of extra-European peoples. His super-academy projected in 1795 he had divided into sections for the major races of mankind, the first and most important being dedicated to the "Celts" and thus to the most advanced European nations, which he supposed to be united by this common ancestry as well as by

---

[87] Moravia: 1973, 162f; cf. F. Péron and L. Freycinet: *Voyages de Découvertes aux Terres Australes*. 3 vols., Paris 1807–16.

[88] van Tieghem: 1917; Gauger: 1987.

[89] Certeau *et al.*: 1975, 88ff.

the cultural-political primacy of France.[90] Volney was thus a main pillar of the *Académie Celtique*.

It is significant that disaffected *Idéologues* took shelter behind this concept of things Celtic after the empire was established in 1804. Apparently their revolutionary internationalism had always hidden a kernel of French imperialism. The replacement of a *Société des Observateurs de l'Homme* by an *Académie Celtique* aptly expresses the transition between the cosmopolitanism of the encyclopaedists to a romantic nationalism, which was equally stimulated by the glory of Napoleon's victories and by the growing dislike of France by the other European nations. The *Académie Celtique* shows how far the *Idéologues* would go in their attempts to maintain good relations with the government. But this alliance was an uneasy one, and it was doomed from the beginning. The *Académie Celtique* was not as innovative in its research methods as the *Observateurs de l'Homme* had been. It mainly relied on research carried out by independent local correspondents.[91] But it wanted to coordinate their research for the whole territory of France and unite them in "one common research centre".[92] For the stimulation and direction of the research of its correspondents, the *Académie* distributed many questionnaires, which are also published in its *Mémoires*. They mainly refer to the manners, customs, dialects, antiquities and social conditions of the regions of France and thus aim at the exploration of the French national character. One of these questionnaires has been hailed by Ozouf as "our first guide for ethnographic fieldwork in France",[93] but on closer examination it cannot stand comparison in terms of originality with Degérando's *Considérations*. Volney submitted a highly sophisticated questionnaire consisting of a list of 369 standard words for which the equivalents in the local dialects were sought. He thus aimed at a dialectology of France by lexico-statistical means. Volney wanted it to be completed for each department by three local correspondents — again without success.[94] Other questionnaires of the *Académie Celtique* are formulated as riddles or parlour games, apparently to entice bored provincial notables into social research — as in the days of the Physiocrats.[95] The *Académie* looked for informants among the "most enlightened persons" in the departments, such as the members of the provincial academies.[96] It also hoped for the support and

---

[90] Volney: 1825, vol. V, 110ff.

[91] Cf. *Mémoires de l'Académie Celtique, ou Recherches sur les Antiquités Celtiques, Gauloises et Françaises*, 5 vols., Paris 1807–12.

[92] *Op. cit.*, vol. V, *Règlement*, Art. III.

[93] Ozouf: 1980, 210.

[94] *Mémoires de l'Académie Celtique* 5 vols., Paris 1807–12, vol. I, 75ff; 87ff; cf. Gaulmier: 1951, 292f, 305.

[95] *Op. cit.*, vol. I, 87.

[96] *Op. cit.*, vol. I, 65.

collaboration of the prefects which these overworked functionaries were but rarely able to give.

The *Académie Celtique* thus competed with Napoleon's *Bureau de Statistique* for the services of the same circle of informants. This explains why it specialized in those areas of research least likely to be considered in the *Statistique générale de la France*, such as antiquities and folklore. It also explains why its endeavours met with so little success. In its membership list, one prominent former *Observateur de l'Homme* is conspicuously absent. Joseph-Marie de Gérando, a devout Catholic and never a fanatic republican, had welcomed Napoleon's reconciliation with the Church and establishment of the empire. In 1804 he had become secretary-general of the Ministry of the Interior and in that capacity also supervisor of the *Bureau de Statistique*. In 1811 he was created *Baron de l'Empire*.[97] Baron de Gérando continued to stand for the governmental branch of empirical social research in which, although it had been inaugurated by him, Volney no longer took part.

Its concept of "Celtic", though it actually meant "Gallic", permitted the *Académie Celtique* to deal also with peoples outside France, where its competition with Napoleon's government was less marked. It was not concerned with the Celts of the British Isles, though it duly referred to the exemplary research of the "British Antiquarians".[98] But England and France were at war now. Instead, the *Académie Celtique* dealt with the ancient Germans and Slavs, with enigmatic peoples like the Basques or the Guanches and even with primitive peoples. Its descent from the *Observateurs de l'Homme* remained obvious. But the *Académie Celtique* was neither interested in isolated man nor in the whole of mankind; it was interested in the people and in peoples. Its attention to peoples outside France made it rely in a subsidiary way on travellers and travel reports. Moreover it had a network of foreign members and correspondents, especially in Austria, linked to France through the Emperor's marriage to the Archduchess Marie Louise. At the end of the empire, the *Académie* abandoned the attribute *Celtique*, now embarrassing because of its lingering revolutionary connotations, and reorganized itself under the name *Société des Antiquaires*. When it sought royal patronage after the Restoration in order to become the *Société Royale des Antiquaires*, the last remaining *Idéologues*, including Volney, left under protest.[99]

After the Restoration Volney continued in his attitude of haughty silence. He did not allow himself to be made a *Pair de France* by Louis XVIII. He wisely took no part in the Hundred Days. After he had married in 1810 a cousin who had been his early love, he and his wife led the busy life of enlightened landowners

---

[97] Trénard, Entry *Gérando* in *Dictionnaire de Biographie Française*.

[98] Johanneau: 1807, 38.

[99] Gaulmier: 1951, 530.

and also kept a suitable residence in Paris, though not seeing much society besides the family and Volney's old *Idéologue* friends. He became something of a philanthropist. In 1818 he funded and endowed a progressive school in his native Craon, a feat on which he was officially felicitated by the Baron de Gérando.[100] Though a high bureaucrat Gérando was concurrently undertaking private social research among the poor, true to his motto *"chercher le vrai et faire le bien"*: by the publication of his *Le visiteur du pauvre* (Paris 1820) he became the leading philanthropist in France. Volney, though by now visibly declining in health, continued his scholarly work in his favourite field of linguistics. He died quietly in 1820 leaving a considerable sum for the institution of an academic prize to encourage an elaborate system of writing applicable to all languages. The prestigious *Prix Volney* exists till today, but has never been assigned according to its founder's intentions.

POSTSCRIPT: *NOTES AND QUERIES*, OR TRAVEL AND SURVEYS IN 19TH AND 20TH CENTURY ETHNOGRAPHIC RESEARCH

At the time of Volney's demise, three strands of empirical social research which he had strived to keep together had been irrevocably separated: (1) statistical inquiries covering political units in their entirety but focusing on topical and preferably quantitative data (origin of present-day official statistics); (2) exploration of living conditions of problem groups, such as the poor, with the intent to solve those problems (the origin of present-day empirical sociology); and (3) encyclopaedic stocktaking of exotic cultures or the cultures of marginal groups at home (the origin of present-day ethnography and folklore); the latter two focusing on qualitative data obtained by travelling or by questioning local experts. On point (3) a few words have still to be said. Travel and the survey remained the two principal instruments of anthropological and folkloristic research till the great vogue of ethnographic fieldwork, which only started around 1920.[101] The time of their preponderance could be called the pre-professional period of these disciplines. In the first half of the 19th century many private persons influenced by the romantic movement collected popular customs, superstitions, songs, tales, dialects, dances and other "antiquities", whose disappearance under the impact of the industrial age they regretted. They did this by methodically questioning local experts, such as country squires, parsons, teachers or doctors, or by observing the people themselves on the spot.[102]

---

[100] *Op. cit.*, 543f.

[101] Stagl: 1993a.

[102] Dorson: 1968.

Originally leading in this field were the antiquaries of England, the mother country of the Industrial Revolution, and later German scholars, such as the brothers Grimm.[103] France lagged behind for some time, probably because of the uncomfortably close association of social research with the government, but it soon caught up in connection with the European expansion overseas. The motives and methods of folklorist research at home were the same as those of ethnographic research overseas, which was felt to be increasingly urgent in view of the colonial transformation of the primitive cultures.[104] From 1834 in London, Paris and other Western metropoles "antiquarian", "literary" or "ethnological" societies were founded with the intention of advancing this research, and often also with philanthropic aims, such as the fight against slavery or deracination.[105] It was in this intellectual climate that the British folklore movement originated, led for more than a generation by William John Thoms, who, deeply impressed with the research of the brothers Grimm, had replaced the term "popular antiquities" by the more Germanic sounding "folklore".[106] In order to record the folklore of the British Isles as extensively as possible, Thoms founded a journal called *Notes and Queries* in 1849, which was an immediate success. It could be described as an immense parlour game among rural notables. The journal was written by its own subscribers. Whoever looked for empirical answers to a question intriguing him, published it and waited for the following issues. In this way, a huge amount of miscellaneous data was amassed, which could be used in the great "evolutionistic" syntheses of the second half of the 19th century.[107]

As in the case of Volney, this nationwide inquiry was followed by a world-wide one. Around 1860 there had been renewed interest in primitive and marginal populations, an interest, however, less motivated by romantic nostalgia than by the consciousness of progress. This new intellectual climate brought the concepts of "science of man" and "anthropology" back to the forefront. From 1859, "anthropological societies" were founded in the Western capitals, beginning with Paris. These societies were not interested in philanthropy, but only in the evaluation of the evidence concerning the early stages of the progress of the human race.[108] Their research methods nevertheless remained conservative. In London, a committee of the leading "anthropologists" chaired by E.B. Tylor drew up research instructions for "travellers, ethnologists and other anthropological observers". They were published under a title expressly referring

---

[103] Bach: 1960, 42ff.

[104] Stagl: 1981c, 31f.

[105] Cohen: 1980, 210ff; Stocking: 1984; Stocking: 1987, 46ff, 240ff.

[106] Schulze: 1949; cf. ch. six, § *On The Early History Of "Ethnography", "Ethnology" And Related Disciplinary Names.*

[107] Dorson: 1968, 53ff.

[108] Stagl: 1981c, 23ff; Stocking: 1987, 245ff.

to the research programme of Thoms, *Notes and Queries in Anthropology, for the Use of Travellers and Residents in Uncivilized Lands*.[109] It has the already familiar form of a huge list of questions structured according to subjects, thus providing a schema for observations (in the first edition, this schema is mainly oriented on Tylor's *Primitive Culture*, London 1873). The intention of this second *Notes and Queries* was to guide research and improve the reports of amateurs travelling or living in exotic countries for the benefit of the professional anthropologists in the metropoles. It was thus distributed to travellers, missionaries, planters and colonial administrators to help them employ their spare time meaningfully in a kind of worldwide parlour game.[110]

Notes and Queries, which I myself was assigned to read as a student of anthropology in Vienna in the early 1960s, is a work which stands in a long line of continuity in intellectual history. On the one hand it looks back to early modern times. It is a lineal descendant of the great collections of questions for travellers of the late 18th century, the intermediate link being Sir John Herschel's *A Manual for Scientific Enquiry* (1849).[111] On the other hand, it looks forward to the 20th century, for unlike Berchtold's *Patriotic Traveller* and Volney's *Questions de Statistique* it has actually fulfilled its intended function and guided ethnographic research in the decades to come. As a "book of authority", it was revised and continued to be reissued till 1951 (1874, 1892, 1899, 1912, 1929, 1951).[112]

It would be tempting indeed — though outside the scope of this book — to compare the subsequent issues of *Notes and Queries*. This would tell us more about the directions and biases of actual ethnographic research than a panorama of the ethnological theories of the same period. For in the course of time *Notes and Queries* also structured the research of professional ethnographic field-workers. In the later editions the simple lists of questions, though not completely disappearing, gradually give way to discursive overviews and methodological reflections. Obviously they were felt to be something archaic. But so is the whole work. The last edition in its encyclopaedic scope as well as in its considerable size rather resembles the *Patriotic Traveller* and probably is rather difficult to use in the field. This might be the reason why no further edition appeared. It had apparently fulfilled its function.

With this, I also have reached the end of my own book. The substitution of intensive fieldwork for extensive ethnographic research inaugurated a new

---

[109] *Notes and Queries in Anthropology, for the Use of Travellers and Residents in Uncivilized Lands*. Drawn up by a Committee appointed by the British Association for the Advancement of Science. London 1874, 1892, 1899, 1912, 1929, 1951.

[110] Urry: 1972; Fowler: 1975.

[111] J.W. Herschel (ed.): *A Manual for Scientific Enquiry Prepared for the use of Her Majesty's Navy and Adapted for Travellers in General*. London 1849, 1851, 1859, 1871, 1886.

[112] See note 109.

"paradigm" in anthropology.[113] Fieldwork means taking over the standpoint of the "native" and exploring the world from there. It thus cannot be too structured by given research instructions. Ethnographical fieldwork, which is by now increasingly also employed in the exploration of "subcultures" and "everyday culture" within our own society[114], if not encyclopaedic, is at least holistic, covering the whole area within the horizon of the researcher. It is the most archaic research technique in existence, since the researcher is involved with his whole person. It also is a special form of travel, which culminates — like medieval pilgrimage — in an extended and momentous sojourn abroad.

Thus ethnographic and sociological fieldwork, though it has made encyclopaedic surveys and instructions for travellers finally obsolete, nevertheless conserves something of the personal and universal orientation of the old *ars apodemica*.

---

[113] Stagl: 1993a.

[114] Stagl: 1985.

References

Aarsleff, Hans, 1982.
From Locke to Saussure. Essays in the Study of Language and Intellectual History. London.

Abraham, James Johnston, 1933.
Lettsom. His life, times, friends and descedants. London.

Académie Celtique, 1807-12.
Mémoires de l'Academie Celtique, ou Recherches sur les Antiquités Celtiques, Gauloises et Francçaises. 5 vols. Paris.

Adams, Percy G., 1962.
Travellers and Travel Liars 1660-1800. Berkeley, Los Angeles.

Agricola, Rudolph, 1528.
De inventione. Dialectica. Cologne. (orig. 1479). Reprint with introduction by Wilhelm Risse. Hildesheim 1976.

Ahrbeck-Wohtge, R., 1971.
Studien über den Philanthropismus und die Dessauer Aufklärung. Halle.

Allen, John L., 1976.
Lands of Myth, Waters of Wonder: The Place of the Imagination in the History of Geographical Exploration. in: *Geographies on the Mind. Essays in Historical Geosophy. In Honor of John Kitland Wright.* Ed. Lowenthal, David and Bowden, Martyn H. New York.

Alpers, Svetlana, 1983.
The Art of Describing. Dutch Art in the Seventeenth Century. London.

Althaus, F., 1884.
Samuel Hartlib: Ein deutsch-englisches Charakterbild. Leipzig.

Altheim, Franz, 1960.
Zarathustra und Alexander. Eine ost-westliche Begegnung. Frankfurt am Main, Berlin.

Althoff, Gerd, 1992.
Vom Zwang zur Mobilität und ihren Problemen, in: Ertzdorff/Neukirch (1992) 91-112.

Amalvy, Isaac d', 1706.
Eclairissements nécessaires pour bien entendre ce que le S.N.F.D.B.R. dit ... par rapport à la conversion de Mr. G. Psalmanazar Japonais, dans son livre intitulé Description de l'isle Formosa. Den Haag.

Anderson, A.W., 1947.
John Tradescant. in: *Gardener's Chronicle of America 1947:* 324-325.

Andreae, Johann Valentin, 1619.
Rei publicae Christianopolitanae descriptio. Strasbourg. (here used in the edition of W. Biesterfeld, Stuttgart 1975).

Andreas, Willy, 1943.
Staatskunst und Diplomatie der Venezianer. Leipzig.

Andrewes, Anthony, 1967.
The Greeks. London.

Anonymus (Ed.), 1591.
De arte peregrinandi. Libri II. Variis exemplis: imprimis vero agri Neapolitani descriptione illustrati Item lib. II dè regimine iter agentium. Quibus acceserunt in fine Quaestiones Forcianae. hoc est, de variis Italorum ingeniis: & de muliebris sexus praestantia, Dialogi II. Singuli accurate denuo recusi. Nürnberg.

Anonymus, 1614.
Fama fraternitatis Rosae Crucis. Kassel.

Anonymus, 1615.
Confessio oder Bekenntnis der Societät und Bruderschaft Rosenkreuz. Kassel.

Anonymus, 1736-65.
An Universal History, from the earliest account of time to the present compiled from the original authors. 23 vols. London. (German ed. by D.F.E. Boysen: *Die allgemeine Welthistorie.* 37 vols. Halle 1769-90).

Antoni, Carli, 1951.
Der Kampf wider die Vernunft. Zur Entstehungsgeschichte des deutschen Freiheitsgedankens. Stuttgart.

Aristotle see Rackham

Assmann, Jan, 1988.
Schrift, Tradition und Kultur. in: Raible, W. (ed.): *Zwischen Festtag und Alltag.* Scriptoralia bei Tübingen: 25-49.

Assmann, Jan, 1992.
Das kulturelle Gedächtnis. Schrift, Erinnerung und politische Identität in frühen Hochkulturen. München.
Aston, Margaret, 1968.
The Fifteenth Century: The Prospect of Europe. New York.
Atkinson, Geoffrey, 1924.
Les relations de voyages au XVIIe siècle et l'evolution des idées. Contribution à l'étude de la formation de l'esprit du XVIIIe siècle. Paris (reprint 1972).
Auerbach, Erich, 1946.
Mimesis. Dargestellte Wirklichkeit in der abendländischen Literatur. Bern.
Augustinus, Aurelius, 1977.
De civitate dei. Vom Gottesstaat. Books 1-22. Ed. Carl Andresen. 2 vols. München.
Bach, Adolf, 1960.
Deutsche Volkskunde: Wege und Organisation, Probleme, System, Methoden, Ergebnisse und Aufgaben. Schrifttum. 3rd ed. Heidelberg.
Bacon, Francis, Lord Verulam, (1740.
The Works. 4 vols. London.
Balázs, Eva H. et al. (eds.), 1979.
Beförderer der Aufklärung in Mittel- und Osteuropa. Freimaurer, Gesellschaften, Klubs. Berlin.
Balbi, Adriano, 1826a.
Atlas Ethnographique du Globe, ou Classification des Peuples Anciens et Modernes d'après Leurs Langues ... Paris.
Balbi, Adriano, 1826b.
Introduction à l'Atlas Ethnographique du Globe Contenant un Discours sur l'Utilité et l'Importance de l'Etude des Langues. t.1 Paris.
Barnett, R.D., 1958.
Early Shipping in the Near East. in: *Antiquity* 32.
Bartholinus, Thomas, 1674.
De peregrinatione medica... Copenhagen.
Bastian, Adolf, 1881.
Die Vorgeschichte der Ethnologie. Berlin.
Bates, Ernest S., , 1911.
Touring in 1600. A Study in the Development of Travel as a Means of Education. London, Boston, New York.
Baudelot de Dairval, Charles César, 1686.
De l'utilité des Voyages, et de l'avantage que la recherche des Antiquitez procure aux scavans. 2 vols. Paris.
Baudelot de Dairval, Charles César, 1688.
Memoire de quelques observation générales, Qu'on peut faire pour ne pas voyager inutilement. Paris, Bruxelles.
Baudet, Henri, 1965.
Paradise on Earth. Some Thoughts on European Images of Non-European Man. New Haven, Conn.
Bauer, W.M., 1969.
Die "Akademielandschaft" in der neulateinischen Dichtung. in: *Euphorion* 63.
Becher, Ursula A.J., 1980.
August Ludwig von Schlözer. in: Wehler (1980) Vol. VII: 7-23.
Beck, Hanno, 1973.
Geographie. Europäische Entwicklung in Texten und Erläuterungen. Freiburg, München.
Beckmann, J., 1807.
Literatur der älteren Reisebeschreibungen. Göttingen.
Beek, Martinus Adrianus, 1973.
Geschichte Israels: Von Abraham bis Bar Kochba. 3rd ed. Stuttgart. (Dutch orig. 1957)
Beck, Hanno, 1955.
Entdeckungsgeschichte und geographische Disziplinhistorie. in: Erdkunde 9: 197-204.
Beck, Hanno, 1959.
Alexander von Humboldt. Vol I: *Von der Bildungsreise zur Forschungsreise 1769-1804.* Wiesbaden.
Beck, Hanno, 1971.
Carsten Niebuhr - der erste Forschungsreisende. in: Beck, Hanno: *Große Reisende.* München: 92-117.
Beck, Hanno, 1973.
Geographie. Europäische Entwicklung in Texten und Erläuterungen. Freiburg, München.
Beck, Hanno, 1980.
Geographie und Statistik - Die Lösung einer Polarität. in: Rassem/Stagl (1980): 269-282.
Behre, Otto, 1905.
Geschichte der Statistik in Brandenburg-Preussen bis zur Gründung des Königlichen Statistischen Bureaus. Berlin.
Behrmann, Walter, 1924.
Die Stammeszersplitterung im Sepikgebiet (Neuguinea und ihre geographischen Ursachen. in: *Petersmanns Mitteilungen* 70.

Belay, Vitomir, 1989.
An Argument for Ethnology as a Historical Science Concerning Ethnic Groups. in: *Studia Ethnologica* 1:9-17.

Belcher, Ursula A.J., 1978.
Politische Gesellschaft. Studien zur Genese der bürgerlichen Öffentlichkeit in Deutschland. Göttingen.

Bellus, Iulius, 1608.
Hermes Politicus Sive De Peregrinatione Prudentia libri tres. Frankfurt.

Beloff, Max, 1966.
The Age of Absolutism 1660-1815. 7th ed. London.

Benham , s.a..
Benham's Book of Quotations, Proverbs and Household Words. rev.ed. London, Melbourne.

Berchtold, Leopold Graf, 1789.
An Essay to direct and extend the Inquiries of Patriotic Travellers; with further Observation on the Means of preserving Life, Health, & Property of the unexperienced in their Journies by Land and Sea. Also a Series of Questions, interesting to Society and Humanity, necessary to be proposed for Solution to Men of all ranks, & employment, & of all Nations and Governments, comprising the most serious Points relative to the Objects of all Travels. To which is annexed a List of English and foreign Works, intended for the Instruction and Benefit of Travellers, & a Catalogue of the most interesting European Travels, which have been publish'd in different Languages form the earliest Times, down to September 8th, 1787. By Count Leopold Berchtold, Knight of Military Order of St. Stephen of Tuscany &c. &c. 2 vols. London.

Berchtold, Leopold Graf, 1791a.
Projet pour prévenir les dangers très-fréquens des inhumations précipitées; presenté à l'Assemblée Nationale par le Comte L.B. Paris.

Berchtold, Leopold Graf, 1791b.
Projet d'une méthode sure et aisée D'approfondir les véritables causes des maladies des gens de mer, et rouver la meilleure manière de les guérir, avec des observations sur la nécessité d'amettre l'art de nager et de plonger dans l'éducation nationale. Présenté à l'Assemblé nationale par le Comte Léopold de Berchtold. Paris.

Berchtold, Leopold Graf, 1791c.
Kurzgefasste Methode alle Arten von Scheinbartodten wiederzubeleben ... Wien.

Berchtold, Leopold Graf, 1791d.
Anweisungen für Reisende, nebst einer systematischen Sammlung zweckmäßiger und nützlicher Fragen. Transl. Paul Jakob Bruns. Brunswick.

Berchtold, Leopold Graf, 1792.
Ensaio de varios meios Comque se intenta salvar, e conservar a vida dos homens em diversos perigos, a que diriamente se acháo expostos ... Parase distribuir gratuitamente a bem da humanidade. Lissabon.

Berchtold, Leopold Graf, 1793.
Ensaio sobre a extensão dos limites da beneficencia a respito, assim dos homens, como dos mesmos animaes ... para se distribuir gratuitamente a bem da humanidade. Lissabon.

Berchtold, Leopold Graf, , 1797a.
Essai pour diriger et étendre les recherches des voyageurs qui se proposent l'utilité de leur patrie, avec observations pour préserver la vie, la santé et ese effets ... Transl. Charles-Philibert Lasteyrie. Paris An V.

Berchtold, Leopold Graf, 1797b.
Nachricht von dem im St. Antons-Spitale in Smirna mit dem allerbesten Erfolg gebrauchten einfachen Mittel, die Pest zu heilen, und sich selber zu bewahren, welche im Lande selbst gesammelt worden ist ... Wien. *(Descritione del nuovo rimedio curativo e preservativo contro la peste ...* Wien, 2nd ed. ital. and croat. Zara 1810).

Berchtold, Leopold Graf, 1800a.
Versuch die Gränzen der Wohlthätigkeit gegen Menschen unt Thiere zu erweitern. Wien.

Berchtold, Leopold Graf, 1800b.
Kurzgefasste Naturgeschichte der schädlichsten Waldinsekten, nebst ihrer Oekonomie und einigen bewährt gefundenen Wehr- und Rettungsmitteln ... s.l.

Berchtold, Leopold Graf, 1809.
Beiträge zur Veredlung des österreichischen Landwehrmannes, von einem Patrioten. s.l.

Berchtold, Leopold Graf, 1893.
Vergangenheit und Gegenwart der Herrenburg Buchlau im mährischen Marsgebirge. Brünn.

Berg, Eberhard, 1982.
Zwischen den Welten. Über die Anthropologie der Aufklärung und ihr Verhältnis zur Entdeckungsreise und Welterfahrung mit besonderem Blick auf das Werk Georg Forsters. Berlin.

Bergson, Henri, 1932.
Les deux sources de la morale et de la religion. Paris.

Berliner, Rudolf, 1928.
Zur älteren Geschichte der allgemeinen Museumslehre in Deutschland. in: *Münchner Jahrbuch für bildende Kunst,* N.F. 59: 327-352.

Berlyne, Daniel E., 1960.
Conflict, arousal and curiosity. New York.

Bernard, Frédéric, 1715-27.
  Recueil de voiages au Commerce & à la Navigation. 3 vols. Amsterdam.
Bertuch, F.J. and Vater, J.S., 1808.
  Allgemeines Archiv für Ethnographie und Linguistik. Weimar.
Bietenholz, Peter G., 1959.
  Der italienische Humanismus und die Blütezeit des Buchdrucks in Basel. Die Baseler Drucke italienischer Autoren von 1530 bis zum Ende des 16. Jahrhunderts. Basel.
Bietenholz, Peter G., 1971.
  Basel and France in the sixteenth Century. The Basle Humanists and Printers in their Contacts With Francophone Culture. Geneva.
Billington, James H., 1980.
  Fire in the Minds of Men: Origins of the Revolutionary Faith. New York.
Biographie universelle ou Dictionnaire Historique. 6 vols. Paris, 1841)
Biondo, Flavio, 1474.
  Italiae Illustratae libri VIII. Rome.
Bitterli, Urs, 1976.
  Die ''Wilden'' und die ''Zivilisierten''. Grundzüge einer Geistes- und Kulturgeschichte der europäisch-überseeischen Begegnung. München.
Blotius, Hugo see Plotius, Hugo
Blumenberg, Hans, 1966.
  Die Legitimität der Neuzeit. Frankfurt am Main.
Blumenberg, Hans, 1975.
  Die Genesis der kopernikanischen Welt. Frankfurt am Main.
Blumenberg, Hans, 1981.
  Die Lesbarkeit der Welt. Frankfurt am Main.
Boas Hall, Marie, 1970-76.
  Hartlib, Samuel. in: *Dictionary of Scientific Biography* vol VI: 140-142.
Bodin, Jean, 1566.
  Methodus ad facilem historiarum cognitionem. Paris.
Boecler, Johann Heinrich, 1701.
  De peregrinatione Germanici Caesaris. in: *Boecler, J.H.: Dissertationes Academicae* 2nd ed. Straßburg.
Boemus, Ioannes, 1520.
  Repertorium librorium trium de omnium gentium ritibus. Augsberg.
Boemus, Ioannes, 1536.
  Omnium Gentium Mores, Leges & Ritus ex multis clarissimis rerum scriptoribus ... Lyon.
Bohnstedt, John Wolfgang, 1968.
  The Infidel Scourge of God. The Turkish Menace as seen by German pamphleteers of the Reformation era. Philadelphia.
Bolgar, R.R. (ed.), 1976.
  Classical Influences on European Culture A.D. 1500-1700. Cambridge.
Bonjour, Edgar, 1960.
  Die Universität Basel von den Anfängen bis zur Gegenwart. Basel.
Bonnefont, G., 1893.
  Un docteur d'autrefois: Théophraste Renaudot. Limoges.
Bonß, Wolfgang, 1982.
  Die Einübung des Tatsachenblicks: Zur Struktur und Veränderung empirischer Sozialforschung. Frankfurt am Main.
Boswell, James, 934-50.
  Life of Johnson. Ed. G. Birkbeck Hill, revised by L.F. Powell. 6 vols. London.
Boucher de la Richarderie, G., 1808.
  Bibliothèque universelle des voyages. Vol. 5. Paris.
Bourde, André J., 1953.
  The influence of England on the French agronomes 1750-1789. Cambridge.
Bourde, André J., 1967.
  Agronomie et Agronomes en France au XVIIIe siècle. 3 vols. Paris.
Bourguet, Marie-Noëlle, 1976.
  Race et Folklore, l'image officielle de la France en 1800. in: *Annales; Economies Sociétés Civilisations* 31/4: 802-823.
Bourguet, Marie-Noëlle, 1984.
  Des prefets aux champs: une ethnographie administrative de la France en 1800. in: Rupp-Eisenreich (1984): 259-272.
Bourne, William, 1578.
  A booke called the Treasure for traueilers, deuided into fiue Bookes or partes, contaynyng very necessary matters, for all sortes of Trauaillers, eyther by Sea or by Lande. London.

Bouwsma, W.J., 1957.
  Concordia Mundi, The Career and Thought of Guillaume Postel. Cambridge, Mass.
Bowen, Emanuel, 1747.
  A Complete System of Geography. Being a description of all the countries of the known world. 2 vols. London.
Boyle, Robert, 1665.
  General heads for a Natural History of a Country, Great or Small. in: *Philosophical Transactions* 1: 186-189.
Boyle, Robert, 1692.
  General heads for the Natural History of a Country, Great or Small; *Drawn out for the use of Travellers and Navigators.* London.
Böcking, E., 1834.
  Über die Notitia Dignitatum utriusque imperii. Bonn.
Böhme, Gernot (ed.), 1989.
  Klassiker der Naturphilosophie. Von den Vorsokratikern bis zur Kopenhagener Schule. Ed. Gernot Böhme. München.
Böhme, Max, 1904.
  Die großen Reisesammlungen des 16. Jahrhunderts und ihre Bedeutung. Strasbourg.
Branca, Vittore (ed.), 1963.
  Umanesimo europeo e umanesimo veneziano. Venice.
Brand, Otto, 1927.
  Heinrich Rantzau und seine Relationen an die dänischen Könige. München, Berlin.
Brather, Hans Stephan (ed.), 1993.
  Leibniz und seine Akademie. Ausgewählte Quellen zur Geschichte der Berliner Sozietät der Wissenschaften 1696-1716. Berlin.
Braudel, Ferdinand (ed.), 1988.
  Europa: Bausteine zu seiner Geschichte. Frankfurt am Main.
Bremer, Ernst, 1992.
  Spätmittelalterliche Reiseliteratur - ein Genre? Überlieferungssymbiosen und Gattungstypologie. in: Ertzdorff-Neukirch (1992) 329-356.
Brenner, Peter J. (ed.), 1989.
  Der Reisebericht. Die Entwicklung einer Gattung in der deutschen Literatur. Frankfurt am Main.
Brinton, Crane, 1948.
  Europa im Zeitalter der Französischen Revolution. Vienna.
British Association for the Advancement of Science, 1929.
  Notes and Queries in Anthropology, for the Use of Travellers and Residents in Uncivilized Lands. Drawn up by a Committee appointed by the British Association for the Advancement of Science. 5th ed. London. (1st ed . 1874, further eds. 1892, 1899, 1912, 1951).
Broc, Numa , 1974.
  La Géographie des Philosophes. Géographes et Voyageurs Français au XVIIIe siècle. Paris.
Broc, Numa , 1980.
  La Géographie de la Renaissance (1420-1620). Paris.
Brown, Harcourt, 1934.
  Scientific Organisations in seventeenth Century France (1620-1680). Baltimore.
Brown, Horatio F., 1891.
  The Venetian Printing Press. London.
Brou, A., 1929.
  Les Statistiques dans les anciennes Missions. in: *Revue d'histoire des Missions* 6/3: 361-384.
Brugi, Biagio, 1905.
  Gli scolari dello Studio de Padova nel Cinquecento. 2nd ed. Verona.
Brummel, L., 1972.
  Twee Ballingen s'Lands Tijdens Onze Opstond Tegen Spanje. Hugo Blotius (1535-1608), Emanuel van Meteren (1535-1612). s'Gravenhage.
Bruni, Leonardo, 1927.
  Historia florentini populi. Ed. Emilio Santini (=Rerum Italicarum Scritpores, n.s. XIX/3). Città di Castello.
Bruni, Leonardo, 1987.
  The Humanism of Leonardo Bruni. Selected Texts. Binghampton.
Brunner, Horst, 1967.
  Die politische Insel. Insel und Inselvorstellungen in der deutschen Literatur. Stuttgart.
Buck, August, 1975a.
  Die ''studia humanitatis'' im italienischen Humanismus. in: Reinhard (1984) 11-24.
Buck, August, 1975b.
  ''Laus Venetiae'' und Politik im 16. Jahrhundert. in: *Archiv für Kulturgeschichte* 57/1 186-194.
Buck, August, 1981.
  Studia Humanitatis. Wiesbaden.

Buck, August, 1986.
Die humanistische Tradition in der Romania. Bad Homburg.

Buck August, 1991.
Juan Luis Vives' Konzeption des humanistischen Gelehrten. in: Buck, A. (ed.) (1991) *Juan Luis Vives.* Hamburg. 11-22.

Buck, Peter, 1977.
Seventeenth Century political arithmetic: civil strife and vital statistics. in: *Isis* 68: 67-84.

Buijnsters, P.J., 1969.
Imaginaire Reisverhalen in Nederland Gedurende de 18e Eeuw. in: *Voordrachten gehouden voor de Geldersche leergangen te Armhem* N. 25: 7-8.

Burckhardt, Jacob, s.a..
Die Kultur der Renaissance in Italien. Vienna.

Burke, Luke, 1848.
Outlines of the Fundamental Doctrines of Ethnology; Or, The Science of Human Races. in: *The Ethnological Journal* 1: 1-8; 129-141; 235-239.

Burmeister, Karl Heinz, 1969.
Sebatian Münster. Versuch eines biographischen Gesamtbildes. Basel, Stuttgart.

Butterfield, Herbert, 1955.
Man on his Past. The study of the history of historical scholarship. Cambridge.

Bühl, Walter L., 1984.
Die Ordnung des Wissens. Berlin.

Bühl, Walter L., 1986.
Kultur als System. in: Neidhart, F., Lepsius M.R., Weiß J. (eds.): *Kultur und Gesellschaft.* (= Kölner Zeitschrift für Soziologie und Sozialpsychologie Sonderheft 27) Opladen: 118-144.

Bühler, Theodor, 1964.
Fosterage. in: *Schweizerisches Archiv für Volkskunde* 60/1.

Bürgi, Andreas, 1989.
Weltvermesser. Die Wandlungen des Reiseberichts in der Spätaufklärung. Bonn.

Büttner, Manfred (ed.), 1979.
Wandlungen im geographischen Denken von Aristoteles bis Kant. Paderborn.

Campbell, Wiliam, 1903.
Formosa under the Dutch. Described from contemporary Records. London

Cardanus, Hieronymus, 1627.
Proxeneta, seu De Prudentia Civili Liber; Recens in Lucem protractus vel e tenebris erutus. Leiden.

Carlson, R.A., 1964.
David, the chosen King. A Traditio-Historical Approach to the Second Book of Samuel. Upsala.

Caron, Pierre, 1913.
Rapports des Agents du Ministre de l'Interieur dans les Départements. Paris.

Carré, Henri, 1980.
Sully. Sa vie et son oeuvre 1559-1641. Paris.

Carrier, Martin and Mittelstraß, Jürgen, 1989.
Johannes Kepler. in: Böhme (1989): 137-157.

Casagrande, Joseph, 1960.
In the Company of Man. New York.

Caselius, Johannes, c. 1578.
Διασκεψ *Qui doctrinae virtutisque gratia peregrinari animum inducunt, quas gentes potissimum adeant eo nomine Italiam autem minime omnium praetereundam, quidque ex ea talis hospes emolumenti capiat.* in: *Collectio Caselianorum,* ed. Joh. Chr. Kiesewetter. Rudelstadt.

Cassirer, Ernst, 1972.
An Essay on Man: An Introduction to a philosophy of Human Culture. 2nd ed. New Haven, London.

Celtis, Conradus Protucius, 1932.
Oratio in gymnasio in Ingolstadio publice recitata cum carminibus ad orationem pertinentibus. Ed. Rupprich, Leipzig.

Certeau, Michel de, 1985.
Histoire et Anthropologie chez Lafitau. in: *Naissance de l'Ethnologie? Anthropologie et Missions en Amérique XVIe - XVIIIe siècle.* Ed. Blanckaert, Claude. Paris.

Certeau, Michel de, Julia, Dominique and Reve, Jaques, 1975.
Une Politique de la Langue: La Révolution Française et les Patois. L'enquête de Grégoire. Paris.

Chadwick, J., 1976.
The Mycenean World. Cambridge.

Chalmers
The General Biographical Dictionary. New ed.

Charles-Roux, François, 1910.
Les Origines de l'Expédition d'Egypte. Paris.

Charles-Roux, François, 1935.
   Bonaparte Gouverneur d'Egypte. Paris.
Chavannes, Alexandre César, 1787.
   Essai sur l'Education Intellectuelle avec le Projet d'une Science Nouvelle. Lausanne. (Nouv. éd. Paris 1886)
Chavannes, Alexandre César, 1788.
   Anthropologie, ou Science Générale de l'Homme. Lausanne.
Chevalley, Abel, 1936.
   Psalmanazar. in: Chevalley, A.: La Bête de Géaudan; Psalmanazar; L'affaire Overbury. Paris.
Churchill, Awsham and John, 1704.
   A Collection of Voyages and Travels ... London.
Chytraeus, Nathan, 1594.
   Variorum in Europa itinerum Deliciae. Herborn.
Chytraeus, Nathan, 1575.
   Hodoeporica, sive Itineraria, a diversis clariss. Doctissimisqu; viris, tum veteribus, tum recentoribus ...
   carmine conscripta ... Frankfurt.
Chytraeus, Nathan, 1568.
   Hodoeporicon, continens itinera Parisiense Anglicum Venetum Romanum Neapolitanum etc. ... Rostock.
Claesen, Henri J.M. and Skalnik, Peter (eds.), 1978.
   The early state. Den Hague.
Clausen, Lars, 1994.
   Krasser sozialer Wandel. Opladen.
Clément, Pierre (ed.), 1867.
   Relation d'un voyage du Marquis de Seignelay ... Paris.
Clifford, James and Marcus, George E. (eds.), 1986.
   Writing Culture. The Poetic and Politics of Ethnography. Berkeley.
Cline, Howard F., 1972.
   The Relaciones Geográficas of the Spanish Indies, 1577-1648. in: Handbook of the Middle American Indians
   XII: Guide to Ethnohistoric Sources, 1. Austin, Texas: 183-242.
Cohen, William B., 1980.
   The French Encounter with Africans. White Response to Blacks. Bloomington, London.
Comenius, Johann Amos, 1668.
   Via Lucis, vestigata & vestiganda, h.e. Rationabilis disquisitio, quibus modis intellectualis Animorum LUX,
   SAPIENTIA, per Omnium Hominum mentes, & jamtandem, sub Mundi vesperam feliciter spargi possit.
   Amsterdam.
Comenius, Johann Amos, 1966.
   De rerum humanarum emendatione catholica. ed. Academia Scientiarum Bohemoslovaca. Prague.
Confino, Michel, 1962.
   Les enquêtes économiques de la "Société d'economie de Saint-Petersbourg" (1765-1820). in: Revue Historique
   227: 155-180.
Conolly, John M. and Keutner, Thomas, 1988.
   Hermeneutics Versus Science. Three German Views. Essays by H.G. Gadamer, E.K. Specht, W. Stegmüller.
   Notre Dame, Indiana.
Conrads, Norbert, 1982.
   Politische und staatsrechtliche Probleme der Kavalierstour. in: Maczak/Teuteberg (1982) 45-64.
Conring, Hermann, 1662.
   De Civili Prudentia Liber unus. Helmstedt.
Copans, J. and Jamin, J., 1978.
   Aux Origines de l'Anthropologie Française. Les Mémoires de la Société des Observateurs de l'homme en
   l'an VIII. Paris.
Cornelius, Paul, 1965.
   Languages in seventeenth and early eighteenth-Century. Imaginary Voyages. Geneva.
Costas, Ilse, 1987.
   Die Sozialstruktur der Studenten der Göttinger Universität im 18. Jahrhundert. in: Herrlitz/Kern
   (1987):127-149.
Crick, Bernard, 1987.
   Introduction. in: Niccolò Machiavelli: The Discourses. Harmondsworth.
Curtius, Ernst Robert, 1973.
   Europäische Literatur.und lateinisches Mittelalter. 8th ed. Bern, München.
D'Olwer, L. Nicolau and Cline, H.F., 1973.
   Bernhardino de Sahagún 1499-1590. in: Handbook of Middle American Indians XIII: Guide to Ethnohistoric
   Sources, 2. Austin, Texas: 186-239.
Dainville, François de, S.J., 1940.
   La géographie des humanistes. Paris.
Dangelmayr, S., 1974.
   Methode und System. Wissenschaftsklassifikation bei Bacon, Locke und Hobbes. Meisenheim am Glan.

Debus, Allen G., 1968.
Mathematics and Nature in the Chemical Texts of the Renaissance. in: Ambix 15: 1-28.
DeFrancis, John, 1989.
Visible Speech: On the diverse Oneness of Writing Systems. Honolulu.
Deger-Jalkotzy, Sigrid, 1978.
E-Qe-Ta. Zur Rolle des Gefolgschaftswesens in der Sozialstruktur mykenischer Reiche. Vienna.
Degérando, Joseph-Marie, 1800a.
Des signes et de l'art de penser dans leurs rapports mutuels. Paris, An VIII.
Degérando, Jopseph-Marie, 1800b.
Considérations sur les diverses méthodes à suivre dans l'observation des peuples sauvages. s.l. s.a. (Paris 1800).
Denecke, Dietrich, 1992.
Straßen, Reiserouten und Routenbücher (Itinerare) im späten Mittelalter und in der frühen Neuzeit. in: Ertzdorff-Neukirch (1992) 227-254.
Désirat, Claude and Hordé, Tristan, 1984.
Volney, l'étude des langues dans l'observation de l'homme. in: Rupp-Eisenreich (1984b): 133-142.
Desmaze, Charles, 1864.
P. Ramus, Professeur au Collège de France. Paris.
Diem, Gudrun, 1962.
Deutsche Schulanthropologie. in: Landmann, Michael et al. (eds.): De Homine. Der Mensch im Spiegel seines Gedankens. Freiburg, München.
Dilthey, Wilhelm, 1962.
Das achtzehnte Jahrhundert und die geschichtliche Welt. in: Wilhelm Dilthey: Gesammelte Schriften vol III: 210-268. 4th ed. Stuttgart, Göttingen.
Dinklage, Karl, 1965.
Gründung und Aufbau der theresianischen Ackerbaugesellschaften. in: Zeitschrift für Agrargeschichte und Agrarsoziologie 13: 200-211.
Dircks, H., 1865.
A Biographical Memoir of Samuel Hartlib, Milton's Familiar Friend; with Bibliographical Notices of Works Published by him, and a Reprint of his Pamphlet entitled "An Invention of Engines of Motion". London.
Diringer, David, 1962.
Writing. London.
Dommanget, M., 1963.
L'Idée de grève générale en France au XVIIIe siècle et pendant la Révolution. in: Revue d'Histoire Economique et Sociale XLI/1.
Donattini, Massimo, 1980.
Giovanni Battista Ramusio e le sue "Navigationi". in: Critica Storica 17: 55-100.
Donnant, Denis-François (ed.), 1805.
Introduction à la science de la statistique suivie d'un coup d'oeil général sur l'étude entière de la politique. D'après l'Allemand de Mr. de Schlözer, avec un discours préliminaire, des additions et des remarques par D.-F. Donnant. Paris. (=French ed. of Schlözer 1804)
Dorson, Richard, 1968.
The British Folklorists. A History. Chicago.
Droysen, Johann Gustav, s.a..
Geschichte Alexander des Großen. Ed. Helmut Berve. Leipzig.
Duerr, Hans Peter (ed.), 1981.
Der Wissenschaftler und das Irrationale. 2 vols. Frankfurt am Main.
Duerr, Hans Peter (ed.), 1987.
Authentizität und Betrug in der Ethnologie. Frankfurt am Main.
Duhamel de Monceau, Henri-Louis, 1752.
Avis pour le transport par mer des arbres, des plantes vivaces, des semences, des animaux différens et de diverses autres morceaux d'histoire naturelle. s.l.
Dupâquier, Jacques and Vilquin, Eric, 1978.
Le pouvoir royal et la statistique démographique. in: Pour une histoire de la statistique. Ed. Jean Mairesse. Paris.
Durkheim, Emile, 1964.
The Elementary Forms of Religiuos Life. 5th ed. London (French orig. 1912).
Durry, M.J., 1929.
L'Academie Celtique et les chansons populaires. in: Revue de Littérature Comparée 9: 62-73.
Dwornik, Francis, 1974.
Origins of Intelligence Service. The Ancient Near East, Persia, Greece, Rome, Byzantium, The Arab Muslim Empires, The Mongol Empire, China, Muscovy. New Brunswick, N.J.
Edwards, William Francis, 1841.
Mémoire sur l'Anthropologie. in: Mémoires de la Société Ethnologique. Paris. I/1: 109-128.

Eibl-Eibesfeldt, Irenäus, 1967.
  Grundriß der vergleichenden Verhaltensforschung. Ethologie. Munich.
Eis, Gerhard, 1962.
  Mittelalterliche Fachliteratur. Stuttgart.
Eisenstadt, Shmuel N., 1993.
  The Political Systems of Empires. New Brunswick, N.J. et al.
Eisenstein, E.L., 1979.
  The Printing Press as an Agent of Change: Communication and Cultural Transformations in Early Modern Europe. 2 vols. Cambridge.
Eisermann, Gottfried, 1956.
  Die Grundlagen des Historismus in der deutschen Nationalökonomie. Stuttgart.
Elesh, David, 1972.
  The Manchester Statistical Society: A Case Study of a Discontinuity in the History of Empirical Social Research. in: *Journal of the History of the Behavioral Sciences* 8: 280-301.
Eliade, Mircea, 1957.
  Schamanismus und archaische Ekstasetechnik. Zürich, Stuttgart. (French orig. 1951).
Emge, Martinus, 1987.
  Saint-Simon. Einführung in ein Leben und Werk, Schule, Sekte und Wirkungsgeschichte. München, Wien.
Engnell, I., 1967.
  Studies in the Divine Kingship in the Ancient Near East. Oxford.
Erasmus Roterodamus, Desiderius, 1542.
  Familiarum Colloquiorum Opus. Basel.
Erpenius, Thomas, 1631.
  De peregrinatione Gallica utiliter instituenda Tractatus. Leiden.
Ersch, Johann S. and Gruber, Johann G. (eds.), 1818-89.
  Allgemeine Encyclopädie der Wissenschaft und Künste. Leipzig.
Ertzdorff, Xenja v. and Neukirch, Dieter (eds.), 1992.
  Reisen und Reiseliteratur im Mittelalter und in der Frühen Neuzeit. Amsterdam.
Esmonin, Edmond, 1964.
  Etudes sur la France des XVIIe et XVIIIe siècles. Paris.
Fabri, Johann Ernst, 1808.
  Encyclopädie der Historischen Haupt-Wissenschaften und deren Hülfs-Doctrinen. Erlangen.
Fabricius, Georg, 1575.
  Hypomnemata hodoeporika ad Christophorum Leuschnerum in Italiam euntem. in: Chytraeus (1575).
Fahim, Hussein (ed.), 1982.
  Indigenous anthropology in non-western countries: proceedings of a Burg Wartenstein Symposium. Durham, N.C.
Faivre, Jean-Paul, 1967.
  Savants et Navigateurs. Un Aspect de la Coopération Internationale Entre 1750 et 1840. in: *Cahiers d'Histoire Mondiale* 10:98-124.
Febvre, L. and Martin, H.J., 1958.
  L'Apparition du livre. Paris
Fechner, Jörg-Ulrich, 1977.
  Die Einheit von Bibliotheken und Kunstkammern im 17. und 18. Jahrhundert dargestellt an Hand zeitgenössischer Berichte. in: *Raabe, Paul (ed.): Öffentliche und Private Bibliotheken im 17. und 18. Jahrhundert.* Wolfenbüttel.
Felwinger, Johann Paul, 1666.
  Dissertationes Politicae ... Altdorf.
Ferguson, Yale H. and Mansbach, Richard W., 1994.
  Polities: Authority, Identities and Ideology. South Carolina.
Finley, M., 1981.
  Economy and Society in Ancient Greece. London.
Finn, R. Welldon, 1963.
  An Introduction to Domesday Book. London.
Firpo, L., 1971.
  Botero, Giovanni. in: *Dizionario Biografico degli Italiani 13.* Roma.
Fischer, Emil, 1952.
  Giovanni Botero. Ein politischer und volkswirtschaftlicher Denker der Gegenreformation. Langnau, Bern.
Fischer, Hans, 1970.
  'Völkerkunde', 'Ethnographie', 'Ethnologie': Kritische Kontrolle der frühesten Belege. in: *Zeitschrift für Ethnologie* 95/1-2: 169-182.
Fischer, Michael W., 1982.
  Die Aufklärung und ihr Gegenteil. Berlin.
Fischer, Michael W. and Strasser, Michaela, 1992.
  Die Rosenkreuzer. Ms Salzburg.

Fontaney, Jean de, 1705.
  Review of George Psalmanaazaar: Description of Formosa. in: *Journal de Trèvoux.*
Fordham, Sir Herbert George, 1912.
  Notes on the British and Irish Road Books. Hertford.
Fordham, Sir Herbert George, 1926.
  Guides-routiers, itinéraires et cartes-routiers de l'Europe de 1500 à 1850. Lille.
Forgách, Michael, 1588.
  Oratio de peregrinatione et eius laudibus ... Wittenberg.
Forster, Johann Reinhold, 1771.
  A Catalogue of the Animals of North America ... To which are added, Short Directions for Collecting, Preserving, and Transporting, all kinds of Natural History Curiosities. London.
Fortius Ringelbergius, Joachim, 1662.
  De Ratione Studii Liber Vere Aurens ed. Thomas Erpenius, Leiden.
Fowler, Don, 1975.
  Notes on inquiries in anthropology: A Bibliographic Essay. in: Thoresen T.H.H. (ed.): *Toward a Science of Man. Essays in the History of Anthropology.* The Hague: 15-32.
Frank, Johann Peter, 1792.
  Oratio Academica De Medicis Peregrinationinus ... in: Frank, J.P.: *Delectus opusculorum medicorum.* vol II. Padua. 357-382.
Frankfort, Henri, 1978.
  Kingship and the Gods. A Study of Ancient Near Eastern Religion and the Integration of Society and Nature. Chicago.
Franklin, Julian H., 1963.
  Jean Bodin and the Sixteenth Century Revolution in the Methodology of Law and History. London.
Frantz, R.W., 1934.
  The English Traveller and the Movement of ideas 1660-1732. Lincoln, Nebr.
Fraser, Russel, 1930.
  The War Against Poetry. Princeton, N.J.
Fried, Morton H., 1967.
  The Evolution of Political Society. New York.
Fried, Johannes, 1983.
  Auf der Suche nach der Wirklichkeit. Die Mongolen und die europäische Erfahrungswissenschaft im 13. Jahrhundert. in: *Historische Zeitschrift* 237. 287-322.
Friedenthal, Richard, 1982.
  Luther. Sein Leben und seine Zeit. München, Zürich.
Fritz, Kurt von, 1971.
  Grundprobleme der Geschichte der antiken Wissenschaft. Berlin, New York.
Frölich, David, 1643/44.
  Bibliotheca sive Cynosura Peregrinantium, hoc est, Viatorium ... 2 vols. Ulm.
Fueter, Eduard, 1936.
  Geschichte der neueren Historiographie. München, Berlin.
Fuhrmann, Horst, 1959.
  Heinrich Rantzaus römische Korrespondenten. in: *Archiv für Kulturgeschichte* XLI/1: 63-89.
Fürst, Friederike, 1928.
  August Ludwig von Schlözer, ein deutscher Aufklärer im 18. Jahrhundert. Heidelberg.
Fürstenberg, Friedrich, 1989.
  Social Regression. in: *Thought* 64/252: 83-93.
Gabriel, Astrik L., 1967.
  Vinzenz von Beauvais, ein mittelalterlicher Erzieher. Frankfurt am Main.
Gadamer, Hans-Georg, 1988.
  On the Circle of Understanding. in: Conolly/Keutner (1988): 68-78.
Gail, Jörg, 1563.
  Ein neuwes nützliches Raißbüchlin der fürnemesten Land vnnd Stett. Augsburg.
Galbraith, V.H., 1961.
  The Making of Domesday Book. Oxford.
Gallizioli, Giovambattista Conte, 1788.
  Della vita degli studi e degli scritti de Guilelmo Grataroli Filosofa e medico. Bergamo
Garat, D.J., 1862.
  Mémoires. Ed. Poulet Malassis. Paris.
Gatterer, Johann Christoph, 1761.
  Handbuch der Universalhistorie, nach ihrem gesamten Umfange von Erschaffung der Welt bis zum Ursprunge der meisten heutigen Reiche und Staaten. Göttingen. (2nd ed. 1765).
Gatterer Johann Chrisoph, 1765.
  Synopsis historiae universalis. Göttingen. (2nd ed. 1769)

Gatterer, Johann Christoph, 1771.
  Einleitung in die synchronistische Universalhistorie, Und Erläuterung seiner synchronistischen Tabellen.
  2 vols. Göttingen.
Gatterer, Johann Christoph, 1775.
  Abriss der Geographie. Göttingen.
Gauger, Hans W., 1987.
  Die Ossianische Verlegenheit. in: Duerr (1987): 333-356.
Gaulmier, Jean, 1951.
  L'Idéologue Volney 1757 -1820. Contribution à l'Histoire de l'Orientalisme en France. Beirut.
Gaulmier, Jean, 1959a.
  Un Grand Témoin de la Révolution et de l'Empire: Volney. Paris.
Gaulmier, Jean, 1959b.
  Introduction. in: Constantin-François Volney: Voyage en Egypte et en Syrie, éd. J. Gaulmier. Paris: 13-19.
Gazley, J.G., 1973.
  The Life of Arthur Young 1741-1820. Philadelphia.
Gehlen, Arnold, 1986a.
  Der Mensch. Seine Natur und seine Stellung in der Welt. 13th ed. Wiesbaden ???
Gehlen, Arnold, 1986b.
  Urmensch und Spätkultur. Philosophische Ergebnisse und Aussagen. 5th ed. Wiesbaden. ???
Gelb, I.J., 1963.
  A Study of Writing. 2nd ed. Chicago.
Gellner, Ernest, 1987.
  Culture, Identity, and Politics. Cambridge
Gennep, Arnold van, 1960.
  The Rites of Passage. London. (French orig. 1909)
Gerando, Baronne de, 1880.
  Lettres de la Baronne de Gérando, Née de Rathsamshausen, Suivies de Fragments d'un Journal Écrit par Elle de 1800 à 1804. Paris.
Gerlo, Aloïs (ed.)
  Juste Lipse (1547-1606) Colloque international tenu en mars 1978. Bruxelles.
Gerlo, Aloïs, 1971.
  The Opus de conscribendis Epistolis of Erasmus and the Tradition of the Ars Epistolaria. in: Bolgar (1976): 103-114.
Giard, L., 1983/84/85.
  Histoire de l'Université et Histoire du Savoir: Padoue (XIVe-XVIe siècle). in: Revue de Synthèse 104:139-169; 105:259-298; 106:419-422.
Gigon, Olof, 1947.
  Sokrates. Sein Bild in Dichtung und Geschichte. Bern.
Gilbert, Neal W., 1960.
  Renaissance Concepts of Method. New York.
Gilly, Carlos, 1977/79.
  Zwischen Erfahrung und Spekulation: Theodor Zwinger und die religiöse und kulturelle Krise seiner Zeit. in: Basler Zeitschrift für Geschichte und Altertumskunde 77:57-137; 79:125-223.
Giraldus, Lillius Gregorius, 1540.
  De re nautica libellus, admiranda quadam et recondita eruditione refertus, nunc primum natus et aeditus. Basel.
Gladden, E.N., 1972.
  A History of Public Administration. 2 vols. London.
Goblet, Louis J.J., 1930.
  La Transformation de la Géographie Politique de l'Irlande au XVIIe siècle dans les cartes et essais anthropogéographiques de Sir William Petty. Nancy, Paris, Strasbourg.
Goldfriedrich, Johann and Fränzel, Walter (ed.), s.a..
  Ritter Grünembergs Pilgerfahrt ins Heilige Land. Leipzig.
Gonnard, 1946.
  La légende du bon sauvage. Paris.
Goody, Jack, 1977.
  The domestication of the savage mind. Cambridge.
Goody, Jack, 1990.
  Die Logik der Schrift und die Organisation der Gesellschaft. Frankfurt am Main.
Goody, Jack and Watt, Ian, 1968.
  The consequences of literacy. in: Goody, Jack (ed.): Literacy in traditional societies. Cambridge: 27-84.
Gove, Philip B., 1961.
  The Imaginary Voyage in Prose Fiction ... London.
Göllner, Carl, 1978.
  Die Türkenfrage in der öffentlichen Meinung Europas im 16. Jahrhundert. Bucuresti, Baden-Baden.

Görlitz, Dietmar and Wohlwill (eds), 1987.
   Curiosity, Imagination, and Play: on the Development of Spontaneous Cognitive and motivational Processes.
   Hillsdale, N.J.
Gratarolus, Guilhelmus, 1561.
   De Regimine iter agentium, vel equitum, vel peditum, vel navi, vel curru seu rheda, &c.viatoribus &
   peregrinatoribus quibusque utilissimi libri duo. Basel.
Graunt, John, 1662.
   Natural and Political Observations mentioned in a following index and made upon the Bills of Mortality
   ... London.
Graves, F.P., 1912.
   Peter Ramus and the educational Reformation of the XVIth century. New York.
Greenacre, Phyllis, 1953.
   The Imposter. in: Psychoanalytic Quarterly 17: 359-382.
Grendler, Paul F., 1969.
   Francesco Sansovino and Italian popular History 1560-1600. in: *Studies in the Renaissance*
   16:139-180
Griep, Wolfgang (ed.), 1991.
   Sehen und Beschreiben. Europäische Reisen im 18. und frühen 19. Jahrhundert. Heide.
Griep, Wolfgang and Jäger, Hans-Wolf, 1983.
   Reisen und soziale Realtät am Ende des 18. Jahrhunderts. Heidelberg.
Growther, J.G., 1960.
   Francis Bacon. The First Statesman of Science. London.
Gruber, Daniel, 1619.
   Discursus historico-politicus de peregrinatione studiosorum ... Heidelberg.
Gryllus, Laurentius , 1566.
   Oratio de peregrinatione studii medicinalis ergo suscepta ... s.l.
Gusdorf, George, 1978.
   La Conscience Révolutionaire: Les Idéologues. Paris.
Haas, Jonathan, 1982.
   The Evolution of the Prehistoric State. New York.
Hagberg, Knut, 1946.
   Carl Linnaeus. Hamburg.
Hahn, Alois, 1982.
   Zur Soziologie der Beichte und anderer Formen institutionalisierter Bekenntnisse. in: *Kölner Zeitschrift*
   für Soziologie und Sozialpsychologie 34: 408-434.
Hahn, Alois and Kapp, Volker (eds.), 1987.
   Selbstthematisierung und Selbstzeugnis: Bekenntnis und Geständnis. Frankfurt am Main.
Hahn, Roger, 1971.
   The Anatomy of a Scientific Institution: The Paris Academy of Sciences, 1666-1803. Berkeley, London.
Halbwachs, Maurice, 1950.
   La Mémoire collective. Paris.
Hald, Anders, 1990.
   A History of Probability and statistics and their Application before 1750. New York.
Hall, Joseph, 1617.
   Quo Vadis? A Just Censure of Travell as it is commonly undertaken by the Gentlemen of our Nation. London.
Halm, Carolus, 1863.
   Rhetores Latini Minores. Leipzig.
Halphen, L., 1947.
   Charlemagne et l'empire carolingien. Paris.
Hamann, Johann Georg, 1952.
   Sämtliche Werke. Ed. Josef Nadler. Vienna.
Hanke, G., 1974.
   Das Zeitalter des Zentralismus. in: Bosl, Karl (ed.): *Handbuch der Geschichte der böhmischen Länder.*
   Stuttgart.
Hantsch, Hugo, 1963.
   Leopold Graf Berchtold. Grandseigneur und Staatsmann. Wien, Köln.
Harbsmeier, Michael, 1982.
   Reisebeschreibungen als mentalitätsgeschichtliche Quellen. Überlegungen zu einer historisch-anthropologischen
   Untersuchung deutscher Reisebeschreibungen. in: Macak/Teuteberg 1982: 1-31.
Harth, Dietrich, 1992.
   Cina: ''Monde Imaginaire'' della letteratura Europaea. in: *Rivista di letterature moderne e comparate* 45/2:
   125-144.
Hartlib, Samuel, 1641.
   A description of the famous Kingdome of Macaria. London.

Hartlib, Samuel, 1643.
   A Faithful and seasonable Advice, or: The necessity of a Correspondencie for the advancement of the Protestant Cause. London.
Hartlib, Samuel, 1647.
   Considerations tending To the Happy accomplishment of Englands Reformation in Church and State. London.
Hartlib, Samuel, 1648.
   A further Discoverie of The Office of Publick Addresse for Accomodations. London.
Hartog, François, 1980.
   Le miroir d'Herodote. Paris
Haskins, Charles Homer, 1911.
   England and Siciliy in the Twelfth Century. in: *English Historical Review* 26: 433-447.
Haskins, Charles Homer, 1927.
   Studies in the History of Medieval Science. 2nd ed. Cambridge, Mass.
Haskins, Charles Homer, 1979.
   The Renaissance of the Twelfth Century. 7th ed. Cambridge, Mass.
Hattaway, Michael, 1978.
   Bacon and Knowledge Broken: Limits for Scientific Method. in: *Journal of the History of Ideas* 39/2: 183-197.
Hawes, William (ed.), 1794.
   The Transactions of the Royal Humane Society from 1774 to 1784. London.
Haym, Rudolf, 1958.
   Herder. Nach seinem Leben und seinen Werken dargestellt. 2 vols. Berlin.
Hazard, Paul, 1961.
   La Crise de la conscience européene (1680 - 1715). Paris.
Hecht, Jacqueline, 1980.
   Imagination et Prospective: Les Origines de la Prévision Démographique. in: Rassem/Stagl (1980): 325-361.
Heer, Friedrich, 1953.
   Europäische Geistesgeschichte. 2nd ed. Stuttgart.
Heer, Friedrich, 1959.
   Die dritte Kraft. Der europäische Humanismus zwischen den Fronten des konfessionellen Zeitalters. Frankfurt am Main.
Heer, Friedrich, 1962.
   Einleitung. in: Heer, F. (ed.): *Erasmus von Rotterdam*. Frankfurt, Hamburg: 7-47.
Heer, Johannes Gall, 1938.
   Mabillon und die Schweizer Benediktiner. Ein Beitrag zur Geschichte der historischen Quellenforschung im 17. und 18. Jahrhundert. St. Gallen.
Heinisch, Klaus J., 1960.
   Der utopische Staat. Morus. Utopia. Campanelle. Sonnenstaat. Bacon. Neu-Atlantis. Hamburg.
Hellmuth, Leopold, 1984.
   Gastfreundschaft und Gastrecht bei den Germanen. Vienna.
Henkel, Arthur and Schöne, Albrecht, 1967.
   Emblemata. Handbuch zur Sinnbildkunst des XVI. und XVII. Jahrhunderts. Stuttgart.
Hennies, Werner, 1985.
   Die politische Theorie August Ludwig von Schlözer's zwischen Aufklärung und Liberalismus. München.
Henningsen, Jürgen, 1966.
   "Enzyklopädie". Zur Sprach- und Deutungsgeschichte eines pädagogischen Begriffes. in: *Archiv für Begriffsgeschichte* 10:271-362.
Hentzner, Paul, 1629.
   Itinerarium Germaniae, Galliae, Angliae, Italiae. 3rd ed. Nürnberg.
Herbst, Ludolf, 1973.
   Briefwechsel/Stats-Anzeigen. in: Fischer, Heinz-Dietrich (ed.): *Deutsche Zeitschriften des 17. - 20. Jahrhunderts*. München.
Herder, Johann Gottfried, 1891.
   A.L. Schlözers Vorstellung seiner Universal-Historie. Göttingen und Gotha bey Dieterich. 8. 16 Bogen. in: *Frankfurter gelehrte Anzeigen* LX (28.VII. 1772): 373-378. Reprinted in: Johann Gottfried Herder: *Sämtliche Werke*. Ed. Bernhard Suphan. Berlin (reprinted Hildesheim 1967), Vol V: 436-440.
Herrmann, S., 1957.
   Untersuchungen zur Überlieferungsgestalt mittelägyptischer Literaturwerke. Berlin.
Herschel, J.W. (ed.), 1849-86.
   A Manual for Scientific Enquiry Prepared for the use of Her Majesty's Navy and Adapted for Travellers in General. London.
Hettner, Alfred, 1932.
   Das länderkundliche Schema. in: *Geographischer Anzeiger* 33:1-6.
Hibbert, Christopher, 1969.
   The Grand Tour. London.

Hill, George Birkbeck (ed.), 1934-50.
   Boswell's Life of Johnson. 6 vols. rev. ed. London.
Hiller, Lotte, 1937.
   Die Geschichtswissenschaft an der Universität Jena in der Zeit der Polyhistorie (1674-1763). Jena.
Hilts, Victor L., 1978.
   Aliis exterendum, or, the Origins of the Statistical Society of London. in: *Isis* 69:21-43.
Hilts, Victor L. and Cohen, I. Bernard (eds.), 1981.
   Statist and statistician. New York.
Hinrichs, Carl, 1943.
   Friedrich Wilhelm I., König von Preussen. Eine Biographie. Hamburg.
Hinske, Norbert and Müller, Manfred E. (ed.), 1979.
   Reisen und Tourismus. (Trierer Beiträge, Sonderheft 3) Trier.
Hirzel, Rudolf, 1895.
   Der Dialog. Ein literaturhistorischer Versuch. 2 vols. Leipzig.
Hodgen, Margaret T., 1936.
   The Doctrine of Survivals. A Chapter in the History of Scientific Method in the Study of Man. London.
Hodgen, Margaret T., 1964.
   Early Anthropology in the Sixteenth and Seventeenth Centuries. Phildelphia.
Horváth, Robert A., 1978.
   Essays in the History of Political Arithmetics and Smithianism. Szeged.
Horváth, Robert A., 1983.
   The rise of demography as an autonomous science. in: Institut für Bevölkerungsforschung und
   Sozialpolitik, Universität Bielefeld: *Materialien* 12. Bielefeld: 1-51.
Horváth, Robert A., 1985.
   La France en 1618 vue par un statisticien hongrois, Marton Szepsi Csombor. in: *Population* 2:335-346.
Houghton, Walter Edwards, 1941.
   *The History of Trades: in relation to seventeenth century thoughts as seen in Bacon, Petty, Evelyn and
   Boyle.* in: *Journal of the History of Ideas* 2: 33-60.
Hooykaas, R., 1958.
   Humanisme, Science et Réforme. Pierre de la Ramée (1515-1572). Leiden.
Howard, Clare, 1914.
   English Travellers of the Renaissance. London, New York, Toronto.
Höltgen, Karl Josef, 1964.
   Synoptische Tabellen in der medizinischen Literatur und die Logik Agricolas und Ramus' in: *Sudhoffs
   Archiv* 48/4:371-390.
Hulsius, Levinus, 1649.
   Die fünff und zweyntzigste Schiffahrt ... Sambt einer Beschreibung der zweyen Insuln Formosa und Japan.
   Frankfurt am Main.
Hurd, Richard, 1764.
   *Dialogues on the Uses of Foreign Travel; considered as a part of an English gentleman's education: between
   Lord Shaftesbury and Mr. Locke.* 2nd ed. London.
Huschenbett, Dietrich, 1985.
   Die Literatur der deutschen Pilgerreisen nach Jerusalem im späten Mittelalter. in: *Deutsche Vierteljahresschrift
   für Literaturwissenschaft und Geistesgeschichte* 59:29-46.
Husserl, Edmund, 1954.
   Die Krisis der europäischen Wissenschaften und die transzendentale Phänomenologie. Den Haag.
Im Hof, Ulrich, 1967.
   Isaak Iselin und die Spätaufklärung. Bern, München.
Imbault-Huard, Camille, 1893.
   L'Ile de Formosa. Histoire et Description. Paris.
Institut d'Egypte, 1809-23.
   *Description de l'Egypet, ou recueil des observations et des recherches qui ont été faites en Egypte pendant
   l'expedient de l'armée française.* 9 vols. + 14 vols. of plates. Paris.
Iselin, Isaak, 1764.
   Über die Geschichte der Menschheit. 2 vols. Frankfurt. (Zürich 1770; 4th ed. Basel 1779; 5th ed. Basel 1787).
Isensee, Josef, 1993.
   Europa - die politische Erfindung eines Erdteils. in: Isensee, J. (ed.): *Europa als politische Idee und als
   rechtliche Form.* Berlin: 103-138.
Jaeckle, Erwin, 1988.
   Die Idee Europa. Berlin.
Jaeger, Werner, 1948.
   Aristotle. Fundamentals of the History of His Development. 2nd ed. Oxford. (German orig. 1923).
Jamin, Jean, 1969.
   Naissance de l'observation anthropologique, la Société des Observateurs de l'Homme (1799-1805). in: *Cahiers
   Internationaux de Sociologie* 67: Seiten!!!

Jaspers, Karl, 1957.
  Vom Ursprung und Ziel der Geschichte. Frankfurt am Main, Hamburg.
Jardine, Lisa, 1974.
  Francis Bacon. Discovery and the Art of Discourse. London
Jäger, Hans-Wolf, 1989.
  Reisefacetten der Aufklärungszeit. in: Brenner (1989): 261-283.
Jedin, Hubert, 1951.
  Die deutsche Romfahrt von Bonifatius bis Winckelmann. Krefeld.
Jellinek, Georg, 1914.
  Allgemeine Staatslehre. 3rd ed. Berlin.
Jensen, De Lamar, 1988.
  La Nouvelle Diplomatie. in: Klaniczay et.al. (1988) 51-62.
Joachimsen, Paul, 1910.
  Geschichtsauffassung und Geschichtsschreibung in Deutschland unter dem Einfluß des Humanismus.
  Leipzig. (reprint Aalen 1968).
Joachimsen, Paul, 1970.
  Loci Communes. (1926) in: Joachimsen, P.: *Gesammelte Aufsätze.* Aalen (Reprint) 387-442.
Johanneau, Eloi, 1807.
  Discours d'ouverture. in: *Académie Celtique* (1807-12), Vol I: 28-64.
John, Viktor, 1884.
  Geschichte der Statistik I: Vom Ursprung der Statistik bis auf Quetelet (1835). Stuttgart.
Jomard, M., 1839.
  Appendice. in: Mengin, Félix (ed.): *Histoire sommarie d'Egypte sous le Gouvernment de Mohammed-Aly.*
  Troisième Partie. Etudes Geographiques et Historiques sur l'Arabie. Paris.
Jonas, Friedrich, 1981.
  Geschichte der Soziologie. 2nd ed. 4 vols. Opladen.
Jones, E.L., 1981.
  The European Miracle: Environments, Economies and Geopolitics in the History of Europe and Asia.
  Cambridge.
Jordan, W.K., 1942.
  *Men of Substance. A Study of the Thought of Two English Revolutionaries. Henry Parker and Henry
  Robinson.* Chicago.
Junius, Melchior, 1955.
  *Orationum. quae Argent. in acad. exercitii causa scriptae ... ad tractandum vero propositae fuerunt a Melch.
  Junio Pars 4.* Montbeliard.
Kaiser, Ernst, 1969.
  Paracelsus. Reinbeck.
Kaiser, Gerhard, 1961.
  Pietismus und Patriotismus im literarischen Deutschland. Ein Beitrag zum Problem der Säkularisation.
  Wiesbaden.
Kant, Immanuel, 1798.
  Anthropologie in pragmatischer Hinsicht. Königsberg. (2nd ed. 1800).
Kantorowicz, Ernst, 1927.
  Kaiser Friederich der Zweite. Berlin.
Kargon, Robert, 1963.
  John Graunt, Francis Bacon, and the Royal Society. in: *Journal of the History of Medicine* 18: 337-348.
Kargon, Robert, 1965.
  William Petty's Mechanical Philosophy. in: *Isis* 56: 63-66.
Karle, Joan, 1972.
  August Ludwig von Schlözer, An Intellectual Biography. Ph.D.Diss. New York.
Kaufhold, Karl Heinrich and Sachse, Wieland, 1987.
  Die Göttinger "Universitätsstatistik" und ihre Bedeutung für die Wirtschafts- und Sozialgeschichte. in:
  Herrlitz, Hans-Georg and Kern, Horst (eds.): *Anfänge Göttinger Sozialwissenschaft. Methoden, Inhalte
  und soziale Prozesse im 18. und 19. Jahrhundert.* Göttingen: 72-95.
Kendall, Maurice and Plackett, Robert L. (eds.), 1987.
  Studies in the History of Statistics and Probability. Vol. II. New York.
Kern, Horst, 1982.
  Empirische Sozialforschung. Ursprünge, Ansätze, Entwicklungslinien. München.
Kerlouegan, François, 1968.
  *Essai sur la mise en nourriture et l'education dans les pays celtiques d'après le témoignage des textes
  hagiographiques latins,* in: *Etudes Celtiques* 12: 101-146.
Kern, Horst, 1987.
  Schlözers Bedeutung für die Methodologie der Empirischen Sozialforschung. in: Herrlitz/Kern (1987).
Klaniczay, Tibor, 1988a.
  L'aristocratie et la pensée politique de Juste Lipse. in: Gerlo (1988):25-36.

Klaniczay, Tibor, 1988b.
   Le Culte des grands personnages. in: Klaniczay et al. (1988): 531-543.
Klaniczay, Tibor et al. (ed.), 1988.
   L'Epoque de la Renaissance 1400-1600. Vol I: L'Avénement de l'Esprit Nouveau, 1400-1480. Budapest.
Klemm, Christian, 1979.
   Weltbedeutung - Allegorien und Symbole im Stilleben. in: *Stilleben in Europa* (catalogue of the exhibition Münster 1979). Eds. Langmeyer, Gerhard and Peters, Albert. Münster.
Kluckhohn, Paul, 1934.
   Die Idee des Volkes im Schrifttum der deutschen Bewegung von Möser und Herder bis Grimm. Berlin.
Knowlson, James R., 1965.
   George Psalmanaazaar: The Fake Formosan. in: *History Today* 15: 871-876.
Koch, Hans-Albrecht, 1991.
   Das Kostümbuch des Lambert de Vos. 2 vols. Graz.
Kohn, Hans, 1953.
   Pan-Slawism. Ist History and Ideology. Notre Dame, Ind.
Kollar, Adam Franz, 1783.
   Historiae iurisque publici regni Ungariae amoenitatis. Vienna.
Koller, H., 1957.
   Εγχυκλιος Παιδεια. in: *Glotta* 34: 174-189.
Kommers, J.H.M., 1982.
   Anthropologie avant la lettre: enige gedachten over de geschiedenis van de etnografie. Nijmegen.
Konetzke, Richard, 1970.
   Die "Geographischen Beschreibungen" als Quellen zur Hispanoamerikanischen Bevölkerungsgeschichte der Kolonialzeit. in: *Jahrbuch für Geschichte von Staat, Wirtschaft und Gesellschaft Lateinamerikas* 7: 1-75.
Kopitzsch, Franklin, 1980.
   Die Hamburgische Gesellschaft zur Beförderung der Künste und nützlichen Gewerbe (Patriotische Gesellschaft von 1765) im Zeitalter der Aufklärung. in: Vierhaus (1980b):71-118.
Koschaker, Paul, 1947.
   Europa und das römische Recht. München, Berlin.
Koselleck, Reinhart, 1959.
   Kritik und Krise. Ein Beitrag zur Pathogenese der bürgerlichen Welt. Freiburg, München.
Koyré, Alexandre, 1957.
   From the closed world to the infinite universe. Baltimore.
Köhler, Johann David, 1762.
   Anweisungen für Reisende Gelehrte, Bibliothecken, Münz-Cabinette, Antiquitäten-Zimmer, Bilder-Säle, Naturalien- und Kunst-Kammern u.a.m. mit Nutzen zu besehen. Frankfurt, Leipzig.
Köllmann, E. and Wirth, Karl-August, 1967.
   Erdteile. in: Heydenreich, Ludwig Heinrich and Wirth, Karl-August (eds.): *Reallexikon zur deutschen Kunstgeschichte.* Bd. 5: 1107-1202. Stuttgart.
Könekamp, Wolf-Dieter, 1988.
   Volkskunde und Statistik: Eine wissenschaftsgeschichtliche Korrektur. in: *Zeitschrift für Volkskunde* 84: 1-25.
Körner, Alfred, 1977.
   Andreas Riedl (1748-1837). Zur Lebensgeschichte eines Wiener Demokraten. in: Reinalter, Helmut (ed.): *Jakobiner in Mitteleuropa.* Innsbruck.
Krafft, Fritz, 1982.
   Theologie der Naturwissenschaft. Die Wende von der Einheit zur Vielheit des Weltbildes. in: Büttner, Manfred (ed.): *Zur Entwicklungsgeschichte der Geographie vom Mittelalter bis zu Carl Ritter.* Paderborn: 43-60.
Kramer, Fritz, 1987.
   Der rote Fes: Über Besessenheit und Kunst in Afrika. Frankfurt am Main.
Kranz, Walther, 1939.
   Kosmos als philosophischer Begriff frühgriechischer Zeit. in: *Philologus* 93: 430-448.
Kranz, Walther, 1955.
   Geschichte der griechischen Literatur. 5th ed. Birsfelden, Basel.
Kranz, Walther, 1971.
   Die griechische Philosophie. 5th ed. München.
Krasnobaev, B.I. et al. (ed.), 1980.
   Reisen und Reisebeschreibungen im 18. und 19. Jahrhundert als Quellen der Kulturbeziehungsforschung. Berlin.
Krauss, Werner, 1963.
   Über die Konstellation der deutschen Aufklärung. in: Krauss, W. (ed.): *Studien zur deutschen und französischen Aufklärung.* Berlin: 309-399.
Krbec, Miloslav and Michálková, Vera (eds.), 1959.
   Der Briefwechesel zwischen Josef Dobrovsk?EC? und Karl Gottlob von Anton. Berlin.
Krempel, Ulla (ed.), 1973.
   Jan van Kessel: Die vier Erdteile (Katalog der Ausstellung alte Pinakothek) München.

Kristeller, Paul Oskar, 1956.
   Studies in Renaissance Thought and Letters. Rome.
Kristeller, Paul Oskar, 1963.
   Giovanni Pico della Mirandola and his Sources. s.l.
Kristeller, Paul Oskar, 1974-76.
   Humanismus und Renaissance. 2 vols. München.
Kroker, Werner, 1971.
   Wege zur Verbreitung technologischer Kenntnisse zwischen England und Deutschland in der zweiten Hälfte des 18. Jahrhunderts. Berlin.
Kropatschek, Josef, 1799.
   Kommentar des Buches für Kreisämter als vermehrter Leitfaden zur Landes- und Kreisbereisung. 2 vols. Wien.
Kulcsár, Péter, 1988.
   L'essor des nationalismes. in: Klaniczay et al. (1988): 63-71.
Kurz, Ernst Georg, 1895.
   Georgius Pictiorius von Villingen, ein Arzt des 16. Jahrhunderts und seine Wissenschaft. Freiburg im Breisgau.
Kutter, Uli, 1978.
   Volks-Kunde - Ein Beleg von 1782. in: Zeitschrift für Volkskunde 74: 161-166.
Kutter, Uli, 1980.
   Apodemiken und Reisehandbücher. Bemerkungen und ein bibliographischer Versuch zu einer vernachlässigten Literaturgattung. in: Das achtzehnte Jahrhundert 4/2:116-131.
Lane, Frederic C., 1981.
   Venice. A Maritime Republic. 3rd ed. Baltimore, London.
Langmeyer, Gerhard and Peters, Albert (eds.), 1979.
   Stillleben in Europa. Münster.
Languet, Hubert, 1633.
   Epistolae Politicae et Historicae, Scripta quondam Ad Illustrem, & Generosum Dominum Philippum Sydnaeum. Frankfurt am Main.
Lasteyrie, C.P., 1797.
   Discours préliminaire. in: Berchtold (1797).
Lasteyrie, C.P., 1802.
   Histoire de l'introduction des moutons à laine fine. Paris.
Lausberg, Heinrich, 1990.
   Handbuch der literarischen Rhetorik. 2 vols. München.
Lawn, Brian, 1963.
   The Salernitan Questions. An Introduction to the History of Medieval and Renaissance Problem Literature. Oxford.
Lazarsfeld, Paul F., 1961.
   Notes on the History of Quantification in Sociology: Trends, Sources and Problems. in: Isis 52:277-333.
Le Roy Ladurie, Emmanuel, 1979.
   Le Carneval de Romans. De la Chandeleur au Mercredi des Cendres. Paris.
Leach, E.R., 1954.
   Political Systems of Highland Burma. London.
Leibniz, Gottfried Wilhelm, 1726.
   Theodicaea, oder Versuch und Abhandlung, wie die Güte und Gerechtigkeit Gottes in Ansehung der Menschlichen Freyheit, und des Ursprungs des Bösen, zu verteidigen. 2nd ed. Amsterdam.
Leibniz, Gottfried Wilhelm, 1864.
   Die Werke von Leibniz. 1. Reihe: Historisch-politische und staatswissenschaftliche Schriften. Ed. Onno Klopp. Hannover.
Leitner, Gertraud, 1968.
   Hugo Blotius und der Straßburger Freundeskreis. Studien zur Korrespondenz des ersten Bibliothekars der Österreichischen Nationalbibliothek. Phil.Diss. Vienna.
Lemay, Edna, 1984.
   Le monde extraeuropéen dans la formation de deux révolutionnaires. in: Rupp-Eisenreich (1984): 117-131.
Lemberg, Eugen, 1950.
   Geschichte·des Nationalismus in Europa. Stuttgart.
Lemberg, Eugen, 1961.
   Voraussetzungen und Probleme des tschechischen Geschichtsbewußtseins. in: Birke, E. and Lemberg, E. (eds.): *Geschichtsbewußtsein in Ostmitteleuropa.* Mahrburg/Lahn.
Lenoir, Dom Jacques, 1760.
   Mémoire Relatif au Projet d'une Histoire Générale de la Province de Normandie. Rouen.
Lepenies, Wolf, 1976.
   Das Ende der Naturgeschichte. Wandel kultureller Selbstverständlichkeiten in den Wissenschaften des 18. und 19. Jahrhunderts. Wien, München.

Lettsom, John Coakley, 1772.
  The Naturalist's and Traveller's Companion, Containing Instructions for Collecting and Preserving objects of Natural History, and for promoting inquiries after Human Knowledge in General. London. (2nd ed. 1773, 3rd. ed. 1799; French transl.: *Le voyageur naturaliste.* Amsterdam 1775).
Lévi-Strauss, Claude, 1955.
  Tristes Tropiques. Paris.
Lévi-Strauss, Claude, 1958.
  Anthropologie structurale. Paris.
Lévi-Strauss, Claude, 1964.
  Mythologiques I: Le Cru et le cuit. Paris.
Lévi-Strauss, Claude, 1973.
  Das wilde Denken. Franffurt am Main (French orig. 1962).
1981/84.
  Lexicon Iconographicon Mythologiae Classicae. Zürich, München., 1981/84)
Lhuyd, Edward, 1691.
  To promote the work; queries in order to the geography, and antiquities of the country, Oxford. (reprinted 1961 in Curiosities of British Archeology)
Lhuyd, Edward, 1707.
  Archaeologia Britannica; an Account of the Languages, Hitories, and Customs of Great Britain, from collections and observations in Travel through Wales, Cornwall, Bas-Bretagne, Ireland and Scotland. London.
Linnaeus, Carolus, 1741.
  Oratio, qua peregrinationum intra patriam asseritur necessitas. Upsala.
Lips, Julius, 1937.
  The savage hits back. London.
Lipsius, Justus, 1586.
  De Ratione cum fructu peregrinandi, & praesertim in Italia Epistola ad Ph. Lanoyum. in: Justi Lipsi *epistolarum selectarum chilias centuria prima.* Antwerp.
Locke, John, 1693.
  Some Thoughts concerning Education. London.
Loebenstein, E.-M., 1966.
  Die adelige Kavalierstour im 17. Jahrhundert, ihre Ziele und Voraussetzungen. Wien.
Lohmeier, Dieter, 1979.
  Von Nutzbarkeit der frembden Reysen. Rechtfertigungen des Reisens im Zeitalter der Entdeckungen. in: Hinske/Müller (1979):2-8.
Luhmann, Niklas, 1971.
  Soziologie als Theorie sozialer Systeme. in: Luhmann, N.: *Soziologische Aufklärung.* 2nd ed. Opladen:113-136.
Luhmann, Niklas, 1975.
  Selbstthematisierung des Gesellschaftssystems. in: Luhmann, N.: *Soziologische Aufklärung II.* Opladen.
Lutz, Gerhard, 1973.
  Johann Ernst Fabri und die Anfänge der Volksforschung im ausgehenden 18. Jahrhundert. in: *Zeitschrift für Volkskunde* 69:19-42.
Lutz, Gerhard, 1980.
  Geographie und Statistik im 18. Jahrhundert. Zur Neueingliederung und Inhalten von 'Fächern' im Bereich der historischen Wissenschaften. in: Rassem/Stagl (1980): 249-268.
Lycosthenes, Conrad, 1555.
  Apophthegmatum sive responsorum memorabilium ... ex autoribus priscis pariter atque recentoribus collect. Loci communes. Basel.
Mackensen, Rainer, 1983.
  Bevölkerungswissenschaft zwischen Forschung und Politikberatung. in: *Zeitschrift für Bevölkerungswissenschaft* 4: 485-497.
Maczak, Antoni and Teuteberg, Hans Jürgen (eds.), 1982.
  Reiseberichte als Quellen europäischer Kulturgeschichte. Aufgaben und Möglichkeiten der historischen Reiseforschung. Wolfenbüttel.
Maddison, R.E.W., 1969.
  The Life of the Honourable Robert Boyle F.R.S. London.
Mader, J., 1787.
  Verzeichniss einiger gedruckten Hilfsmittel einer Programmatischen Landes- Volks- und Staatskunde Böhmens. in: Riegger, J.A.v. (ed.): *Materialien zur alten und neuen Statistik von Böhmen I.* Prag.
Maignan, E., 1578.
  Petit Discours de l'Utilité des voyages ou Pelerinages, tiré de plusieurs passages de la Saincte Escriture, & autres Autheurs. Mis en lumière du Commandement de la Royne de France. Paris.
Mair, Lucy, 1962.
  Primitive Government. Harmondsworth.

Makdisi, G. et al. (ed.), 1985.
La Notion de liberté au Moyen Age, Islam, Byzance, Occident. Paris.

Mandrou, Robert, 1973.
Histoire de la pensée européene. Vol 3: Des humanistes aux hommes de science. Paris.

Manheim, Henry L., 1977.
Sociological research: Philosophy and methods. Homewood, Ill.

Marquard, Odo, 1965.
Zur Geschichte des philosophischen Begriffs 'Anthropologie' seit dem Ende des 18. Jahrhunderts. in: *Collegium Philosophicum.* Festschrift für Joachim Ritter. Basel, Stuttgart: 209-239.

Marquard, Odo, 1971.
Anthropologie. in: Ritter, Joachim (ed.): *Historisches Wörterbuch der Philosophie.* Vol I.: 362-374. Basel, Stuttgart.

Marrou, H.-I., 1957.
Geschichte der Erziehung im klassischen Altertum. Ed. R. Harder. Freiburg, München. (French orig. 1948).

Martin, Julian, 1988.
Knowledge ist Power: Francis Bacon, The State and the Reform of Natural Philosophy. Cambridge.

Martin-Allanic, Jean-Etienne, 1964.
Bougainville navigateur et les découvertes de son temps. 2 vols. Paris.

Maus, Heinz, 1973.
Zur Vorgeschichte der empirischen Sozialforschung. in: König, René (ed.): *Handbuch der empirischen Sozialforschung.* 3rd ed. Stuttgart: 21-56.

Mauss, Marcel, 1978.
Soziale Morphologie. Über den jahreszeitlichen Wandel der Eskimo-Gesellschaften. in: Mauss, M.: *Soziologie und Anthropologie,* vol I.: 183-278. Frankfurt, Berlin, Wien. (French orig. 1906)

McClelland, Charles E., 1980.
State, Society and University in Germany 1700-1914. Cambridge.

Mead, William Edward, 1914.
The Grand Tour in the eighteenth Century. Boston, New York (reprint 1972).

Meek, Ronald, 1973.
Turgot on Progress, Sociology and Economics. Cambridge.

Meek, Ronald, 1976.
Social Science and the Ignoble Savage. Cambridge.

Meier, Albert, 1989.
Von der enzyklopädischen Studienreise zur ästhetischen Bildungsreise. Italienreisen im 18. Jahrhundert. in: Brenner (1989): 284-305.

Meier, Christian, 1975.
Geschichte, Historie, II: Antike. in: Brunner, O., Conze, W., Koselleck, R. (eds.): *Geschichtliche Grundbegriffe.* Vol 2. Stuttgart.

Meier, Christian, 1986.
Caesar. München.

1897.
Meiers Konversations-Lexikon. 5th ed. Leipzig, Wien.

Meinecke, Friedrich, 1929.
Die Idee der Staatsräson in der neueren Geschichte. 3rd ed. in: Meinecke, F.: *Werke,* vol I, München 1960.

Meinecke, Friedrich, 1965.
Die Entstehung des Historismus. (= Meinecke, F.: *Werke* 3). Ed. C. Hinrichs. 4th ed. München.

Meitzen, August, 1903.
Theorie und Technik der Statistik. Stuttgart, Berlin.

Menhardt, Hermann, 1957.
Das älteste Handschriftenverzeichnis der Wiener Hofbibliothek von Hugo Blotius 1576. Vienna.

Menzel, Adolf, 1936.
Griechische Soziologie. Wien, Leipzig.

Mersenne, Marin, 1636.
Harmonie Universelle. Paris.

Meyer, Eduard, s.a..
Urgeschichte des Christentums. 2 vols. Stuttgart.

Michaelis, Johann David, 1762.
Fragen an eine Gesellschaft Gelehrter Männer, die auf Befehl Ihro Majestät des Königs von Dännemark (sic) nach Arabien reisen. Frankfurt am Main.

Michéa, René, 1945.
Le ''Voyage en Italie'' de Goethe. Paris.

Mieszkowski, Petrus, 1625.
Institutio peregrinationum peregrinantibus peropportuna ... Louvain.

Milanesi, Marica, 1976.
   Introduzione. in: *Giovanni Battista Ramusio: Navigationi e Viaggi.* Torino (Vol. I; xi-xxiii).
Milanesi, Marica, 1982.
   Giovanni Battista Ramusios Sammlung von Reiseberichten des Entdeckungszeitalters "Delle Navigazione e Viaggi" (1550-1559) neu betrachtet. in: Maczak/Teuteberg (1982):33-44.
Milic, Louis Tonko (ed.), 1971.
   Studies in the Eighteenth Century Culture. Vol I: *The Modernity of the Eighteenth Century.* Cleveland, London.
Mirabeau, Victor Riqueti, Marquis de, 1759/60.
   L'Ami des Hommes, ou Traité de la Population. Nouv. éd. Paris.
Mohl, Robert von, 1856.
   Die Geschichte und Literatur der Staatswissenschaften. In Monographien dargestellt. Erlangen.
Mol, H., 1976.
   Identity and the Sacred. Oxford.
Momigliano, Arnaldo D., 1966.
   Studies in Historiography. London.
Mommsen, Theodor, 1871-88.
   Römisches Staatsrecht. 3 vols. Leipzig.
Montaigne, Michel de, 1965.
   Essais. Ed. Pierre Michel. 3 vols. Paris.
Montesquieu, Charles Louis de Secondat, Baron de, 1721.
   Lettres Persanes. Amsterdam (originally anonymous)
Mooney, Michael, 1985.
   Vico in the Tradition of Rhetoric. Princeton, N.J.
Moore, F.C.T., 1969.
   Translator's Introduction. in: *The Observation of Savage Peoples,* by Joseph-Marie Degérando, translated by F.C.T. Moore. London.
Moore, O'Brien, 1935.
   Senatus. in: Pauly and Wissowa: *Realencyclopädie der Classischen Altertumswissenschaften,* Suppl 6.
Moravia, Sergio, 1967.
   Philosophie et Géographie à la Fin du XVIIIe siècle. in: *Studies on Voltaire and the eighteenth Century* 57: 937-1011.
Moravia, Sergio, 1970.
   La scienza dell'uomo nel Settecento. Bari.
Moravia, Sergio, 1973.
   Beobachtende Vernunft. Philosophie und Anthropologie in der Aufklärung. München.
Moravia, Sergio, 1974.
   Il Pensiero degli Idéologues. Scienza e Filosofia in Francia 1780-1815. Florence.
Moravia, Sergio, 1982.
   Filosofia e Scienze Umane nell' età dei Lumi. Florence.
Moraw, Peter, 1992.
   Reisen im europäischen Spätmittelalter im Licht der neueren historischen Forschung. in: Ertzdorff/Neukirch (1992) 113-140.
Morhof, Daniel Georg, 1747.
   Polyhistor. 4th ed. Lübeck.
Morris, C., 1976.
   Master design of the Inca. in: *Natural History* 85/10: 58-67.
Morus, Thomas, 1517.
   De optimo reip. statu, deque nova insula Utopia ... Basel.
Mouchel, Christian, 1990.
   Cicéron et Sénèque dans la rhétorique de la Renaissance. Marburg.
Möller, Helmut, 1964.
   Volkskunde, Statistik, Völkerkunde 1787. Aus den Anfängen der Volkskunde als Wissenschaft. in: *Zeitschrift für Volkskunde* 60: 218-233.
Muchembled, R., 1978.
   Culture populaire et culture des élites dans la France moderne (XVe - XVIIIe siècles). Paris.
Mühlmann, W.E., 1956.
   Ethnologie als soziologische Theorie der interethnischen Systeme. in: *Kölner Zeitschrift für Soziologie und Sozialpsychologie* 8: 186-205.
Mühlmann, W. E., 1964.
   Rassen Ethnien Kulturen. Moderne Ethnologie. Neuwied, Berlin.
Mühlmann, W.E., 1968.
   Geschichte der Anthropologie. 2nd ed. Frankfurt, Bonn.
Müller, Klaus E., 1972-80.
   Geschichte der antiken Ethnographie und ethnologischen Theoriebildung. Von den Anfängen bis auf die byzantinischen Historiographen. 2 vols. Wiesbaden.

Müller, Klaus E., 1987.
Das magische Universum der Identität. Elementarformen sozialen Verhaltens. Frankfurt, New York.

Mylaeus, Christophorus, 1548.
Consilium historiae universitatis scribendae. Florence. (Further ed. 1668).

Mylaeus, Christophorus, 1551.
De scribenda universitatis rerum historia libri quinque. Basel. Further eds. Basel 1576, 1579; Jena 1624).

Nagler, Georg Kaspar, 1835-52.
Neues allgemeines Künstler-Lexikon oder Nachrichten von dem Leben und den Werken der Maler, Bildhauer, Baumeister ... 22 vols. München.

Nance, John, 1975.
The Gentle Tasaday: A Stone Age People in the Philippine Rain Forest. New York.

Narr, Dieter and Bausinger, Hermann, 1964.
Volkskunde 1788. in: Zeitschrift für Volkskunde 60/2: 233-241.

Neal, Gilbert W., 1960.
Renaissance Concepts of Method. New York.

Nebesky, Wenzel, 1868.
Geschichte des Museums des Königreichs Böhmen. Prag.

Needham, Rodney, 1985.
Exemplars. Berkeley, Los Angeles, London.

Neickel, C.F., 1727.
Museographia Oder Anleitung Zum rechten Begriff und nützlicher Anlegung der Museorum, Oder Raritäten-Kammern ... In bliebter Kürtze zusammengetragen und curiösen Gemüthern dargestellt. Leipzig, Breslau.

Neitzschitz, Georg Christoph von, 1673.
Des weilant Hoch Edlen Herrn Georgen Christophs von Neitzschitz Sieben Jährige und gefährliche WELT-BESCHAUUNG. Also beschrieben und in Druck gegeben von M. Christph Jägern zu S. Afra und der Churf. S. berühmten Landschul daselbst Past. Prim. Bautzen.

Nestle, W., 1941.
Vom Mythos zum Logos. Die Selbstentfaltung des griechischen Denkens. Stuttgart.

Neuber, Wolfgang, 1989.
Zur Gattungspoetik des Reiseberichts. Skizze einer historischen Grundlegung im Horizont von Rhetorik und Topik. in: Brenner (1989) 50-66

Neuber, Wolfgang, 1991.
Fremde Welt im europäischen Horizont. Zur Topik deutscher Amerika.Reiseberichte der Frühen Neuzeit. Berlin.

Neugebauer, Salomon, 1605?.
Tractatus de peregrinatione. Methodo naturali conscriptus ac Historicis, Ethicis, Politicisque exemplis illustratus ... Basel.

Newell, Allen, 1980.
Physical Symbol Systems. in: Cognitive Science 4: 135-183.

Newhauser, Richard, 1982.
Towards a History of Human Curiosity. A Prolegomenon to ist Medieval Phase. in: Deutsche Vierteljahreszeitschrift für Literaturwissenschaft und Geistesgeschichte 56:559-575.

Niebuhr, Carsten, 1772.
Beschreibung von Arabien aus eigenen Beobachtungen und im Lande selbst gesammelten Nachrichten. Kopenhagen.

Niebuhr, Carsten, 1774-1834) Reisebeschreibung nach Arabien und den umliegenden Ländern. 3 vols. Ed. Henze, D. (reprint Graz 1968). Vgl. Kap. 7 FN 2!!!!!

Nippel, Wilfried, 1990.
Griechen, Barbaren und ''Wilde''. Alte Geschichte und Sozialanthropologie. Frankfurt am Main.

Nordblad, Erik, 1759.
Instructio Peregrinatoris, quam, consent. Nobiliss. Facultat. Medica in Regia Academia Upsaliensi, sub praesidio viri nobiliss. et experientiss. Dn. Doct. Linnaei ... publicae censurae submittit ... Upsala.

Norden, Eduard, 1958.
Die antike Kunstprosa. 2 vols. 5th ed. Stuttgart.

Oates, Joan, 1986.
Babylon. rev. ed. London.

Oberschall, Anthony, 1972.
The Establishment of Empirical Sociology: Studies in Continuity, Discontinuity and Institutionalization. New York.

Oestreich, Gerhard, 1976.
Die antike Literatur als Vorbild der praktischen Wissenschaft im 16. und 17. Jahrhundert. in: Bolgar (1976) 315-324.

Ong, Walter J., 1958a.
Ramus. Method, and the Decay of Dialogue. From the Art of Discourse to the Art of reason. Cambridge, Mass.

Ong, Walter J., 1958b.
 Ramus and Talon Inventory. Cambridge, Mass.
Ong, Walter. J., 1961.
 Ramist Method and the Commercial Mind. in: *Studies in the Renaissance* 8:155-172.
Ong, Walter J., 1971.
 Rhetoric, Romance, and Technology. Ithaca, London.
Ong, Walter J., 1976.
 Commonplace Rhapsody: Ravisius Textor, Zwinger, and Shakespeare. in: Bolgar (1976) 91-126.
Ong, Walter J., 1982.
 Orality and Literacy: The Technologizing of the Word. London, New York.
Ornstein, Martha, 1963.
 The Role of Scientific Societies in the Seventeenth Century. Hamden, London.
Osterhammel, Jürgen, 1989.
 Reisen an die Grenze der alten Welt. Asien im Reisebericht des 17. und 18. Jahrhunderts. in: Brenner (1989): 224-260.
Owen, David, 1965.
 English Philanthropy 1660-1960. Cambridge, Mass.
Ozouf, Mona, 1980.
 L'Invention de l'Etnhographie Française: Le Questionnaire de l'Académie Celtique. in: *Annales. Economies Sociétés Civilisations* 36: 210-230.
Pacioli, Luca, 1494.
 Summa de Arithmetica, Geometria, Proportioni e Proportionalità. Venice.
Padgen, Anthony, 1982.
 The fall of natural man: The American Indians and the origins of comparative ethnology. Cambridge.
Pallas, Peter Simon, 1771-76.
 Reisen durch verschiedene Provinzen des russischen Reiches. 3 vols. St. Petersburg.
Papalekas, Johannes Chr., 1989.
 Kulturelle Integration und Kulturkonflikt in der technischen Zivilisation. Frankfurt, New York.
Pareto, Vilfredo, 1935.
 The Mind and Society. New York.
Parkin, Frank, 1986.
 Krippendorf's Tribe. London.
Pearson, E.S. and Kendall, Maurice (eds.), 1987.
 Studies in the History of Statistics and Probability. Vol. I. New York.
Pelz, Annegret, 1991.
 "Ob und wie Frauenzimmer reisen sollen?" Das "reisende Frauenzimmer" als eine Entdeckung des 18. Jahrhunderts. in: Griep (1991) 125-135.
Penrose, Boies, 1975.
 Travel and Discovery in the Renaissance 1420 -1620. New York.
Perelman, Ch. and Olbrechts-Tyteca, L., 1971.
 The New Rhetoric. A Treatise on Argumentation. 2nd ed. Notre Dame, London (French orig. 1958).
Péron, F. and Freycinet, L., 1807-16.
 Voyage de Découvertes aux Terres Australes. 3 vols. Paris.
Perrot, Jean-Claude, 1978.
 L'âge d'or de la Statistique Régionale (an IV-1804). Paris.
Perrot, Jean Claude and Woolf, Joseph, 1984.
 State and statistics in France 1789-1815. Chur.
Péter, Katalin, 1987.
 Der rosenkruzerische Patriotismus. Die Verbreitung der Ideen der Rosenkreuzer in Mittel- und Osteuropa. in: Buck, August and Klaniczay, Tibor (eds.): *Das Ende der Renaissance. Europäische Kultur um 1600*. Wiesbaden: 125-134.
Peters, Edward, 1985.
 Libertas Inquirendi and the Vitium Curiositatis in Medieval Thought. in: Makdisi et al. (1985) 89-98.
Petty, Sir William, 1647.
 The Advice of W.P. to Mr. Samuel Hartlib, For the Advancement of some Particular Parts of Learning. London.
Petty, Sir William, 1690.
 Political Arithmetick. London.
Petty, Sir William, 1691.
 The Political Anatomy of Ireland. London.
Petty, Sir William, 1851.
 The History of the Survey of Ireland, commonly called the Down Survey. Ed. Thomas Aiskew Larcom. Dublin.
Peuchet, J., 1801.
 Essai d'une Statistique Générale de France. Paris, An IX.

Pfister, F., 1961.
   Das Alexander-Archiv und die hellenisch-römische Wissenschaft. in: *Historia* 10.
Piccolomini, Enea Silvio, 1509.
   Cosmographia Pii Papae ... Paris.
Pictorius, Georg, 1577.
   Raiss Büchlin. Ordnung wie sich zu halten/ so einer raisen will in weite und onerfarne Land/ unnd wie man allen zufällen/ so dem raisenden zustehn mögen/ mit guten mitteln der artzney begegnen soll. Strasbourg, Mühlhausen.
Pitsius, Johannes, 1602.
   De peregrinatione libri septem. Düsseldorf.
Pitt-Rivers, Julian, 1977.
   The Fate of Shechem or The Politics of Sex. Essays in the Anthropology ofthe Mediterranian. Cambridge.
Plackett, P.L., 1988.
   Data analysis before 1750. in: *International Statistical Review* 2:180-195.
Plaschka, Richard Georg, 1955.
   Von Palack?EC? bis Pekar. Geschichtswissenschaft und Nationalbewußtsein bei den Tschechen. Graz, Köln.
Plischke, Hans, 1937.
   Johann Friedrich Blumenbachs Einfluß auf die Entdeckungsreisenden seiner Zeit. Göttingen.
Plotius, Hugo (recte Blotius, Hugo), 1629.
   Tabula Peregrinationis continens capita Politica. in: Hentzner (1629).
Pluskal, F.S., 1859.
   Leopold Graf von Berchtold, der Menschenfreund. Brünn.
Polanyi, Karl, Arensberg Conrad M., Pearson, Harry W., 1962.
   Trade and Market in the Early Empires. Glencoe, Ill. 1957.
Polaschek, E., 1936.
   Notitia Dignitatum. in: RE 33:1077-1116.
Poliakov, Léon, 1974.
   The Aryan Myth. A History of racist and nationalist ideas in Europe. Brighton.
Popper, Sir Karl, 1950.
   The Open Society and its Enemies. Princeton.
Posselt, Franz, 1795.
   Apodemik oder die Kunst zu reisen. Ein systematischer Versuch zum Gebrauch junger Reisenden (sic!) *aus den gebildeten Ständen überhaupt und angehender Gelehrter und Künstler insbesondere.* 2 vols. Leipzig.
Pratt, Marie Louise, 1986.
   Fieldwork in common places. in: Clifford/Marcus (1986): 27-50.
Prichard, J.C., 1836.
   Researches into the Physical History of Man. 3rd ed. London.
Psalmanazar, George, 1704.
   An Historical and Geographical Description of Formosa, An Island subject to the Emperor of Japan. Giving an Account of the Religion, Customs, Manners, etc. of the Inhabitants. London. (2nd ed. London 1705; French: *Description de l'isle Formosa en Asie ...* 1st ed. Amsterdam 1705, 2nd ed. Amsterdam 1708, 3rd ed. Amsterdam 1712, 4th ed: *Description dressée sur les mémoires du sieur George Psalmanaazaar.* Paris 1739; Dutch: *Beschryvinge van het eyland Formosa in Asia ...* Rotterdam 1708 (of which an extract was reprinted in John Toland: *Van den oorspronk en de kracht der Vooroordelen ...* Amsterdam 1710); German: *Historische und Geographische Beschreibung der Insul Formosa.*
Psalmanazar, George, 1707.
   A Dialogue Between A Japanese and A Formosan, About some Points of the Religion of the Time. By G.P.-m-r. London.
Psalmanazar, George, 1710.
   An Enquiry into the objections against George Psalmanaazaar of Formosa ... to which is added G. Psalmanaazaar's answer to M. d'Amalvy of Sluice. London s.a.
Psalmanazar, George, 1753.
   Essays on the Following Subjects: I. On the Reality and Evidence of Miracles ..., II. On the Extraordinary Adventure of Balaam ..., III. On the Surprising March and final Victory, gained by Joshua over Jabin, King of Hazor ..., IV. On the Religious War of the Israelitish Tribes ..., V. On the Amazing speedy Relief which Saul ... Brought to the besigned Inhabitants of Jabesh-Gilead ... Wherein the Most considerable Objections raised against each respective subject, are fully answered; The difficulties removed; and each of these remarcable Transactions accounted for, in a rational Way. Written some Years since, and at the desire, and for the Use of, a young Clergyman in the Country, by a Layman in Town. London.
Psalmanazar, George, 1764.
   Memoirs of **** *Commonly known by the Name of George Psalmanazar; A Reputed Native of Formosa. Written by Himself In Order to be published After his Death.* London.
Purver, Margery, 1967.
   The Royal Society: Concept and Creation. London.

Pyrckmair, Hilarius, 1577.
   Commentariolus de Arte Apodemica, seu Vera Peregrinandi Ratione. Ingolstadt.
Quichelberg, Samuel, 1565.
   Inscriptiones vel tituli theatri amplissimi. Munich.
Rackham, H. (ed.), 1961.
   Aristotle: The Athenian Constitution; The Eudemian Ethics; On Virtues and Vices. Introduction: 2-5.
   London, Cambridge, Mass.
Rad, Gerhard von, 1957.
   Theologie des Alten Testamentes. vol. I: *Die Theologie der geschichtlichen Überlieferung Israels.* München.
Ramée, Pierre de la, 1555.
   Dialectique. Paris.
Ramus, Petrus, 1543.
   Institutiones dialecticae (Aristotelis Anidmadversationes) (reprint Stuttgart, Bad Cannstadt 1964).
Ramus, Petrus, 1944.
   Basilea ad Senatum Populumque Basiliensem (1569) Ed. Hans Fleig. Basel.
Ramusio, Giovanni Battista, 1550, 1556, 1559) Delle Navigationi et viaggi. 3 vols. Venice.
Randall, John H., jr., 1940.
   The Development of Scientific Method in the School of Padua. in: *Journal of the History of Ideas* I:177-206.
Ranzovius, Henricus, 1739.
   Cimbricae Cheronesi eiusdemque partium, urbium, insularum, et fluvium ... descriptio nova. First published
   in E.J. de Westphalen, Monumenta inedita I.
Rappaport, R.A., 1967.
   Pigs for the Ancestors: Ritual in the Ecology of a New Guinea People. New Haven.
Rassem, Mohammed, 1979.
   Die Vokstumswissenschaften und der Etatismus. 2nd ed. Mittenwald.
Rassem, Mohammed, 1980.
   Stichproben aus dem Wortfeld der alten Statistik. in: Rassem/Stagl (1980): 17-31.
Rassem, Mohammed, 1992.
   Wohlfahrt, Wohltätigkeit, Caritas. in: Brunner, Otto, Conze, Werner, Koselleck, Reinhart (eds.):
   Geschichtliche Grundbegriffe. Historisches Lexikon zur politisch-sozialen Sprache in Deutschland.
   Vol. 7: 595-636. Stuttgart.
Rassem, Mohammed and Stagl, Justin (eds.), 1980.
   Statistik und Staatsbeschreibung in der Neuzeit, vornehmlich im 16. - 18. Jahrhundert. Paderborn,
   München, Wien Zürich.
Rassem Mohammed and Stagl, Justin (eds.), 1994.
   Geschichte der Staatsbeschreibung. Ausgewählte Quellentexte 1458-1813. Berlin.
Ratzel, Friedrich, 1897.
   Politische Geographie. 2nd ed. München.
Redfield, Robert, 1968.
   The Folk Culture of Yucatan. Chicago.
Redlich, Josef, 1920.
   *Das österreichische Staats- und Reichsproblem. Geschichtliche Darstellung der inneren Politik der
   habsburgischen Monarchie von 1848 bis zum Untergang des Reiches.* Vol. I. Leipzig.
Reichert, Folker, 1988.
   Columbus und Marco Polo - Asien und Amerika. Zur Literaturgeschichte der Entdeckungen. in: *Zeitschrift
   für historische Forschung* 15: 1-63.
Reill, P.H., 1980.
   Johann Christoph Gatterer. in: Wehler (1980), Vol. VI: 7-22.
Reinhard, W. (ed.), 1984.
   Humanismus im Bildungswesen des 15. und 16. Jahrhunderts. Weinheim.
Renaudot, Théophraste, 1630.
   *Inventaire du Bureau de Recontre, ou chacun peut donner & recevoir avis de toutes les necessitez, & commoditez
   de la vie & societé humaine ...* Paris (Bureau d'adresse).
Renaudot, Theophraste, 1636.
   Seconde Centurie des Questions traitées ez conferences du Bureau d'adresse. Paris (Bureau d'adresse).
Renaudot, Theophraste, 1642.
   *La Presence des Absens, ou facile moyen de rendre présent au Médecin l'estat d'un malade absent. Dressé
   par les docteurs en Médecine Consultans charitablement à Paris pour les pauvres malades.* Paris (Bureau
   d'adresse).
Ricard, Robert, 1933.
   *La "Conqête Spirituelle" du Mexique. Essai sur l'Apostolat et les Méthodes des Ordres Mendiants en Nouvelle
   Espagne de 1523 à 1572.* Paris.
Richardson, John, 1778.
   A Dissertation on languages, literature, and manners of the Eastern Nations. Oxford.

Richter, Melvin, 1973.
  Despotism. in: *Dictionary of the History of Ideas.* Ed. Wiener, Phillip. Vol. 2: 1-18. New York.
de Ridder-Symoens, Hilde, 1989.
  Die Kavalierstour im 16. und 17. Jahrhundert. in: Brenner (1989) 197-223.
Risse, Wilhelm , 1963.
  Zur Vorgeschichte der Cartesianischen Methodenlehre. in: *Archiv für Geschichte der Philosophie* 45/3:269-291.
Robinson, Henry, 1650.
  The office of addresses and encounters: where all people of each rancke and quality may receive direction and advice for the most cheap and speedy way of attaining whatsoever they can lawfully desire ... London.
Rohan-Csermak, Géza de, 1967.
  La Premiere Apparition du Terme 'Ethnologie'. in: *Ethnologia Europaea* I/3.
Rohan-Csermak, Géza de, 1970.
  Ethnographie. in: *Encyclopedia Universalis.* Vol. 6: 704-707.
Rossi, Paolo, 1968.
  Francis Bacon: From Magic to Science. London.
Rothkrug, Lionel, 1965.
  Opposition to Louis XIV. Princeton.
Rothkrug, Lionel, 1980.
  Religious Practices and Collective Perceptions. Hidden Homologies in the Renaissance and Reformation. in: *Historical Reflections* 10/1.
Le Roux, C.C.F.M., 1948-50.
  De Bergpapoeas van Nieuw Guinea en hun woongebied. 3 vols. Leiden.
Röhricht, R., 1963.
  Bibliotheca Geographica Palästinä. Jerusalem.
Rupp-Eisenreich, Britta, 1983.
  Des Choses Occultes en Histoire des Sciences Humaines: Le Destin de la 'Science Nouvelle' de Christoph Meiners. in: *L'Ethnographie* CXXV/LXXIX, Numéro Spécial 90-91: 131-183.
Rupp-Eisenreich, Britta, 1984a.
  Aux 'origines' de la Völkerkunde Allemande: de la Statistik à l'Anthropologie de Georg Forster. in: Rupp-Eisenreich (1984b): 89-116.
Rupp-Eisenreich, Britta (ed.), 1984b.
  Histoires de l'anthropologie: XVI-XIX siècles. Paris.
Rupp-Eisenreich, Britta, 1986.
  Christoph Meiners et Joseph-Marie de Gérando: un chapitre du comparatisme anthropologique. in: Droixhe, D. and Gossiaux, P.P. (eds.): *L'Homme de Lumières et la Découverte de l'autre.* Brussels.
Rühl, Edith, 1958.
  Die nachgelassenen Zeitungssammlungen und die gelehrte Korrespondenz Hugo Blotius', des ersten Bibliothekars der Wiener Hofbibliothek. Phil. Diss. Vienna.
Saage, Richard, 1987.
  August Ludwig Schlözer als politischer Theoretiker. in: Herrlitz/Kern (1987): 55-71.
Sabellico, Marcantonio Coccio, 1487.
  Historiae rerum venetiarum. Venice.
Sabellico, Marcantonio Coccio, 1488.
  De venetis magistratibus. Venice.
Saggs, H.W.F., 1989.
  Civilization Before Greece and Rome. London.
Salomon-Delatour, Gottfried, 1965.
  Moderne Staatslehren. Neuwied, Berlin.
Sansovino, Francesco, 1561.
  Del Governo de i regni et delle republiche cosi antiche come moderne. Venice.
Sauder, Gerhard, 1983.
  Sternes "Sentimental Journey" und die "empfindsamen Reisen" in Deutschland. in: Griep/Jäger (1983) 303-319
Schalk, Fritz, 1977.
  Von Erasmus' "Res publica literaria" zur Gelehrtenrepublik der Aufklärung. in: Schalk, F.: *Studien zur französichen Aufklärung.* 2nd ed. Frankfurt am Main: 143-163.
Schindler, Norbert, Bonß, Wolfgang, 1980.
  Praktische Aufklärung - Ökonomische Sozietäten in Süddeutschland und Österreich im 18. Jahrhundert. in: Vierhaus (1980b): 255-353.
Schindling, Anton, 1977.
  Humanistische Hochschule und Freie Reichsstadt. Gymnasium und Akademie in Straßburg 1538-1621. Wiesbaden.
Schipperges, Heinrich, 1989.
  Paracelsus (1493-1541) in: Böhme (1989): 99-116.

Schlözer, August Ludwig, 1771.
   Allgemeine Nordische Geschichte (= Allgemeine Welthistorie XXXI: Theil, Historie der Neuern Zeiten 13. Theil (Fortsetzung erster Theil). Halle.
Schlözer, August Ludwig, 1772.
   August Ludwig Schlözers Prof. in Göttingen: Vorstellung seiner Universal-Historie. Göttingen und Gotha. (2nd ed. 1775).
Schlözer, August Ludwig, 1773.
   August Ludwig Schlözers Prof. in Göttingen: Vorstellung seiner Universal-Historie. Zweeter Teil. Göttingen und Gotha.
Schlözer, August Ludwig, 1775.
   Briefwechsel meist statistischen Inhalts. Gesammelt, und zum Versuch herausgegeben. Göttingen.
Schlözer, August Ludwig, 1776-82.
   Briefwechsel meist historischen und politischen Inhalts. 10 parts. Göttingen.
Schlözer, August Ludwig, 1777.
   Entwurf zu einem Reise-Collegio ... nebst einer Anzeige seines Zeitungs-Collegii. Göttingen.
Schlözer, August Ludwig, 1779.
   Vorbereitung zur Weltgeschichte für Kinder. Göttingen.
Schlözer, August Ludwig, 1782-93.
   Stats-Anzeigen/Gesammelt und zum Druck befördert. 18 vols. Göttingen.
Schlözer, August Ludwig, 1785-89.
   Weltgeschichte, nach ihren HauptTheilen im Auszug und Zusammenhange von August Ludwig Schlözer D. 2 vols. Göttingen.
Schlözer, August Ludwig, 1802-09.
   Nestors Russische Annalen in ihrer Slavonischen Grund-Sprache Verglichen, Übersetzt, und Erklärt. 5 Parts. Göttingen.
Schlözer, August Ludwig, 1804.
   Theorie der Statistik. Nebst Ideen über das Studium der Politik überhaupt ... Göttingen. (French ed. Donnant: 1805; dutch eds. Tijdeman: 1807 and 1814).
Schlözer, August Ludwig, 1962.
   Vorlesungen über Land- und Seereisen, nach dem Kollegheft des stud. iur. E.F. Haupt. (ed. Wilhelm Ebel). Göttingen.
Schlözer, Christian v. (ed.) , 1828.
   August Ludwig Schlözers Öffentliches und Privatleben aus Originalurkunden ... Vollständig beschrieben von dessen Ältesten Sohne. Leipzig.
Schlözer, Leopold v., 1923.
   Dorothea von Schlözer, der Philosophie Doctor. Ein deutsches Frauenleben um die Jahrhundertwende 1770-1825. Stuttgart, Berlin, Leipzig.
Schmandt-Basserat, Denise, 1978.
   The earliest precursor of writing. in: *Scientific American* 238/6: 50-59.
Schmidt, Paul Gerhard, 1978.
   Mittelalterliches und humanistisches Städtelob (Manuscript).
Schmidt-Biggemann, Wilhelm, 1963.
   Topica universalis. Eine Modellgeschichte humanistischer und barocker Wissenschaft. Hamburg.
Schmied-Kowarzik, Wolfdietrich and Stagl, Justin (eds.), 1993.
   Grundfragen der Ethnologie. Beiträge zur gegenwärtigen Theorie-Diskussion. 2nd rev. ed Berlin. (1st ed. 1980).
Schnapper-Arndt, G., 1908.
   Sozialstatistik (Ed. Leon Zeitlin). Leipzig.
Schneider, Ivo, 1980.
   Mathematisierung des Wahrscheinlichen und Anwendung auf Massenphänomene im 17. und 18. Jahrhundert. in: Rassem/Stagl (1980): 53-66.
Schoeck, R.J., 1990.
   Erasmus of Europe: The Making of a Humanist, 1467-1500. Savage, Maryland.
Schöne, Walter, 1924.
   Zeitungswesen und Statistik. Eine Untersuchung über den Einfluß der periodischen Presse auf die Entstehung und Entwicklung der staatswissenschaftlichen Literatur, speziell der Statistik. Jena.
Schramm, Percy Ernst, 1928.
   Die deutschen Kaiser und Könige in Bildern ihrer Zeit. Leipzig, Berlin.
Schudt, Ludwig, 1959.
   Italienreisen im 17. und 18. Jahrhundert. Wien, München.
Schulze, Fritz Willy, 1949.
   Folklore. Zur Ableitung der Vorgeschichte einer Wissenschaftsbezeichnung. Halle an der Saale.
Schüling, H., 1963.
   Die Geschichte der axiomatischen Methode im 16. und beginnenden 17. Jahrhundert. Hildesheim.

Schütz, Alfred, 1972.
   Studien zur soziologischen Theorie. Den Haag.
Schwart, Anton Wilhelm, 1693.
   Der Adeliche Hofmeister. Frankfurt am Main.
Seidlmayr, Michael, 1965.
   Wege und Wandlungen des Humanismus. Göttingen.
Seifert, Arno, 1976.
   Cognitio historica. Die Geschichte als Namengeberin der frühneuzeitlichen Empirie. Berlin.
Seifert, Arno, 1980.
   Staatenkunde. Eine neue Disziplin und ihr wissenschaftstheoretischer Ort. in: Rassem/Stagl (1980) 217-248.
Selle, Götz v., 1937.
   Die Georg-August-Universität. Göttingen.
Sergeant, Phillip W., 1925.
   Liars and Fakers. London.
Service, Elman, R., 1977.
   Ursprünge des Staates und der Zivilisation. Frankfurt am Main. (Engl. orig. 1975).
Severi, Carlo, 1993.
   La memoria rituale. Follia e immagine del Bianco in una tradtzione sciamanica amerindiana. Florence.
Shackleton, Robert, 1971.
   The Grand Tour in the Eighteenth Century. in: Milic (1971) 127-142.
Shumaker, Wayne, 1972.
   The Occult Sciences in the Renaissance. A Study in Intellectual Patterns. Berkeley, Calif.
Simmel, Georg, 1908.
   Soziologie. Untersuchungen über die Formen der Vergesellschaftung. Leipzig.
Smith, Adam, 1933.
   An Inquiry into the Nature and Causes of the Wealth of Nations (1776). London.
Sobrevilla, David, 1971.
   Der Ursprung des Kulturbegriffs, der Kulturphilosophie und der Kulturkritik. Eine Studie über deren Entstehung und deren Voraussetzungen. Phil. Diss. Tübingen.
Soden, Wolfram von, 1965.
   Leistung und Grenze sumerischer und babylonischer Wissenschaft. Darmstadt.
Solomon, Howard M., 1972.
   Public Welfare, Science and propaganda in Seventeenth Century France. The Innovations of Théophraste Renaudot. Princeton, N.J.
Sommerfeld, Martin, 1924.
   Die Reisebeschreibung der deutschen Jerusalempilger im ausgehenden Mittelalter. in: *Deutsche Vierteljahresschrift für Literaturwissenschaft und Geistesgeschichte* 2:816-851.
Sorokin, Pitrim A., 1957.
   Dynamics of Cultural Change. A study in major systems of art, truth, ethics, law and relationships. London.
Spethmann, Hans, 1932.
   Länderkundliches Schema und Kausalität. in: *Geographischer Anzeiger* 33:193-197.
Sprat, Thomas, 1667.
   The History of the Royal Society of London. For the Improving of Natural Knowledge. London.
Srbik, Heinrich von, 1950.
   Geist und Geschichte vom deutschen Humanismus bis zur Gegenwart. München, Salzburg.
Stagl, Justin, 1971.
   Der Geschlechtsantagonismus in Melanesien. Vienna.
Stagl, Justin, 1974a.
   Die Morphologie segmentärer Gesellschaften. Dargestellt am Beispiel des Hochlandes von Neuguinea. Meisenheim/Glan.
Stagl, Justin, 1974b.
   August Ludwig Schlözers Entwurf einer 'Völkerkunde' oder 'Ethnographie' seit 1772. in: *Ethnologische Zeitschrift Zürich* 2: 73-91.
Stagl, Justin, 1979.
   Vom Dialog zum Fragebogen. Miszellen zur Geschichte der Umfrage. in: *Kölner Zeitschrift für Soziologie und Sozialpsychologie* 31/3:611-638.
Stagl, Justin, 1980a.
   Die Apodemik oder ''Reisekunst'' als Methodik der Sozialforschung vom Humanismus bis zur Aufklärung. in: Rassem/Stagl (1980) 131-204.
Stagl, Justin, 1980b.
   Der wohl unterwiesene Passagier. Reisekunst und Gesellschaftsbeschreibung vom 16. bis zum 18. Jahrhundert. in: Krasnobaev et.al. (1980) 353-384.
Stagl, Justin, 1980c.
   Szientistische, hermeneutische und phänomenologische Grundlagen der Ethnologie. in: Schmied-Kowarzik/Stagl (1980), reprinted in Schmied-Kowarzik/Stagl (1993):15-50.

Stagl, Justin, 1981a.
   Das Reisen als Kunst und als Wissenschaft (16.-18. Jahrhundert). in: *Mitteilungen der anthropologischen Gesellschaft in Wien* 111:78-92. reprinted in: *Zeitschrift für Ethnologie* 108/1:15-43.
Stagl, Justin, 1981b.
   Die Beschreibung des Fremden in der Wissenschaft. in: Duerr 1981, vol I: 273-295.
Stagl, Justin, 1981c.
   Kulturanthropologie und Gesellschaft. 2nd ed. Berlin.
Stagl, Justin, 1983.
   Apodemiken. Eine räsonnierte Bibliographie der reisetheoretischen Literatur des 16., 17. und 18. Jahrhunderts. Paderborn, München, Wien, Zürich.
Stagl, Justin, 1985.
   Feldforschung als Ideologie. in: Fischer, Hans (ed.): *Feldforschungen: Berichte zur Einführung in Probleme und Methoden.* Berlin: 289-310.
Stagl, Justin, 1989a.
   Die Methodisierung des Reisens im 16. Jahrhundert. in: Brenner (1989) 140-177.
Stagl, Justin, 1989b.
   Zur Soziologie der Repräsentativkultur. in: Papalekas (1989) 43-67.
Stagl, Justin, 1990.
   The Methodising of Travel in the 16th Century. A Tale of Three Cities. (English version of Stagl (1989)) in: *History and Anthropology* 4: 303-338.
Stagl, Justin, 1992.
   Ars Apodemica: Bildungsreise und Reisemethodik von 1560 bis 1600. in: Ertzdorff/Neukirch (1992):141-189.
Stagl, Justin, 1993a.
   Malinowskis Paradigma. in: Schmied-Kowarzik/Stagl (1993): 93-106.
Stagl, Justin, 1993b.
   Der Kreislauf der Kultur. in: *Anthropos* 88.
Stark, Werner, 1934.
   Ursprung und Aufstieg des landwirtschaftlichen Großbetriebs in den böhmischen Ländern. Brünn.
Stark, Werner, 1972.
   The Sociology of religion. A Study of Christendom. Vol. V: Types of Religious Culture. London.
Stehr, Nico, 1992.
   Experts, Counsellors and Advisers. in: Stehr, Nico and Ericson, Richard V. (eds.): *The Culture and Power of Knowledge. Inquiries into Contemporary Societies.* Berlin, New York: 107-156.
Steinmetz, Sebald Rudolf, 1928.
   De "fosterage" of opvoeding in freemde families. in: Steinmetz, S.R.: Gesammelte kleinere Schriften zur Ethnologie und Soziologie. Band 1: 1-113. Groningen.
Sterne, Laurence, 1768.
   A Sentimental Journey through France and Italy, by Mr. Yorick. 2 vols. London.
Stewart, Susan, 1989.
   Antipodal expectations: Notes on the Formosa "Ethnography" of George Psalmanazar. in: Stocking, George W. jr. (ed.): *Romantic Motives. Essays on Anthropological Sensibility* (=History of Anthropology, vol. 6) Madison, Wisc.: 44-73.
Stewart, William E., 1978.
   Die Reisebeschreibung und ihre Theorie im Deutschland des 18. Jahrhunderts. Bonn.
Stigler, Stephen M., 1975.
   Napoleonic Statistics: The Work of Laplace. in: *Biometrica* 62/2.
Stigler, Stephen M., 1986.
   The History of Statistics. The measurement of uncertainty before 1900. Cambridge, Mass., London.
Stimson, D., 1940.
   Hartlib, Haak, and Oldenburg, Intelligencers. in: *Isis* 31.
Stocking, George W., 1973.
   From Chronology to Ethnology: James Cowles Prichard and British Anthropology, 1800-1850. in: Prichard. J.C.: *Researches into the Physical History of Man (1813).* Chicago: IX-CX.
Stocking, George W., 1982.
   French Anthropology in 1800. in: Stocking, G.W. (ed.): *Race, Culture and Evolution. Essays in the History of Anthropology.* 2nd ed. Chicago, London: 13-41.
Stocking, George W., 1983.
   Observers Observed. Essays on Ethnographic Fieldwork (=History of Anthropology, vol I). Madison, Wisc.
Stocking, George W., 1984.
   Qu'est-ce qui est en jeu dans un nom?; La "Société d'Ethnographie" et L'historiographie de l'anthropologie en France. in: Rupp-Eisenreich (1984b):421-431.
Stocking, George W., 1987.
   Victorian Anthropology. New York.

Stradling, Sir John, 1592.
A Direction for Traueilers. Taken out of Justus Lipsius, and enlarged for the behoofe of the right honorable Lord, the young Earl of Bedford, being now ready to trauell. London.

Strasburger, Hermann, 1966.
Die Wesensbestimmung der Geschichte durch die antike Geschichtsschreibung. Wiesbaden.

Strasburger, Hermann, 1977.
Überblick im Trümmerfeld der griechischen Geschichtsschreibung. in: *Historiographia Antiqua. Commentationes Lovanienses in honorem W. Perelmans septuagenarii editae.* Leuven: 3-52.

Strathern, Andrew, 1979.
The Rope of Moka. Big-men and Ceremonial Exchange in Mount Hagen, New Guinea. Cambridge.

Strauss, E., 1954.
Sir William Petty. Protrait of a Genius. London.

Strauss, Gerald, 1959.
Sixteenth Century Germany. Ist Topography and Topographers. Madison, Wisc.

Stuck, Gottlieb Heinrich, 1784/87.
Verzeichnis von aeltern und neuern Land- und Reisebeschreibungen. Ein Versuch eines Hauptstückes der geographischen Litteratur mit einem vollständigen Realregister, und einer Vorrede von M Johann Ernst Fabri. 2 parts, Halle.

Sturm, Heribert, 1979.
Biographisches Lexikon zur Geschichte der böhmischen Länder. Vienna.

Sudhoff, Karl, 1911.
Ärztliche Reiseregimina für Land und Seereisen aus dem 15. Jahrhundert. in: *Archiv für Geschichte der Medizin* 4:263-281.

Swift, Jonathan, 1957.
The Examiner and other Pieces Written in 1710-11. Ed. Herbert Davis. Oxford.

Syme, Ronald, s.a..
Die römische Revolution. München. (Engl. orig. 1939).

Szalay, Miklós, 1972.
"Coree the Soldanian": Europäisch-afrikanische Beziehung am Kap der guten Hoffnung 1613-1627. in: *Wiener Ethnohistorische Blätter* 5.

Szalay, Miklós, 1985.
Historismus und Kulturrelativismus. in: *Anthropos* 80: 587-604.

Szepsi Csombor, Márton, 1620.
Europica Varietas. in: *M. Szepsi Csombor. Complete Works* (in Hungarian), ed. S.I. Kovacs and P. Kulcsar. Budapest 1968.

Tadmor, H., 1986.
Monarchy and the Elite in Assyria and Babylonia: The Question of Royal Accountability. in: Eisenstadt, s.N. (ed.): *The Origins and Diversity of Axial Civilisations.* Albany, New York.

Tambiah, S.J., 1985.
Culture, Thought and Social Action. Cambridge, Mass.

Tankard, James W., 1984.
The statistical Pioneers. Cambridge, Mass.

Teggart, F.J., 1925.
Theory of History. New Haven.

Tenbruck, Friedrich, 1989a.
Die kulturellen Grundlagen der Gesellschaft. Der Fall der Moderne. Opladen.

Tenbruck, Friedrich, 1989b.
Gesellschaftsgeschichte oder Weltgeschichte? in: *Kölner Zeitschrift für Soziologie und Sozialpsychologie* 41/3: 417-443.

Thieme, Ulrich and Becker, 1907-47.
Allgemeines Lexikon der bildenden Künstler von der Antike bis zur Gegenwart. Leipzig.

Thienen-Adlerflycht, Christoph, 1967.
Graf Leo Thun im Vormärz. Grundlagen des böhmischen Konservativismus im Kaisertum Österreich. Graz, Wien, Köln.

Thommen, R., 1889.
Geschichte der Universität Basel. Basel.

Thomson, J. Oliver, 1948.
History of Ancient Geography. Cambridge.

Thorndike, Lynn, 1966.
Renaissance. in: *Encyclopedia Britannica,* ed. 1966: 126.

Thyssen, Johannes, 1960.
Geschichte der Geschichtsphilosophie. 3rd ed. Bonn.

Tibenský, Ján, 1978.
"Barokový historizismus" a zaciatky slovensky slavistiky. in: *Studie z dejín svetory slavisziky do poovice 19. storicia.* Bratislava: 93-124.

Tibenský, Ján, 1983.
Slovenský Sokrates. Zivot a dielo Frantiska Kollára. Bratislava.
Tieghem, P. van, 1917.
Ossian en France. 2 vols. Paris.
Tijderman, Henrik Willem, 1807.
Theorie der Statistiek. Naar het Hoogduitsch van August Ludwig von Schlözer. 1st ed. Groningen (2nd ed. 1814) (=Dutch ed. of Schlözer 1804)
Todorov, Tsvetan, 1985.
Die Eroberung Amerikas. Das Problem des Anderen. Frankfurt am Main.
Topitsch, Ernst, 1972.
Vom Ursprung und Ende der Metaphysik. Eine Studie zur Weltanschauungskritik. München.
Toscanini, Ignazio, 1980.
Etatistisches Denken und erkenntnistheoretische Überlegungen in den venezianischen Relazionen. in: Rassem/Stagl (1980) 111-130.
Trénard, Louis, 1958
Lyon. De l'Encyclopédie au Préromantisme. Paris.
Trevor-Roper, Hugh, 1967.
Three Foreigners: The Philosophers of the Puritan Revolution. in: Trevor-Roper, H.: *Religion, the Reformation and Social Change and other Essays.* London.
Trier, Jost, 1957.
Reihendienst. Münster.
Trier, Jost, 1964.
Umfrage und Meinung. in: *Archiv für Begriffsgeschichte* 9: 189-201.
Troeltsch, Ernst, 1925.
Deutscher Geit und Westeuropa: Gesammelte kulturphilosophische Aufsätze und Reden. Ed. H. Baron. Tübingen.
Tschirnhaus auf Hackenau, Wolf Bernhard v., 1727.
Getreuer Hofmeister auf Academien und Reisen, welcher Hn. Ehrenfr. Walthers von Tschirnhauß auf Kißlingswaldau, für Studierende und Reisende, sonderlich Standes-Personen und Deroselben Hofmeister zu einer sicheren Anleitung zur anständigen Conduite auf Universitäten und Reisen, in Manuscripto hinterlassene XXX Nützliche Anmerkungen mit XLVI Erläuterungen und XII beylagen vermehrter, wohlmeynend ans Licht stellet. Hannover.
Tucker, Josiah, 1757.
Instructions for Travellers. s.l. (London)
Turgot, Etienne François, 1758.
Mémoire instructifs sur la manière de rassembler, de préparer, de conserver et d'envoyer les diverses curiosités d'histoire naturelle ... Paris, Lyon.
Turler Hieronymus, 1569.
Oikonomia Institutionum Iustiniani Imperatoris. Totius Iuris Civilis Epitomen Continens. Scripta in Gratiam Studiosorum. Wittenberg.
Turler, Hieronymus, 1574.
De peregrinatione et agro Neapolitano Libri II. Straßburg.
Turler, Hieronymus, 1575.
The Taveiler, devided into two Bookes. London. Reprint Gainsville, Florida 1951. (English Translation of Turler 1574).
Turnbull, G.H., 1947.
Hartlib, Dury and Comenius. Gleanings from Hartlib's Papers. London.
Turner, Victor, 1969.
The Ritual Process. Structure and Anti-Structure. Chicago.
Turner, Victor and Turner, Edith, 1978.
Image and Pilgrimage in Christian Culture. New York.
Unterkirchner, Franz, 1968.
Hugo Blotius und seine ersten Nachfolger (1575-1663). in: Stummvoll, Josef (ed.): *Geschichte der österreichischen Nationalbibliothek.* Vienna. Vol I.
Urry, James, 1972.
Notes and Queries in Anthropology and the development of field methods in British Anthropology, 1870-1920. in: *Proceedings of the Royal anthropological Institute* 1972: 45-57.
Valjavec, Fritz, 1945.
Der Josephinismus. Zur geistigen Entwicklung Österreichs im achtzehnten und neunzehnten Jahrhundert. 2nd ed. München.
Valla, Lorenzo, 1499.
Dialecticae disputationes contra Aristoteleos. Venice.
Van Dülmen, Richard, 1978.
Die Utopie einer christlichen Gesellschaft. Stuttgart, Bad Cannstadt.

Van Dülmen, Richard, 1986.
  Die Gesellschaft der Aufklärer. Zur bürgerlichen Emanzipation und aufklärerischen Kultur in Deutschland.
  Frankfurt am Main.
Varagnac, André, 1938.
  Definition du Folklore. Paris.
Varenius, Bernhard, 1649.
  Descriptio regni Japoniae ... Amsterdam.
Venturi, Angelo, 1976.
  Introduzione A Relazioni degli ambascatori al senato. Bari.
Vermeer, Hans J., 1972.
  Johann Lochners Reisekonsilia. in: *Sudhoffs Archiv* 56/2:145-196.
Vermeulen, Han F., 1988.
  Het ontstaan van de Volkenkunde ca 1770 in Göttingen. Leiden.
Vermeulen, Han F., 1992a.
  Footnotes for the History of Anthropology. The Emergence of 'Ethnography' ca. 1770 in Göttingen. in:
  History of Anthropology Newsletter 19/2: 6-22.
Vermeulen, Han F., 1992b.
  *Origins and Institutionalization of Völkerkunde (1771-1843). Formation and distribution of the concepts
  'Völkerkunde', 'Ethnographie', 'Volkskunde' and 'Ethnologie' in the late 18th and early 19th century in
  Europe and the USA.* Ms. to appear in: *Ethnograficheskoe Obozrenie* (Moscow).
Vetter, Verena, 1952.
  Baslerische Italienreisen vom ausgehenden Mittelalter bis in das 17. Jahrhundert. Basel.
Vierhaus, Rudolf, 1980a.
  "Patriotismus" - Begriff und Realität einer moralisch-politischen Haltung. in: Vierhaus (1980b): 9-29.
Vierhaus, Rudolf (ed.), 1980b.
  Deutsche patriotische und gemeinnützige Gesellschaften. München.
Vilquin, Eric (ed.), 1977.
  Observations naturelles et politiques ... faites sur les Bulletins de mortalité. Paris.
Vinandus Pighius, Stephanus, 1587.
  *Hercules Prodicius, Seu Principis Iuventutis Vita Et Peregrinatio ... Historia Principis Adolescentis institutrix:
  & antquitatum, rerumque scitu dignarum varietate non minus utilis quam iucunda ...* Antwerp.
Vinas y Mey, Carmelo, 1951.
  Las Relaciones de Felipe II. in: *Studios Geográficos* 42: 131-136.
Voigt, Georg, 1880/81.
  Die Wiederbelebung des classischen Altertums oder das erste Jahrhundert des Humanismus. 2 vols. Berlin.
Volney, Constantin-François, 1795a.
  Leçons d'histoire prononcées à l'Ecole Normale, en l'an III de la République Française. in: Volney (1825)
Volney, Constantin-François, 1795b.
  Questions d'économie publique par le citoyen Volney. in: *Magasin Encyclopédique* I: 352-362.
Volney, Constantin-François, 1803.
  Tableau du climat et du sol des États-Unis d'Amerique. Paris.
Volney, Constantin-François, 1809.
  Chronologie d'Hérodote. Paris.
Volney, Constantin-François, 1813.
  Questions de Statistique à l'usage des Voyageurs. Paris.
Volney, Constantin-François, 1821.
  Mémoires. Paris.
Volney, Constantin-François, 1825.
  Oeuvres. Paris.
Volney, Constantin-François, 1860.
  Oeuvres Complètes. Paris.
Volney, Constantin-François, 1959.
  Voyage en Egypte et en Syrie. (orig. 1787) Ed. J. Gaulmier. Paris.
Waddington, Charles, 1855.
  Ramus (Pierre de la Ramée). Sa Vie, Ses Ecrits et Ses Opinions. Paris.
Wandruszka, Adam, 1963.
  *Leopold II. Erzherzog von Österreich Großherzog von Toskana König von Ungarn und Böhmen Römischer
  Kaiser.* 2 vols. Wien, München.
Warlich, Bernd, 1972.
  *August Ludwig von Schlözer 1735-1809 zwischen Reform und Revolution. Ein Beitrag zur Pathogenese
  frühliberalen Staatsdenkens im späten 18. Jahrhundert.* Phil.Diss. Erlangen, Nürnberg.
Wassmann, Jürg, 1982.
  *Der Gesang an den Fliegenden Hund. Untersuchungen zu den totemistischen Gesängen und geheimen
  Namen des Dorfes Kandzngei am Mittelsepik (Papua New Guinea) anhand der kirugu-Knotenschnüre.* Basel.

Weber, Max, 1958.
   The Protestant Ethic and the Spirit of Capitalism. London 1930, New York 1958. (German orig. 1904/05).
Weber, Max, 1978.
   Economy and Society. An Outline of Iterpretative Sociology. Eds. G. Roth and C. Wittich. Berkeley,
   Los Angeles, London.
Webster, Ch., 1970.
   "Macaria": Samuel Hartlib and the Great Reformation. in: *Acta Comeniana* 26: 147-164.
Webster, Noah, 1928.
   An American Dictionary of the English Language. New York.
Wehler, H.-U. (ed.), 1980.
   Deutsche Historiker. Göttingen.
Wells, Herbert George, 1895.
   The Time Machine. New York.
Wesendonck, H., 1876.
   *Die Bergündung der neueren deutschen Geschichtsschreibung durch Gatterer und Schlözer. Nebst Einleitung
   über Gang und Stand derselben vor diesen.* Leipzig.
Wiegand, Hermann, 1984.
   *Hodoeprica. Studien zur neulateinischen Reisedichtung des deutschen Kulturraums im 16. Jahrhundert.
   Mit einer Bio-Bibliographie der Autoren und Drucke.* Baden-Baden.
Wiegand, Hermann, 1989.
   Hodoeporica. Zur neulateinischen Reisedichtung des sechzehnten Jahrhunderts. in: Brenner (1989) 117-139.
Wijngarden, Nicolaas van, 1952.
   Les Odysées philosophiques en France entre 1616 et 1781. Haarlem.
Wilson, Thomas, 1553.
   The Arte of Rhetorique, for the use of all such as are studious of eloquence ... London.
Winbauer, Alois, 1971.
   August Ludwig von Schlözer (1735-1809). in: Fischer, Heinz Dietrich (ed.): *Deutsche Publizisten des
   15. - 20. Jahrhunderts.* München, Berlin.
Windelband, Wilhelm, 1980.
   Lehrbuch der Geschichte der Philosophie. 17th ed. Tübingen. (1st ed. 1892).
Winnett, A. R., 1971.
   George Psalmanazar. in: *The New Rambler* 110: 6-17.
Winter, Eduard (ed.), 1961.
   August Ludwig von Schlözer und Rußland. Berlin.
Winter, Eduard, 1962.
   Der Josefinismus. Die Geschichte des österreichischen Reformkatholizismus 1740-1848. Berlin.
Winter, Eduard, 1968.
   Frühliberalismus in der Donaumonarchie. Religiöse, nationale und wissenschaftliche Strömungen 1790-1868.
   Berlin.
Witthöft, Harald, 1980.
   Reiseanleitungen, Reisemodalitäten, Reisekosten im 18. Jahrhundert. in: Krasnobaev et.al. (1980) 39-50.
Wittkower, Rudolf and Wittkower, Margot, s.a.
   Les enfants de Saturne. Psychologie et comportement des artistes, de l'Antiquité à la Revolution française.
   Paris.
Wittfogel, Karl August, 1962.
   Die orientalische Despotie. Köln, Berlin. (Engl. orig. 1957)
Wohlwill, 1987.
   Curiosity. in: Görlitz/Wohlwill (1987).
Wolf, Gerhard, 1989.
   Die deutschsprachigen Reiseberichte des Spätmittelalters. in: Brenner (1989) 81-116.
Woolley, Leonard, 1963.
   The beginnings of civilisation. in: *History of Mankind: Cultural and Scientific Development,* Vol I Part
   2. London.
Wurzbach, Constant von, 1856-89.
   Biographisches Lexikon des Kaiserthums Österreich. Wien.
Wurzbacher, Gerhard, 1972.
   *Die öffentliche freie Vereinigung als Faktor soziokulturellen, insbesondere emanzipatorischen Wandels im
   19. Jahrhundert. Beiträge zur Geschichte historischer Forschung in Deutschland.* (Veröffentlichungen
   des Max-Planck-Instituts für Geschichte, Bd. 1). Göttingen.
Wuthenow, Ralph-Rainer, 1980.
   Die erfahrene Welt. Europäische Reiseliteratur im Zeitalter der Aufklärung. Frankfurt am Main.
Yates, Frances A., 1947.
   The French Academies of the sixteenth Century. London.
Yates, Frances A., 1964.
   Giordano Bruno and the Hermetic Tradition. London.

Yates Frances A., 1966.
The art of memory. London.
Yates, Frances A., 1969.
Theatre of the World. London.
Yates, Frances A., 1972.
The Rosicrucian Enlightenment. London, Boston.
Young, Arthur, 1792.
Travels, during the years 1787-89. Undertaken more particulary with a view of ascertaining the cultivation, wealth, resources and national prosperity of the Kingdom of France. 2 vols. Bury St. Edmunds.
Zacher, Christian K., 1976.
Curiosity and Pilgrimage: The Literature of discovery in Fourteenth-Century England. Baltimore, London.
Zacharasiewicz, Waldemar, 1977.
Die Klimatheorie in der englischen Literatur und Literaturkritik. Von der Mitte des 16. bis zum frühen 18. Jahrhundert. Stuttgart.
Zäunemannin, Sidonia Hedwig, 1737.
Curieuser und immer währender Astronomisch-Meteorologisch-Oeconomischer Frauenzimmer- Reise- und Handkalender ... 6th ed. Erfurt.
Zeisel, Hans, 1960.
Zur Geschichte der Soziographie. in: Jahoda, Marie, Lazarsfeld, Paul, Zeisel, Hans: *Die Arbeitslosen von Marienthal.* 2nd ed. Allensbach, Bonn: 101-138.
Zelger, Renate, 1953.
Der historisch-politische Briefwechsel und die Staatsanzeigen A.L.v. Schlözers als Zeitschrift und Zeitbild. Phil.Diss. München.
Zeller, Eduard, 1883.
Grundriß der Geschichte der griechischen Philosophie. Stuttgart.
Zobel, Ernst Friedrich, 1734.
Neu eingerichtetes Hand- und Reisebuch. für alle und jede in die Fremde ziehende junge Personen. 2 parts, Altdorf.
Zorn, W., 1967.
Die Physiokraten und die Idee der individualitischen Gesellschaft. in: Montaner, Antonio (ed.): *Geschichte der Volkswirtschaftslehre.* Köln, Berlin: 25-33.
Zwicker, S., 1638.
Breviarium apodemicum methodice concinnatum. Danzig.
Zwinger, Theodor, 1565.
Theatrum vitae Humanae, Omnium fere eorum, quae in hominem cadere possunt, Bonorum atque Malorum Exempla historice, Ethicae philosophiae praeceptis accomodata, et in XIX Libros digesta ... Basel.
Zwinger, Theodor , 1577.
Methodus apodemica in eorum gratiam qui cum fructu in quocunq; tandem vitae genere peregrinari cupiunt, a Thod. Zvingero Basiliense typis delineata, & cum aliis, tum quator praesertim Athenarum vivis exemplis illustrata. Cum indice. Basel. (2nd ed. Strasbourg 1594).
Zwinger, Theordor, 1631.
Magnum Theatrum Vitae Humanae ... Ed. Laurentius Beyerlinck, 8 vols. in folio. Cologne (re-edited Venice 1707).

Subject Index

Académie Celtique 287–292
Académie des Sciences 147, 151
Academies 35, 85, 86, 92, 98, 99, 104, 105,
    112, 113, 119–122, 137, 140, 143, 144,
    147–155, 209, 230, 240, 244, 246, 279,
    282–285, 287, 290–294
Advisory writings 53–55, 58, 75, 76, 92, 223,
    278, 288
Africa 159, 164, 167, 168, 289
Age of barbarism 103, 117, 125, 130
Age of discoveries 49, 55, 57, 103, 204
Age of enlightenment *see* Enlightenment
Age of ideology 198
Agriculture 140, 150, 152, 209, 212, 213,
    218, 224–226, 229, 257, 272, 273, 275,
    277, 284, 286
Aides-mémoire 6, 7, 15, 17, 18, 110, 112
Allegory 155–170, 197, 198, 252
America 126, 127, 164, 166, 168, 190, 285
Anatomy, political 43, 142, 146
Ancient Near East 10, 17, 20–29, 39, 41–43,
    244
Anglicans 76, 142, 176, 180, 181, 186, 197
Anthropology (cultural) 86, 153, 196, 198,
    206, 207, 233, 234, 237–241, 258, 266,
    268, 287–289, 293
Antiquarians, antiquities 36, 38, 39, 54, 85,
    114, 152, 153, 221, 242, 286, 292–294
Aphorism 132, 134, 223
Arabs, Araby 81, 89, 216, 223, 244, 270, 288
Arcana imperii 22, 23, 29, 42, 150
Archaic societies 8, 10, 13, 17, 29, 36, 186,
    290
Archives 22, 52, 85, 97, 110, 112, 119, 121,
    128, 131, 224
Arithmetic, political 146–149, 213, 262, 268
Ars apodemica (art of travel) 57–93, 96–99,
    107, 113, 120, 121, 223, 229, 247, 277,
    278, 280, 296
Ars epistolaria (*ars dictaminis*) 102, 103,
    111, 118, 120
Ars memorativa 110–112, 118, 120, 129, 130,
    134

Asia 159, 164, 166, 167, 175, 183, 198
Asia Minor 29, 30
Astrology 78, 128, 138, 144, 146
Athens 13–15, 30, 34, 58, 104
Australia 16, 168, 288–290
Austria 14, 89, 211, 216, 218, 220, 228–230,
    237–240, 273, 283, 292
Austroslavism 230, 231
Authenticity 51, 116, 198–207
Authority (books of) 119, 204, 205, 295
Autopsy 79, 93, 94, 113, 145, 224
Average 126, 210, 212, 215, 279

Babylonia 19, 24, 169
Barbaresque states 215, 216, 221, 225, 226
Baroque 83, 157–163, 170, 173
Basel 56–58, 62, 64–70, 73, 87, 90, 117, 120,
    122, 123, 238
Basques 292
Benedictines 153
Berlin 149
Bible 107, 109, 167, 244, 249, 250, 253, 260
Bohemia 89, 92, 93, 130, 140, 212, 213, 218,
    220, 221, 228–231, 239, 283
Book of nature 101, 116, 117, 149
Bookkeeping 50, 80, 120
Bureaucracy 8, 13, 18–24, 27–29, 40–45,
    127, 149, 211, 212, 229, 243, 247,
    255, 293

Cabbala 57, 65, 78, 111, 134
Calvinism *see* Reformation
Cambridge 139
Canaan 25–27
Cannibalism 51, 183, 185, 189, 195, 197, 202
Capuchins *see* Franciscans
Catalogue 85, 89, 113, 115, 131, 141, 149,
    185
Catechism 35, 176, 181, 227, 275
Catholicism 76, 130, 136, 141, 147, 175, 176,
    181, 185, 197, 211, 215, 238, 292
Celts 152, 260, 290–292
Censorship 100, 149

Census 14, 16, 17, 20, 21, 25, 26, 28, 39, 42, 145, 147
Centralization 18, 24, 125, 126, 211, 272, 274
Chanceries 95, 97, 101, 102
Chiliasm 129, 140, 143, 146
Christendom, Christianity 25, 31, 43, 47, 100, 125, 130, 131, 156, 157, 176, 180, 181, 190, 193, 211, 216, 252, 260, 264, 270, 273, 290
Climates 73, 77, 78, 80, 81, 167, 168, 226, 227, 288
Closed cosmos 156, 166, 168
Closed questions 138, 275
Closing 8, 9, 24
Collection 3, 7, 13, 20, 21, 31, 37, 39, 41, 43, 45, 54–58, 62, 65, 71, 79, 84, 85, 88, 95–99, 107, 109–115, 117, 119, 121–130, 132, 134, 137, 138, 140–143, 146, 148, 150–152, 224, 227, 235, 256, 261, 267, 270, 276, 280–282, 284–286, 288, 293, 295
College (invisible) 131, 133, 134, 143
Colonies, colonization 100, 126, 128, 145, 199, 226, 270, 294, 295
Common places 31, 79, 82, 185, 258
Common sense 102, 210, 243, 278, 279
Community rituals 16, 17, 20, 26, 27, 39
Comparison 16, 20, 24, 29, 32, 44, 77, 85, 102, 104, 146, 156, 239, 261, 276, 280, 282, 287
Compilation, compendia 38, 43–45, 53, 55, 78, 81, 109, 110, 115–121, 123, 124, 130, 132–134, 145, 261
"Constitutions" (Aristotle) 37–39, 43, 56, 81, 124
Continents 56, 155–170
Correspondence 34, 38, 56, 62, 77, 85, 92, 97–100, 112, 113, 116, 119, 121–123, 126, 128, 137, 139, 141, 148, 151, 152, 224, 247, 249, 274, 279, 282, 285, 287, 291, 292
Cosmography 56, 80, 169, 259, 267
Cosmos 29, 33, 34, 36, 111, 155–157, 168, 169
Crisis 9, 10, 13, 21, 27, 128, 156
Culture 6, 9, 15, 17, 51, 64, 66, 90, 100, 128, 156, 168, 189, 190, 211, 213, 216, 253, 255, 257, 258, 293, 296
Cuna 17
Curiosity (curisiositas) 2, 3, 11, 14, 29, 35, 36, 38, 43, 46–50, 72, 79, 112, 113, 136, 139, 149, 163, 170, 175, 196, 212, 286, 287

Demography 88, 145, 225, 262, 277, 280

Denmark see Scandinavia
Description 37, 38, 43, 77–82, 88–95, 103, 104, 107–110, 114, 115, 118, 123–126, 128, 129, 151, 170, 171, 175, 189, 190, 196, 203, 204, 213, 223–226, 229, 237, 239, 243, 245, 257, 261, 267, 270, 278, 285, 288, 290
Dialectic 30, 33, 34, 57, 58, 66, 68, 69, 72, 101, 104–110, 131, 132, 181
Dialogue 32, 33, 35, 73, 185, 186
Diary 50, 78, 80, 81, 92, 95, 148, 224
Diplomacy 21, 23, 52, 122, 151, 272, 275, 284
Documentation 6, 7, 16, 22, 31, 34, 41, 64, 96, 110–121, 213, 229, 276, 279, 281
Documentation centres see Research-and-documentation centres
"Domesday Book" 44, 145
Dominicans 126, 129, 178
Dutch see Netherlands

Early civilizations 10, 17, 23, 32, 36
Education 30, 35, 40, 47–49, 52, 54–57, 66, 70–75, 82, 84, 88–93, 97–103, 106, 107, 112, 113, 117, 118, 122, 139, 144, 173, 190, 212, 213, 224, 226, 227, 242–244, 247, 278, 288
Egypt 17, 19, 23, 24, 27, 30, 240, 256, 272, 285, 286, 289
Empiry, empiricism 7–10, 14, 19, 22, 23, 30–32, 35–37, 44–46, 50–53, 55, 57, 64–66, 69, 81, 84–89, 95–110, 115, 119, 121–153, 235, 243, 244, 250, 281, 282, 287, 288, 293, 294
England 60, 75, 84, 88, 92, 93, 114, 128, 130, 139–141, 144, 148, 152, 175, 180, 181, 183, 186, 187, 199, 217, 234, 240–243, 246, 250, 256, 260, 261, 292, 294
England, Church of see Anglicans
Encyclopaedia, Encylopaedists 30, 55, 58, 70, 81, 86, 89, 109, 116–118, 123, 130, 148, 237, 238, 244, 269, 272, 278, 279, 281, 284, 287–289, 291, 293, 295, 296
Enlightened absolutism 89, 149, 150, 211
Enlightenment (age of) 88, 147, 150, 153, 156, 163–166, 170, 209–211, 213, 215, 216, 228, 246–248, 252, 267–270, 283, 285, 291
Episteme 36, 37
Epistemological curiosity 3, 5, 7
Eskimo 11
Ethnographic present 21, 22

Ethnography 4, 10, 11, 19, 27–29, 36, 38, 41, 42, 51, 56, 78, 81, 86, 89, 90, 115, 125, 134, 152, 153, 170–173, 175, 181, 184, 189, 190, 193, 195, 196, 199, 203–207, 233–237, 239–241, 248, 251, 254, 257–267, 270, 277, 285, 289–296

Ethnohistory 261, 264

Ethnology 2, 233–241, 256, 266–268, 282, 287, 288, 294, 295

Europe 56, 70, 73, 75, 82, 84, 88, 94–97, 119, 123, 128, 149–153, 155, 159, 160, 164–168, 173, 175, 180, 183, 189, 195, 209, 216, 234, 240, 242, 251, 256, 262–264, 270, 274, 280, 282, 290, 294

Evolution 282, 288, 294

Exempla 109, 157, 166, 210, 213, 284

Experienced world (*Lebenswelt*) 4, 6, 20, 200, 202, 204, 206

Experiment 132, 134, 137, 141, 143, 148, 149, 152, 288

Experts 4, 5, 8, 12–14, 21, 23, 31, 44, 45, 93, 100, 293

Exploration 2–4, 10–12, 15, 16, 20, 21, 25, 27–29, 33, 38, 49, 77, 81, 84, 89, 96, 100, 101, 103, 106, 129, 150, 151, 166, 212, 230, 270, 275, 279, 280, 289, 293, 296

Exploratory expeditions 85, 89, 152, 223, 227, 229, 270, 285, 288

Fieldwork 4, 86, 89, 90, 145, 203, 205, 206, 289, 291, 293, 295, 296

Florence 116, 147

Folklore 2, 115, 153, 213, 234, 242, 268, 292–294

Foreign service *see* Diplomacy

Formosa 171, 173, 175, 180, 183, 187–189, 193, 195, 200, 205

Fosterage 11

France 60, 68, 75, 85, 92, 93, 106, 130, 136, 137, 141, 144, 151, 153, 175, 178, 183, 184, 237–242, 246, 247, 250, 270, 272–280, 282–288, 291–294

Franciscans 126, 136, 137, 178

French Revolution 84, 89, 123, 145, 151, 218, 228–231, 243, 248, 272–276, 279, 280, 283, 284, 287, 289–292

Geography 19, 29, 42, 49, 56, 81, 92, 95, 104, 120, 125, 128, 145, 152, 153, 167, 187, 190, 201, 213, 215, 234–237, 240, 241, 244, 249, 254–260, 263, 267, 272, 277, 280, 286

Germany 55, 56, 64, 66, 68, 70, 73, 75, 84, 87–93, 103, 104, 110, 115, 120, 125, 128–130, 139, 147–149, 155–157, 160, 161, 163, 165, 166, 176, 178, 179, 184–187, 209, 211, 212, 217, 230, 233, 234, 237–243, 246–250, 256, 260–263, 267, 277, 278, 289, 290, 292, 294

Göttingen 84, 85, 88, 89, 217, 228, 235–246, 248–250, 253, 258–261, 267, 270, 278, 281, 283, 284, 288

Grand tour 73, 75, 82–84, 227, 229

Greece 10, 23, 28–46, 116, 167, 168, 173, 235, 250, 256, 267

Guanches 292

Halle 88, 163, 196, 237, 242, 243, 250

Harmony (of the universe) 144–147, 212

Hearsay 79, 224

Hebrew *see* Old Testament

Hellas *see* Greece

Hellenism *see* Greece

Hermeneutics 4

Heuresis see Inventio

Hippies 198, 205

History (*historia*) 30, 35–37, 50, 79, 81, 104, 108–110, 116, 118, 125, 128, 131, 132, 148, 152, 153, 163, 167, 169, 213, 224, 234, 243–249, 252, 256–258, 260, 261, 264, 266, 267, 273, 281, 282, 288

Holland *see* Netherlands

Holy *see* Pope

Homecomer 12

Humanism 31, 43, 46–53, 55, 59–66, 72–76, 78, 80, 82, 90–92, 97–107, 113–117, 119, 122, 124–128, 133, 134, 138, 145, 233, 260, 261

Hungary 91–93, 236, 240

Identity 7–10, 12, 17, 24, 36, 206, 270, 290

Idéologues 287–293

Images 110, 111, 129, 130, 155–170, 252

Imaginary travels 82, 188, 190, 199, 200, 206

Information 15, 16, 20–22, 32, 37, 38, 42, 43, 46, 50, 51, 57, 62, 66, 77, 79, 81, 82, 85, 93, 95, 96, 98–102, 106, 108, 112, 115, 118, 119, 126, 127, 133, 137, 141, 148, 226, 227, 235, 257, 276, 279, 280, 286

Inquisition 150, 176

Inspection 2, 3, 13

Institutionalization 34, 35, 53, 64, 96, 98, 99, 121–123, 132, 133, 149, 183

Instruction 25, 26, 52, 55, 73, 78, 85, 86, 90, 113, 122–124, 127, 145, 152, 226, 228, 269, 270, 276, 279, 289, 290, 294, 296

Intellectuals 24, 29, 34, 35, 43, 45, 101, 122, 126, 129, 130, 144, 198, 247, 286, 287, 290

Interrogation 5, 12, 34, 35, 40, 44, 145, 148, 150

Interrogatorium see Questionnaire

Interview 3, 5, 14, 15, 19, 21, 25, 26, 31, 38, 39, 126

Inventio 31, 106–108, 110, 113, 115, 129, 132–134, 202, 216, 254

Inventory 132, 133, 141

Ireland 143, 145, 147, 152, 179, 180

Islam 168, 190

Island *see* Scandinavia

Israel 10, 25–28, 39, 173, 178, 187

Italy 54, 60, 62, 64, 65, 75, 76, 85, 90, 97, 98, 103, 104, 106, 112, 114, 120, 173, 247

Itinerary 53, 78, 95, 148, 203

Iudicium 106–108, 110, 113, 115, 131

Jerusalem 160, 216

Jesuits 76, 126, 130, 140, 143, 144, 150, 175, 176, 178, 179, 181, 183, 184, 193, 195, 196, 204

Jews 178, 186, 256

Josephinism 209–216, 228, 229, 231, 236

Knowledge 5–15, 20–26, 30–32, 36–40, 42, 44–46, 48–52, 55–57, 64, 65, 69, 70, 76, 79, 82, 84–87, 94, 96–153, 166, 199, 202, 203, 222–226, 233, 235, 246, 261, 276, 278, 280, 287, 289

Koinoi topoi see Common places

Kosmos see Cosmos

Laus see Praise

Lebenswelt see Experienced world

Libraries 110, 112, 119, 121, 125, 129, 131, 141, 224

Lists 19, 25, 27, 28, 44, 62, 105, 106, 110, 123, 126, 127, 131, 141, 150, 224, 226, 279, 291, 294

Literary travels 85, 153

Loci see Places

Loci communes see Common places

Logic *see* Dialectic

Logographoi 35–38

London 87, 114, 141–143, 146, 147, 171, 176, 185, 186, 222, 294

Low Countries *see* Netherlands

Lutheranism *see* Reformation

Macedonia 17, 38

Macrocosmos 78, 111, 112, 114, 119, 139, 141, 143

Manipulation 2, 3, 7

Mankind 99, 122, 129–131, 133, 134, 139, 140, 148–150, 160, 169, 224, 233, 234, 237, 241, 244, 246, 252, 253, 255, 258, 264, 282, 283, 287, 292

Memorabilia see Memory

Memory 4, 8, 9, 15, 18, 31, 35, 50, 78, 81, 102, 108, 110, 112, 116–118, 120, 121, 132, 136, 178, 184, 257, 263

Mesopotamia 17, 23, 27, 30

Messianism *see* Chiliasm

Method, methodology 1, 3–5, 7, 11, 15, 19, 25, 32, 33, 46–94, 96, 104–106, 108–110, 131, 132, 147, 207, 213, 221, 223, 224, 226, 227, 230, 231, 246, 254, 257, 259–266, 270, 273, 275, 277, 278, 285, 289–291, 293–295

Microcosmos 78, 111, 112, 114, 115, 119, 121, 125, 139, 141, 143, 189

Middle Ages (medieval) 10, 31, 43–50, 52, 54, 72, 75, 78, 87, 95, 98, 100–102, 111, 115, 116, 136, 242, 246, 256, 296

Mirror (of the world) 114, 118, 134, 230, 274

Mission 95, 100, 122, 123, 128, 130, 137, 139, 151, 155, 175, 176, 181, 196, 197, 199, 195

Mnemonics *see Ars memorativa*

Moravia *see* Bohemia

Museums 112–116, 119, 125, 131, 213, 230, 231

Names 81, 91, 124, 233–235

Naples 60, 129

Narration 80, 108, 195, 281

Nationalism 229

Naturalization 12

Navigatio 49, 53, 56, 78, 152, 226

Neoplatonism 65, 78, 100, 111, 129, 130, 144, 230

Netherlands 57, 64, 75, 92, 93, 106, 114, 126, 128, 143, 144, 171, 176, 183–185, 235, 240, 270

New Guinea 16

Noble savage 4, 176, 180, 181, 184, 185, 189, 193, 195, 197, 199

Notitia (*rerum publicarum*) 43, 56, 82, 88, 110, 149, 237
Numbers 25–28, 32, 42, 93, 190, 226, 257, 276
Nürnberg 60, 63, 80, 157, 159

Observation 2, 4, 50, 55, 70, 71, 77–80, 90, 99, 132, 134, 152, 167, 227, 272, 274, 276, 278, 284, 285, 287, 289, 293, 294
Oikoumene 23–25, 38, 39, 167–169
Old Testament 20, 24–26, 180, 186, 187, 190, 244
Open questions 138
Open universe 156, 166, 168
Opening 8–10, 23, 26, 41, 42, 66, 77
Opinion poll 33, 34, 132
Orality 13, 14, 18–20, 23, 28, 30–34, 40, 44, 52, 54, 78, 93, 102
Otherness 5, 7, 16, 17, 179
Oxford 114, 141, 143, 145, 176, 184, 185

Padua 57, 58, 60, 65–70, 71, 73, 120
Paris 57, 58, 62, 65–70, 87, 92, 137–140, 147, 151, 218, 228, 241, 269, 273, 282, 289, 293, 294
Participant observation 4
"Patriotic Traveller" (Berchtold) 217, 218, 221–227, 229, 275–277, 280, 295
Patriotism 104, 150, 209, 210, 212, 213, 220–224, 227–229, 231, 247, 248, 283
Peoples 233–235, 239, 241, 244, 246, 248, 252–258, 260–266, 281, 282, 292
Perceptive curiosity 3, 5
Periodicals 119, 137, 139, 141, 151, 163, 247, 279
Persia 17, 23, 30, 36, 37, 216, 256
Philanthropy 131, 136–138, 141–144, 148, 150, 209–212, 215, 216, 218, 220–222, 224, 226, 238, 290, 293, 294
Philology 243, 246, 250, 255
Phoenicia 19, 28, 29, 167, 256
Physiocrats 210, 216–218, 222, 238, 277, 281, 291
Pietism 209–213, 215, 229, 243
Pilgrimage 12, 47–49, 53–54, 72, 75, 84, 160–164, 176, 179, 197, 216, 225, 296
Pilgrim's guides 52, 53, 75–78
Places 31, 32, 48, 69, 80, 91, 105–113, 116–119, 124, 128–132
"Polities" (Aristotle) *see* "Constitutions"
Pope 52, 102, 126, 129, 155, 176, 179, 195

Portugal 55, 185, 216, 240
Postal service 53, 119, 243, 247
Praise 80, 91, 123
Pre-judgments 4, 5, 8
Primitive societies (people, cultures) 4, 8, 10, 11, 13, 292, 294
Printing 57, 58, 64, 66, 92, 98, 111, 113, 115–121, 131, 137, 188, 199, 206
Problemata see Questions
Progress 99, 133, 233, 238, 246, 250, 253, 258, 273, 278, 281, 282, 294
Protestantism *see* Reformation
Prussia 211, 242
Public opinion 98, 100, 103, 137, 286
Publishing *see* Printing
Puritans 142, 144, 199, 202

Quaestiones see Questions
Quantification 81, 213, 280, 284, 293
Questions 3, 5, 13–15, 19–23, 25–27, 31, 33–35, 37–39, 44, 45, 49, 56, 62, 69, 86, 93, 96, 98, 105–108, 110, 119, 123–128, 131, 132, 134, 137, 138, 141, 150–152, 221–223, 225, 226, 231, 277, 279, 280, 285, 290, 293, 295
Questionnaire (*see* also Survey) 1, 19, 27, 37, 45, 64, 85, 89, 96, 123, 124, 127, 134, 138, 148, 152, 153, 181, 273–277, 281, 283, 285, 286, 291

Race 155, 168, 241, 263
Ramism 68–70, 84, 88, 107–109, 118, 131
Reconnoitering 25, 41
Recording *see* Register
Reformation 64, 66, 68, 69, 72, 75, 76, 84, 87, 92, 100, 110, 114, 119, 125, 130, 136, 139–141, 148, 149, 161, 176, 170, 179, 193, 195, 197, 211, 213, 238, 239, 243, 244, 249, 264
Register 9, 26, 27, 35, 78, 88, 96, 99, 115, 119, 122, 138, 141–143, 146, 148, 150–152
Reihendienst 13, 16, 20, 26, 31, 35, 37, 40
Relativism 70, 156, 189, 258
Renaissance 41, 52, 53, 65, 70, 78, 81, 87, 89, 110–112, 123, 129, 133, 137, 139, 230, 231
Representatives 5, 8, 13, 14, 23, 26, 27, 33
Republic of letters (*res publica literaria, réplublique des lettres*) 34, 52, 57, 65, 73, 77, 97–100, 104, 106, 113, 120–122, 125, 128, 149–151

Research 3, 4, 8, 19–21, 25, 27, 35–39, 45, 53, 71, 96–98, 101–107, 109, 113–116, 124, 127, 129, 130, 133, 137, 138, 144, 147, 149, 152, 153, 206, 230, 276, 281–289, 291–296 (*see* also Social research)

Research-and-documentation centres 64, 95–153, 230, 274, 279, 284, 285, 291, 292

Resistance against social research 15, 20, 23, 25–38, 42, 44, 145, 147, 276, 284

Rhetoric 30–33, 40, 42, 50, 62, 80, 81, 91, 101–106, 111–113, 120, 123, 147, 225

Rites de passage 12, 15, 16

Road books *see* Itinerary

Romanticism 229, 231, 241, 258, 293, 294

Rome 10, 31, 39–43, 46, 48, 60, 66, 76, 167, 176, 179, 250, 256, 264

Rosicrucians 130, 138, 140, 282

Royal Society 114, 140, 143, 146–148, 151, 152, 170, 181, 185

Russia 85, 244, 246, 248, 249, 260, 267

Saint Petersburg 149, 244, 246, 267

Sample 14, 25, 27

Scandinavia 75, 84, 85, 92, 93, 114, 128, 239, 244, 246, 249, 260, 270, 288

Schemata 31, 32, 37, 62, 70, 80–82, 91, 102, 128, 203, 258, 278, 289, 295

Scholasticism 66, 68, 101–104, 119, 242

Science (social, cultural, political, of man) 2, 19, 21, 24, 25, 29–33, 35–39, 43, 45, 46, 50, 64, 66, 68, 78, 81, 85–87, 89, 93, 102, 105, 108–110, 121–123, 126, 127, 130–133, 138, 139, 141, 143, 146, 147, 149–151, 153, 156, 157, 165, 166, 168, 170, 202, 233, 234, 237, 238, 243, 246, 257, 258, 269, 270, 273, 276–283, 285–289, 294

Science de l' homme see Science

Scribes 8, 18, 19, 22, 43

Secrecy 21–23, 130, 133, 142, 206, 247 (*see* also *Arcana imperii*)

Secret societies 130, 143, 150, 209

Self-thematizazion 16

Sentimental journeys (ethnographies) 87, 200, 204, 205

Significant objects (phenomena) 3, 5, 7, 15, 25, 119

Slavs 230, 239, 246, 256, 260, 261, 264, 292

Social reform 130, 136, 210–212, 229, 288

Social research 1, 2, 7, 10, 19, 25–27, 32, 33, 37–42, 100–107, 124, 129, 137, 148, 150,

209, 212–216, 227, 230, 273, 276, 283, 284, 287, 291–294

Société des Observateurs de l'Homme 287–292

Societies, learned, *see* Academies

Sociology 2, 132, 150, 153, 190, 198, 205, 246, 256, 267, 282, 293, 296

Sodalities *see* Academies

Songhai 17

Space, spiritual 11

Spain 57, 106, 126, 127, 173, 218

Speier 43, 125

Standardization 13–15, 19, 20, 44, 52, 54, 124, 126, 127, 141, 150, 275, 279, 280

Statistics (statiscal bureaux) 28, 56, 64, 78, 80, 86, 88, 92, 93, 138, 144–147, 149, 150, 163, 213, 235, 237, 239–249, 256, 258, 262, 264–267, 277, 280–284, 287, 288, 292, 293

Stocktaking 19, 44, 115, 124, 126, 127, 212, 282, 283, 296

Strangers 9, 12

Strasbourg 56, 58, 60, 62, 63, 68, 72, 91, 92, 123

Survey (*see also* Questionnaire) 5, 7, 13–16, 19, 20, 23, 27, 28, 37, 38, 41–45, 78, 95–153, 213, 225–227, 230, 241

Survival 242, 282, 290

Sweden *see* Scandinavia

Switzerland 66, 114, 116, 120, 218, 234, 238–240

Systems theory 70, 169, 253, 282

Tables 58, 61, 68, 69, 81, 144, 226, 252

Technology (technography) 107, 125, 132–134, 141, 143, 144, 146, 152, 212, 213, 254, 263

Theater (of the world) 114, 118, 148

"Theatrum vitae humanae" (Zwinger) 55, 58, 68, 72, 117, 118, 122, 124, 130

Topic *see* Places

Topicality 21, 22, 32, 35, 44, 52

Topoi see Places

Tourist guides 75, 78, 89

Travel 4, 5, 7, 12, 14, 21, 24, 26, 29, 30, 38, 40, 42, 44, 47–100, 107, 112–114, 121–125, 129, 133, 134, 151–153, 175, 200, 202, 206, 213, 215, 221, 222, 224, 226–230, 239, 244, 247, 269–296

Travel books (reports) 4, 32, 38, 49–52, 55, 65, 71, 80–82, 89, 91–93, 99, 119, 155–157, 163, 188–193, 197, 199–203, 217, 223, 235, 237, 247, 267, 268, 272, 277–279, 286
Travel guides *see* Tourist guides
Travel regimina 54, 73, 75
Turks 100, 117, 125, 128, 157, 159, 160, 164, 166, 216, 218, 270, 272, 275

Universal history 186, 236, 249–264, 266, 268, 281, 282
Universities 35, 48, 57, 58, 62, 64, 66, 68, 69, 73, 75, 84, 88, 91, 101, 104, 105, 110, 114, 116, 119, 120, 144, 149, 226, 235, 240, 242–244, 249
Untrustworthiness of travellers 12, 77, 79, 82, 199, 200
Urbarii 44
USA 275, 284, 285

Utopianism 99, 100, 112, 113, 122, 129–134, 181, 189, 231, 279
Venice 52, 55, 60, 65–70, 80, 87, 120, 122–124, 240
Vienna 62, 125, 149, 160, 212, 215, 220, 230, 236, 295
Viri illustres 76, 80, 91, 92, 97, 115, 123, 125, 226
Völkerkunde 234–236, 241, 248, 251, 257, 258, 262–267, 288
Völkskunde 234, 239, 242, 268

Wittenberg 128, 244
World view 8, 86, 87, 156, 166, 168
Writing 7, 10, 17–20, 27, 28, 31, 36, 43, 52, 79, 102, 110, 111, 115, 173, 260, 288

Yaqui 205

Name Index

Aaron 25–27
Achenwall, Gottfried 88, 246, 249, 252
Adams, Percy G. 188
Agricola, Rudolph 104–108, 110, 114, 116, 124, 127, 132
Alexander (the Great) 36–39, 41
Alexander I (Tsar) 248
Amalvi, Isaac d'185
Ambrose (Saint) 75
Ampére, Jean-Marie 238
Andreae, Johann Valentin 130, 133, 139, 140, 148
Antisthenes 34
Antoni, Carlo 244
Aristotle 29, 32, 33, 35–39, 43, 45, 46, 56, 81, 104, 105, 107, 108, 116, 124, 160, 231
Arrian (Flavius Arrianus) 30
Ashmole, Elias 114
Aston, Margaret 49
Aubrey, John 152
Auerbach, Erich 250, 267
Augustus (Emperor) 41, 42

Bacon, Francis 95, 109, 110, 116, 123, 130–133, 139, 140, 144, 146, 148, 276, 282, 287
Balbi, Adriano 240
Baldwin, George 216, 217
Bartholinus, Thomas 84
Bates, Ernest S. 63
Baudelot de Dairval, Charles-César 85
Baudin, Nicholas-T 288–290
Beauvais, Vincent of 115, 116
Beck, Hanno 204
Behre, Otto 45
Berchtold, Friedrich 230, 231
Berchtold, Leopold 89, 209, 214–231, 273, 274, 276–280, 286, 295

Berchtold, Leopold (Foreign Minister) 215, 218
Berlyne, Daniel E. 3
Bersmann, Gregor 60
Bersuire, Pierre 116
Biondo, Flavio 103
Blotius, Hugo 57, 60, 62–65, 68, 70, 80, 114, 121, 123–125, 127, 128
Blumenbach, Johann Friedrich 237, 240, 241, 253
Boates, Arnold 140
Bodin, Jean 78, 96
Boecler, Johann Heinrich 79
Boemus, Ioannes 115
Boisgirais, (=Voley) 269, 270
Boldensele, Wilhelm von 52
Boorde, Andrew 49
Bonß, Wolfgang 1
Bossuet, Jacques-Bénigne (Bishop) 250, 252
Boswell, James 180, 187
Botero, Giovanni 96, 126
Bougainville, Louis Antoine de 86
Bourne, William 53
Boyle, Robert 143, 147, 151, 152
Breidenbach, Bernhard von 52
Bruni, Leonardo 102
Bruno, Giordano 111, 140
Bruns, Paul J. 218, 228
Budé, Guillaume 106
Burnet, Gilbert (Bishop) 183
Butterfield, Herbert 249

Cabanis, Pierre Jean Georges 288, 289
Caesar, Gaius Iulius 41
Caligula (Emperor) 42
Calvin, John 195
Campanella, Thomaso 129, 130, 133, 139, 140, 148

Candidus, Georgius 171, 187, 189, 205
Cardanus, Hieronymus 55
Caron, Pierre 275
Caselius, Johannes 54
Cassirer, Ernst 6, 234
Castaneda, Carlos 205, 206
Castiglione, Baldassare 60
Celtis, Conrad 51, 80, 103, 106
Chaptal, Jean Antoine Claude 283, 284
Charlemagne (Emperor) 44
Charles II (King of England) 146
Charles IV (Emperor) 45
Charles V (Emperor) 128
Chasseboeuf, Constantin-François (=Volney) 269, 270
Chavannes, Alexandre César 237, 238, 240, 268
Chevalley, Abel 190, 198, 202
Chosroes (King) 45
Chytraeus, Nathan 54, 61, 62
Cicero, Marcus Tullius 39, 40, 46, 102, 108
Coccio, Sabellico, Marcantonio 103
Colbert, Jean-Baptiste 86
Comenius, Johann Amos 116, 123, 130, 139–134, 143, 144
Compton, Henry (Bishop) 181, 185
Comte, Auguste 116, 283
Condorcet, Marie Jean Marquis de 269, 273
Conring, Hermann 149
Croesus (King) 29
Cromwell, Oliver 143, 145

Daedalus 72
Dairval, Baudelot de see Baudelot de Dairval
David (King) 26, 28, 42
Defoe, Daniel 183, 202
Degerando, Joseph-Marie 86, 289–293
Descartes, René 116
Dilthey, Wilhelm 248
Diogenes, Laërtius 34
Dobrovský, Josef 239
Don Juan (alleged shaman of the Yaqui) 205
Du Bois, Nicolas F. 184–186
Duchamp, Marcel 206
Duerr, Hans Peter 206
Durkheim, Emile 8, 24

Edwards, William F. 241
Eibl-Eibesfeldt, Irenäus 3
Ekkard, Friedrich 239
Elias, Norbert 53
Eliot, T.S. 155
Erasmus of Rotterdam 47, 49, 66, 97, 102, 106, 115, 117, 120
Erpenius, Thomas 79

Fabri, Ernst 237, 239, 268
Fabricius, Georg 54
Félix 276
Fernandez, Valentin 55
Fischer, Hans 235, 267
Fischer, J.E. 267
Fontaney, Jean de 181, 183, 185, 197
Forgách, Mihály 91–94
Forster, Georg 234, 238, 279
Fortius Ringelbergius, Joachim 48–50, 73
Francis (Emperor) 221
François de Neufchâteau, Nicolas Louis 283, 289
Frank Johann Peter 84
Frederick II (Emperor) 45
Freige, Johann Thomas 68
Fueter, Eduard 250

Gail, Jörg 53
Galilei, Galileo 147
Garat, Dominique Joseph 274, 275, 283, 289
Gatterer, Johann Christoph 235–237, 241, 249–252, 254, 257, 258, 262, 263, 282
Gaulmier, Jean 275
Gehlen, Arnold 3, 4, 34
Gellner, Ernest 18
Gennep, Arnold van 12
Gérando, Joseph-Marie de see Dégerando
Gesner, Conrad von 114, 116, 119
Giraldus, Lilius Gregorius 53
Goethe, Johann Wolfgang von 11
Gogol, Nikolai 233, 246, 248
Gratarolus Guilhelmus 54, 73, 74
Graunt, John 146, 147, 149
Grégoire, Henri 285, 286, 288
Grimm, Jacob and Wilhelm 294
Grünemberg, Conrad von 52

Guérin, François 150
Gusdorf, George 288
Gryllus, Laurentius 54

Hakluyt, Richard 56
Hall, Joseph (Bishop) 73
Hamann, Johann Georg 259
Hanau-Lichtenberg, Ludwig von 52
Hantsch, Hugo 218
Hartlib, Samuel 130, 139–146, 148, 149, 282
Haschke, Cajetan 215
Hawes, William 216, 220, 222, 225
Hay (Bishop) 213
Heer, Friedrich 66
Helvétius, Mmé 269, 272
Henry IV (King) 136
Hentzner, Paul 63
Herder, Johann Gottfried von 255, 258, 259,
    263, 265, 266, 281
Herodotos 23, 30, 35, 36, 38, 81, 160, 281
Herschel, John 295
Hobbes, Thomas 96, 144
Holbach, Paul-Henri Thiry, Baron d' 269,
    272
Horace (Q. Horatius Flaccus) 47, 79, 171
Hurd, Richard (Bishop) 73
Husserl, Edmund 4, 87

Innes, Alexander 176, 180, 184, 185, 188
    195–197, 199
Iselin, Isaak 238, 253
Iselin, Ludwig 90, 92–94

Jäger, Christoph 157, 161
Jaeger, Werner 36
James I (King) 133
Jamin, Jean 288
Jellinek, Georg 255
Jesus Christ 42
Joab 26
Johann (Archduke) 213, 215, 230, 283
Johnson, Samuel 180, 187, 188
Joseph II (Emperor) 213, 215
Junius, Melchior 72
Justinian (Emperor) 39

Kant, Immanuel 233
Karl (Archduke) 221
Keckermann, Bartholomäus 92, 93, 109, 110,
    132, 140, 148
Komensky, Jan A. see Comenius
Kollár, Adam Franz 236, 237, 239, 268
Köhler, Johann David 85
Könekamp, Wolf-Dieter 235
Kramer, Fritz 17
Krügner, Johann Gottfried 157
Kutter, Uli 235, 239, 268

Lafayette, Marie Joseph Marquis de 218
Laffermas, Barthélémy de 136
Lane, F.C. 55
Langlès, 218, 285, 286, 288
Languet, Hubert 54
Lannoy, Philippe de 54
Laplace, Pierre Simon 284
Lasteyrie, Charles-Philibert, Maquis de 218,
    276, 279, 288
Lausberg, Heinrich 31
Law, William 187
Lazarsfeld, Paul 1, 2
Leclerc du Tremblay, François (Pére Joseph)
    136, 137, 139
Le Play, Frédéric 225
Leibniz, Gottfried Willhelm 147–149, 181
    211, 242, 261, 265, 282, 287, 288
Leopold (Grand Duke) 215, 218, 224
Lettsom, John Coakley 222
Levaillant, François 289, 290
Lévi-Strauss, Claude 11, 204
Lhuyd, Edward 152
Linné, Carl von (Linnaeus) 85, 115, 244, 258,
    261
Lipsius, Justus 54, 91, 92
Locke, John 73, 116
López de Velasco, Juan 127
Lorenz, Konrad 3
Louis XVI (King) 218, 273
Louis XVIII (King) 292
Luhmannn, Niklas 16
Lullus, Raimundus 116, 139
Luther, Martin 107
Lutz, Gerhard 235

Lycosthenes, Conrad 58, 117, 120
Lydus, Priscianus 45

Machiavelli, Nicolò 60, 96
Maffei, Raphael 116
Maignan, E. 53
Manutius, Aldus 120
Marie Louise (Archduchess) 292
Maurois, André 171
Maus, Heinz 1
Mauss, Marcel 11
Maximilian II (Emperor) 62, 63, 117, 122, 124, 125
Mazarin, Jules (Cardinal) 139
Meierus, Albertus (Meier, Albrecht) 127, 128
Meiners, Christoph 240, 253, 288, 289
Melanchthon, Philipp 249
Mersenne, Marin 144, 146, 148, 149
Michaelis, Johann David 223, 228, 239, 244, 246, 258, 270, 282
Mieszkowski, Petrus 73
Milanesi, Marica 56
Mirabeau, Victor Riqueti, Marquisde 210, 222
Mirabeau, Honoré Gabriel Riqueti, Comte de 273
Mohl, Robert von 246
Molyneux, William 152
Montaigne, Michel de 51
Montesquieu, Charles de Secondat, Baron de 164, 168, 181, 244, 246, 248, 250, 253, 257, 281
Moravia, Sergio 288
Morellet, André 275, 277
Morhof, Daniel Georg 116, 117
Morus, Thomas 56, 112
Moser, Friedrich C. von 209
Moses 25–28, 186
Morzart, Wolfgang Amadeus 164
Möller, Helmut 235
Müller, Gerhard F. 233, 244, 267
Münchhausen, Gerlach Adolf von 243, 246
Münster, Sebastian 56, 118–120
Mylaeus, Christophorus 116–118, 125

Napoleon (Emperor) 284–287, 290–292
Necker, Jacques 272, 273, 289

Needham, Rodney 190, 203, 207
Neickel, F.C. 114
Neitzschitz, Georg Christoph von 157, 158, 161
Nestor 246, 248
Neufchâteau, François de see François de Neufchâteau
Newton, Isaac 148, 150
Nicolai, Friedrich 278
Niebuhr, Carsten 89, 223, 228, 270, 278
Nordblad, Erik 85

Oberschall, Anthony 1
Ogilby, John 152
Oporinus, Johannes 117, 120
Ossian 290
Oswald, Dr. 184
Otto, von Freising 166
Ovando y Godoy, Juan de 127, 128

Pallas, Peter Simon 267
Paracelsus, Theophrastus 111, 117, 138, 139
Pareto, Vilfredo 33
Parkin, Frank 205
Parmenides 33
Pausanias 30, 39, 42, 81
Pelicanus, Conrad 120
Pére Joseph see Leclerc du Tremblay
Perez, Marco 68
Péron, François 290
Petty, William 143–149, 151, 152
Philip II (King of Spain) 117, 126–128
Piccolomini, Enea Silvio (Pope Pius II) 102
Pictorius, Georg 54
Pighius, Stephanus Vinandus 72
Pitsius, Johannes 53, 75
Plato 13, 32–36, 98, 100, 104, 105, 121–123, 230
Plinius (Gaius Plinius Cäcilius Secundus) 42, 115
Pluskal, F.S. 215, 218, 230
Plutarch 41
Polo, Marco 204, 205
Polybius 30, 252
Poseidonius 30
Posselt, Franz 89, 228, 278

Postel Guillaume 139
Prichard, James Cowley 241
Psalmanazar (Psalmanaazaar), George 171–207, 250, 256, 260
Pufendorf, Samuel 255
Pyrckmair, Hilarius 60, 62, 65, 68, 70, 81, 93

Quichelberg, Samuel 114
Quincey, Thomas de 187

Ramus, Petrus 57, 66–70, 107–110, 114, 116, 121, 124, 287
Ramusio, Giovanni Battista 56, 81, 118
Ranzovius, Henricus (Rantzau, Heinrich) 128
Ratzel, Friedrich 11
Ray, John 114–116, 119
Renaudot, Théophraste 130, 134–142, 144, 145, 148, 149
Richelieu, Armand de (Cardinal) 136–139
Riedl, Andreas 218
Rimbaud, Arthur 197
Ringelbergius see Fortius Ringelbergius
Robinson, Henry 142
Rollin, Charles 250, 252
Rousseau, Jean-Jacques 198
Rupp-Eisenreich, Britta 235, 238, 288
Rziha, Heinrich 215

Sabellico Marcantonio see Coccio Sabellico
Sahagún, Bernardino de 126
Saint-Simon, Claude-Henri de 283
Sansovino, Francesco 56, 118, 120, 124
Schlözer, August Ludwig von 88, 89, 228, 233, 237, 239, 242, 244–268, 278, 281, 282, 288
Schmeitzel, Martin 163, 252
Schönemann, Friedrich 163
Seifert, Arno 234
Seignelay, Marquis de 86
Sidney, Philip 54
Simmel, Georg 9, 12
Sloane, Hans 114, 181
Smith, Adam 242
Socrates 32–34, 104, 105
Soden, Wolfram von 19
Solon 29

Sorokin, Pitrim 8
Sprat, Thomas 151
Staël, Mme de 289
Sterne, Laurence 87
Stewart, Susan 189, 196
Stilicho 43
Stocking, G.W. 241, 288
Strabo 30, 42, 81, 115
Stuck, Gottlieb H. 223, 228, 237
Swift, Jonathan 197, 202, 207
Szepsi Csombor, Márton 92, 93

Tacitus, Cornelius 41, 42
Talleyrand, Helie de (Bishop) 52
Tiberius (Emperor) 42
Thoms, William J. 242, 294, 295
Thucydides 30
Toland, Johne 184, 189
Trier, Jost 13
Tschirnhaus auf Kißlingswaldau, E.W. 86
Tucker, Josiah 222
Turgot, Anne Robert Jacques 238, 250, 253
Turler, Hieronymus 60, 62, 65, 68, 70, 71, 73, 93
Tylor, Eduard Burnett 282, 294, 295

Vairasse, Denis 181
Valla, Giorgio 116
Valla, Lorenzo 104, 105
Varenius, Bernhard 189
Varro, Marcus Tullius 115
Vergennes, Charles de 272, 275
Vermeulen, H.F. 235, 236, 239, 251, 252, 260–262, 266
Vetter, Gottfried 161
Vierhaus, Rudolf 209
Villon, François 197
Vives, Juan Luis 57, 64, 69, 106, 107, 127, 136
Volney, Constantin-François 218, 269–295
Voltaire 246, 250, 253, 256, 257, 270, 281

Wallraff, Günter 206
Wargentin, Pehr 244
Washington, George 286
Weber, Max 6, 9, 13

Wells, Herbert George 204
Wesley, John 187
Wilkins, John 143, 145, 181
William the Conqueror 44
Wilson, Thomas 49
Wittfogel, Karl August 22
Wittkower, Rudolf and Margot 53
Woolley, Leonard 21
Worm, Ole 114

Xenophon 31, 32, 34
Xerxes (Great King) 23

Young, Arthur 217, 218, 222, 273, 274

Zäunemannin, Sidonia Hedwig 84
Zeisel, Hans 1
Zeno 33
Zobel, Ernst F. 84
Zwicker, Samuel 71, 75
Zwinger, Theodor 55, 57–60, 62, 64, 65,
    68–73, 80, 81, 91, 93, 116–118, 121–124,
    128, 130, 148